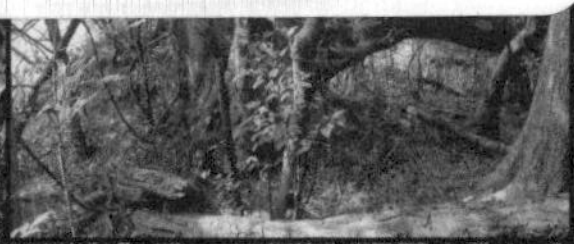

## BOICHI

I came to a certain decision when drawing Japanese landscapes untouched by man for 3,700 years. I shouldn't draw flat forests filled with Japanese cedar trees growing straight up. There can't be a lot of cedar trees because, in real life, people have developed the land. They can't grow straight up because that requires careful pruning and engineering. And the forests can't be level because it's an easy cop-out for someone who's lived on the flat plains of Kanto. For 13 years I lived there, and the first image of a forest that comes to mind is a flat one with cedar trees—manicured to uniform average height. That's why I draw as few cedars as possible, and I never make them straight. The trees have been growing freely for hundreds or even thousands of years.

I won't draw level forests. I modeled the plains of Kanto that appear in the story after Russian airspace images of the tundra. I'm always striving to impart these scenes with a sense of majesty, showing the power of nature in all its glory.

But even with all that thought put into it, I still haven't quite pulled it off. The problem lies in my abilities. I'm only capable of so much...

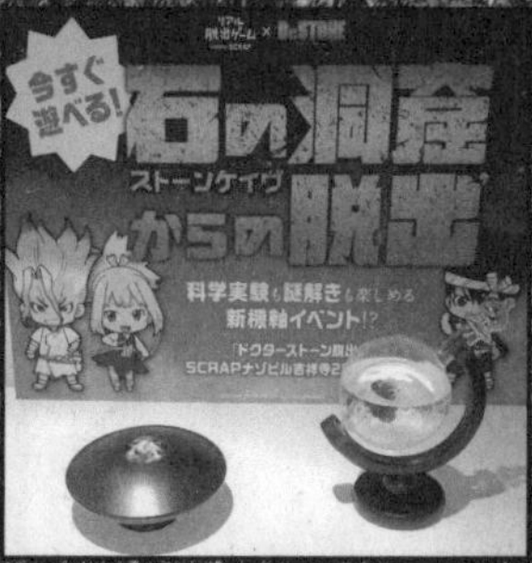
今すぐ遊べる!
石の洞窟からの脱出
ストーンケイヴ
科学実験も謎解きも楽しめる
新機軸イベント!?

## RIICHIRO INAGAKI

They came out with a *Dr. Stone*-themed escape room! You use science experiments to solve puzzles, making it an experience pretty much unlike any other. They let me try it out as a test run, and I managed to clear the game (after receiving some hints)! It was lots of fun! If you get the chance, definitely give it a shot.

There's also a *Dr. Stone* stamp rally event, a special *Dr. Stone* skin for train cars, a *Dr. Stone* science exhibit... I'm thrilled that the series is inspiring all these events!

**Boichi** is a Korean-born artist currently living and working in Japan. His previous works include *Sun-Ken Rock* and *Terra Formars Asimov*.

**Riichiro Inagaki** is a Japanese manga writer from Tokyo. He is the writer for the sports manga series *Eyeshield 21*, which was serialized in *Weekly Shonen Jump*.

# Dr. STONE

## 15

### SHONEN JUMP Manga Edition

Story **RIICHIRO INAGAKI**
Art **BOICHI**

Science Consultant/**KURARE** with Yakuri Classroom of Doom: Aruma Zirou, Cyrano, POKA
Translation/**CALEB COOK**
Touch-Up Art & Lettering/**STEPHEN DUTRO**
Design/**JULIAN [JR] ROBINSON**
Editor/**JOHN BAE**

Printed in Canada

Published by VIZ Media, LLC
P.O. Box 77010
San Francisco, CA 94107

10 9 8 7 6 5 4 3 2 1
First printing, February 2021

## Consulted Works:

• Asari, Yoshito, *Uchu e Ikitakute Ekitainenryo Rocket wo DIY Shite Mita (Gakken Rigaku Sensho)*, Gakken Plus, 2013

• Dartnell, Lewis, *The Knowledge: How to Rebuild Civilization in the Aftermath of a Cataclysm*, translated by Erika Togo, Kawade Shobo Shinsha, 2015

• Davies, Barry, *The Complete SAS Survival Manual*, translated by Yoshito Takigawa, Toyo Shorin, 2001

• Harari, Yuval Noah, *Sapiens: A Brief History of Humankind*, translated by Hiroyuki Shibata, Kawade Shobo Shinsha, 2016

• Jackson, Donald Dale, *The Aeronauts: The Epic of Flight*, translated by Asajiro Nishiyama and Kazuo Oyauchi, Time-Life Books, 1981

• Kazama, Rinpei, *Shinboken Techo (Definitive Edition)*, Shufu to Seikatsusha, 2016

• *Mechanism Encyclopedia*, Edited by Shigeru Ito, Ohmsha, 2013

• McNab, Chris, *Special Forces Survival Guide*, translated by Atsuko Sumi, Hara Shobo, 2016

• Olsen, Larry Dean, *Outdoor Survival Skills*, translated by Katsuji Tani, A&F, 2014

• *Sagara Oil Field: History and Mysterious Origin*, Haibara Public High School Hometown History Research Club, 2018

• Weisman, Alan, *The World Without Us*, Translated by Shinobu Onizawa, Hayakawa Publishing, 2009

• Wiseman, John, *SAS Survival Handbook, Revised Edition*, Translated by Kazuhiro Takahashi and Hitoshi Tomokiyo, Namiki Shobo, 2009

VIZ MEDIA
viz.com

SHONEN JUMP

# Dr.STONE

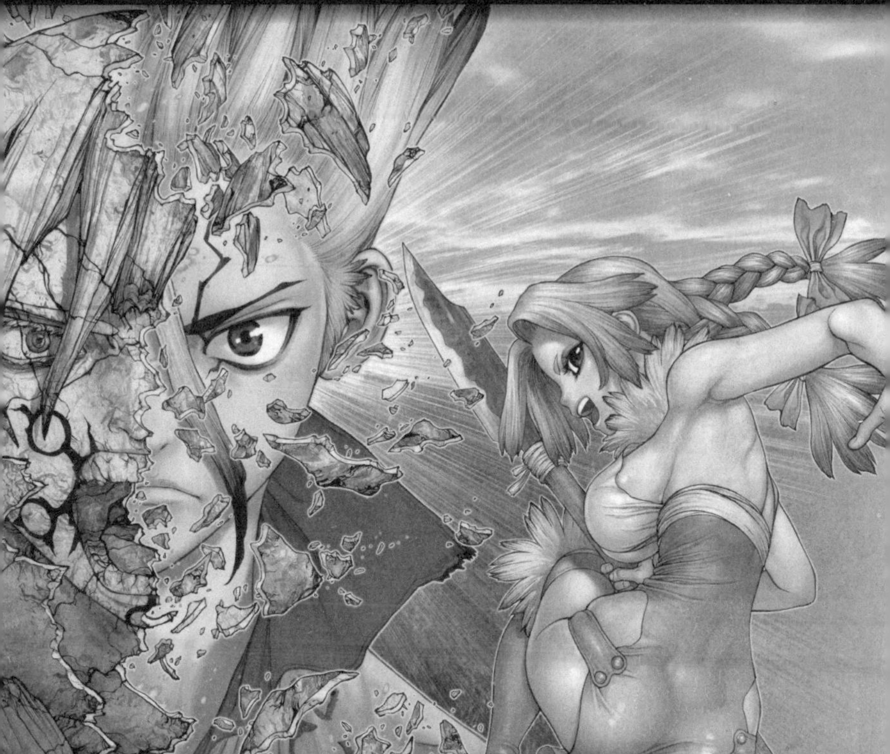

STORY **RIICHIRO INAGAKI**
ART **BOICHI**

**15**

**THE STRONGEST WEAPON IS...**

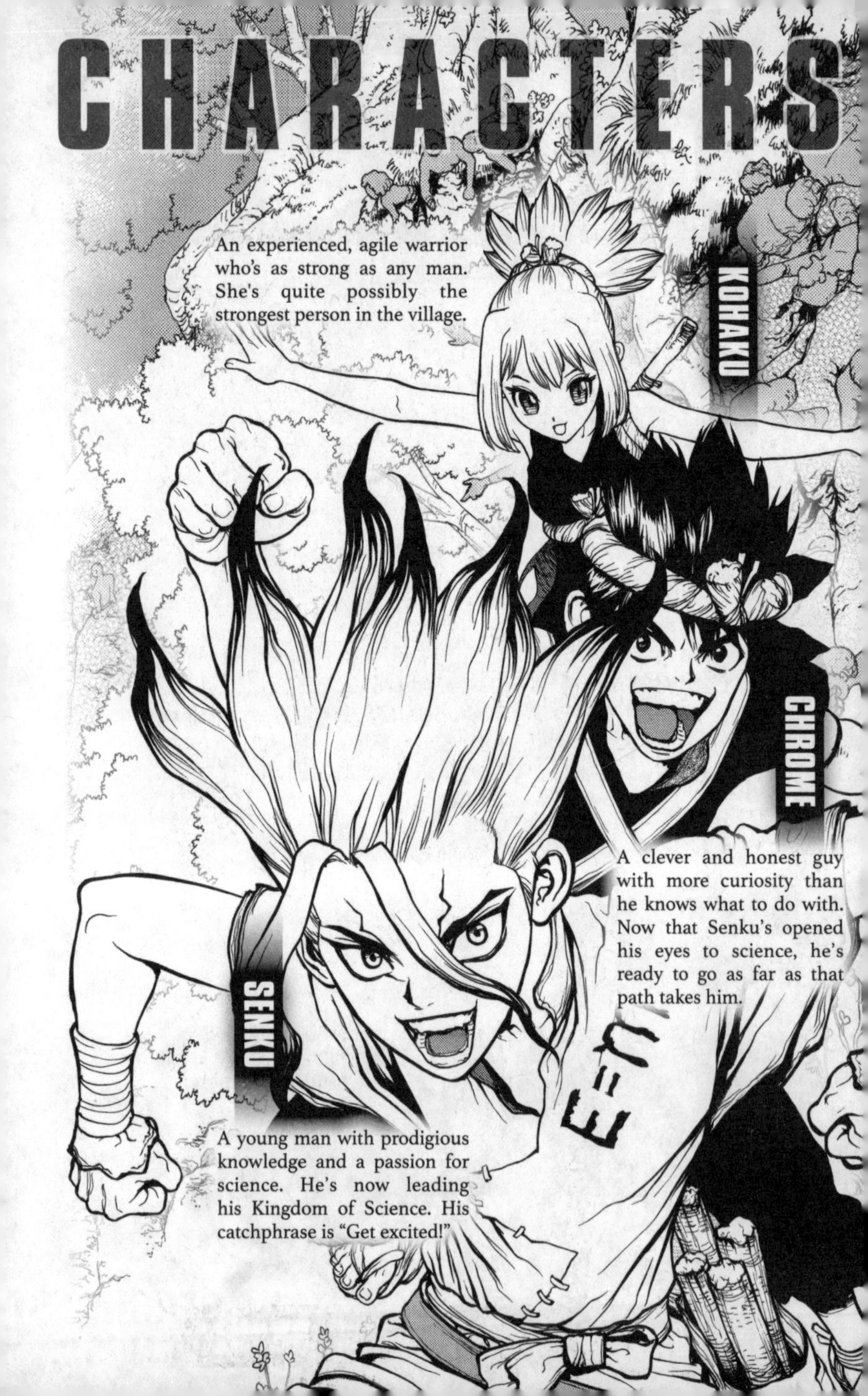
CHARACTERS
KOHAKU
An experienced, agile warrior who's as strong as any man. She's quite possibly the strongest person in the village.
CHROME
A clever and honest guy with more curiosity than he knows what to do with. Now that Senku's opened his eyes to science, he's ready to go as far as that path takes him.
SENKU
A young man with prodigious knowledge and a passion for science. He's now leading his Kingdom of Science. His catchphrase is "Get excited!"

# Dr.STONE

## STORY

Every human on earth is turned to stone by a mysterious phenomenon, including high school student Taiju. Nearly 3,700 years later, Taiju awakens and finds his friend Senku, who revived a bit earlier. Together, they vow to restore civilization, but Tsukasa, once considered the strongest high schooler alive, nearly kills Senku in order to put a stop to his scientific plans.

After being secretly revived by his friends, Senku arrives at Ishigami Village. But when word of Senku's survival gets back to Tsukasa, the war between the two forces begins! Eventually, the two factions make peace, but the traitorous Hyoga skewers Tsukasa. Senku cryogenically freezes Tsukasa's body.

Seeking to unravel the mysteries behind the petrification phenomenon, Senku and friends arrive at the so-called "Treasure Island," but soon after landing, those who stayed behind on the ship are turned to stone by the Petrification Kingdom—the island's ruling group. But thanks to the revival fluid, the Kingdom of Science is slowly reviving its crew. Meanwhile, the gang has formed an alliance with Moz and is ready to go on the offensive!

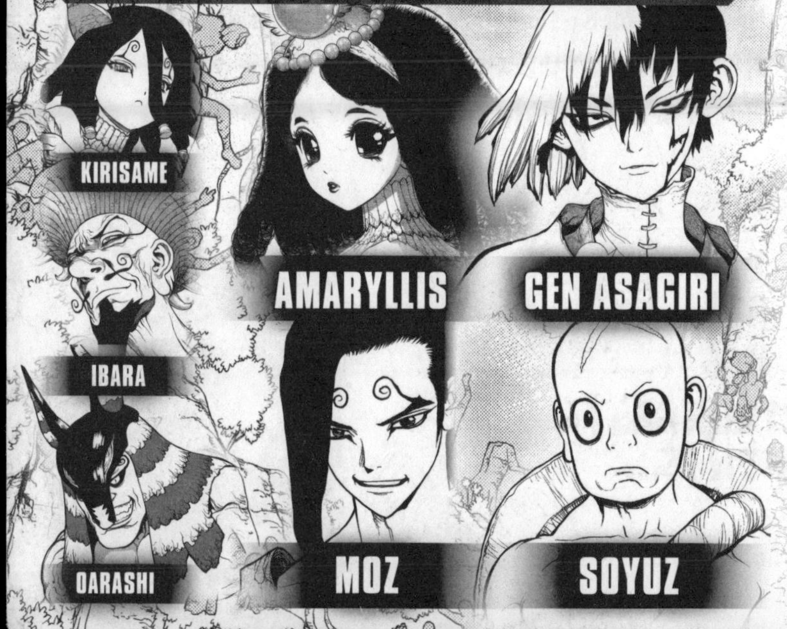
KIRISAME
AMARYLLIS
GEN ASAGIRI
IBARA
OARASHI
MOZ
SOYUZ

# CONTENTS

# 15
## THE STRONGEST WEAPON IS…

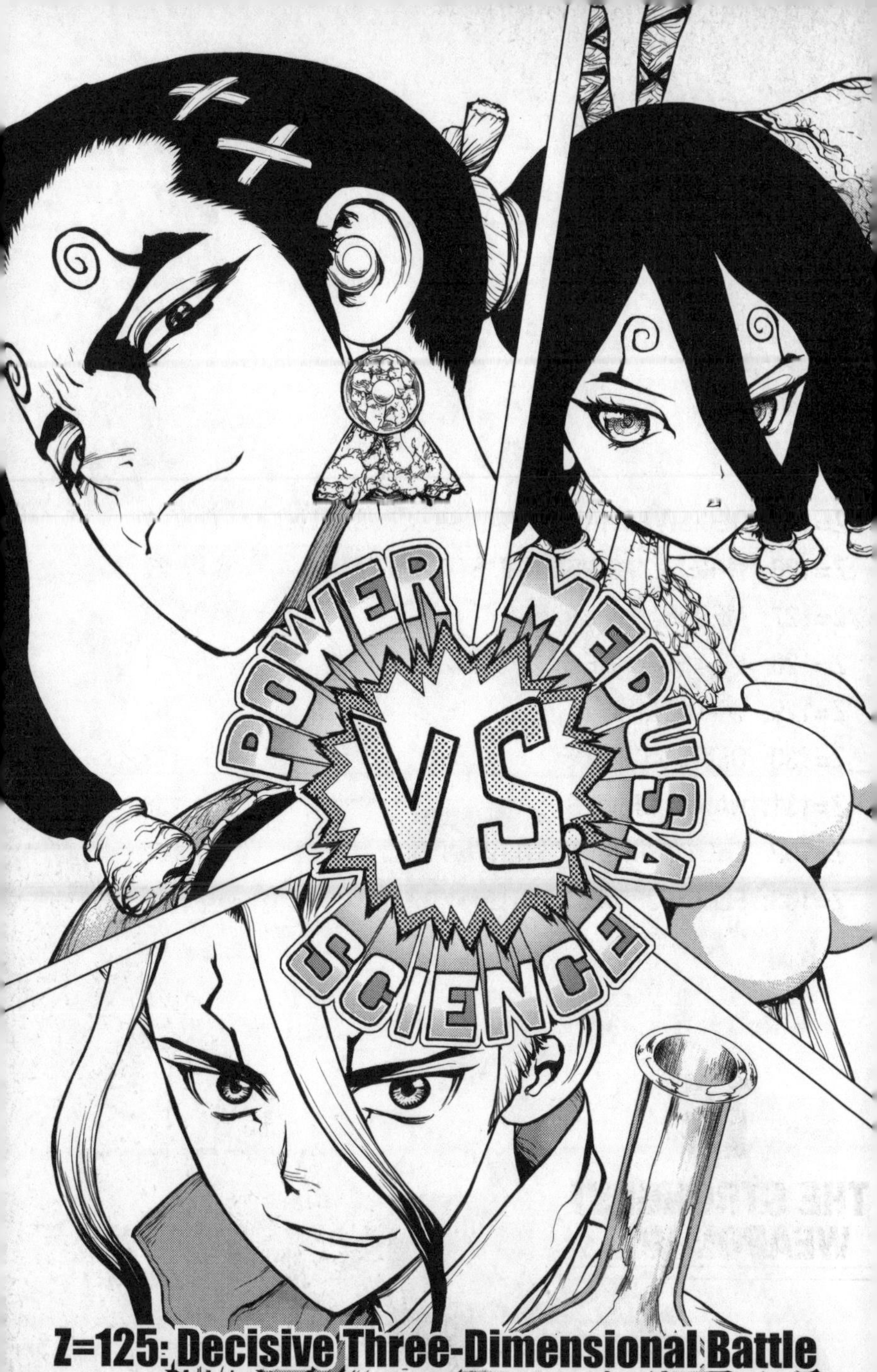
POWER
MEDUSA
V.S.
SCIENCE

## Z=125: Decisive Three-Dimensional Battle

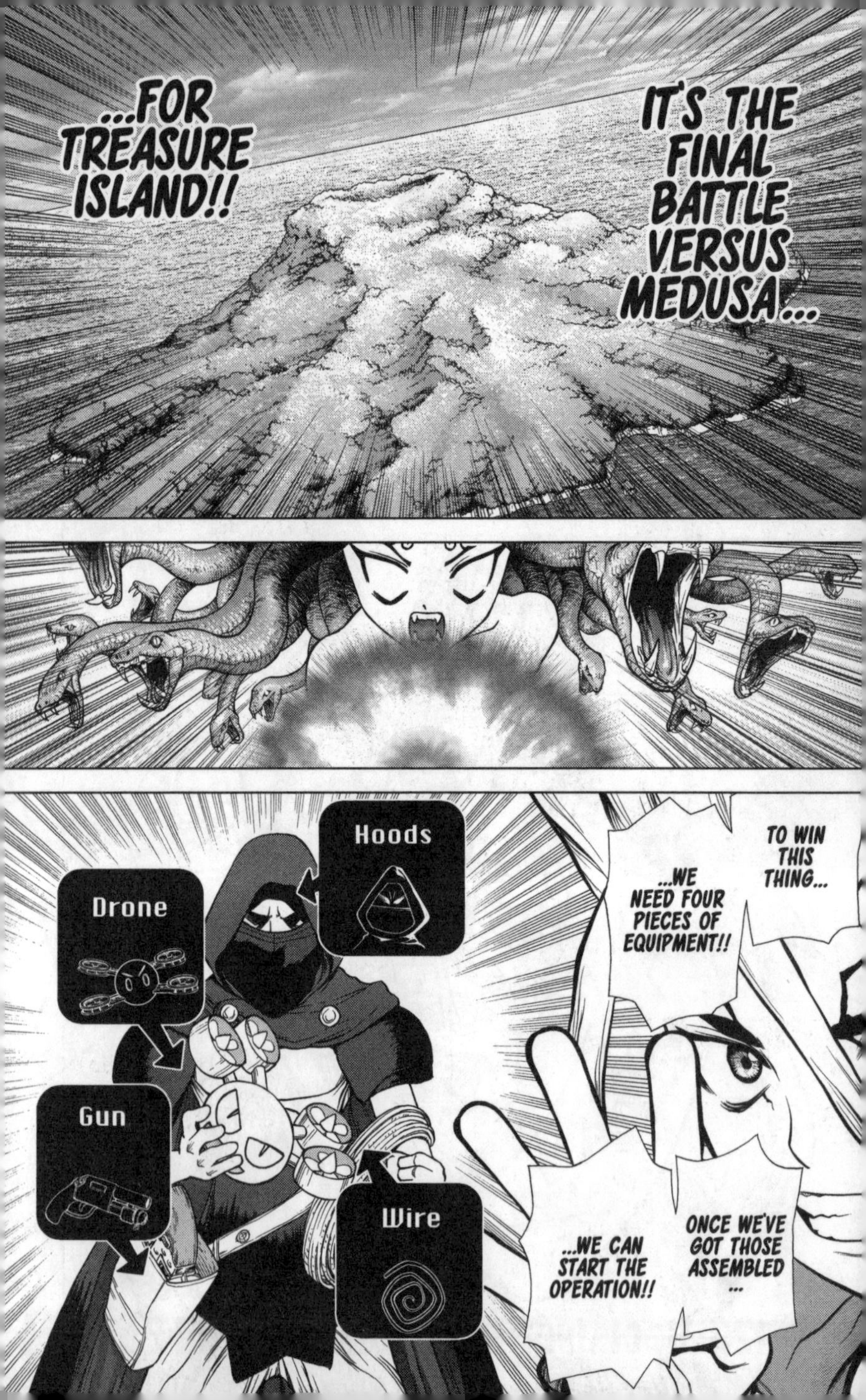
IT'S THE FINAL BATTLE VERSUS MEDUSA...
...FOR TREASURE ISLAND!!
TO WIN THIS THING...
...WE NEED FOUR PIECES OF EQUIPMENT!!
ONCE WE'VE GOT THOSE ASSEMBLED...
...WE CAN START THE OPERATION!!
Hoods
Drone
Gun
Wire

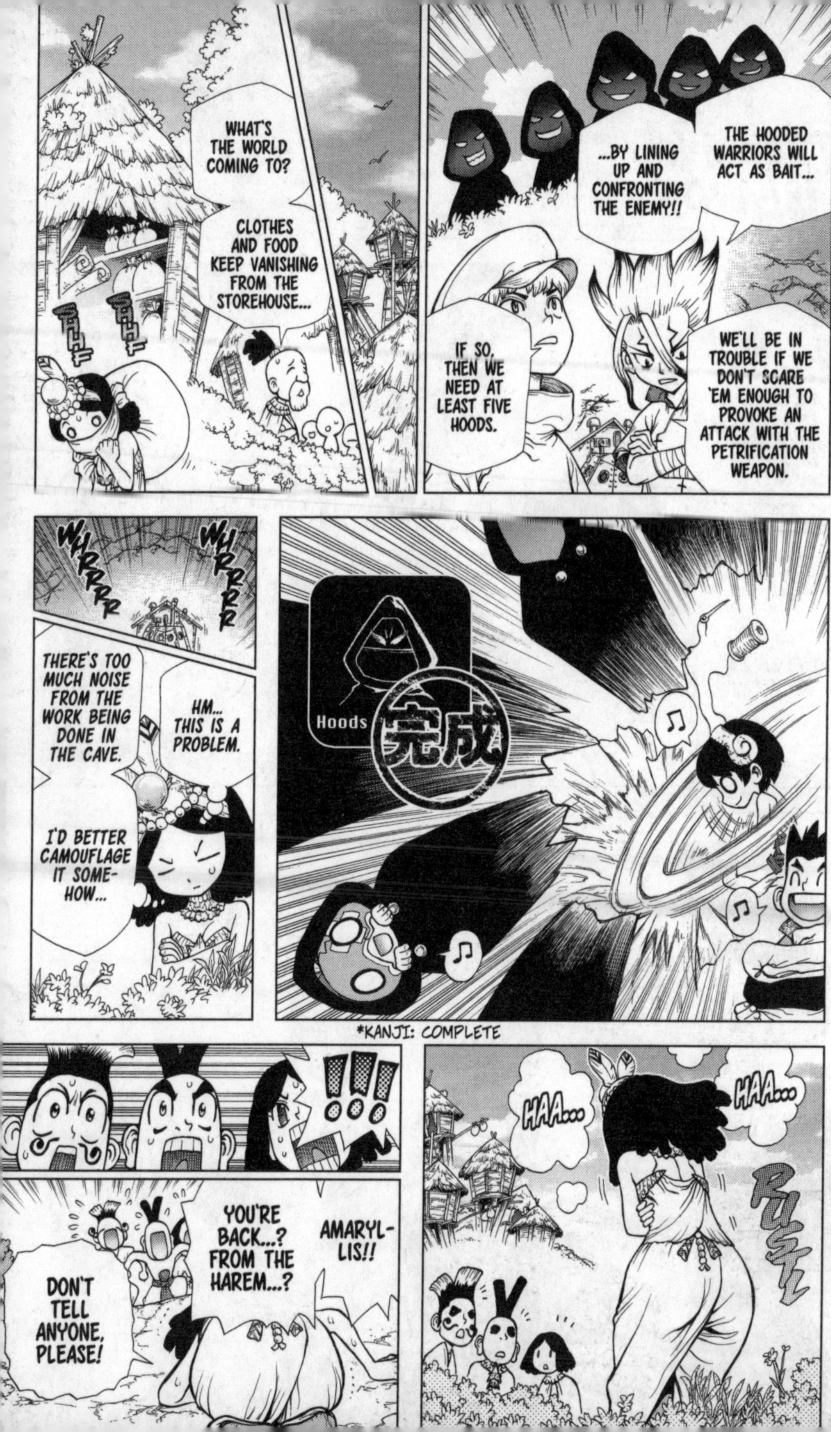
THE HOODED WARRIORS WILL ACT AS BAIT...
...BY LINING UP AND CONFRONTING THE ENEMY!!
WE'LL BE IN TROUBLE IF WE DON'T SCARE 'EM ENOUGH TO PROVOKE AN ATTACK WITH THE PETRIFICATION WEAPON.
IF SO, THEN WE NEED AT LEAST FIVE HOODS.
WHAT'S THE WORLD COMING TO?
CLOTHES AND FOOD KEEP VANISHING FROM THE STOREHOUSE...
Hoods
完成
♪
♪
♪
WHRRRR
WHRRRR
HM... THIS IS A PROBLEM.
THERE'S TOO MUCH NOISE FROM THE WORK BEING DONE IN THE CAVE.
I'D BETTER CAMOUFLAGE IT SOME-HOW...
*KANJI: COMPLETE
HAA...
HAA...
!!!
AMARYL-LIS!!
YOU'RE BACK...? FROM THE HAREM...?
DON'T TELL ANYONE, PLEASE!

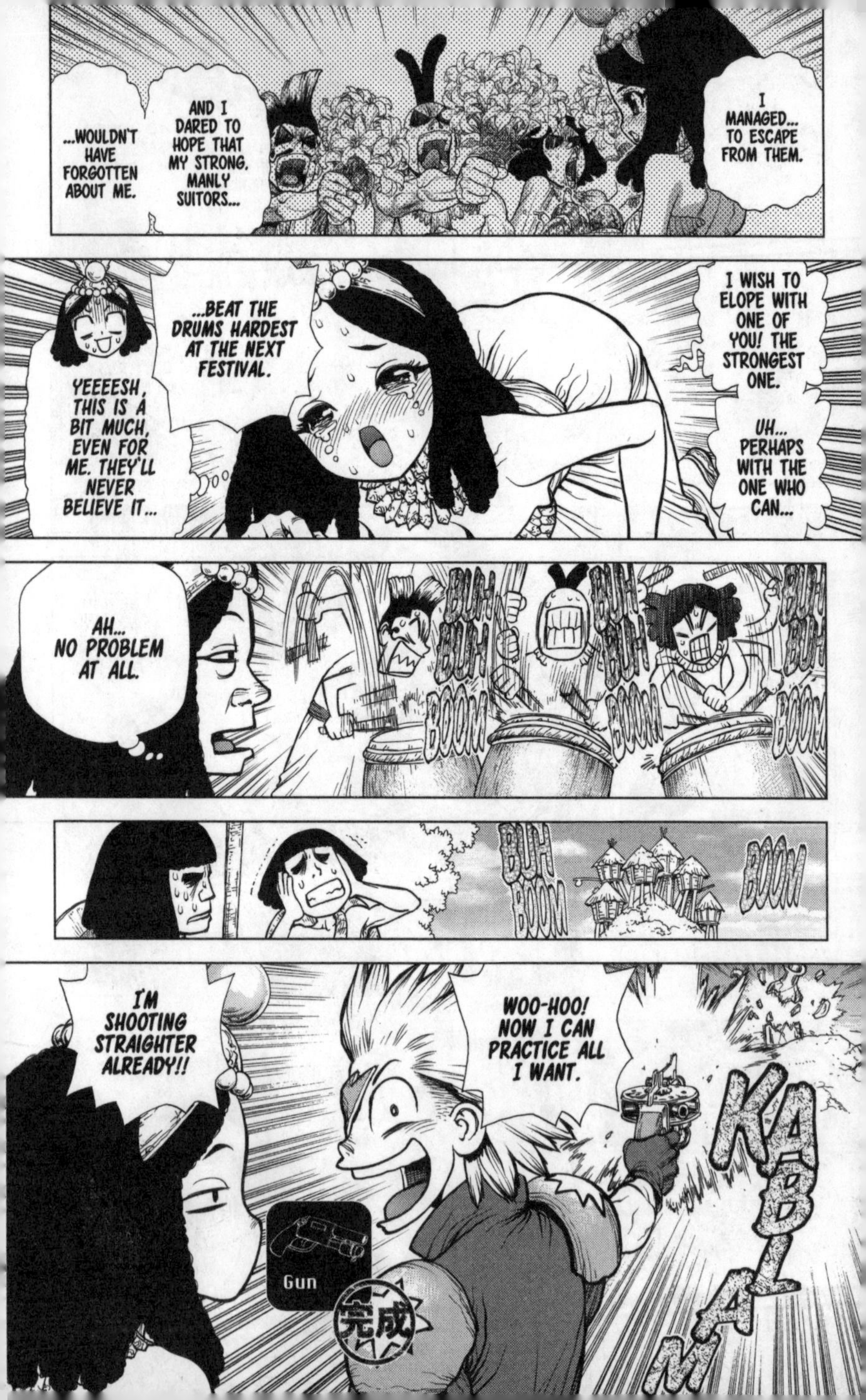
I MANAGED... TO ESCAPE FROM THEM.
AND I DARED TO HOPE THAT MY STRONG, MANLY SUITORS...
...WOULDN'T HAVE FORGOTTEN ABOUT ME.
I WISH TO ELOPE WITH ONE OF YOU! THE STRONGEST ONE.
UH... PERHAPS WITH THE ONE WHO CAN...
...BEAT THE DRUMS HARDEST AT THE NEXT FESTIVAL.
YEEEESH, THIS IS A BIT MUCH, EVEN FOR ME. THEY'LL NEVER BELIEVE IT...
BUH BUH BOOM
BUH BUH BOOM
BUH BUH BOOM
AH... NO PROBLEM AT ALL.
BOOM
BUH BOOM
KABLAM
WOO-HOO! NOW I CAN PRACTICE ALL I WANT.
I'M SHOOTING STRAIGHTER ALREADY!!
Gun
完成

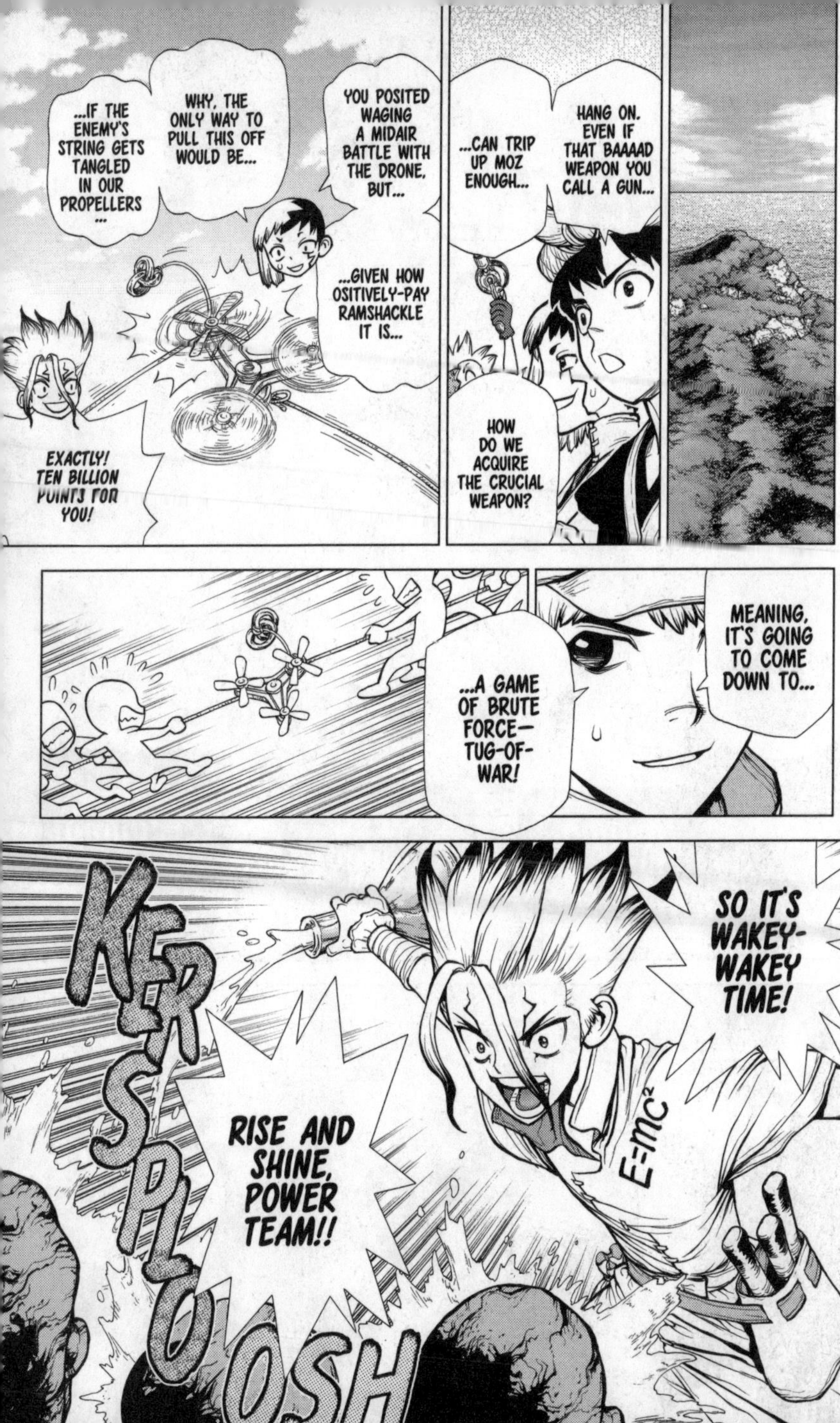
HANG ON. EVEN IF THAT BAAAAD WEAPON YOU CALL A GUN...
...CAN TRIP UP MOZ ENOUGH...
HOW DO WE ACQUIRE THE CRUCIAL WEAPON?
YOU POSITED WAGING A MIDAIR BATTLE WITH THE DRONE, BUT...
...GIVEN HOW OSITIVELY-PAY RAMSHACKLE IT IS...
WHY, THE ONLY WAY TO PULL THIS OFF WOULD BE...
...IF THE ENEMY'S STRING GETS TANGLED IN OUR PROPELLERS...
EXACTLY! TEN BILLION POINTS FOR YOU!
MEANING, IT'S GOING TO COME DOWN TO...
...A GAME OF BRUTE FORCE— TUG-OF-WAR!
SO IT'S WAKEY-WAKEY TIME!
E=mc²
RISE AND SHINE, POWER TEAM!!
KERSPLOOSH

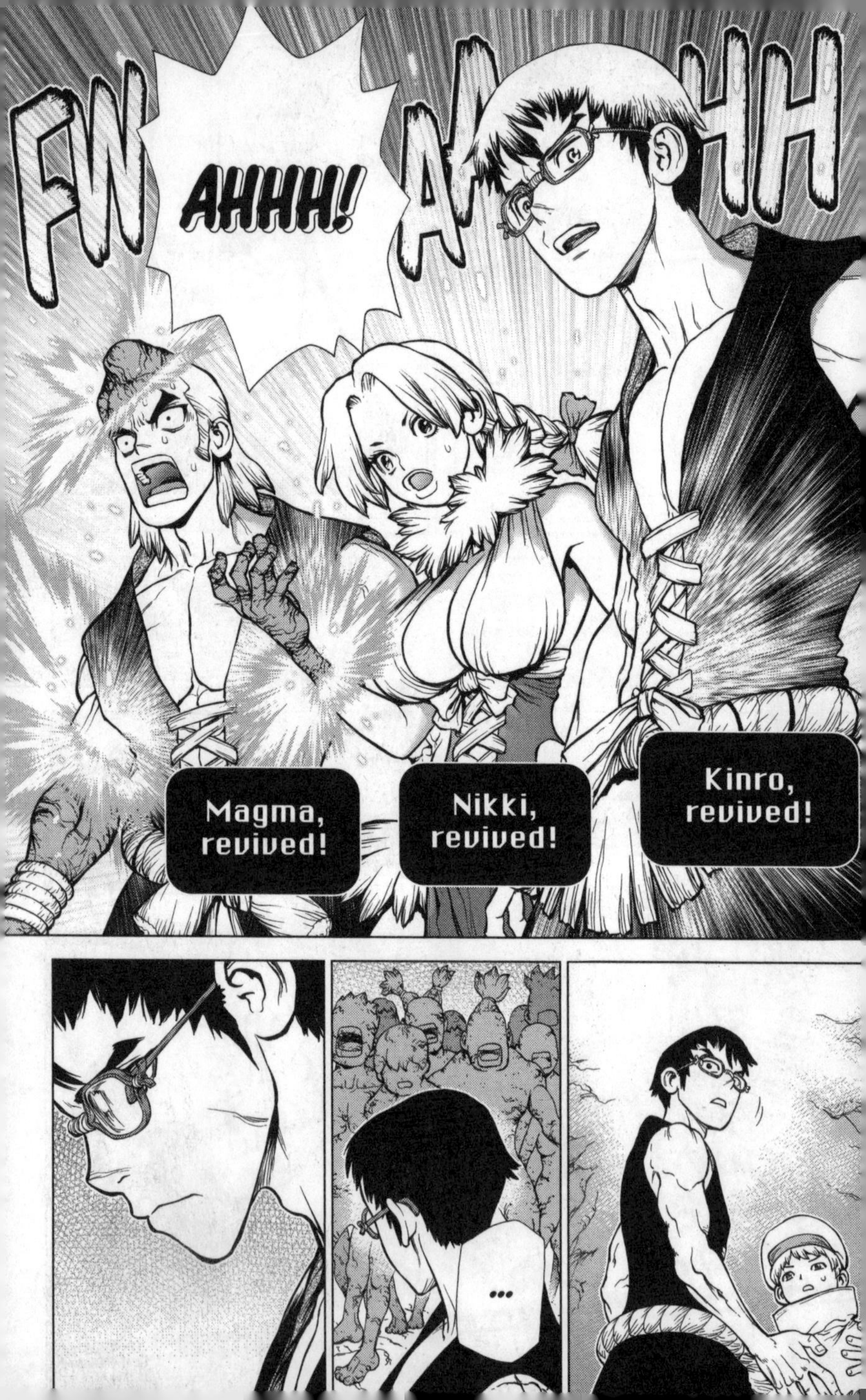

AHHHH!
Kinro, revived!
Nikki, revived!
Magma, revived!
...

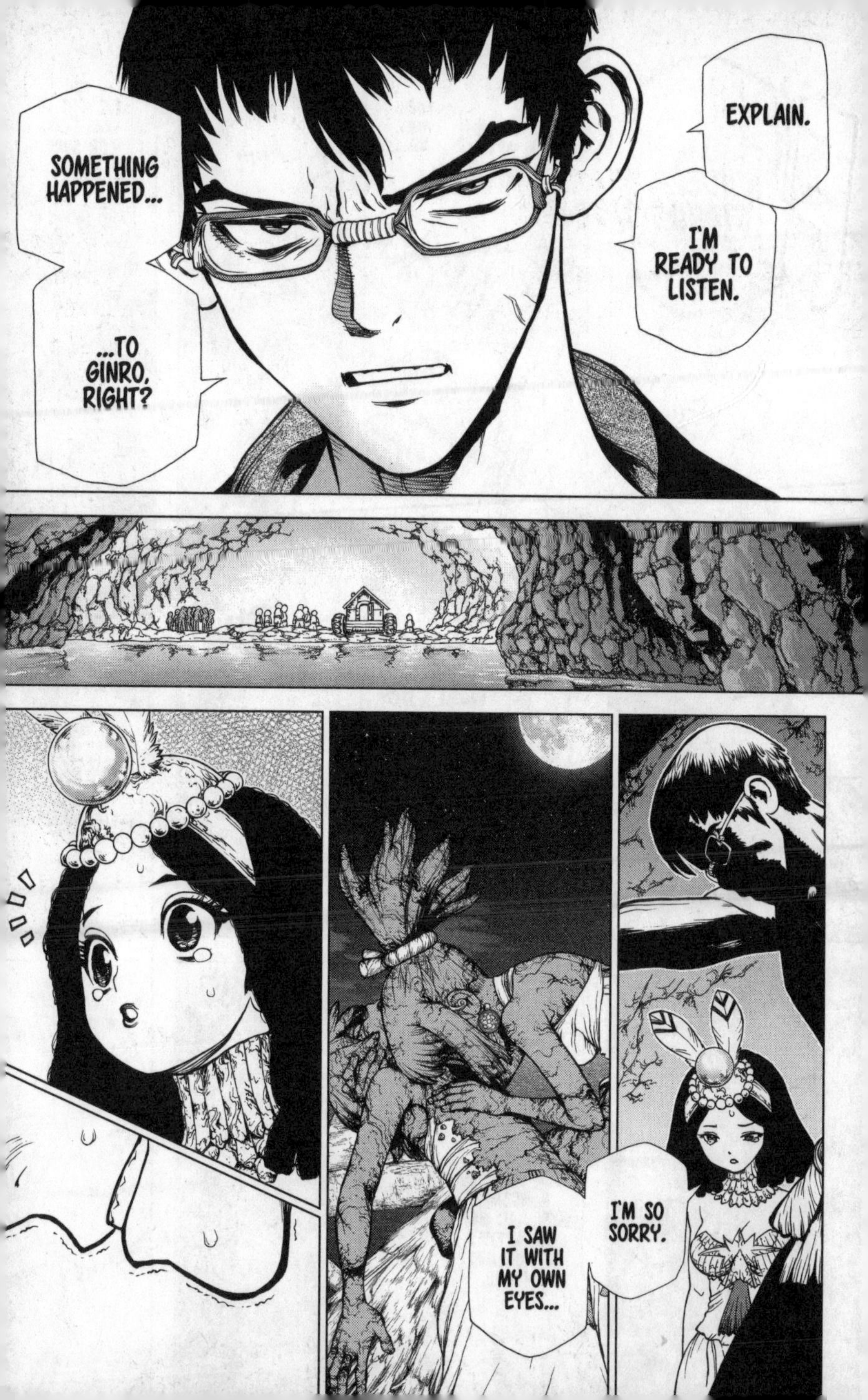
EXPLAIN.
I'M READY TO LISTEN.
SOMETHING HAPPENED...
...TO GINRO, RIGHT?
I'M SO SORRY.
I SAW IT WITH MY OWN EYES...

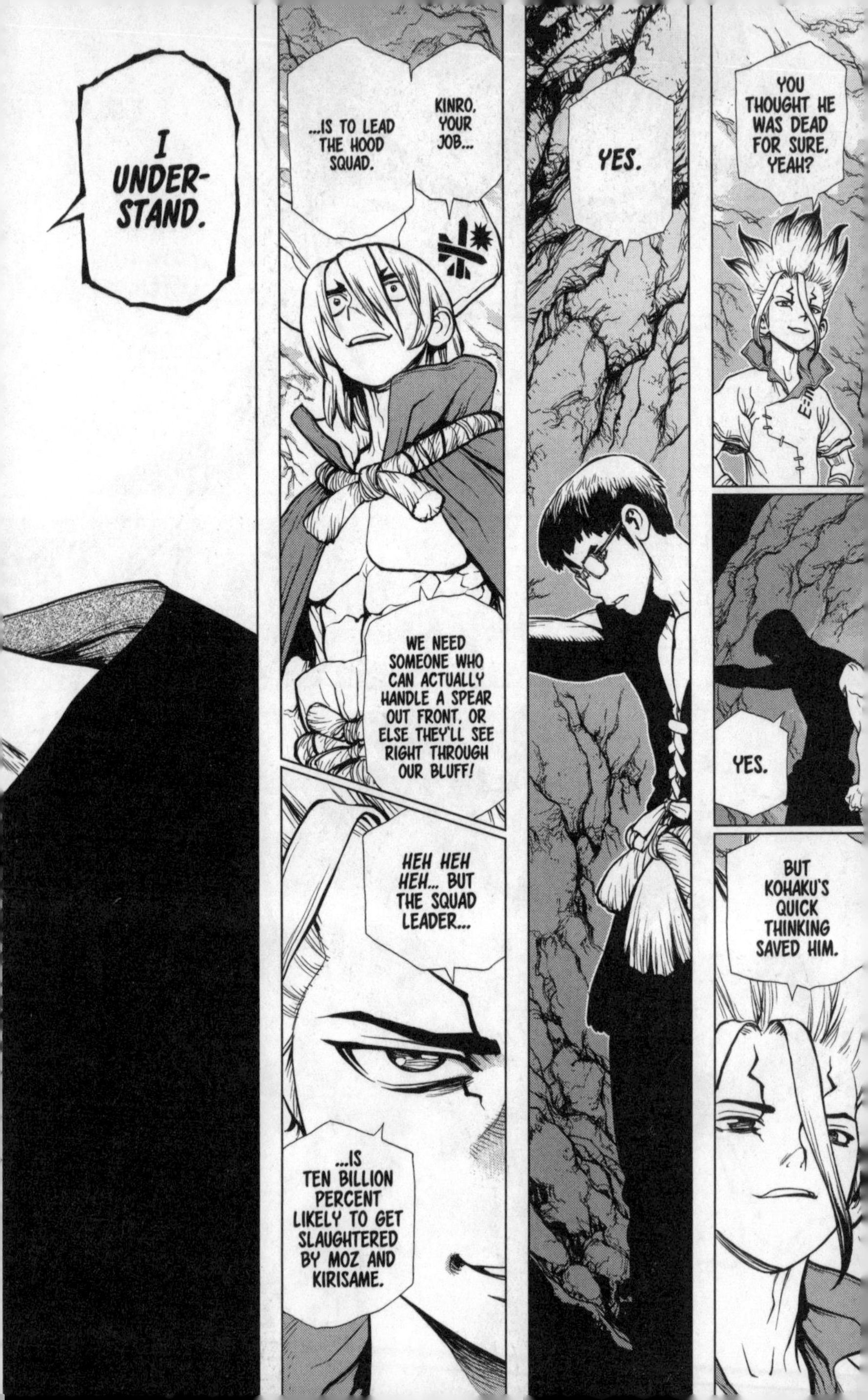
YOU THOUGHT HE WAS DEAD FOR SURE, YEAH?
YES.
BUT KOHAKU'S QUICK THINKING SAVED HIM.
YES.
KINRO, YOUR JOB...
...IS TO LEAD THE HOOD SQUAD.
WE NEED SOMEONE WHO CAN ACTUALLY HANDLE A SPEAR OUT FRONT, OR ELSE THEY'LL SEE RIGHT THROUGH OUR BLUFF!
HEH HEH HEH... BUT THE SQUAD LEADER...
...IS TEN BILLION PERCENT LIKELY TO GET SLAUGHTERED BY MOZ AND KIRISAME.
I UNDER-STAND.

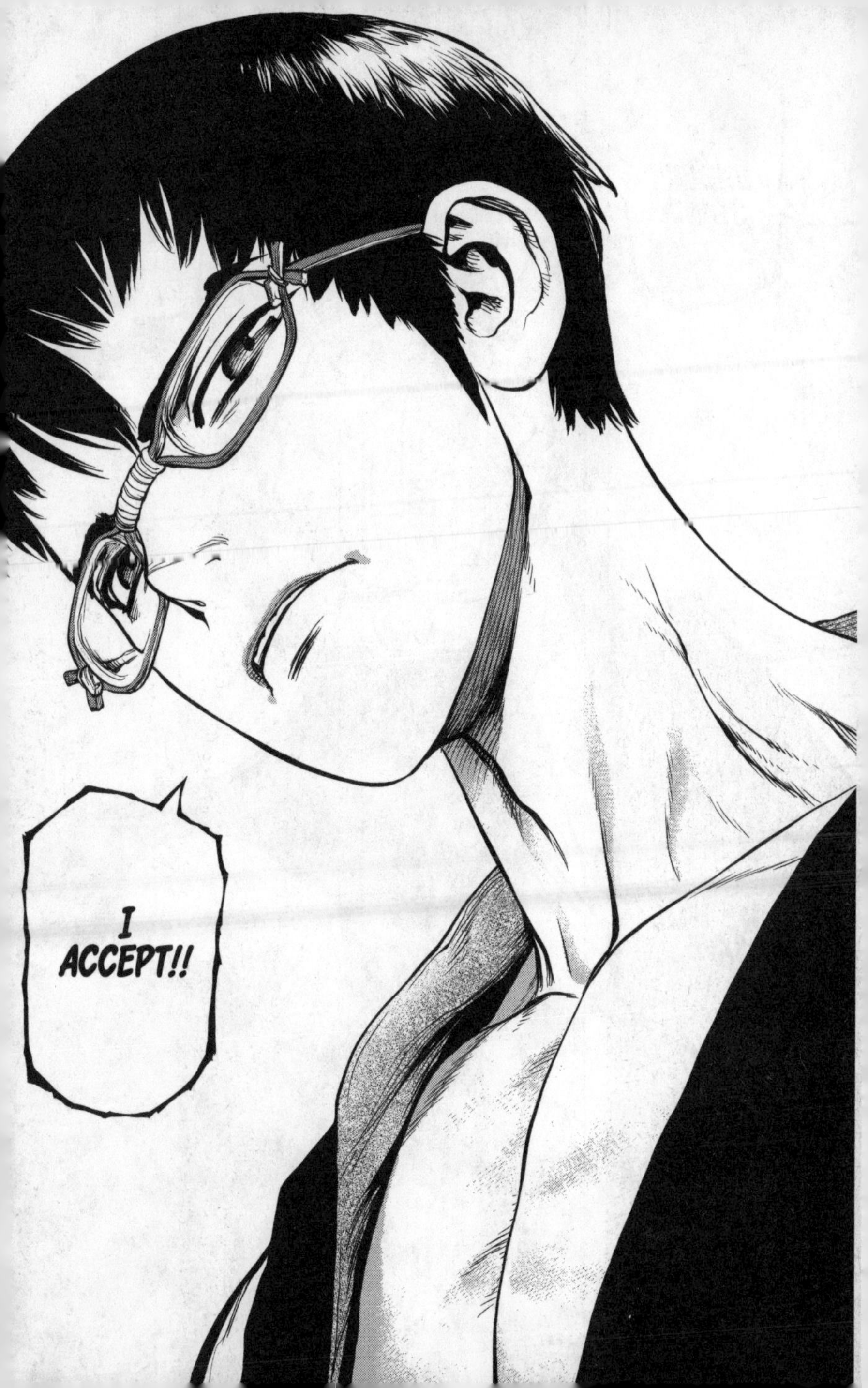
I ACCEPT!!

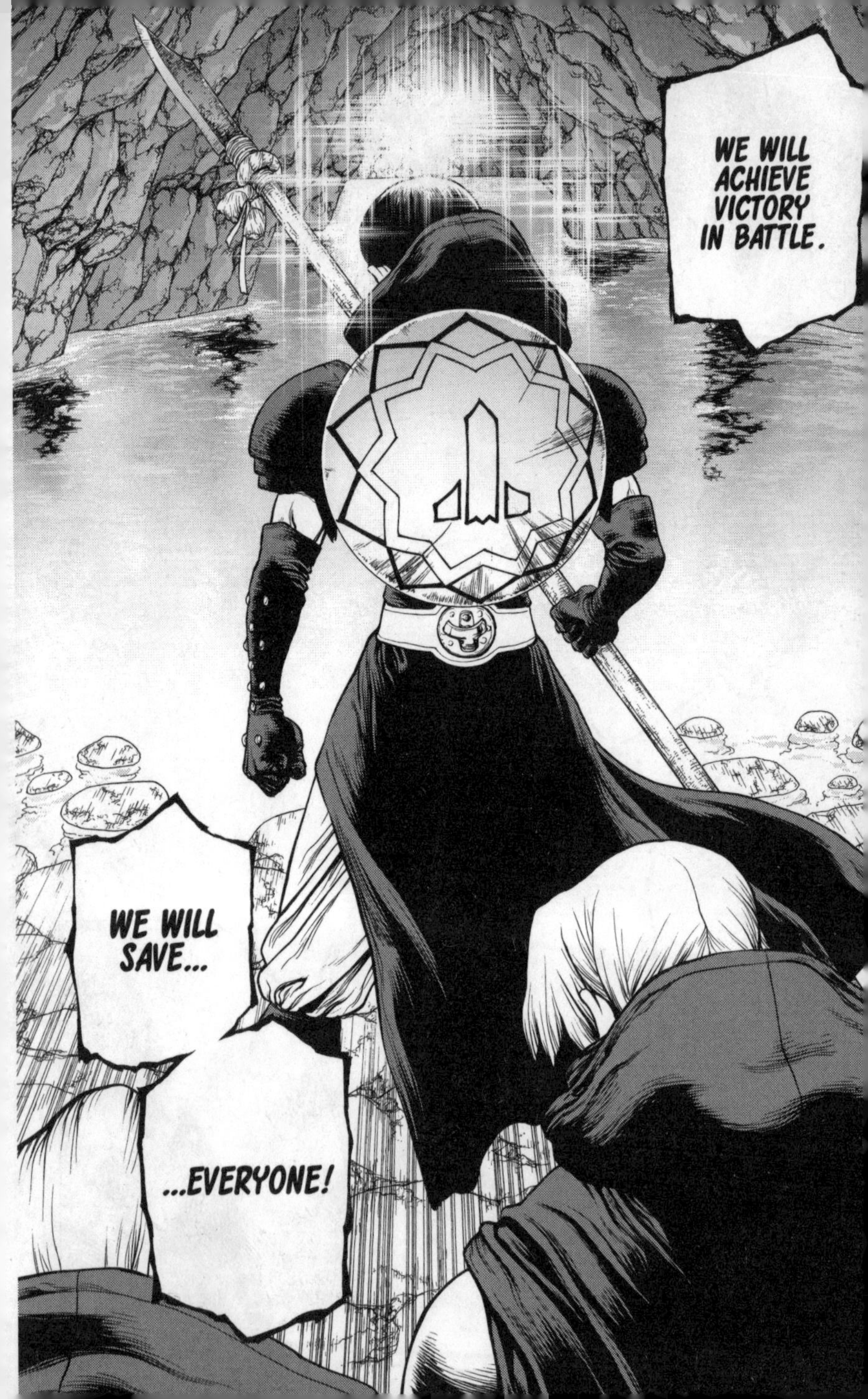
WE WILL ACHIEVE VICTORY IN BATTLE.
WE WILL SAVE...
...EVERYONE!

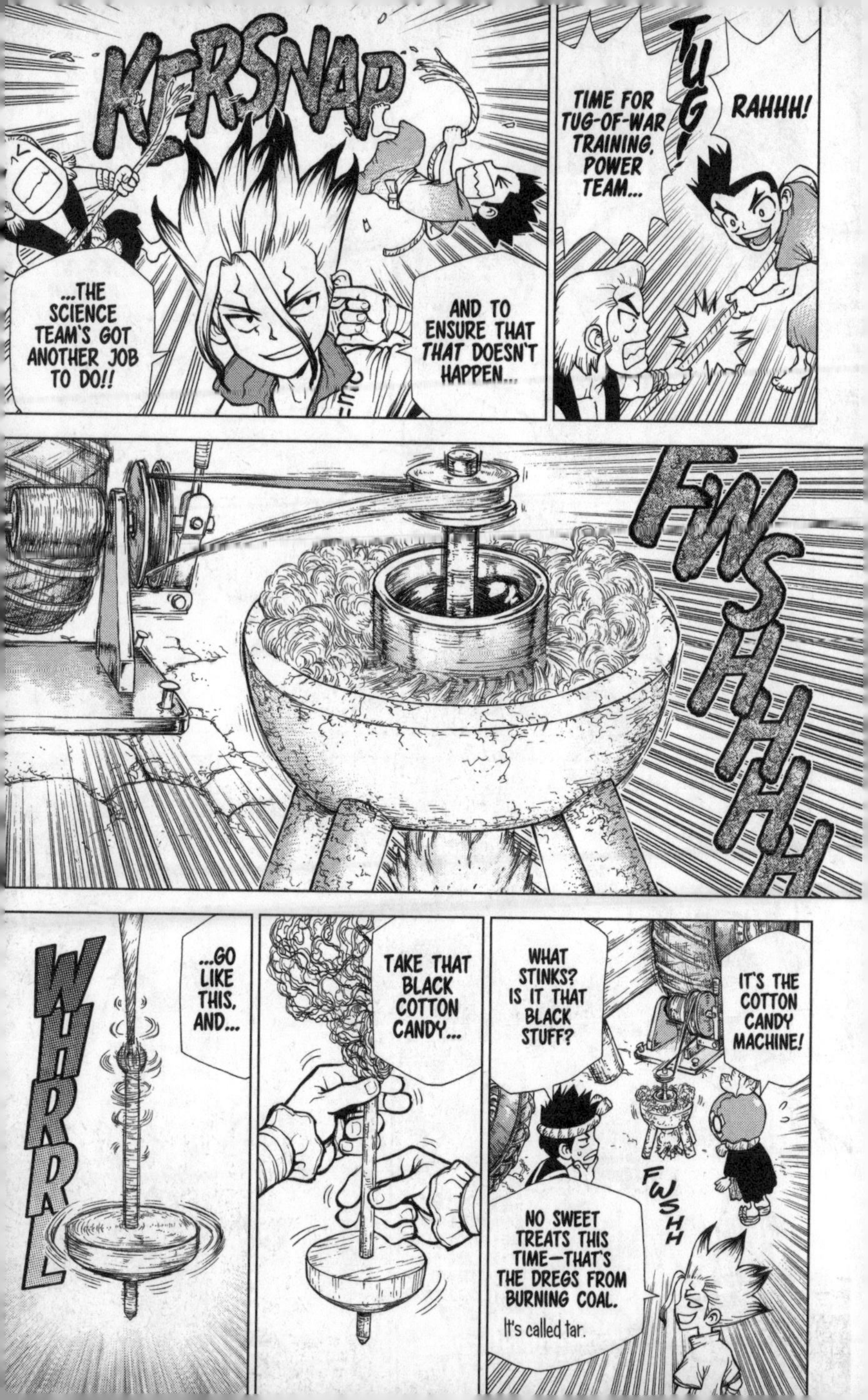
TIME FOR TUG-OF-WAR TRAINING, POWER TEAM...
TUG!
RAHHH!
KERSNAP
AND TO ENSURE THAT THAT DOESN'T HAPPEN...
...THE SCIENCE TEAM'S GOT ANOTHER JOB TO DO!!
FWSHHHHH
IT'S THE COTTON CANDY MACHINE!
WHAT STINKS? IS IT THAT BLACK STUFF?
FWSHH
NO SWEET TREATS THIS TIME—THAT'S THE DREGS FROM BURNING COAL.
It's called tar.
TAKE THAT BLACK COTTON CANDY...
...GO LIKE THIS, AND...
WHRRL

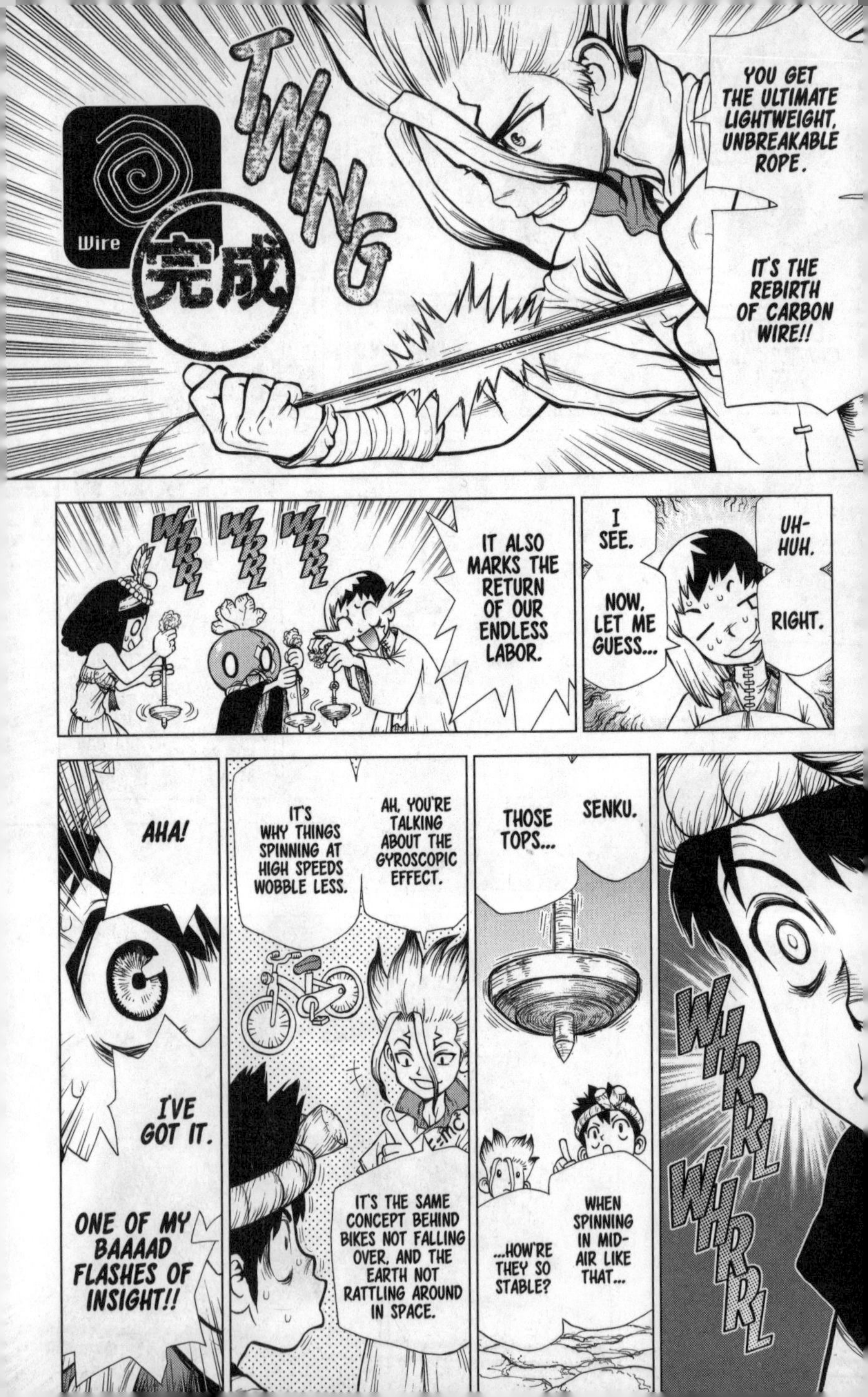
YOU GET THE ULTIMATE LIGHTWEIGHT, UNBREAKABLE ROPE.
IT'S THE REBIRTH OF CARBON WIRE!!
TWING
Wire
完成
UH-HUH.
I SEE.
RIGHT.
NOW, LET ME GUESS...
IT ALSO MARKS THE RETURN OF OUR ENDLESS LABOR.
WHRRL
WHRRL
WHRRL
WHRRL
WHRRL
SENKU.
THOSE TOPS...
WHEN SPINNING IN MID-AIR LIKE THAT...
...HOW'RE THEY SO STABLE?
AH, YOU'RE TALKING ABOUT THE GYROSCOPIC EFFECT.
IT'S WHY THINGS SPINNING AT HIGH SPEEDS WOBBLE LESS.
IT'S THE SAME CONCEPT BEHIND BIKES NOT FALLING OVER, AND THE EARTH NOT RATTLING AROUND IN SPACE.
AHA!
I'VE GOT IT.
ONE OF MY BAAAAD FLASHES OF INSIGHT!!

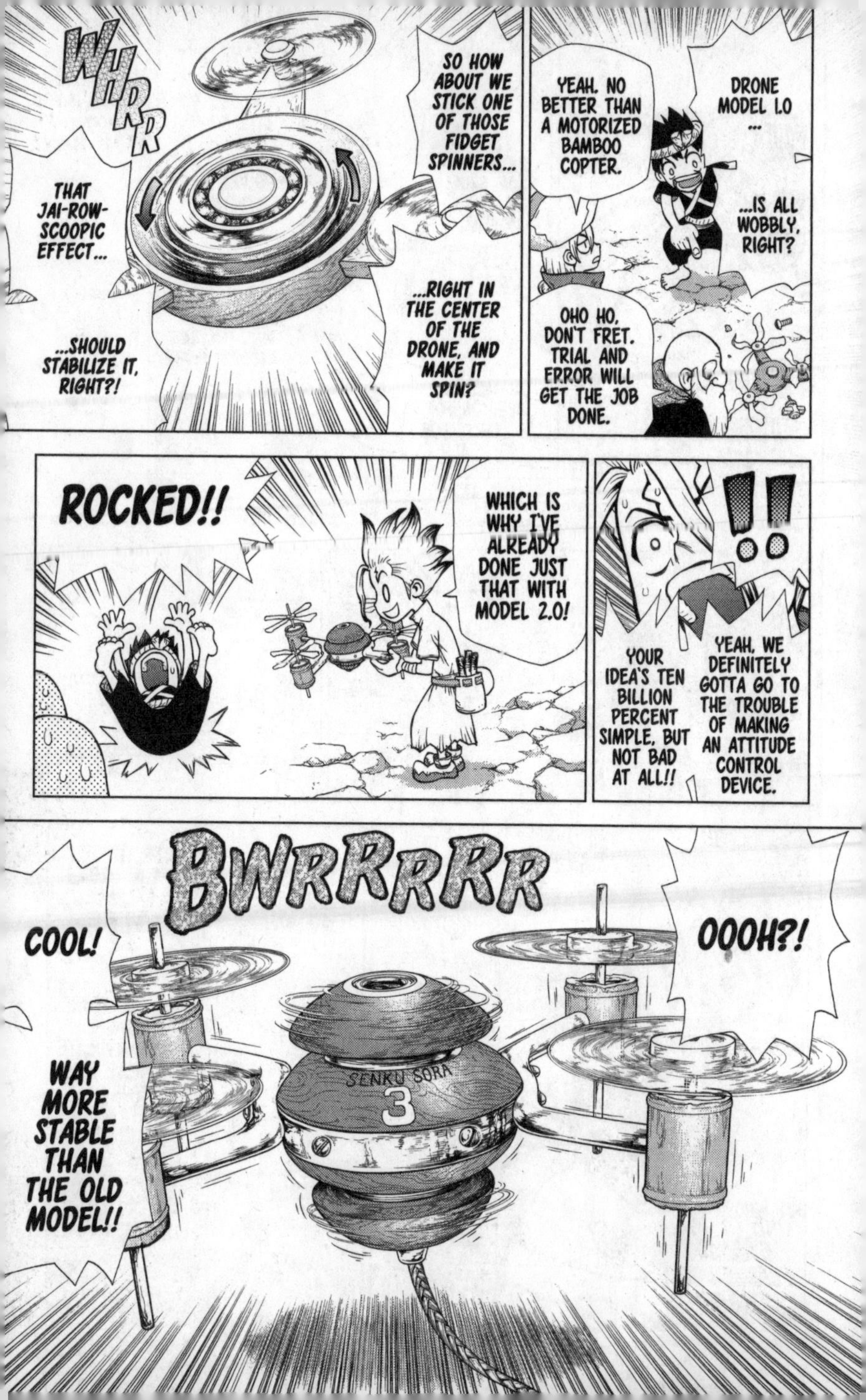
DRONE MODEL 1.0 ...
...IS ALL WOBBLY, RIGHT?
YEAH. NO BETTER THAN A MOTORIZED BAMBOO COPTER.
OHO HO, DON'T FRET. TRIAL AND ERROR WILL GET THE JOB DONE.
SO HOW ABOUT WE STICK ONE OF THOSE FIDGET SPINNERS...
...RIGHT IN THE CENTER OF THE DRONE, AND MAKE IT SPIN?
WHRRR
THAT JAI-ROW-SCOOPIC EFFECT...
...SHOULD STABILIZE IT, RIGHT?!
!!
YEAH, WE DEFINITELY GOTTA GO TO THE TROUBLE OF MAKING AN ATTITUDE CONTROL DEVICE.
YOUR IDEA'S TEN BILLION PERCENT SIMPLE, BUT NOT BAD AT ALL!!
WHICH IS WHY I'VE ALREADY DONE JUST THAT WITH MODEL 2.0!
ROCKED!!
BWRRRRR
OOOH?!
COOL!
SENKU SORA
3
WAY MORE STABLE THAN THE OLD MODEL!!

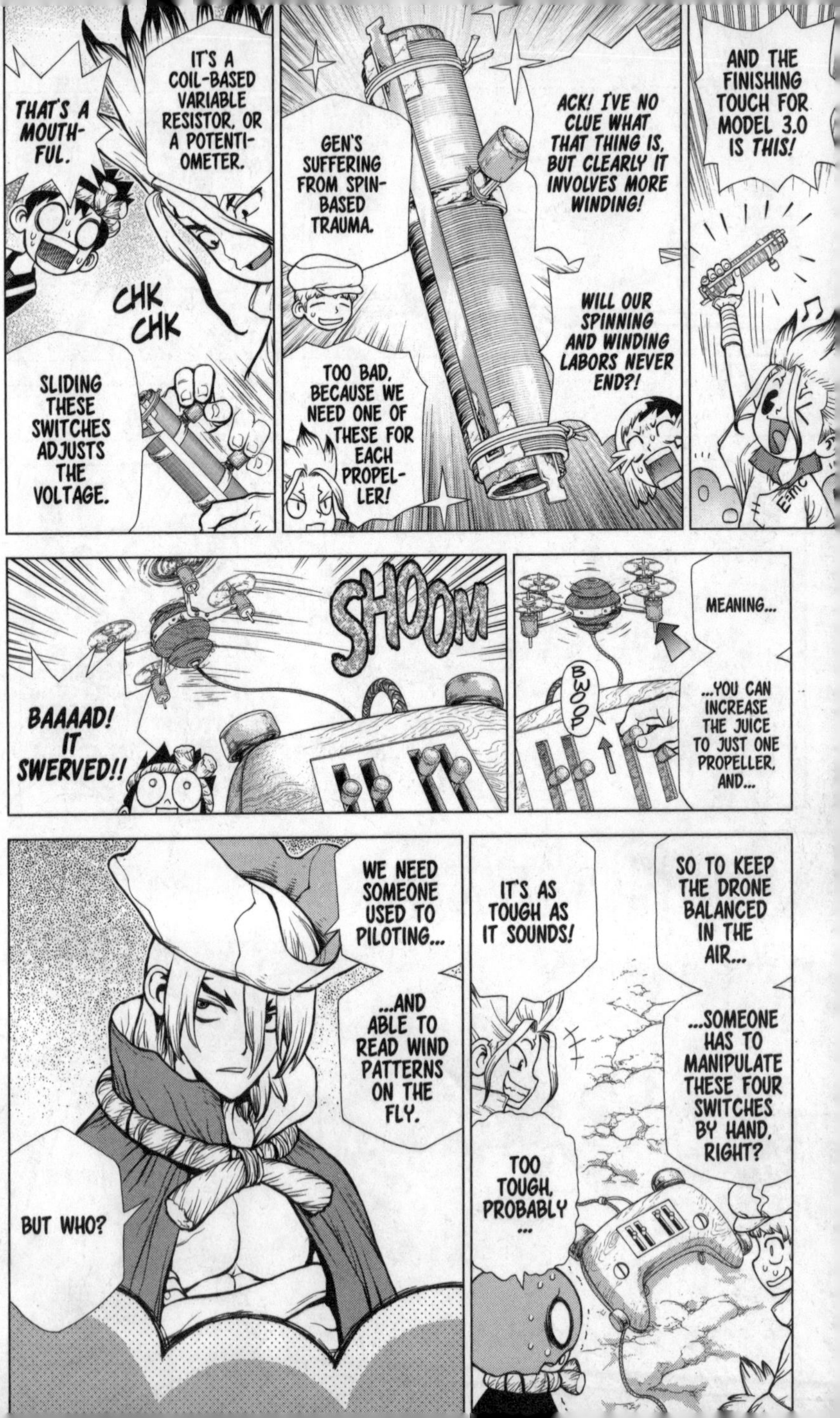
AND THE FINISHING TOUCH FOR MODEL 3.0 IS THIS!
ACK! I'VE NO CLUE WHAT THAT THING IS, BUT CLEARLY IT INVOLVES MORE WINDING!
GEN'S SUFFERING FROM SPIN-BASED TRAUMA.
WILL OUR SPINNING AND WINDING LABORS NEVER END?!
TOO BAD, BECAUSE WE NEED ONE OF THESE FOR EACH PROPELLER!
IT'S A COIL-BASED VARIABLE RESISTOR, OR A POTENTIOMETER.
THAT'S A MOUTHFUL.
CHK CHK
SLIDING THESE SWITCHES ADJUSTS THE VOLTAGE.
MEANING...
BWOOP
...YOU CAN INCREASE THE JUICE TO JUST ONE PROPELLER, AND...
SHOOM
BAAAAD! IT SWERVED!!
SO TO KEEP THE DRONE BALANCED IN THE AIR...
IT'S AS TOUGH AS IT SOUNDS!
...SOMEONE HAS TO MANIPULATE THESE FOUR SWITCHES BY HAND, RIGHT?
TOO TOUGH, PROBABLY...
WE NEED SOMEONE USED TO PILOTING...
...AND ABLE TO READ WIND PATTERNS ON THE FLY.
BUT WHO?

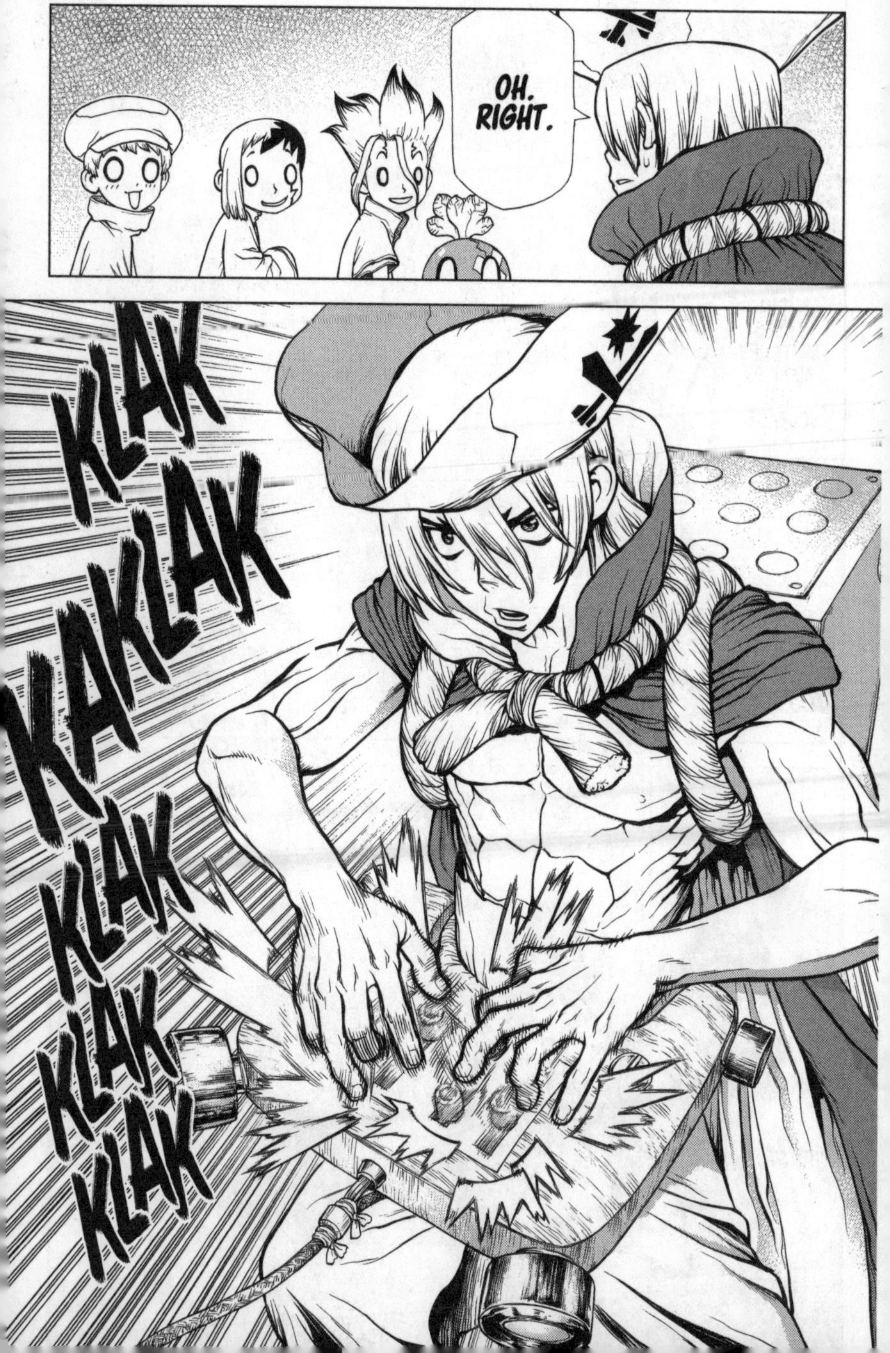
OH. RIGHT.
KLAK KLAK KAKLAK
KAKLAK KLAK KLAK KLAK KLAK KLAK

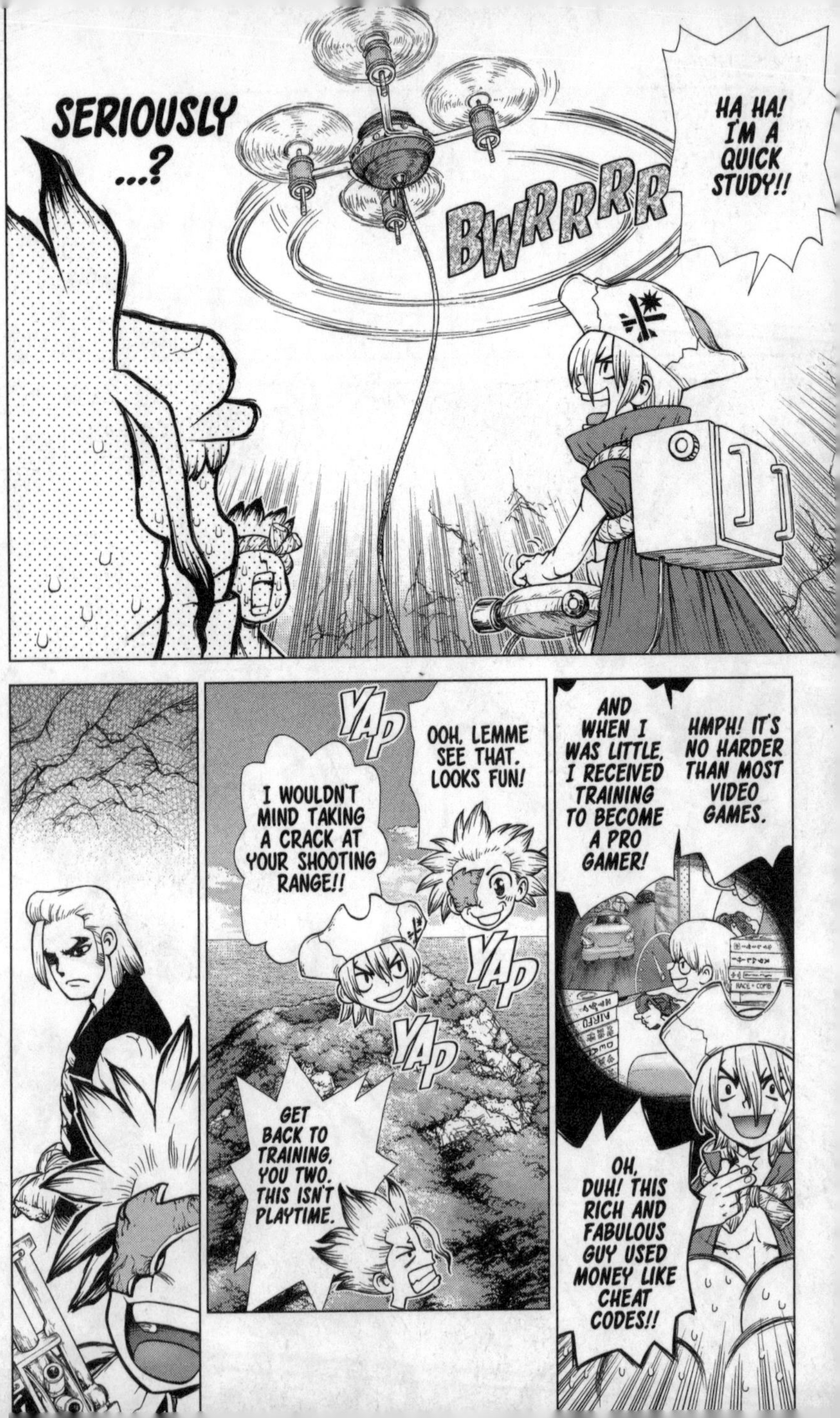
HA HA! I'M A QUICK STUDY!!
BWRRRR
SERIOUSLY ...?
HMPH! IT'S NO HARDER THAN MOST VIDEO GAMES.
AND WHEN I WAS LITTLE, I RECEIVED TRAINING TO BECOME A PRO GAMER!
OH, DUH! THIS RICH AND FABULOUS GUY USED MONEY LIKE CHEAT CODES!!
OOH, LEMME SEE THAT. LOOKS FUN!
YAP
I WOULDN'T MIND TAKING A CRACK AT YOUR SHOOTING RANGE!!
YAP
YAP
GET BACK TO TRAINING, YOU TWO. THIS ISN'T PLAYTIME.

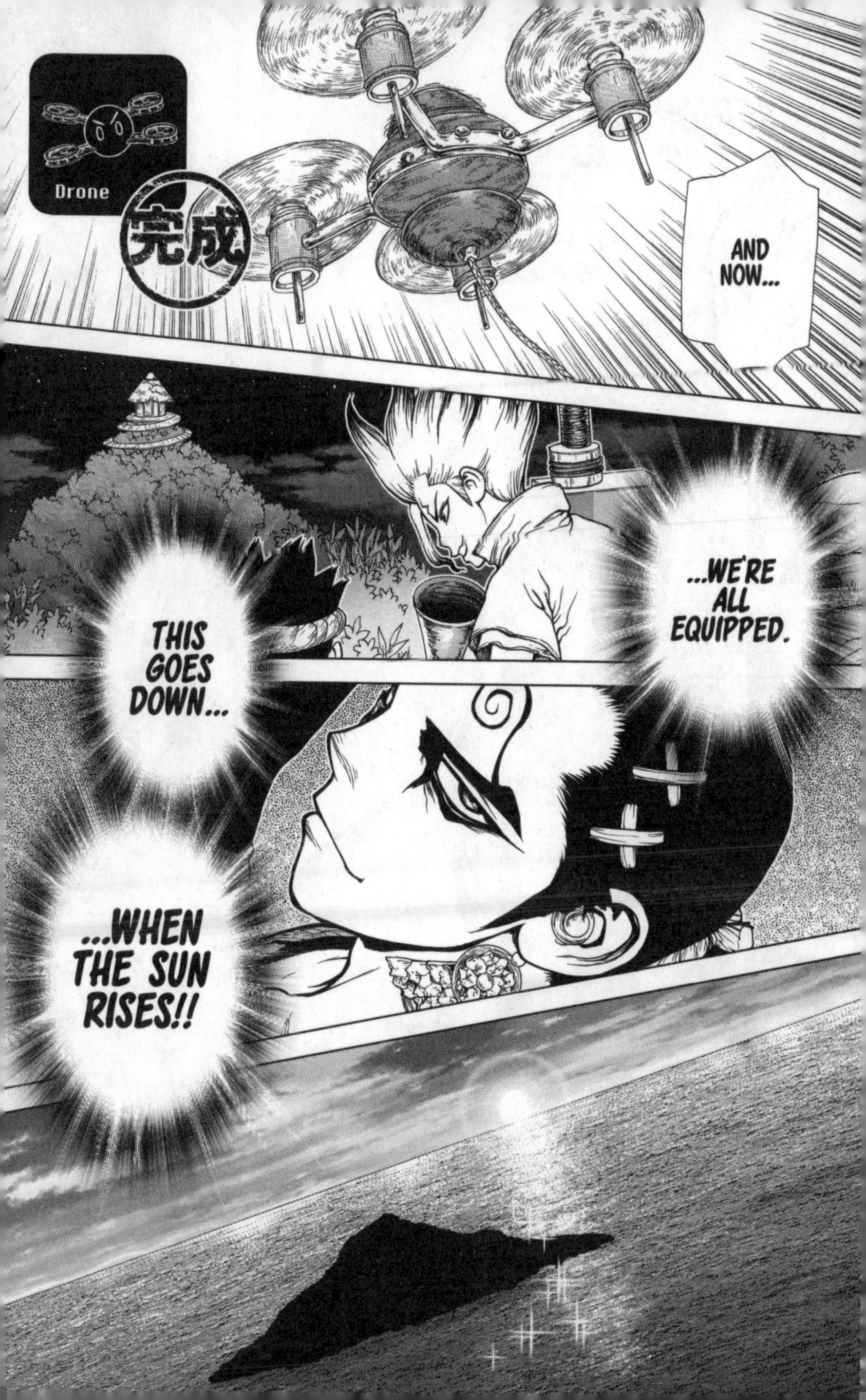

Drone
完成
AND NOW...
...WE'RE ALL EQUIPPED.
THIS GOES DOWN...
...WHEN THE SUN RISES!!

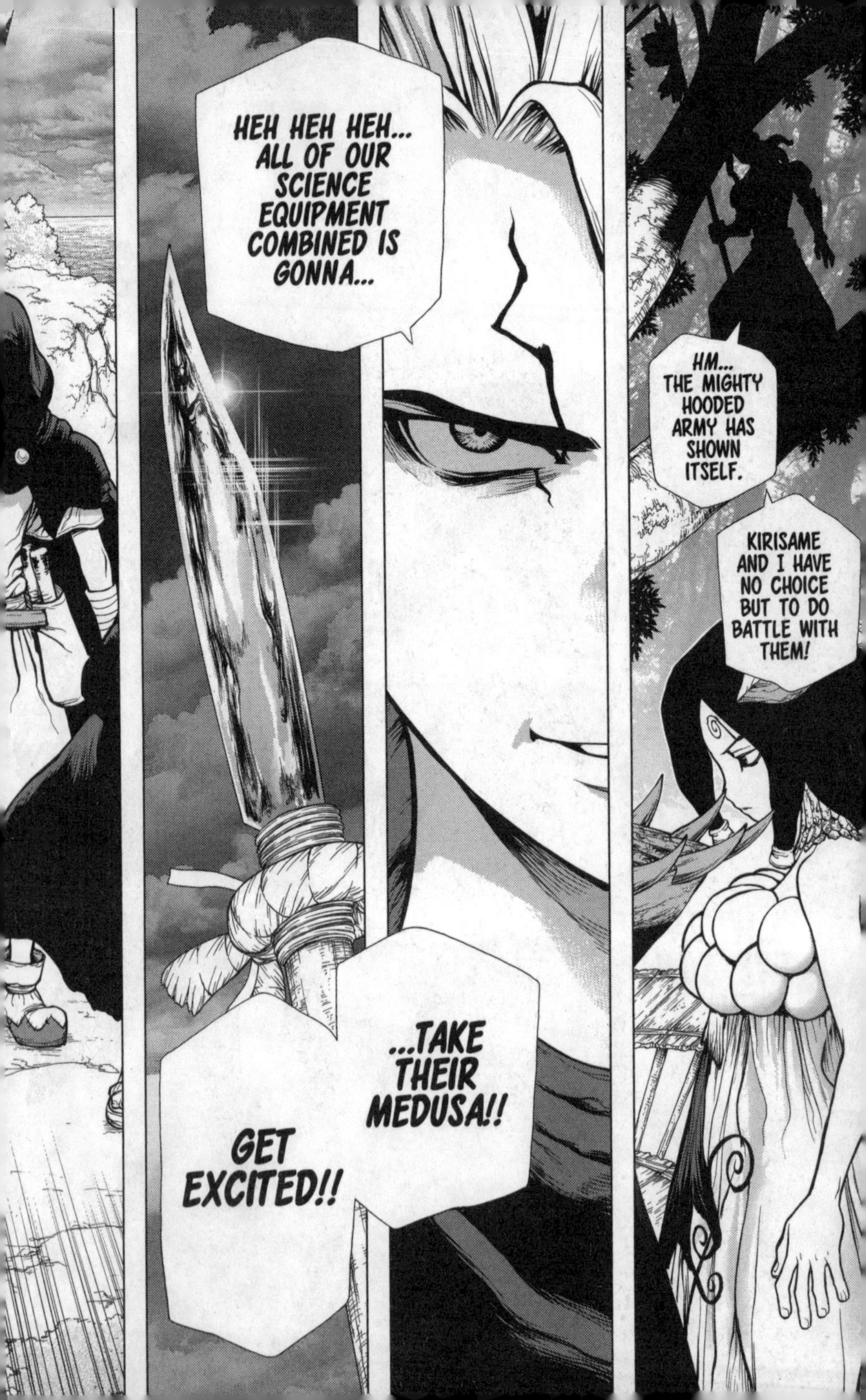
HM... THE MIGHTY HOODED ARMY HAS SHOWN ITSELF.
KIRISAME AND I HAVE NO CHOICE BUT TO DO BATTLE WITH THEM!
HEH HEH HEH... ALL OF OUR SCIENCE EQUIPMENT COMBINED IS GONNA...
...TAKE THEIR MEDUSA!!
GET EXCITED!!

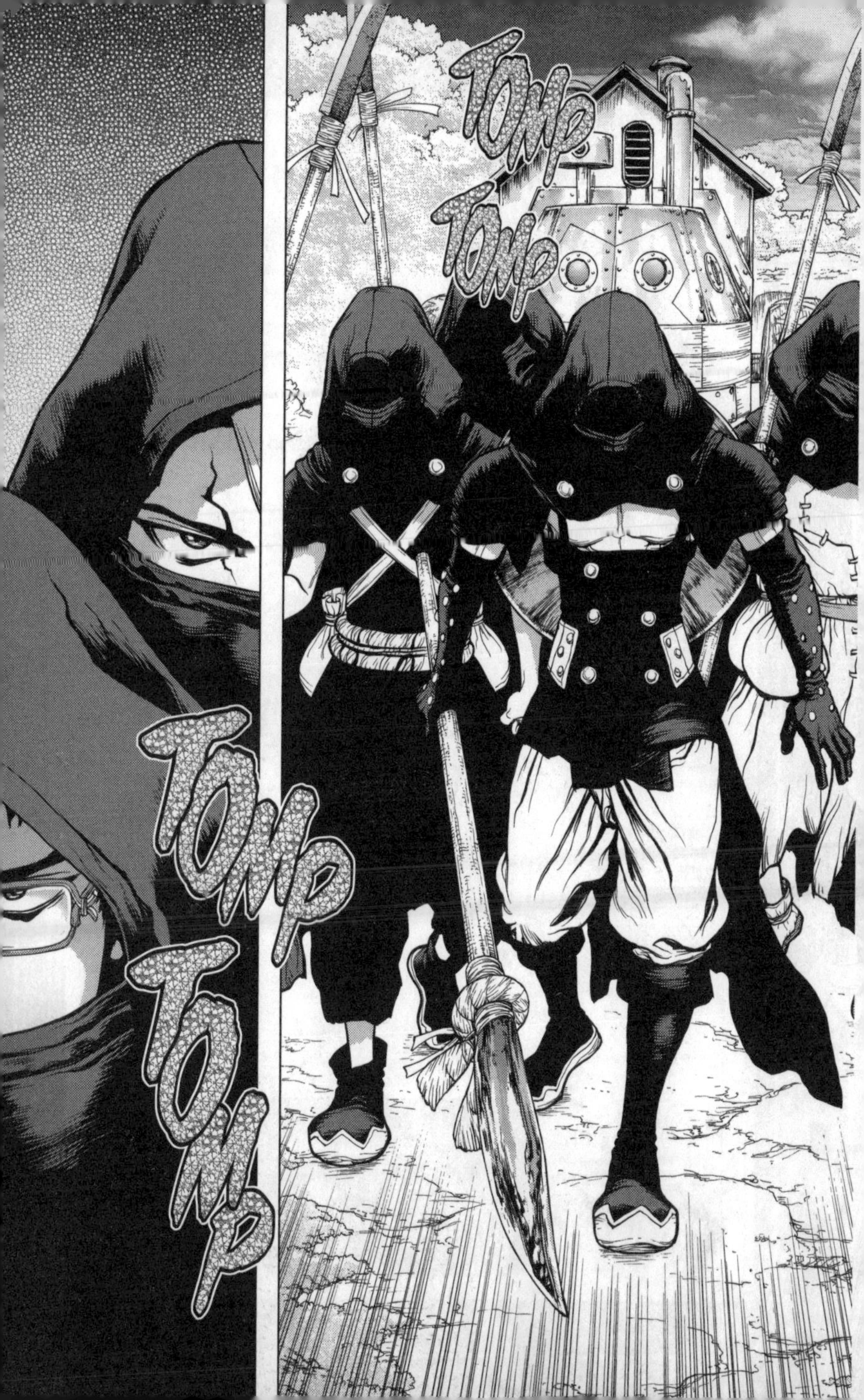
TOMP
TOMP
TOMP
TOMP

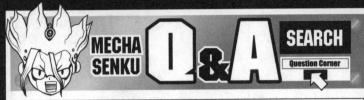

# MECHA SENKU Q&A

SEARCH

Question Corner

**How are people saving and storing all those dragos they get from Ryusui? Aren't they worried about being robbed?**

Suemitsu of Ibaraki Prefecture

SEARCH

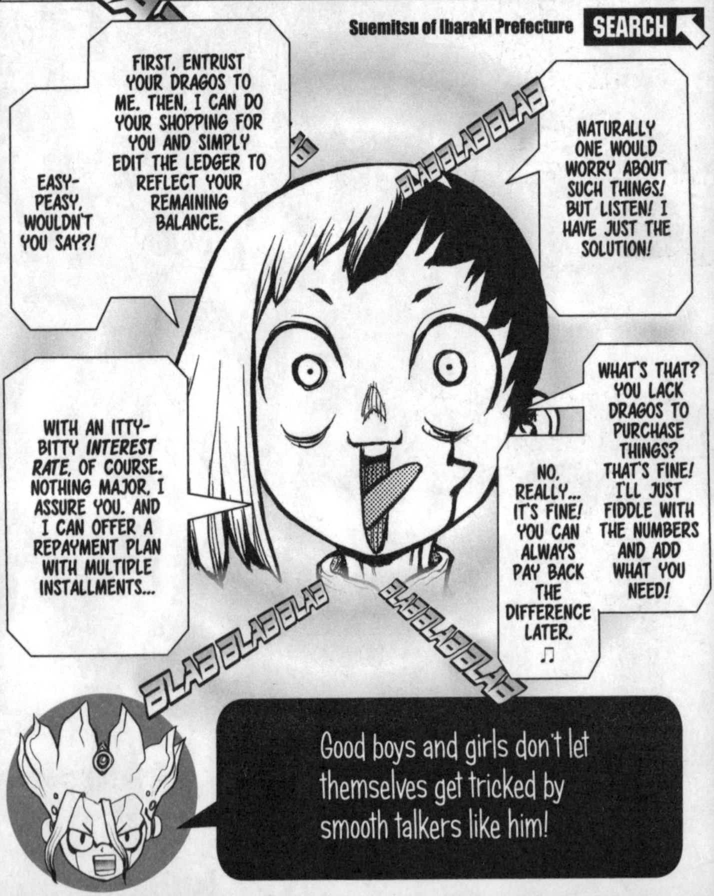

NATURALLY ONE WOULD WORRY ABOUT SUCH THINGS! BUT LISTEN! I HAVE JUST THE SOLUTION!
FIRST, ENTRUST YOUR DRAGOS TO ME. THEN, I CAN DO YOUR SHOPPING FOR YOU AND SIMPLY EDIT THE LEDGER TO REFLECT YOUR REMAINING BALANCE.
EASY-PEASY, WOULDN'T YOU SAY?!
BLAB BLAB BLAB
WHAT'S THAT? YOU LACK DRAGOS TO PURCHASE THINGS? THAT'S FINE! I'LL JUST FIDDLE WITH THE NUMBERS AND ADD WHAT YOU NEED!
NO, REALLY... IT'S FINE! YOU CAN ALWAYS PAY BACK THE DIFFERENCE LATER. ♫
WITH AN ITTY-BITTY *INTEREST RATE*, OF COURSE. NOTHING MAJOR, I ASSURE YOU. AND I CAN OFFER A REPAYMENT PLAN WITH MULTIPLE INSTALLMENTS...
BLAB BLAB BLAB
Good boys and girls don't let themselves get tricked by smooth talkers like him!

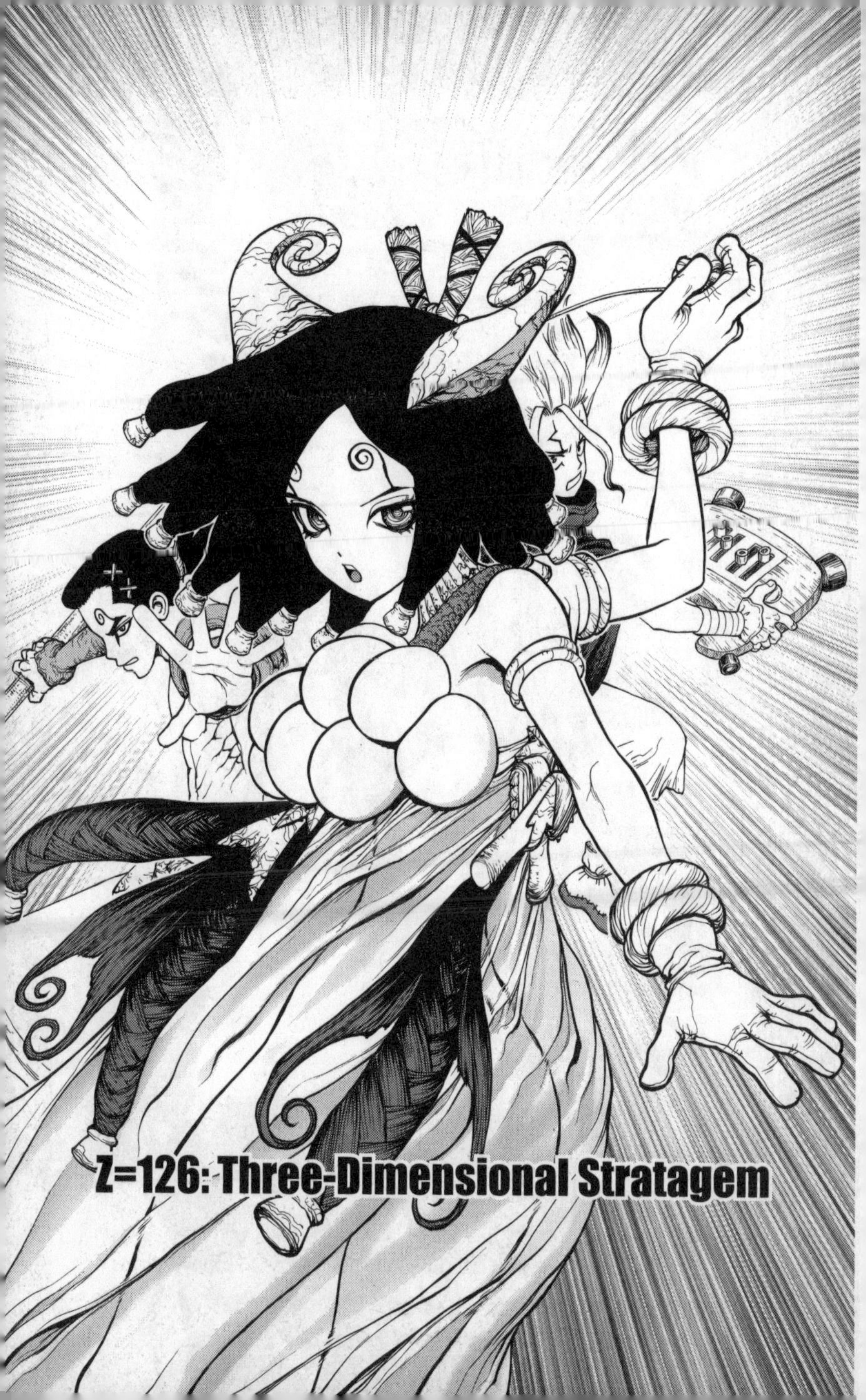
Z=126: Three-Dimensional Stratagem

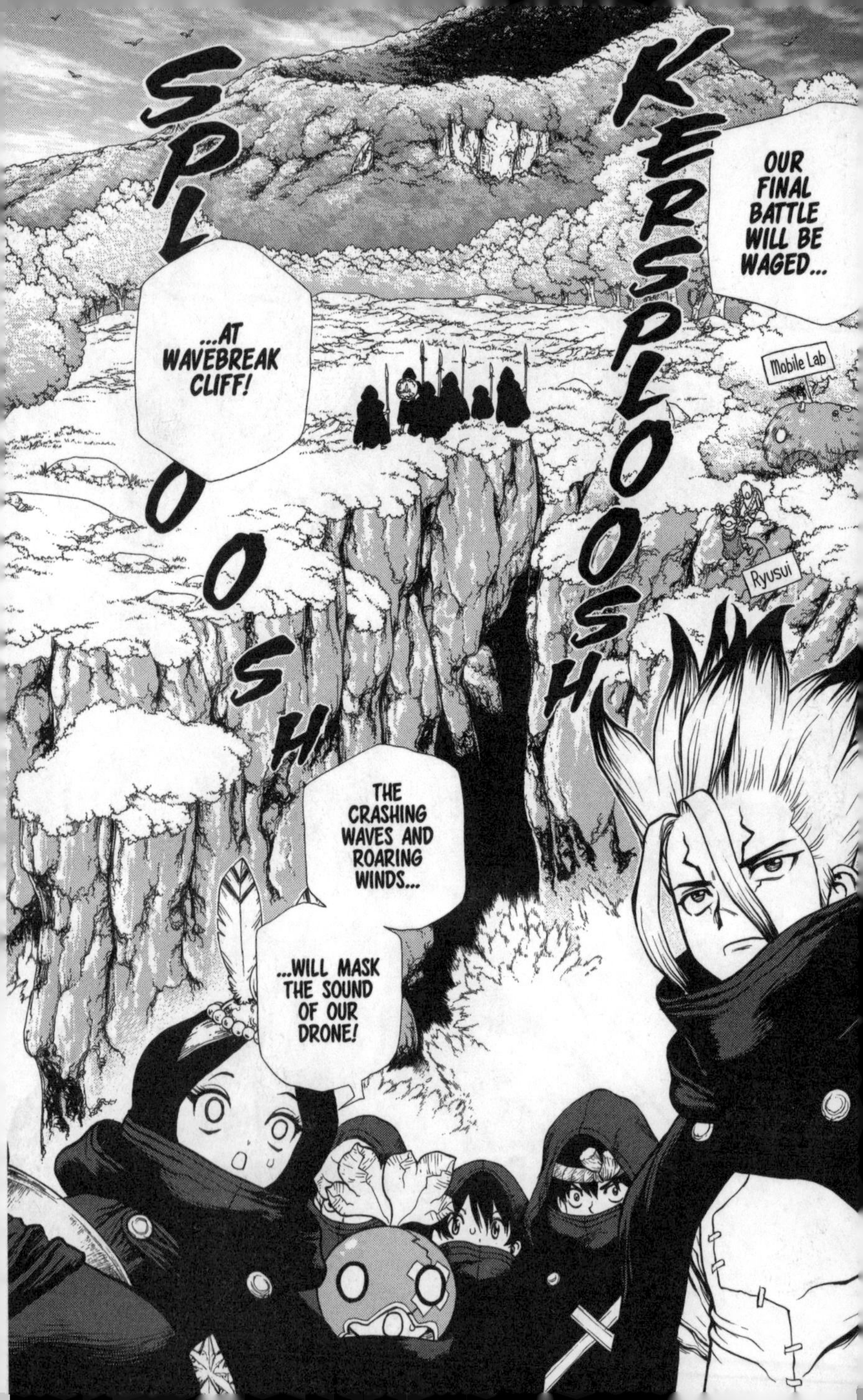
OUR FINAL BATTLE WILL BE WAGED...
KERSPLOOSH
SPLOOSH
...AT WAVEBREAK CLIFF!
Mobile Lab
Ryusui
THE CRASHING WAVES AND ROARING WINDS...
...WILL MASK THE SOUND OF OUR DRONE!

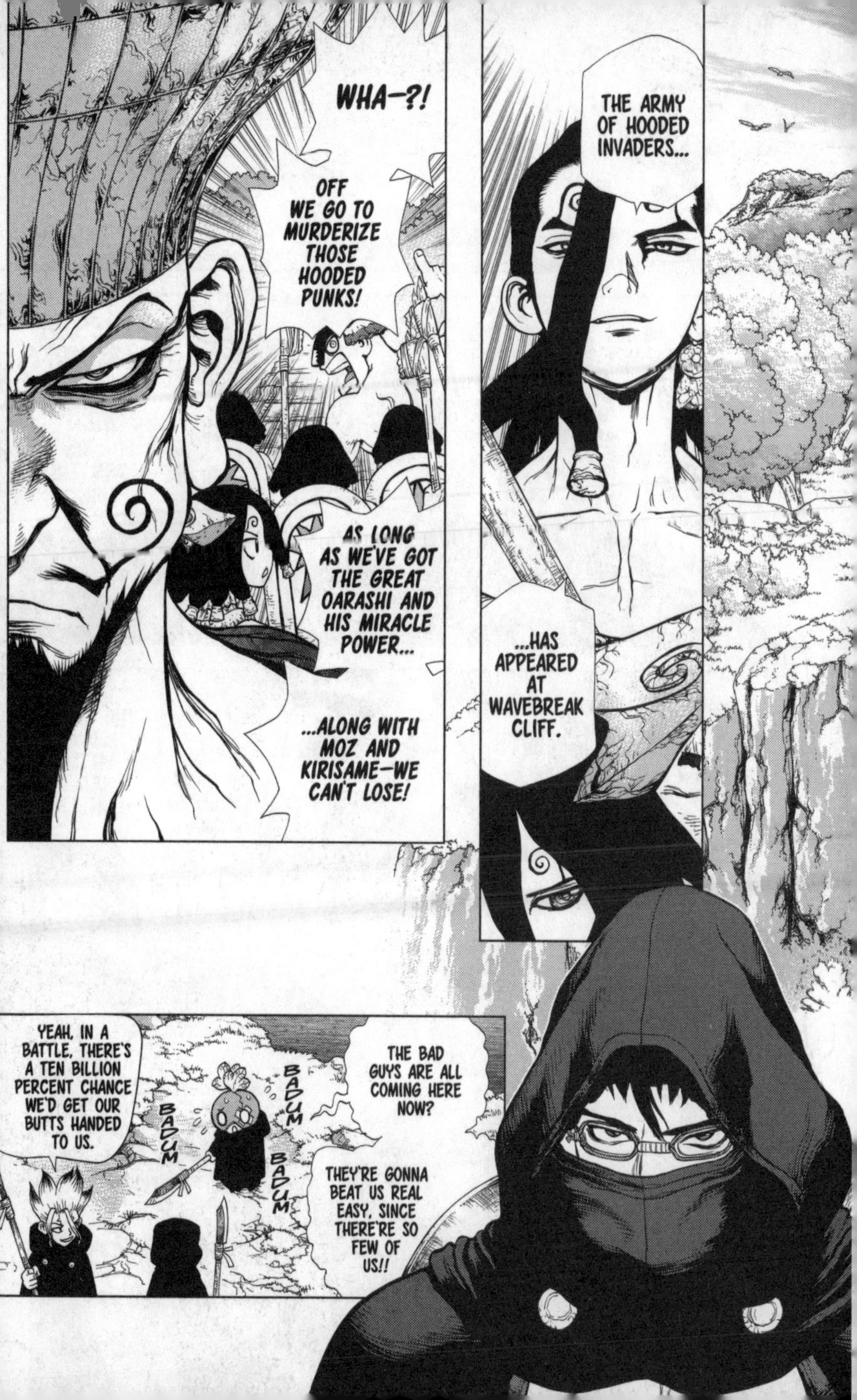
THE ARMY OF HOODED INVADERS...
...HAS APPEARED AT WAVEBREAK CLIFF.
WHA-?!
OFF WE GO TO MURDERIZE THOSE HOODED PUNKS!
AS LONG AS WE'VE GOT THE GREAT OARASHI AND HIS MIRACLE POWER...
...ALONG WITH MOZ AND KIRISAME—WE CAN'T LOSE!
THE BAD GUYS ARE ALL COMING HERE NOW?
BADUM
BADUM
BADUM
THEY'RE GONNA BEAT US REAL EASY, SINCE THERE'RE SO FEW OF US!!
YEAH, IN A BATTLE, THERE'S A TEN BILLION PERCENT CHANCE WE'D GET OUR BUTTS HANDED TO US.

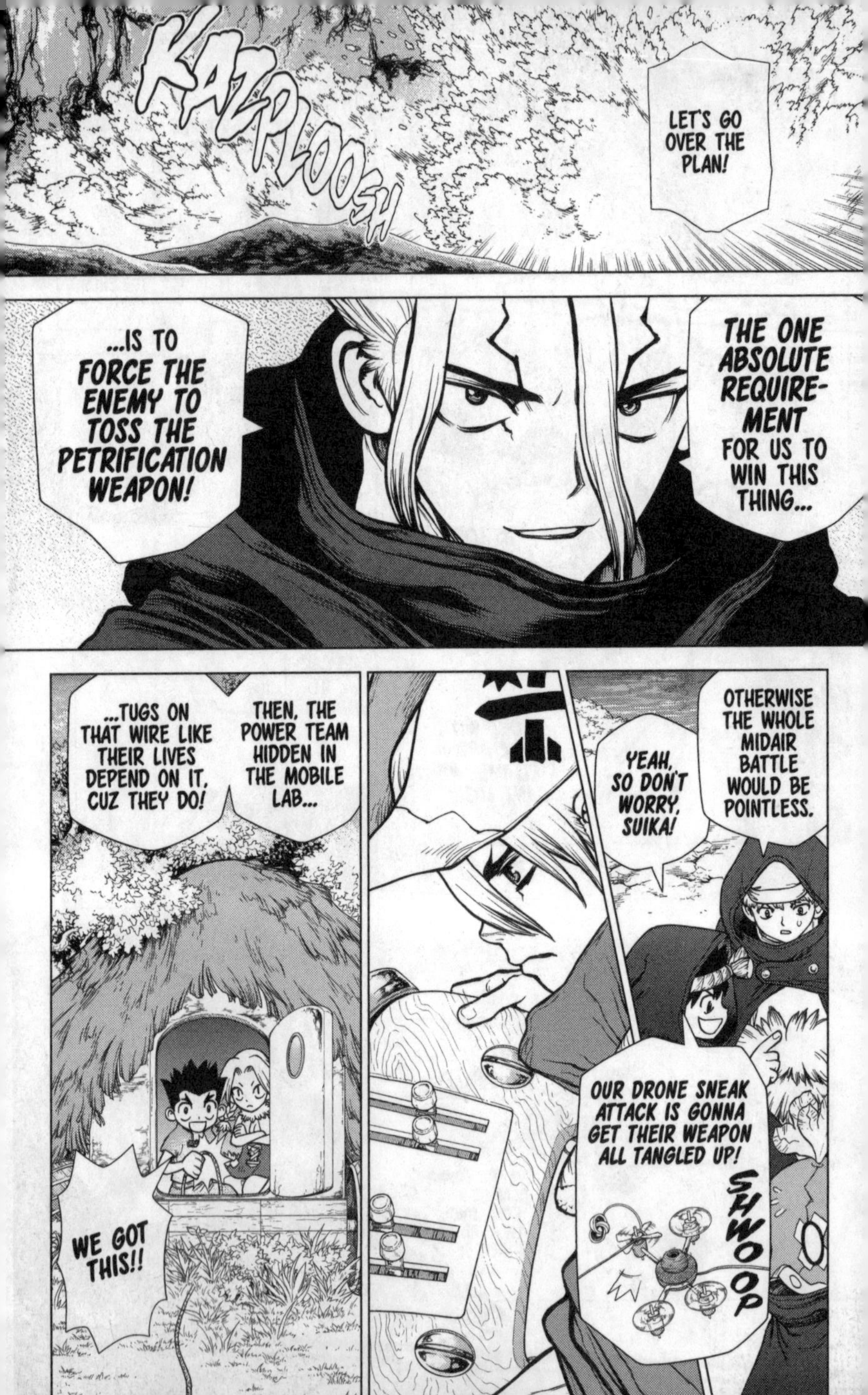
LET'S GO OVER THE PLAN!
KAZPLOOSH
THE ONE ABSOLUTE REQUIRE-MENT FOR US TO WIN THIS THING...
...IS TO FORCE THE ENEMY TO TOSS THE PETRIFICATION WEAPON!
OTHERWISE THE WHOLE MIDAIR BATTLE WOULD BE POINTLESS.
YEAH, SO DON'T WORRY, SUIKA!
OUR DRONE SNEAK ATTACK IS GONNA GET THEIR WEAPON ALL TANGLED UP!
SHWOOP
THEN, THE POWER TEAM HIDDEN IN THE MOBILE LAB...
...TUGS ON THAT WIRE LIKE THEIR LIVES DEPEND ON IT, CUZ THEY DO!
WE GOT THIS!!

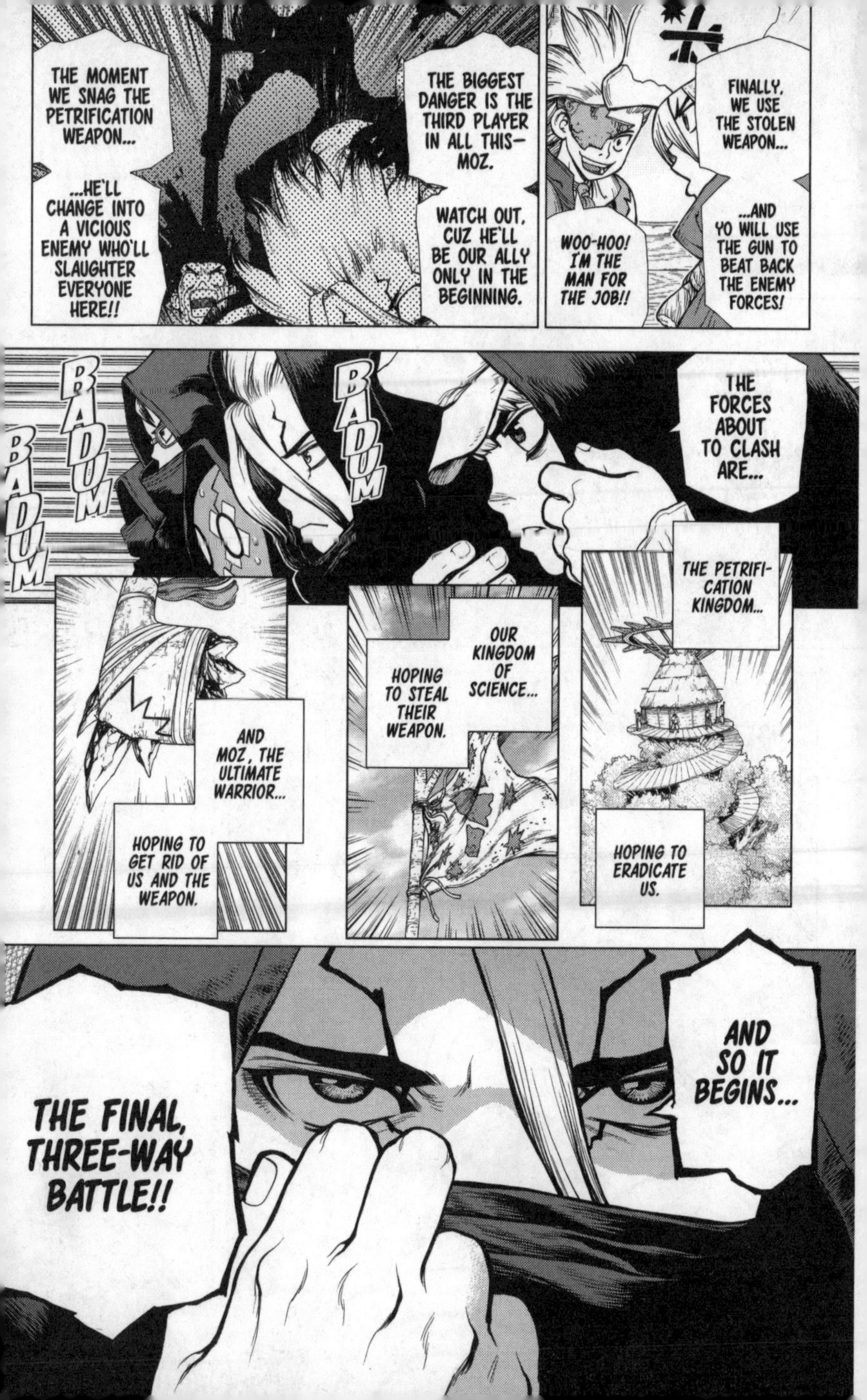
FINALLY, WE USE THE STOLEN WEAPON...
...AND YO WILL USE THE GUN TO BEAT BACK THE ENEMY FORCES!
WOO-HOO! I'M THE MAN FOR THE JOB!!
THE BIGGEST DANGER IS THE THIRD PLAYER IN ALL THIS—MOZ.
WATCH OUT, CUZ HE'LL BE OUR ALLY ONLY IN THE BEGINNING.
THE MOMENT WE SNAG THE PETRIFICATION WEAPON...
...HE'LL CHANGE INTO A VICIOUS ENEMY WHO'LL SLAUGHTER EVERYONE HERE!!
THE FORCES ABOUT TO CLASH ARE...
BADUM
BADUM
BADUM
THE PETRIFICATION KINGDOM...
HOPING TO ERADICATE US.
OUR KINGDOM OF SCIENCE...
HOPING TO STEAL THEIR WEAPON.
AND MOZ, THE ULTIMATE WARRIOR...
HOPING TO GET RID OF US AND THE WEAPON.
AND SO IT BEGINS...
THE FINAL, THREE-WAY BATTLE!!

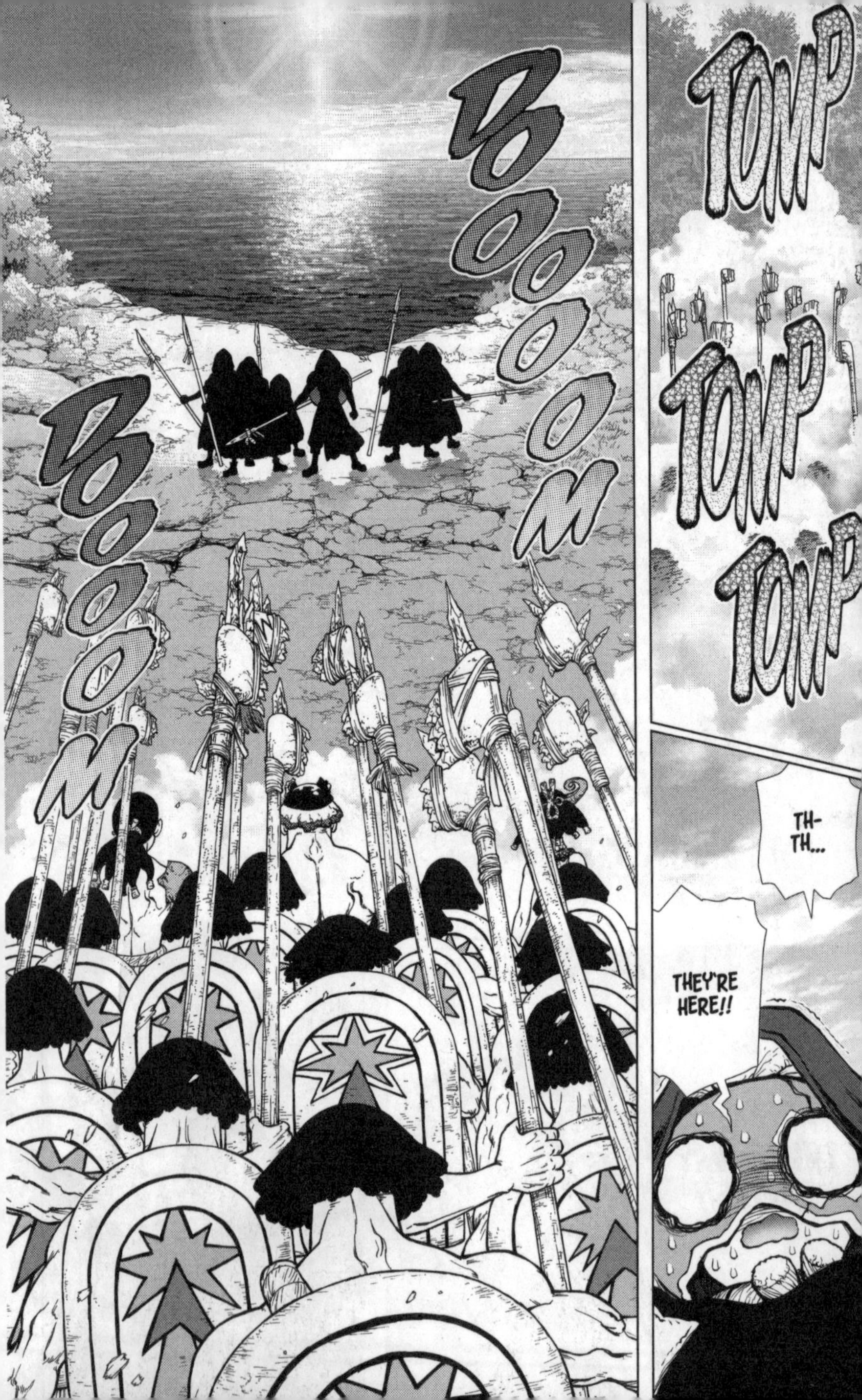
TOMP
TOMP
TOMP
TOMP
TH- TH...
THEY'RE HERE!!
DOOOOOOM
DOOOOOM

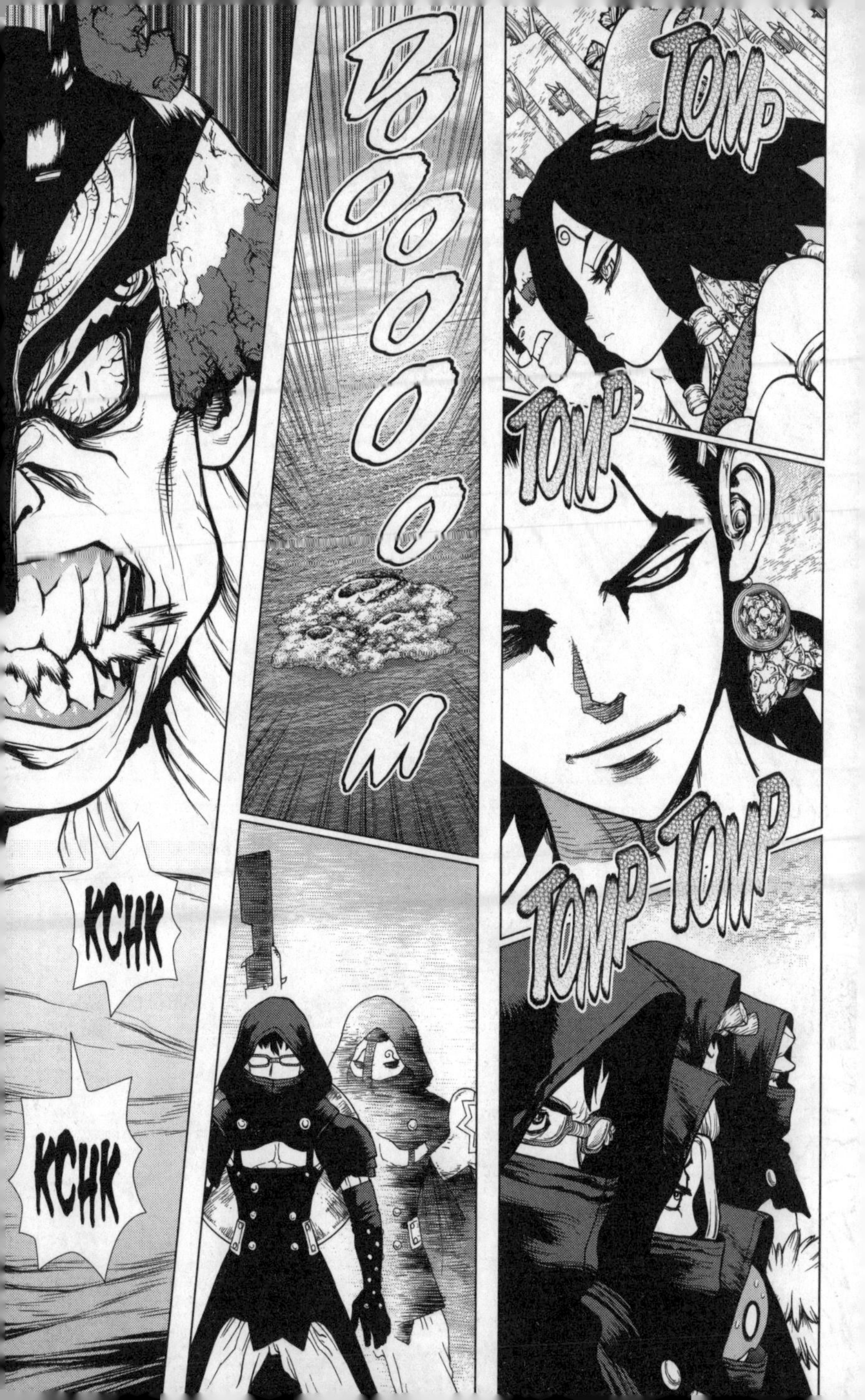
TOMP
TOMP
TOMP
TOMP
DOOOOOOOM
KCHK
KCHK

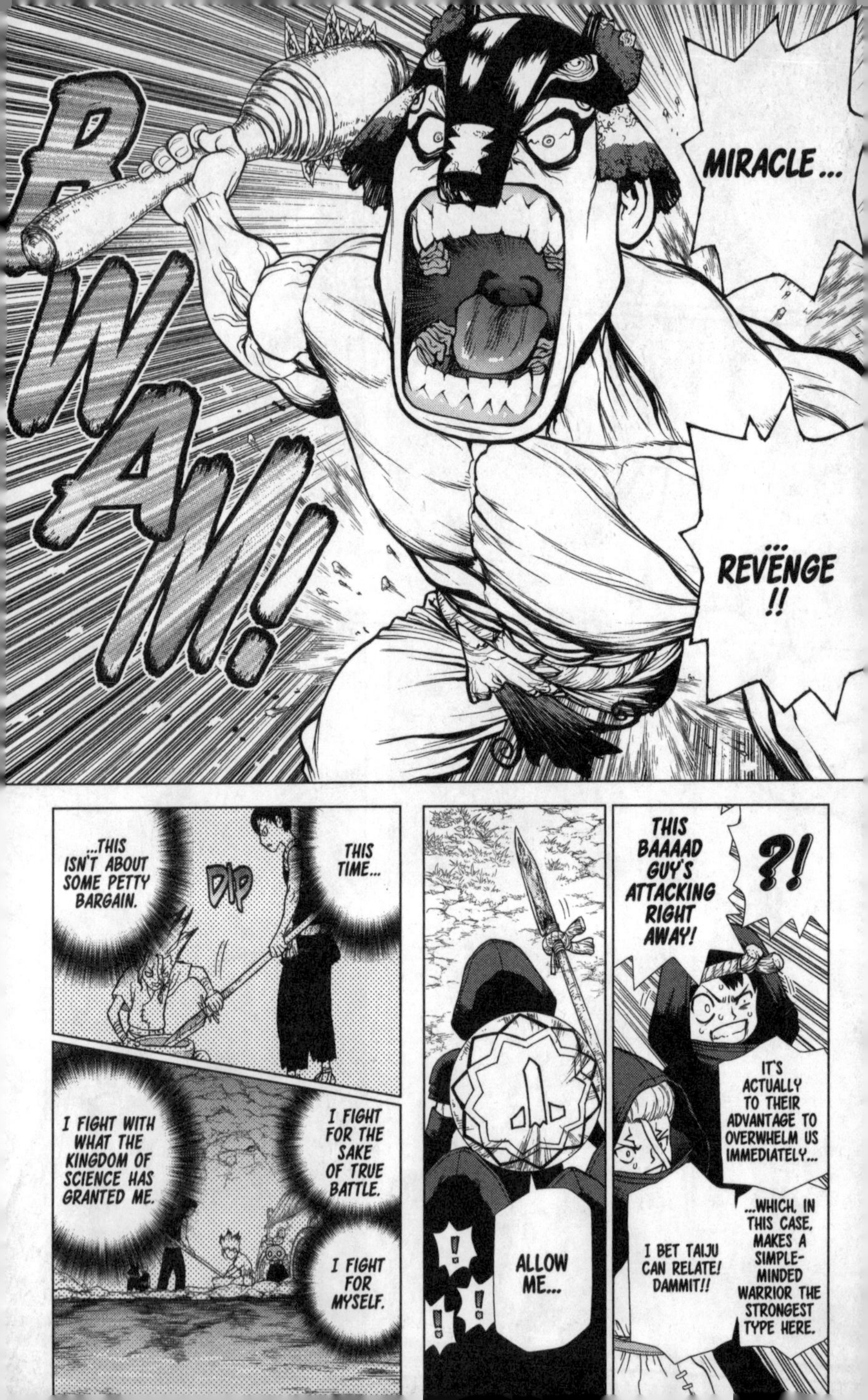
MIRACLE...
...REVËNGE !!
PWAM!
?!
THIS BAAAAD GUY'S ATTACKING RIGHT AWAY!
IT'S ACTUALLY TO THEIR ADVANTAGE TO OVERWHELM US IMMEDIATELY...
...WHICH, IN THIS CASE, MAKES A SIMPLE-MINDED WARRIOR THE STRONGEST TYPE HERE.
I BET TAIJU CAN RELATE! DAMMIT!!
ALLOW ME...
THIS TIME...
DIP
...THIS ISN'T ABOUT SOME PETTY BARGAIN.
I FIGHT FOR THE SAKE OF TRUE BATTLE.
I FIGHT WITH WHAT THE KINGDOM OF SCIENCE HAS GRANTED ME.
I FIGHT FOR MYSELF.

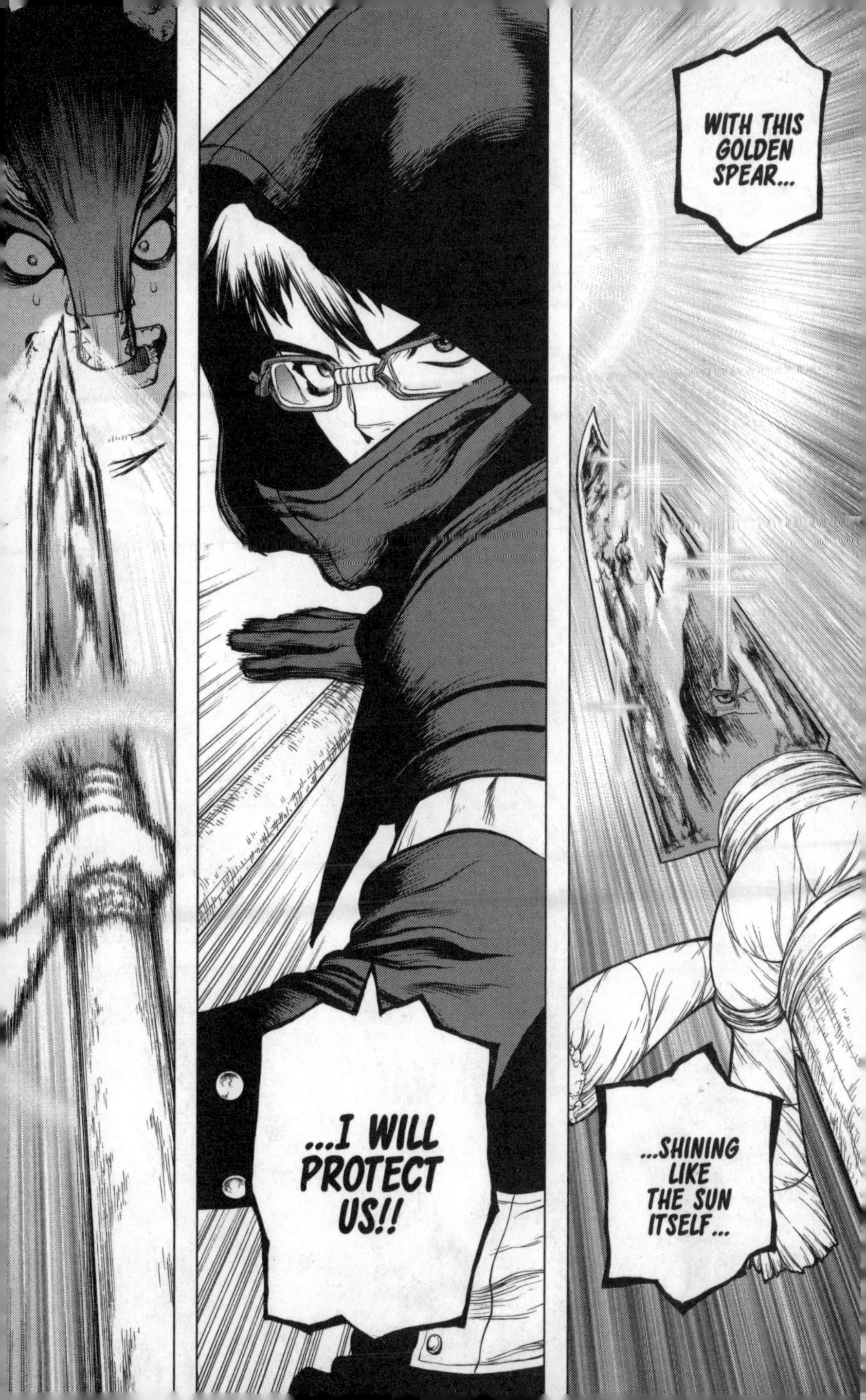
WITH THIS GOLDEN SPEAR...
...SHINING LIKE THE SUN ITSELF...
...I WILL PROTECT US!!

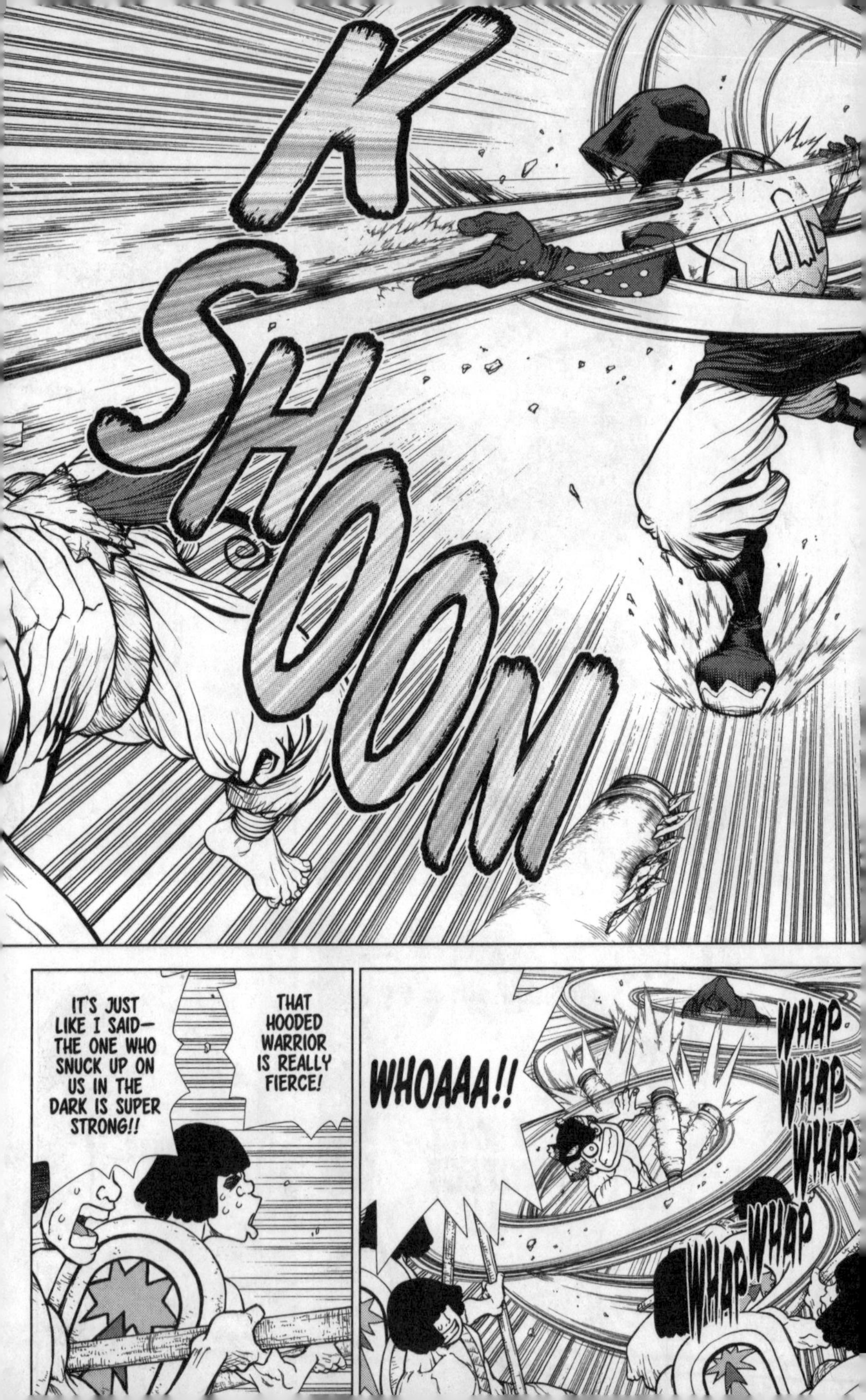
KSHOOOM
WHOAAA!!
WHAP WHAP WHAP WHAP WHAP WHAP
THAT HOODED WARRIOR IS REALLY FIERCE!
IT'S JUST LIKE I SAID— THE ONE WHO SNUCK UP ON US IN THE DARK IS SUPER STRONG!!

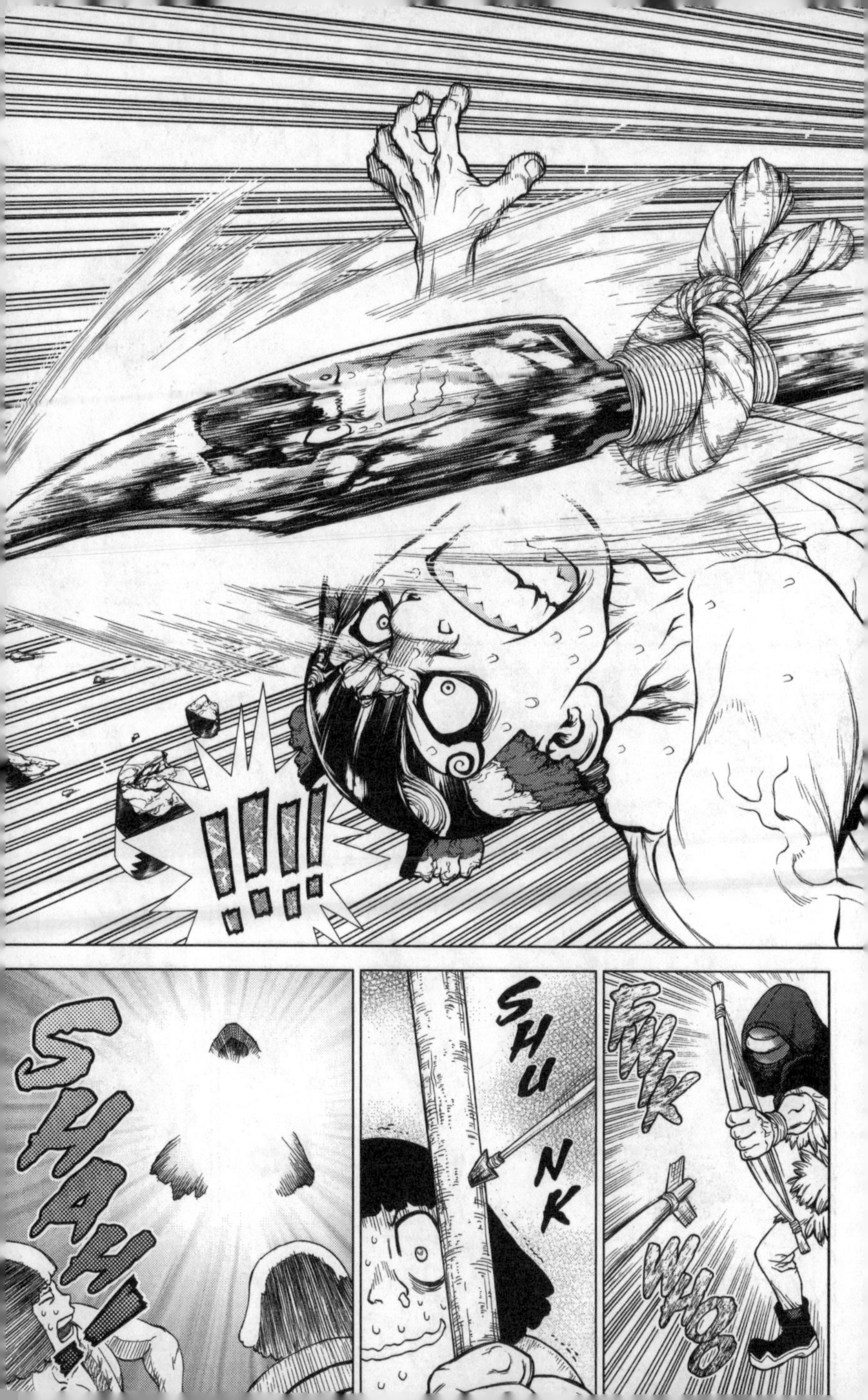
!!!!
FWK
WHOO
SHUNK
SHAH!!

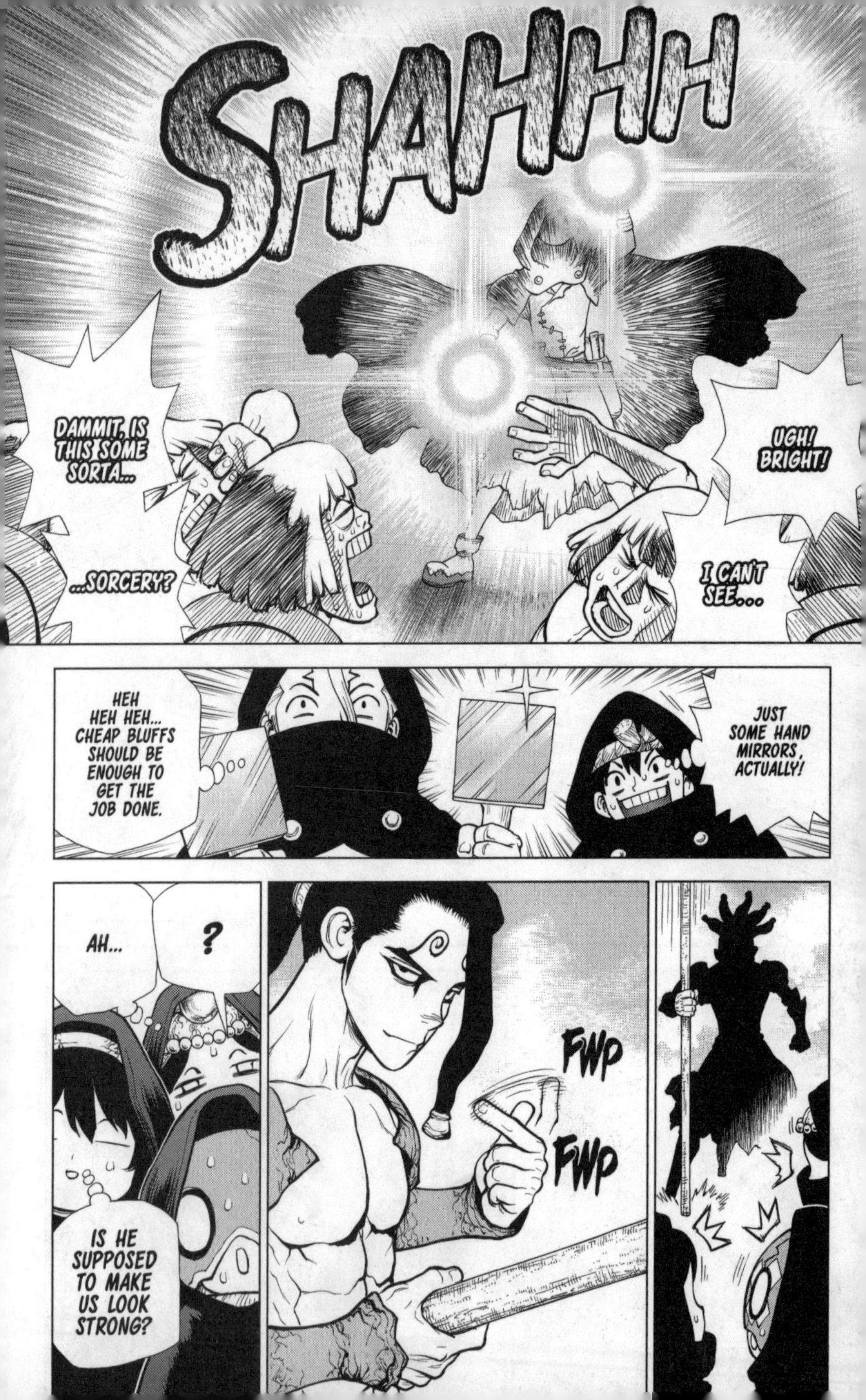
SHAHHH
UGH! BRIGHT!
I CAN'T SEE...
DAMMIT, IS THIS SOME SORTA...
...SORCERY?
JUST SOME HAND MIRRORS, ACTUALLY!
HEH HEH HEH... CHEAP BLUFFS SHOULD BE ENOUGH TO GET THE JOB DONE.
FWP
FWP
?
AH...
IS HE SUPPOSED TO MAKE US LOOK STRONG?

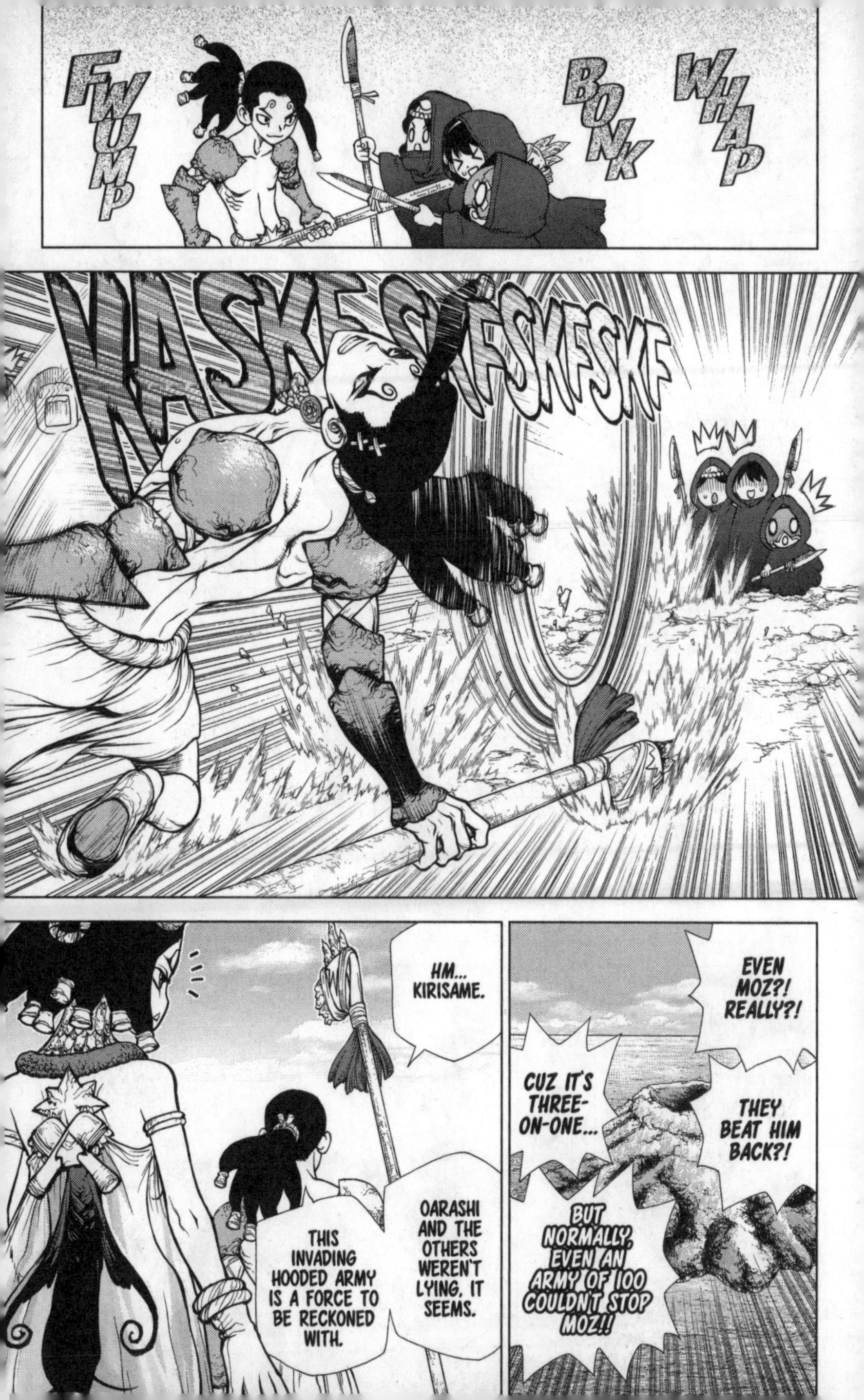
WHAP
BONK
FWUMP
EVEN MOZ?! REALLY?!
THEY BEAT HIM BACK?!
CUZ IT'S THREE-ON-ONE...
BUT NORMALLY, EVEN AN ARMY OF 100 COULDN'T STOP MOZ!!
HM... KIRISAME.
OARASHI AND THE OTHERS WEREN'T LYING, IT SEEMS.
THIS INVADING HOODED ARMY IS A FORCE TO BE RECKONED WITH.

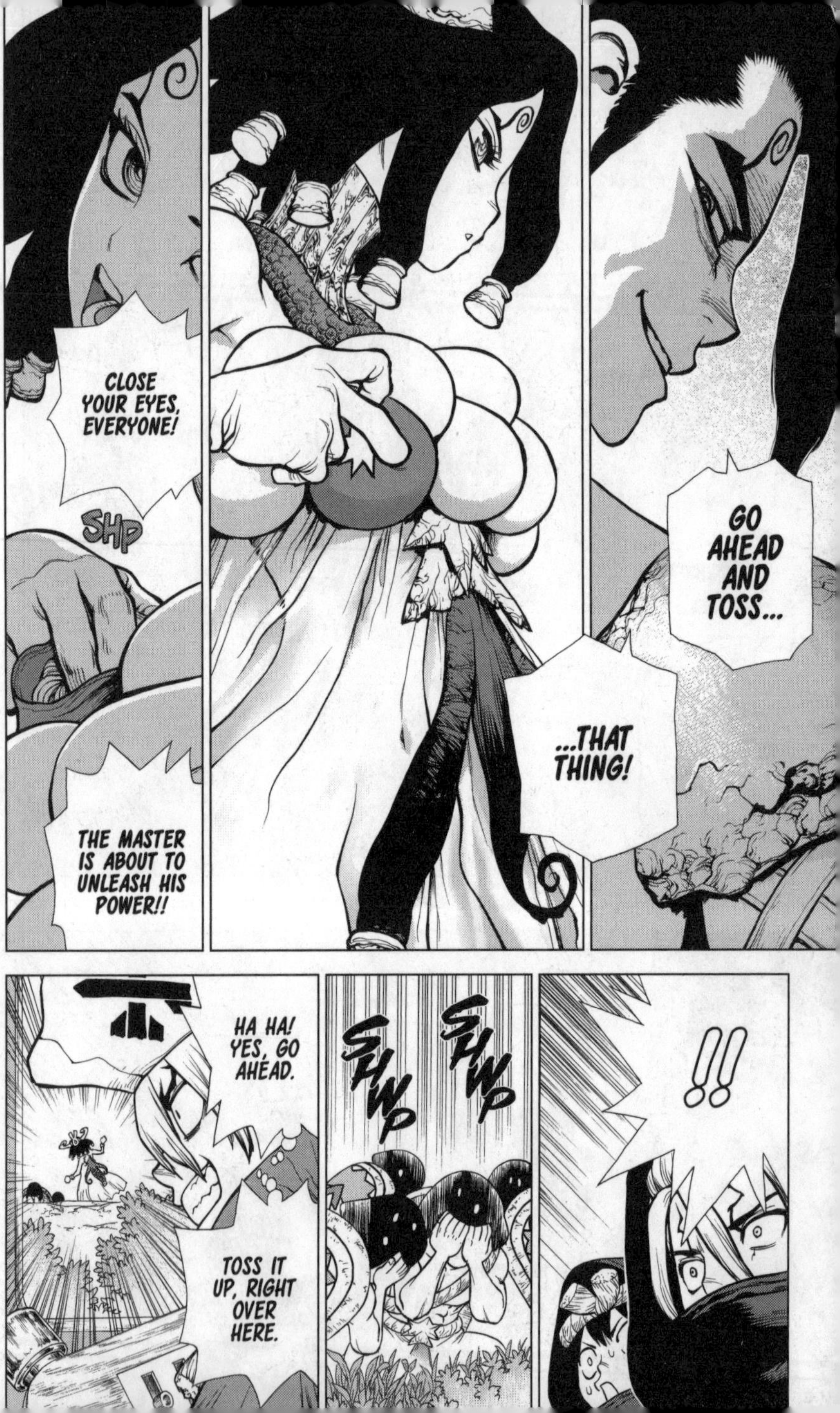
GO AHEAD AND TOSS...
...THAT THING!
CLOSE YOUR EYES, EVERYONE!
SHP
THE MASTER IS ABOUT TO UNLEASH HIS POWER!!
!!
SHWP
SHWP
HA HA! YES, GO AHEAD.
TOSS IT UP, RIGHT OVER HERE.

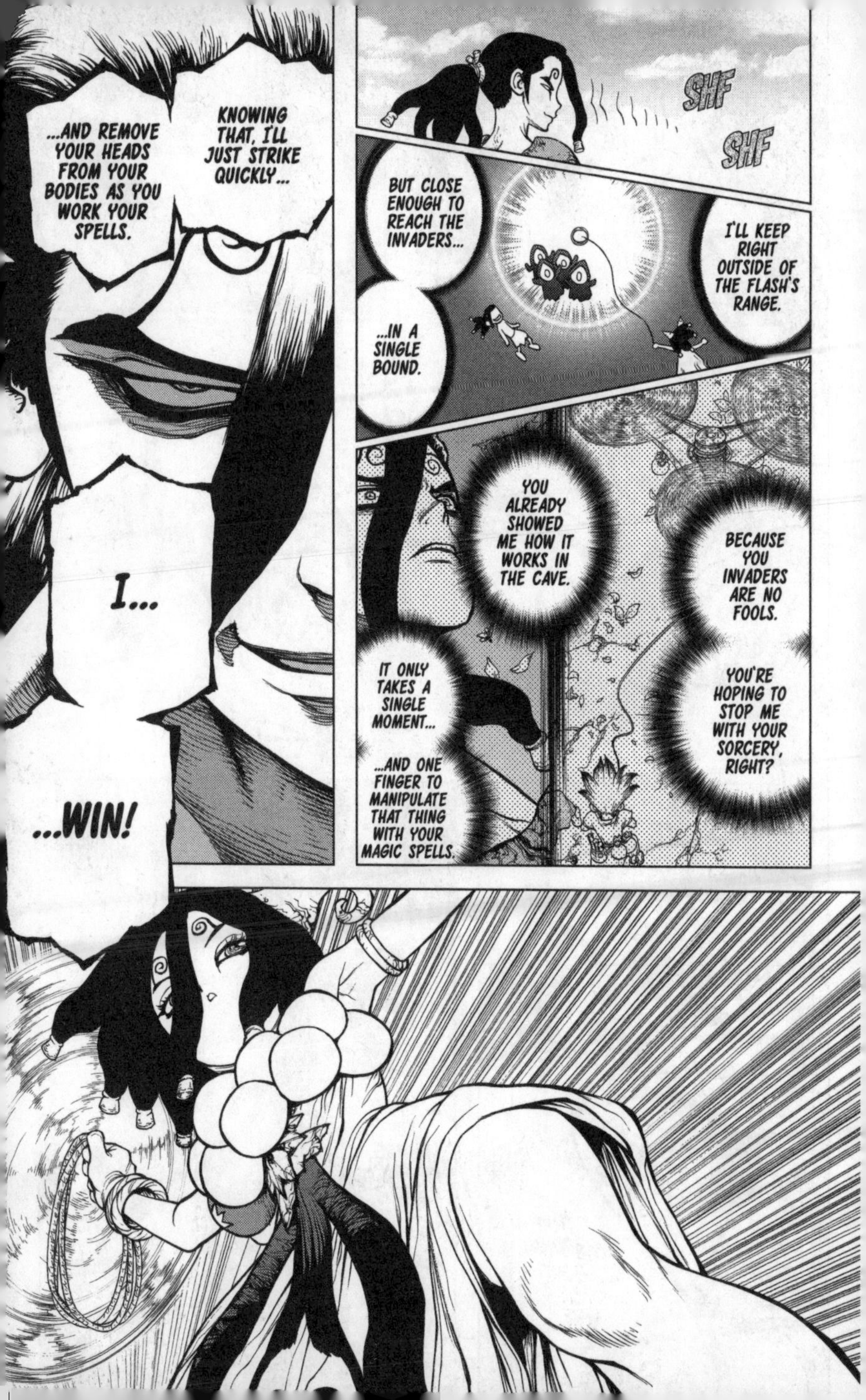
SHF
SHF
I'LL KEEP RIGHT OUTSIDE OF THE FLASH'S RANGE.
BUT CLOSE ENOUGH TO REACH THE INVADERS...
...IN A SINGLE BOUND.
BECAUSE YOU INVADERS ARE NO FOOLS.
YOU'RE HOPING TO STOP ME WITH YOUR SORCERY, RIGHT?
YOU ALREADY SHOWED ME HOW IT WORKS IN THE CAVE.
IT ONLY TAKES A SINGLE MOMENT...
...AND ONE FINGER TO MANIPULATE THAT THING WITH YOUR MAGIC SPELLS.
KNOWING THAT, I'LL JUST STRIKE QUICKLY...
...AND REMOVE YOUR HEADS FROM YOUR BODIES AS YOU WORK YOUR SPELLS.
I...
...WIN!

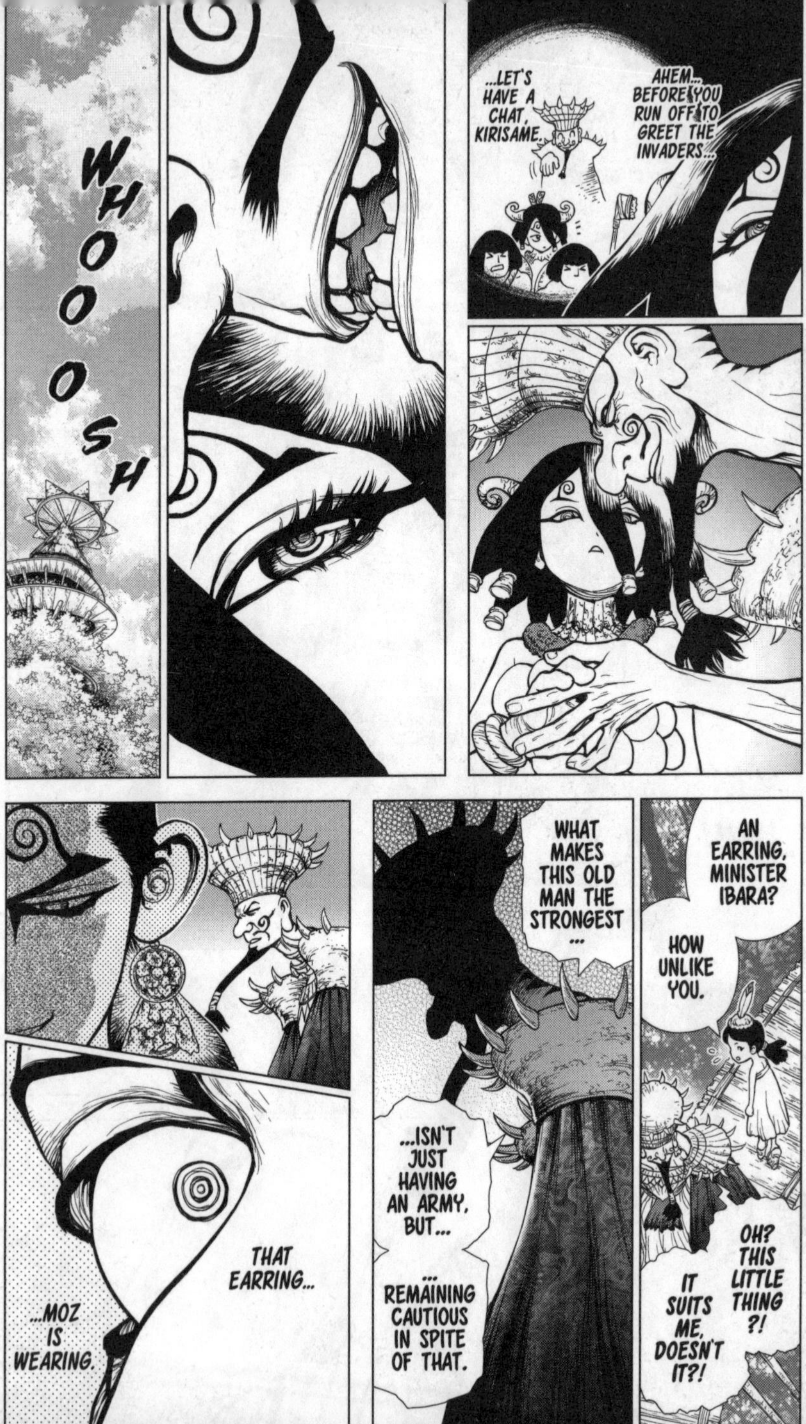
AHEM... BEFORE YOU RUN OFF TO GREET THE INVADERS...
...LET'S HAVE A CHAT, KIRISAME.
WHOOOOOSH
AN EARRING, MINISTER IBARA?
HOW UNLIKE YOU.
OH? THIS LITTLE THING?!
IT SUITS ME, DOESN'T IT?!
WHAT MAKES THIS OLD MAN THE STRONGEST...
...ISN'T JUST HAVING AN ARMY, BUT...
...REMAINING CAUTIOUS IN SPITE OF THAT.
THAT EARRING...
...MOZ IS WEARING.

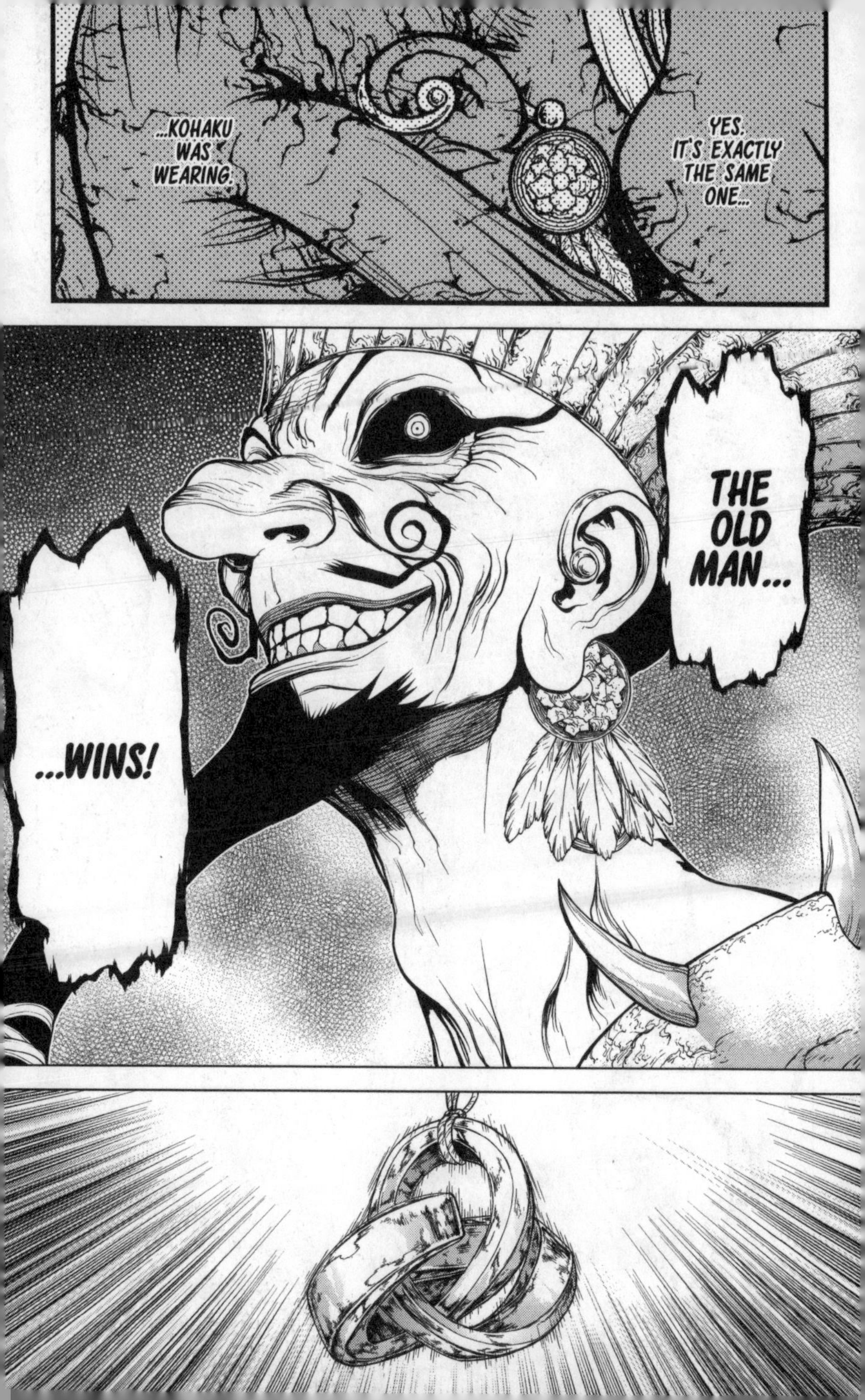
YES. IT'S EXACTLY THE SAME ONE...
...KOHAKU WAS WEARING.
THE OLD MAN...
...WINS!

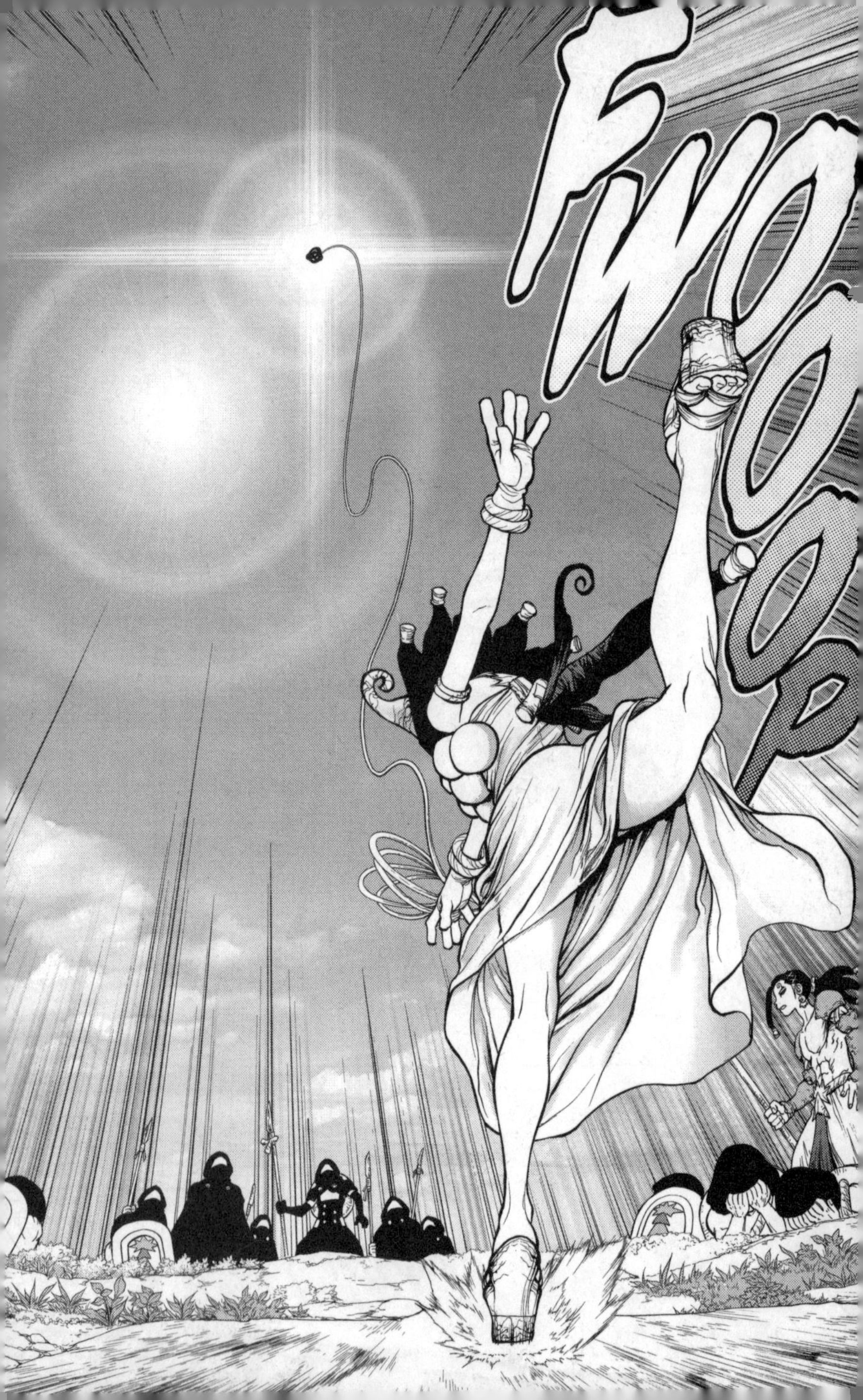
FWOOOOP

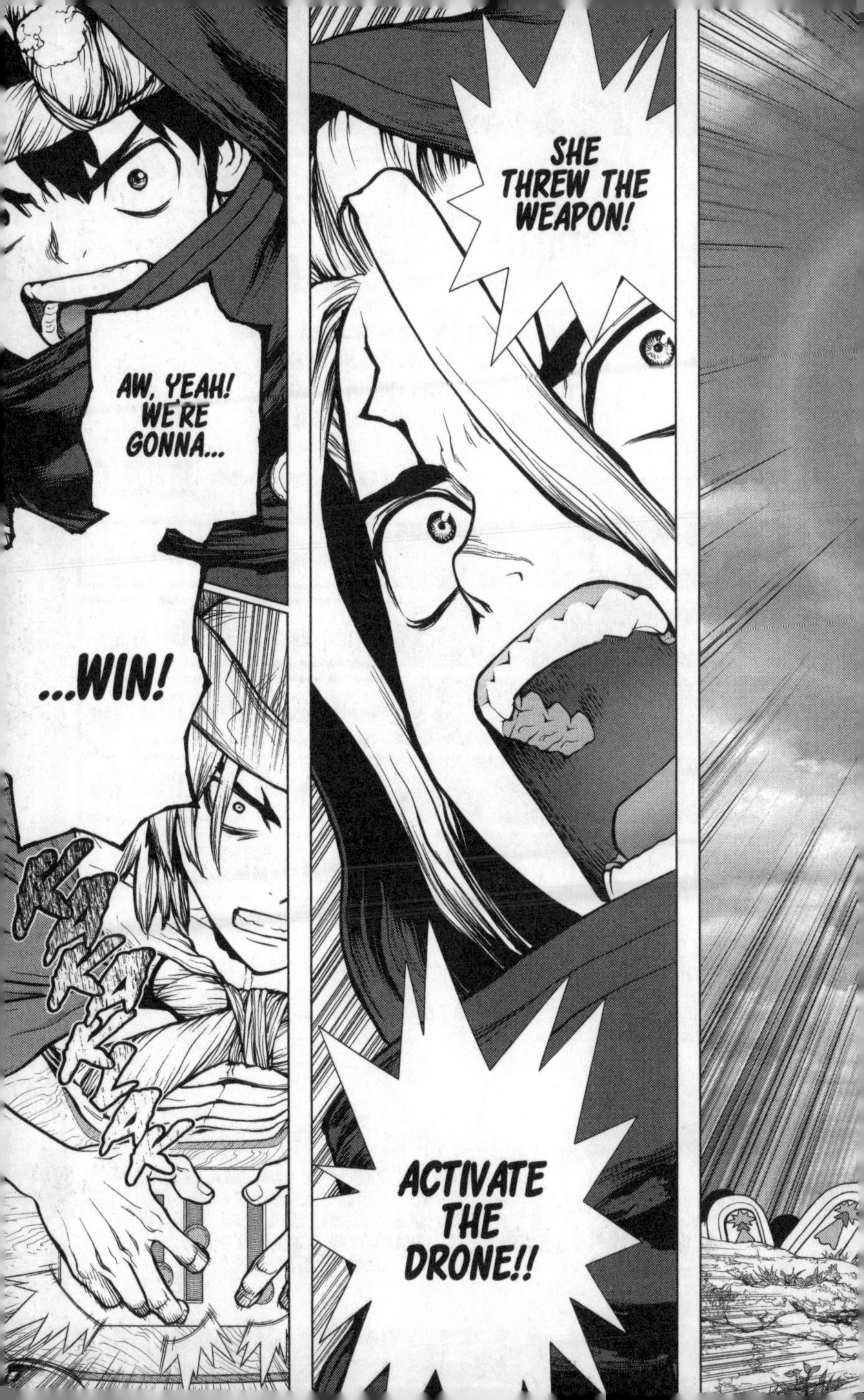
SHE THREW THE WEAPON!
ACTIVATE THE DRONE!!
AW, YEAH! WE'RE GONNA...
...WIN!

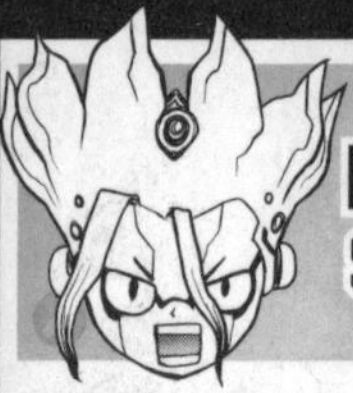

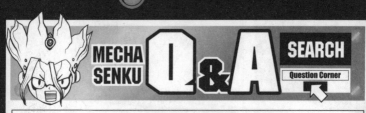

# MECHA SENKU Q&A

**SEARCH**

Question Corner

**Ryusui learned to be a pro gamer, but what other things did he learn? (I love Ryusui so I want to learn the same things as him!)**

N.T. of Miyagi Prefecture

**SEARCH**

| | |
|---|---|
| Race Car Driving | Monthly Fee 2,000,000 Yen |
| Gaming | Monthly Fee 500,000 Yen |
| Exercising | Monthly Fee 2,000,000 Yen |
| Piloting | Monthly Fee 3,000,000 Yen |
| Weather Forecasting | Monthly Fee 500,000 Yen |

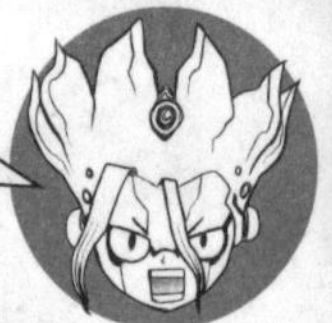
That's quite a tidy sum... And yet, none of the activities listed are related to nautical affairs.

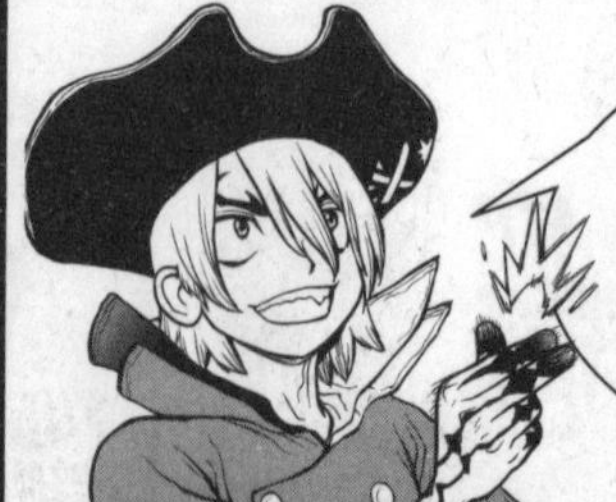
SELF-STUDY AND LEARNING VIA LESSONS ARE EFFECTIVE IN DIFFERENT WAYS! AM I WRONG?! SO IF FORGING YOUR OWN PATH APPEALS TO YOU, THERE SHOULD BE A METHOD THAT DOESN'T INVOLVE A HEAP OF CASH! THAT'S HOW CONQUERING THE SEAS FELT FOR ME!

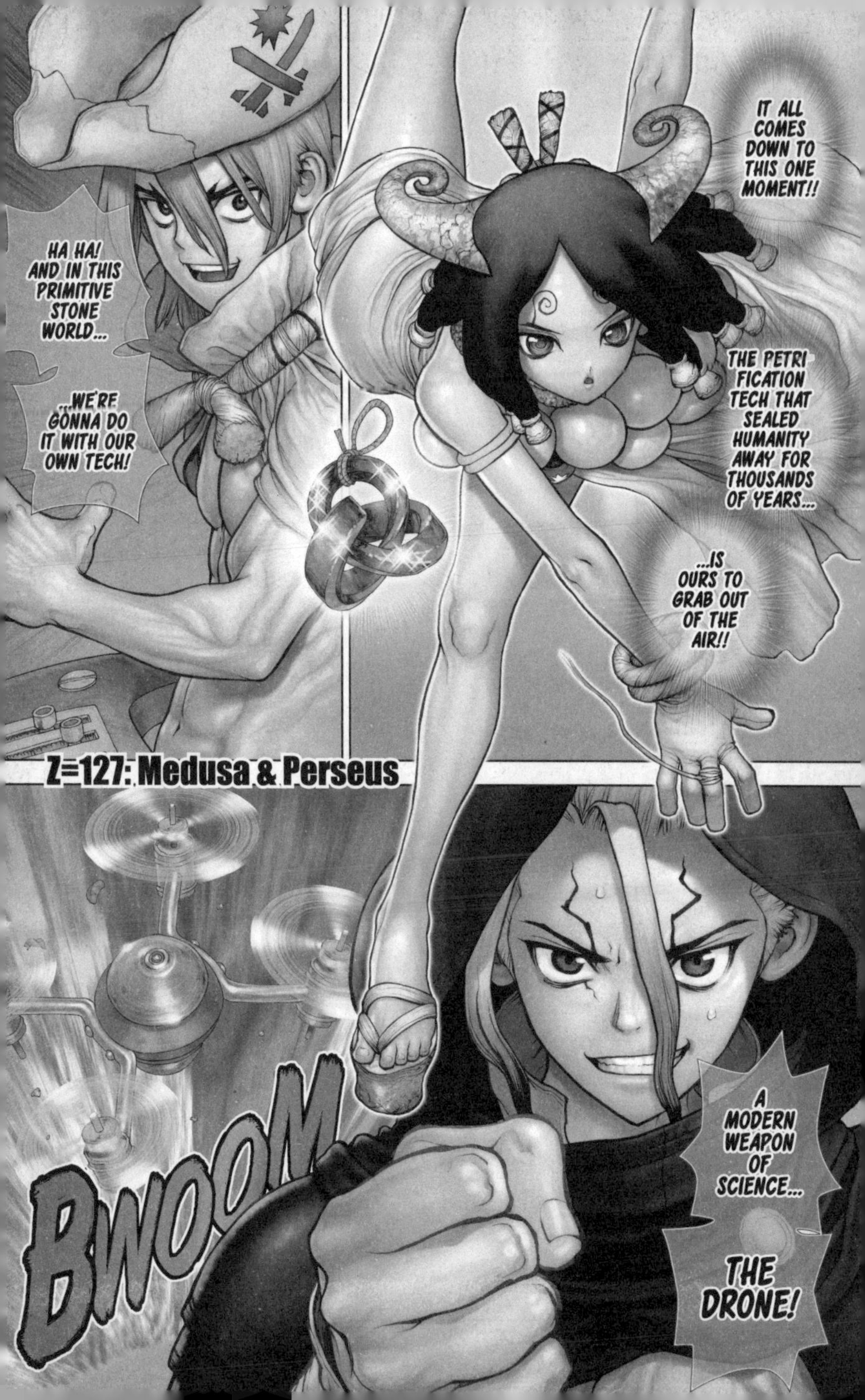
IT ALL COMES DOWN TO THIS ONE MOMENT!!
THE PETRIFICATION TECH THAT SEALED HUMANITY AWAY FOR THOUSANDS OF YEARS...
...IS OURS TO GRAB OUT OF THE AIR!!
HA HA! AND IN THIS PRIMITIVE STONE WORLD...
...WE'RE GONNA DO IT WITH OUR OWN TECH!
Z=127: Medusa & Perseus
A MODERN WEAPON OF SCIENCE...
THE DRONE!
BWOOM

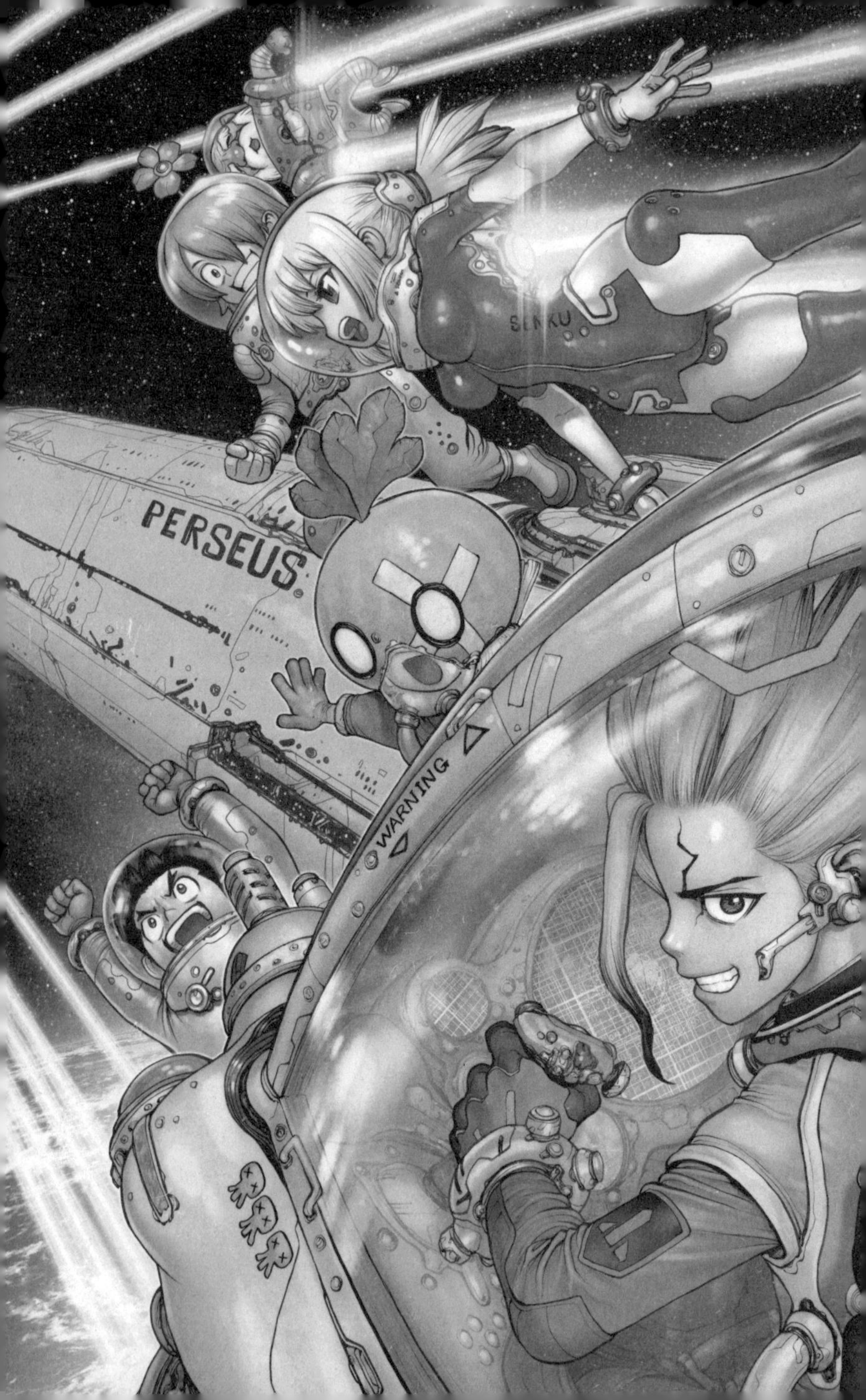
PERSEUS
WARNING

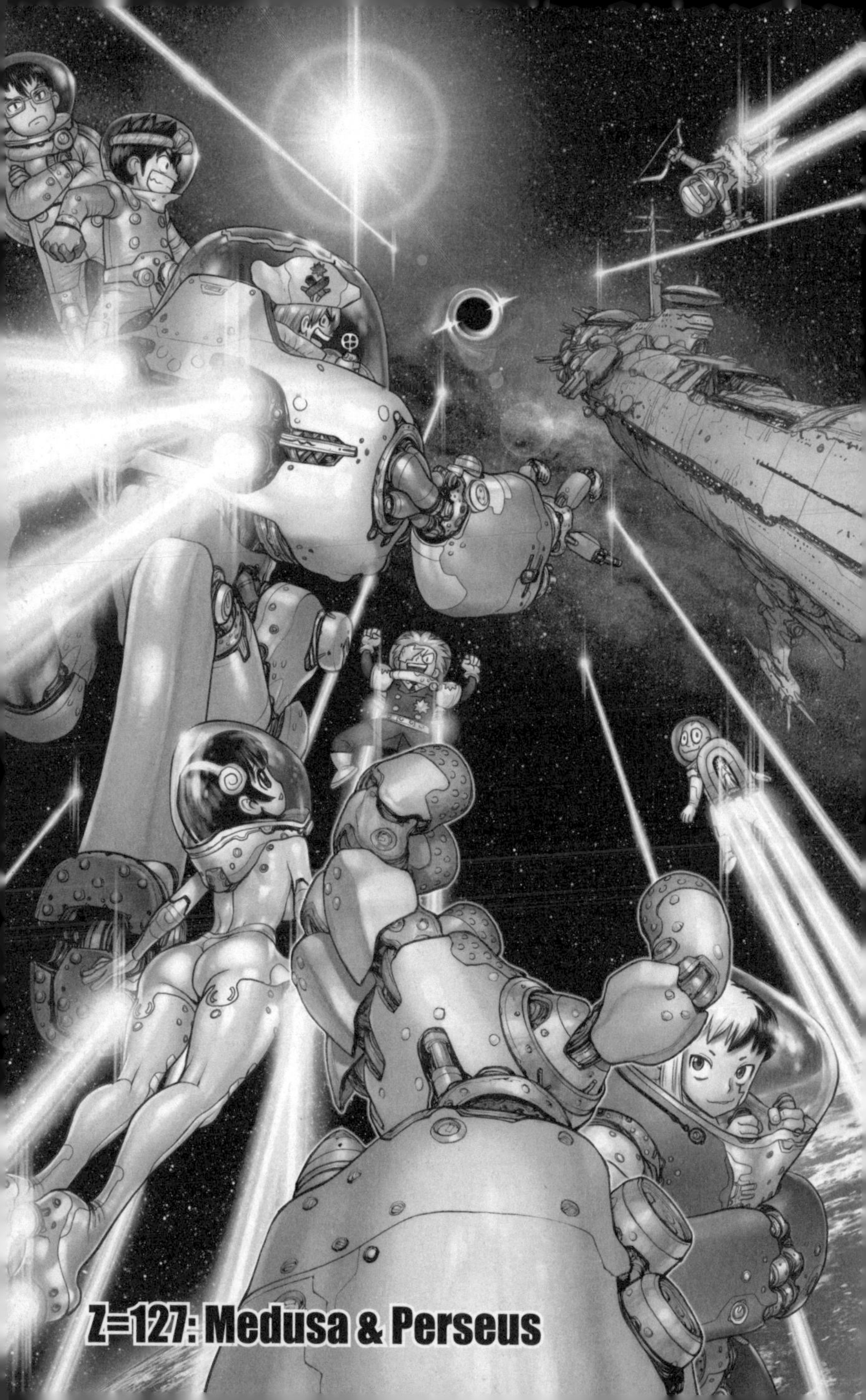

# Z=127: Medusa & Perseus

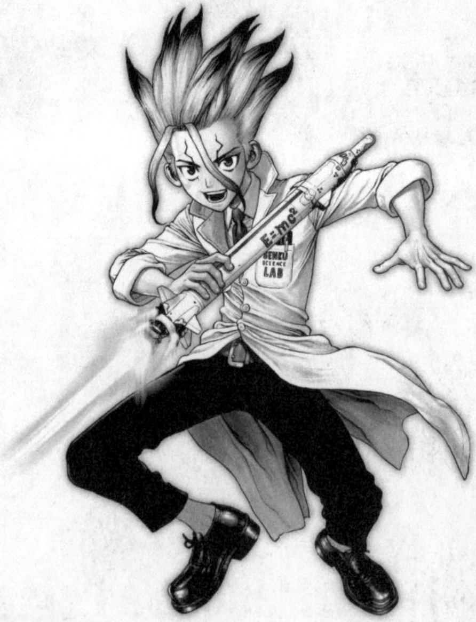
$E=mc^2$
SCIENCE
LAB

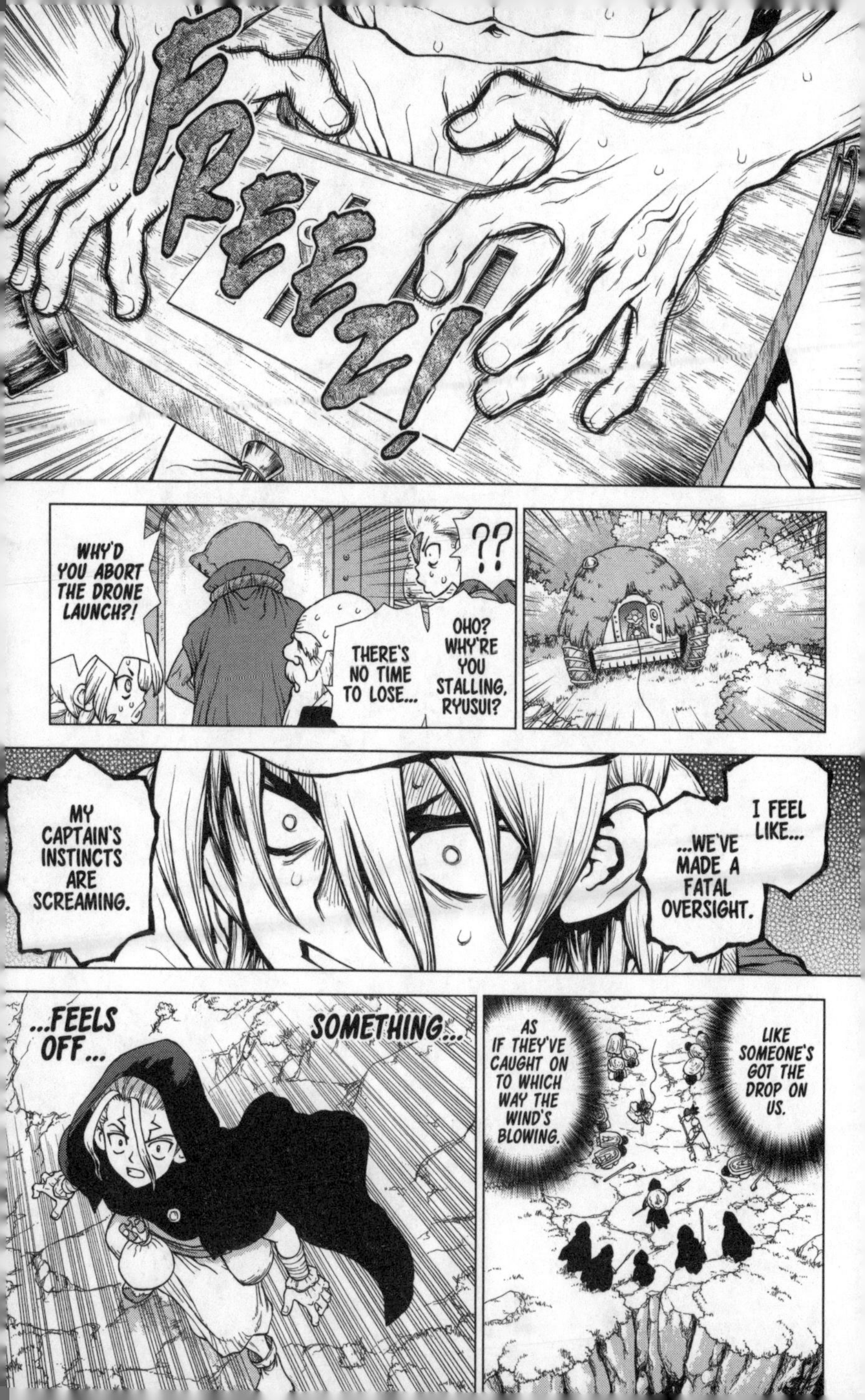
FREEZ!
??
OHO? WHY'RE YOU STALLING, RYUSUI?
THERE'S NO TIME TO LOSE...
WHY'D YOU ABORT THE DRONE LAUNCH?!
I FEEL LIKE...
...WE'VE MADE A FATAL OVERSIGHT.
MY CAPTAIN'S INSTINCTS ARE SCREAMING.
LIKE SOMEONE'S GOT THE DROP ON US.
AS IF THEY'VE CAUGHT ON TO WHICH WAY THE WIND'S BLOWING.
SOMETHING...
...FEELS OFF...

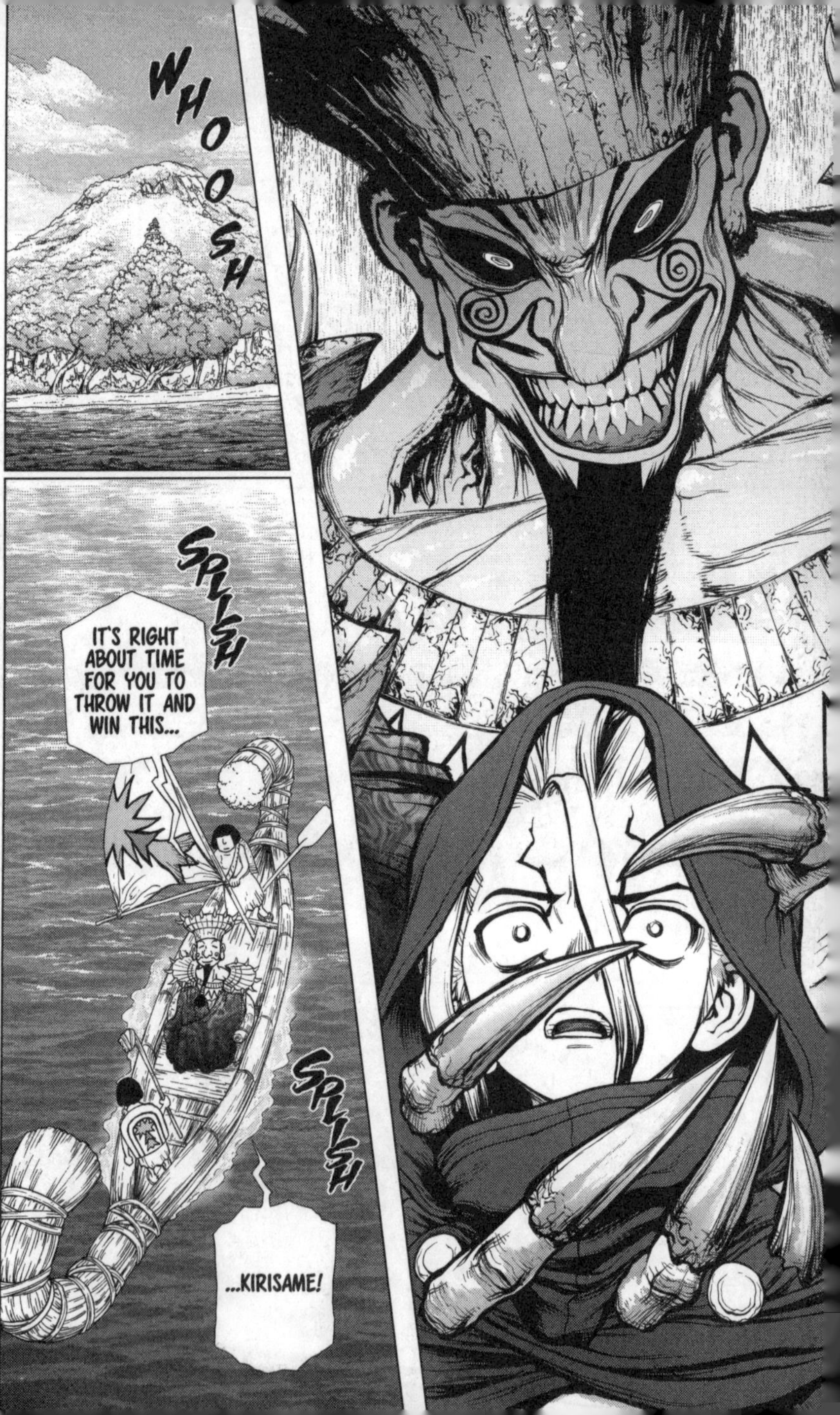
WHOOSH
SPLISH
IT'S RIGHT ABOUT TIME FOR YOU TO THROW IT AND WIN THIS...
SPLISH
...KIRISAME!

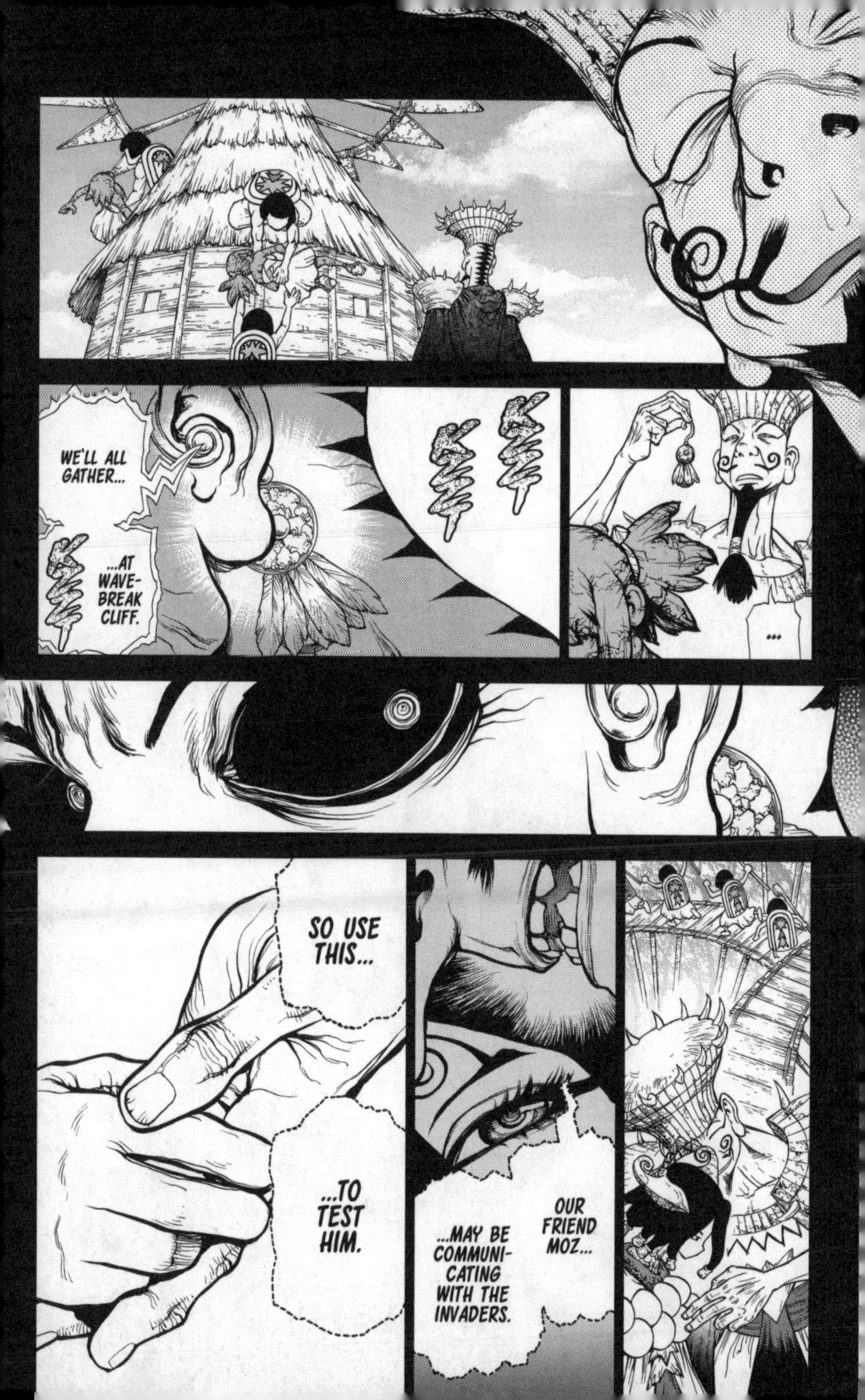
...
WE'LL ALL GATHER...
...AT WAVE-BREAK CLIFF.
OUR FRIEND MOZ...
...MAY BE COMMUNICATING WITH THE INVADERS.
SO USE THIS...
...TO TEST HIM.

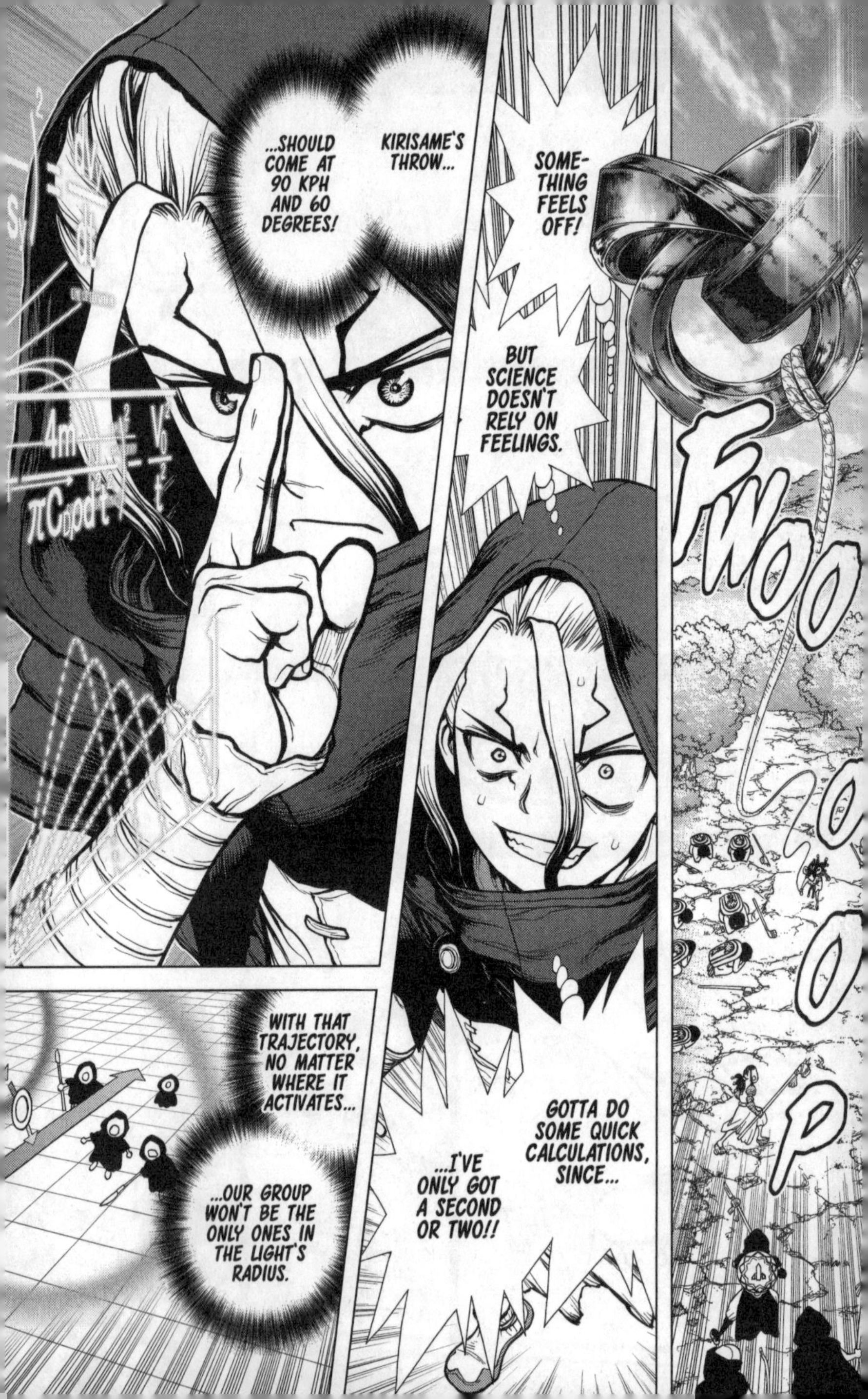
FWOOOOOP
SOME-THING FEELS OFF!
BUT SCIENCE DOESN'T RELY ON FEELINGS.
KIRISAME'S THROW...
...SHOULD COME AT 90 KPH AND 60 DEGREES!
GOTTA DO SOME QUICK CALCULATIONS, SINCE...
...I'VE ONLY GOT A SECOND OR TWO!!
WITH THAT TRAJECTORY, NO MATTER WHERE IT ACTIVATES...
...OUR GROUP WON'T BE THE ONLY ONES IN THE LIGHT'S RADIUS.

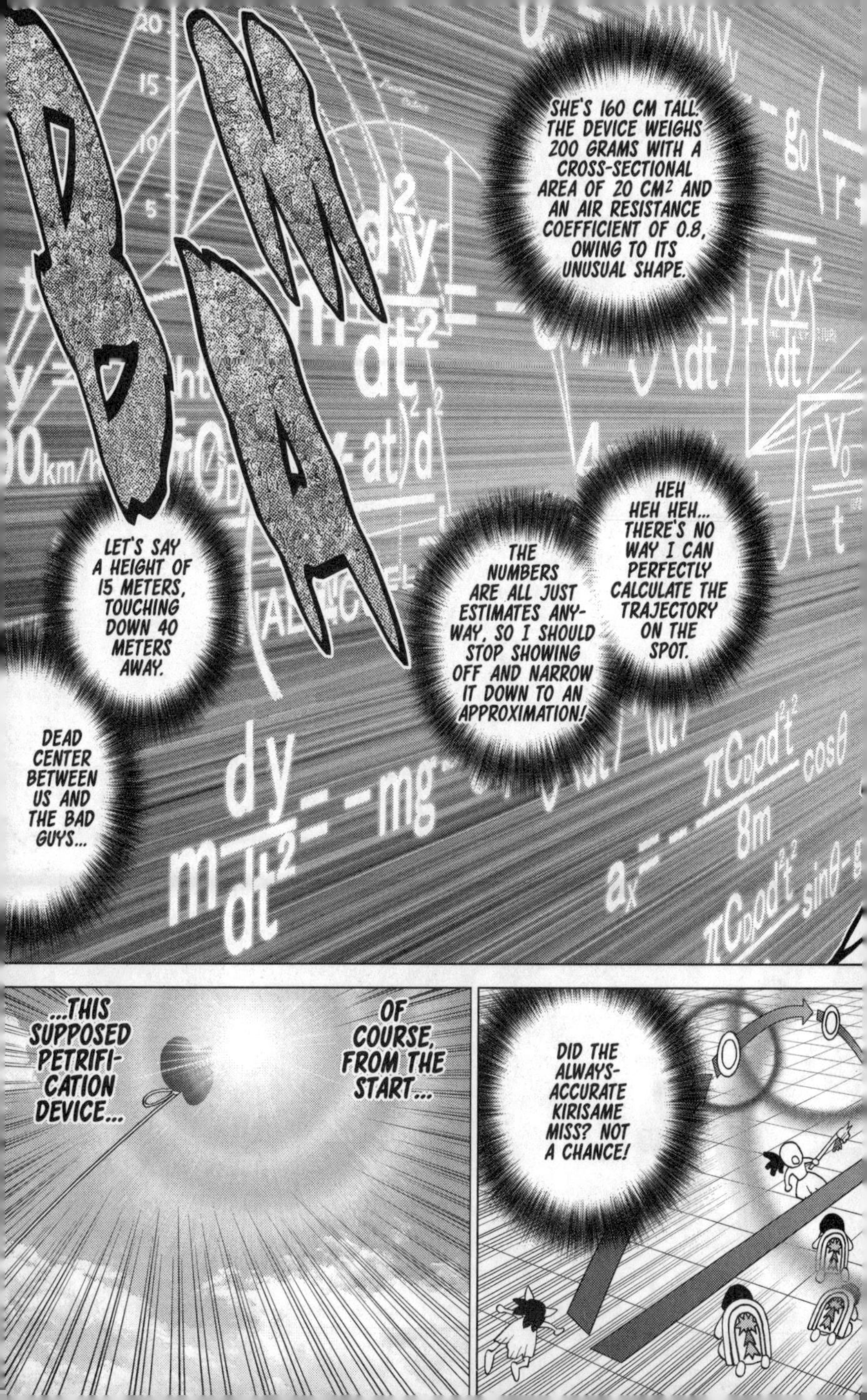
SHE'S 160 CM TALL. THE DEVICE WEIGHS 200 GRAMS WITH A CROSS-SECTIONAL AREA OF 20 CM² AND AN AIR RESISTANCE COEFFICIENT OF 0.8, OWING TO ITS UNUSUAL SHAPE.
HEH HEH HEH... THERE'S NO WAY I CAN PERFECTLY CALCULATE THE TRAJECTORY ON THE SPOT.
THE NUMBERS ARE ALL JUST ESTIMATES ANY-WAY, SO I SHOULD STOP SHOWING OFF AND NARROW IT DOWN TO AN APPROXIMATION!
LET'S SAY A HEIGHT OF 15 METERS, TOUCHING DOWN 40 METERS AWAY.
DEAD CENTER BETWEEN US AND THE BAD GUYS...
DID THE ALWAYS-ACCURATE KIRISAME MISS? NOT A CHANCE!
OF COURSE, FROM THE START...
...THIS SUPPOSED PETRIFI-CATION DEVICE...

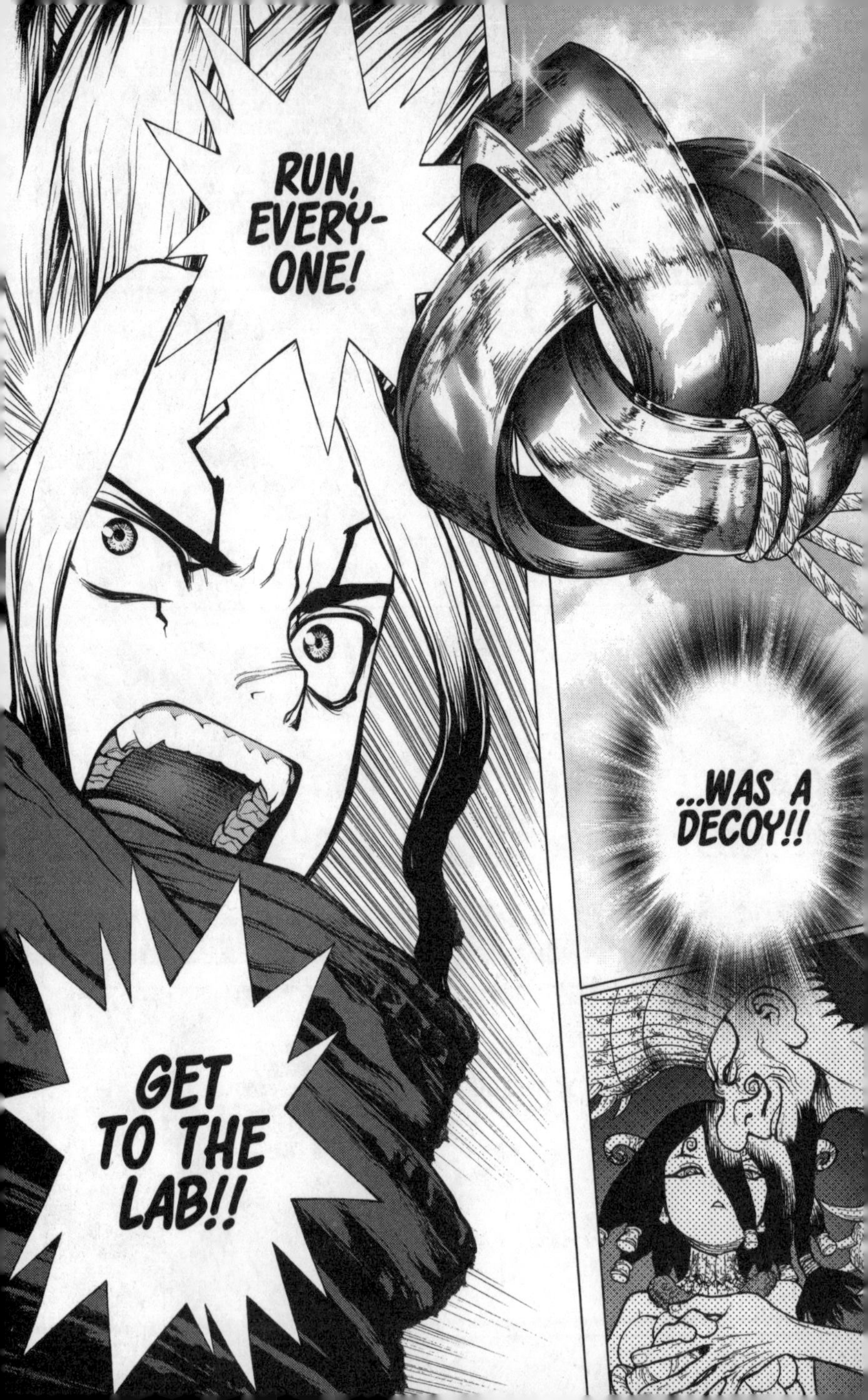
...WAS A DECOY!!
RUN, EVERY-ONE!
GET TO THE LAB!!

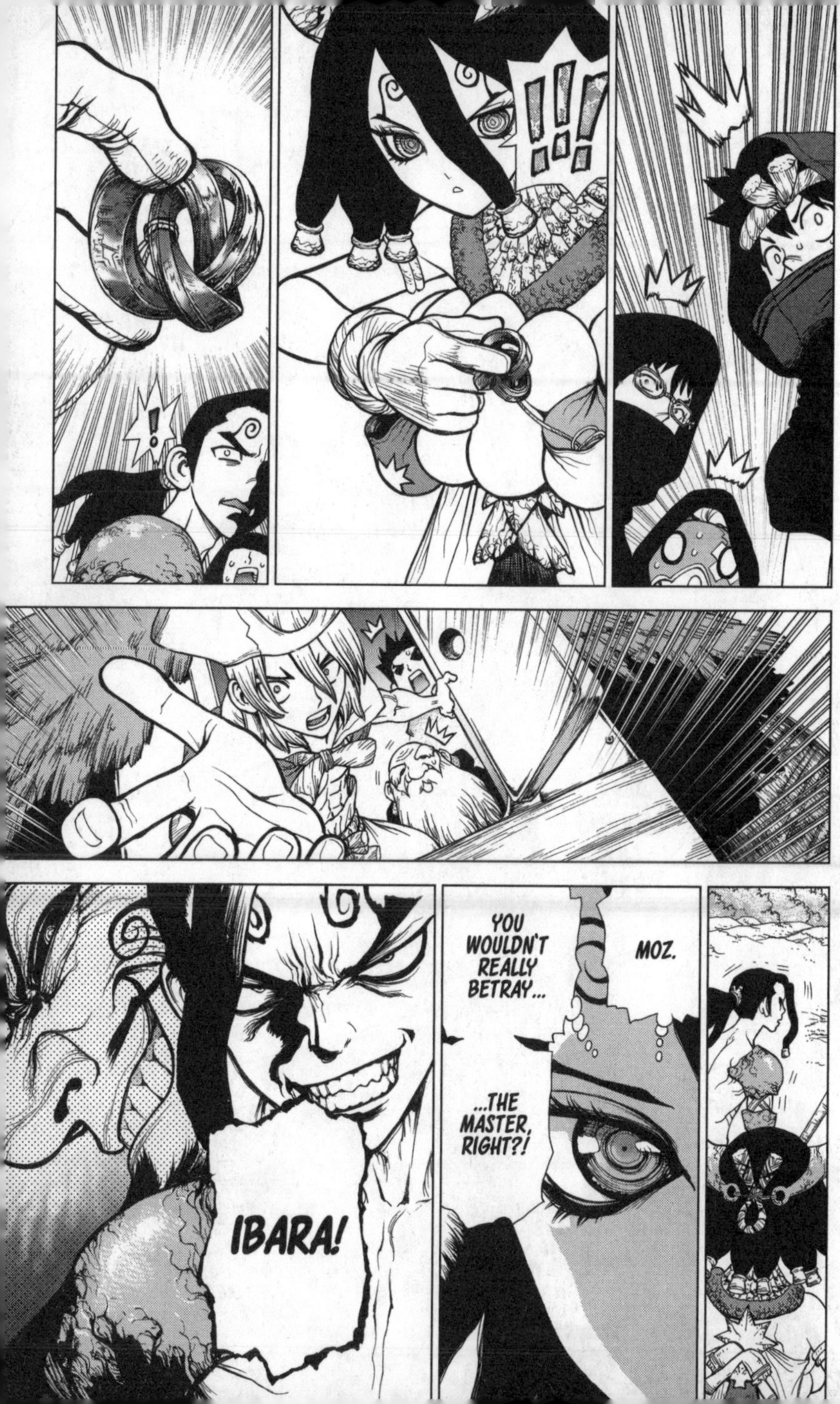
MOZ.
YOU WOULDN'T REALLY BETRAY...
...THE MASTER, RIGHT?!
IBARA!

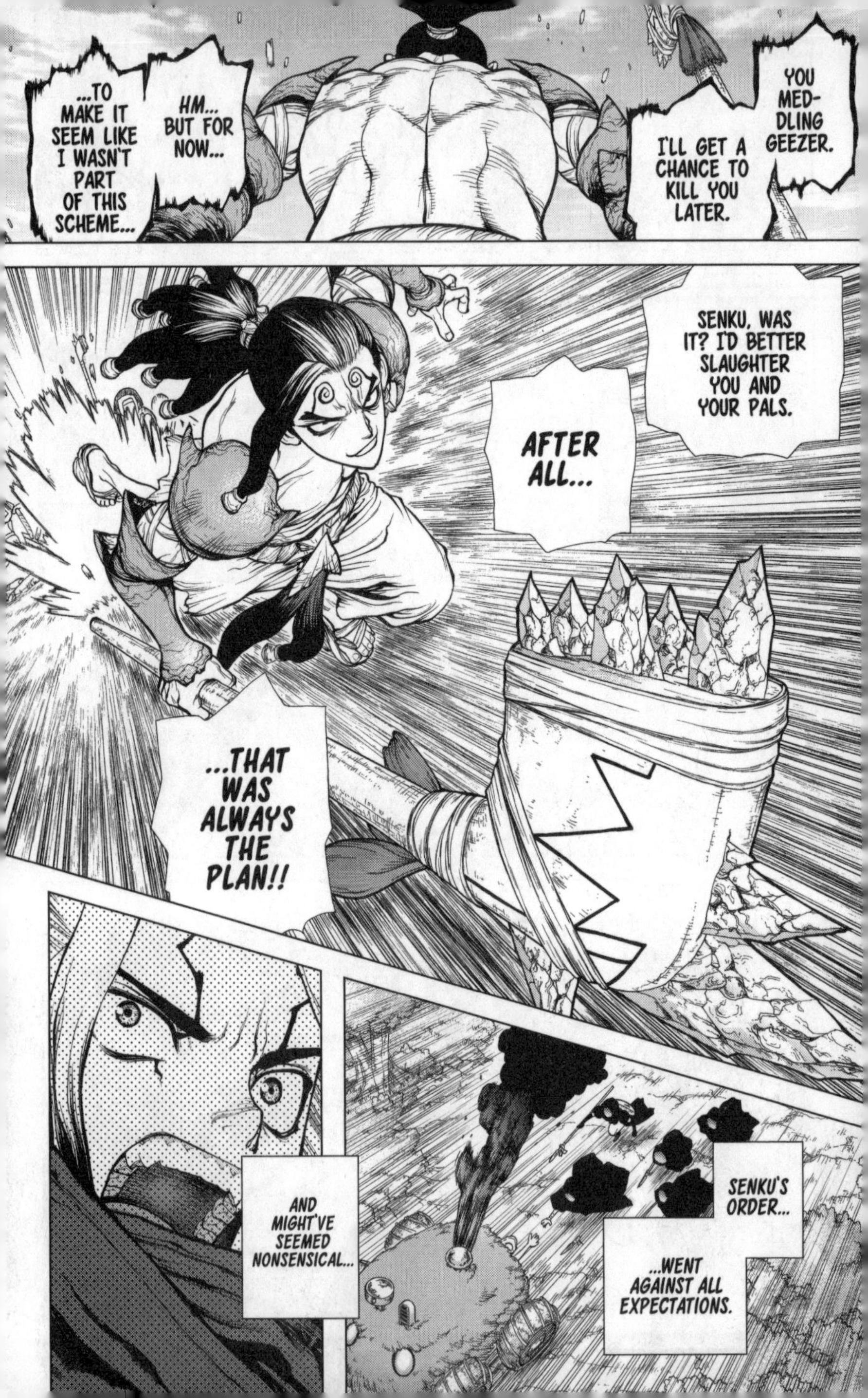
YOU MEDDLING GEEZER.
I'LL GET A CHANCE TO KILL YOU LATER.
HM... BUT FOR NOW...
...TO MAKE IT SEEM LIKE I WASN'T PART OF THIS SCHEME...
SENKU, WAS IT? I'D BETTER SLAUGHTER YOU AND YOUR PALS.
AFTER ALL...
...THAT WAS ALWAYS THE PLAN!!
SENKU'S ORDER...
...WENT AGAINST ALL EXPECTATIONS.
AND MIGHT'VE SEEMED NONSENSICAL...

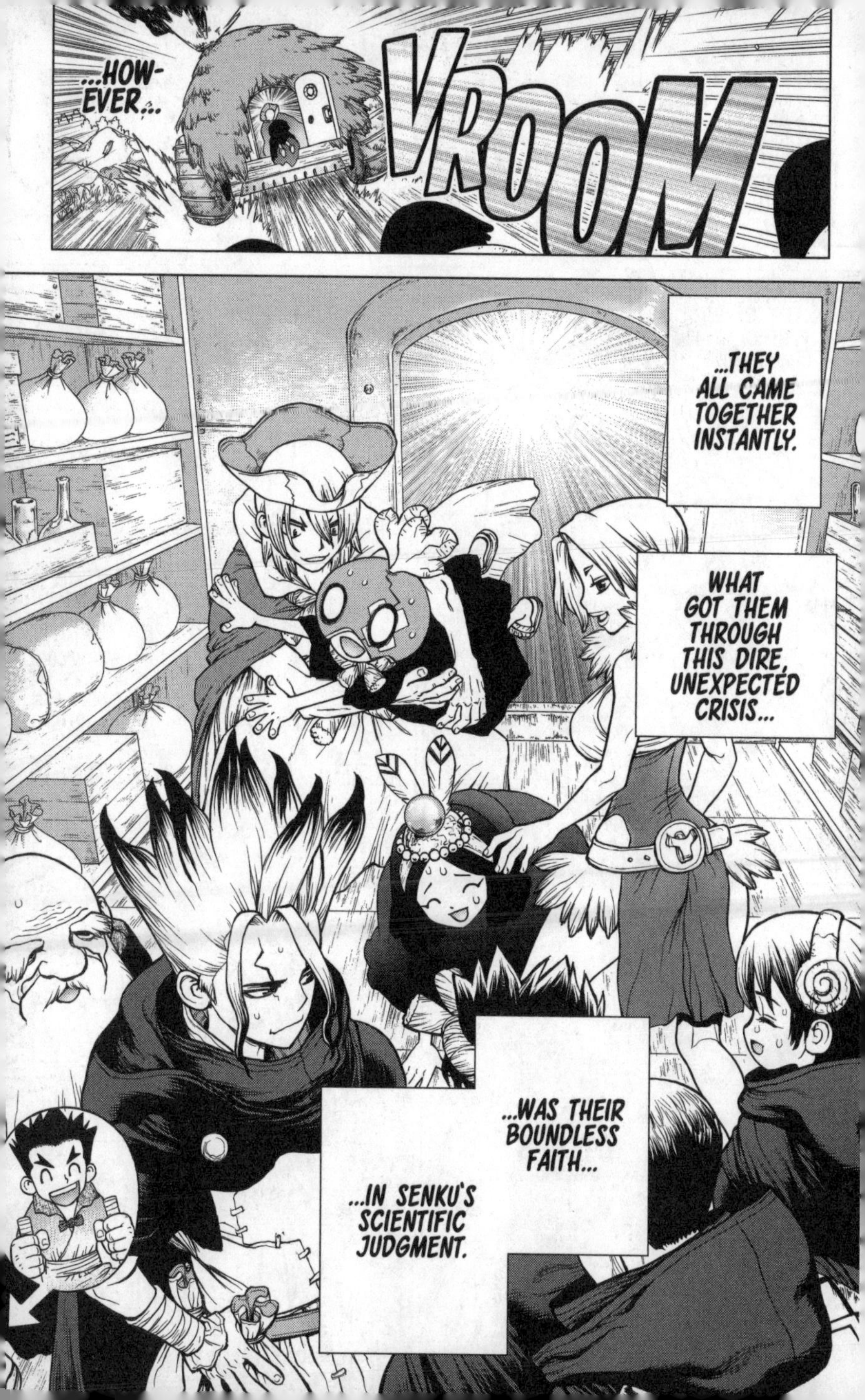
...HOW-
EVER...
VROOM
...THEY ALL CAME TOGETHER INSTANTLY.
WHAT GOT THEM THROUGH THIS DIRE, UNEXPECTED CRISIS...
...WAS THEIR BOUNDLESS FAITH...
...IN SENKU'S SCIENTIFIC JUDGMENT.

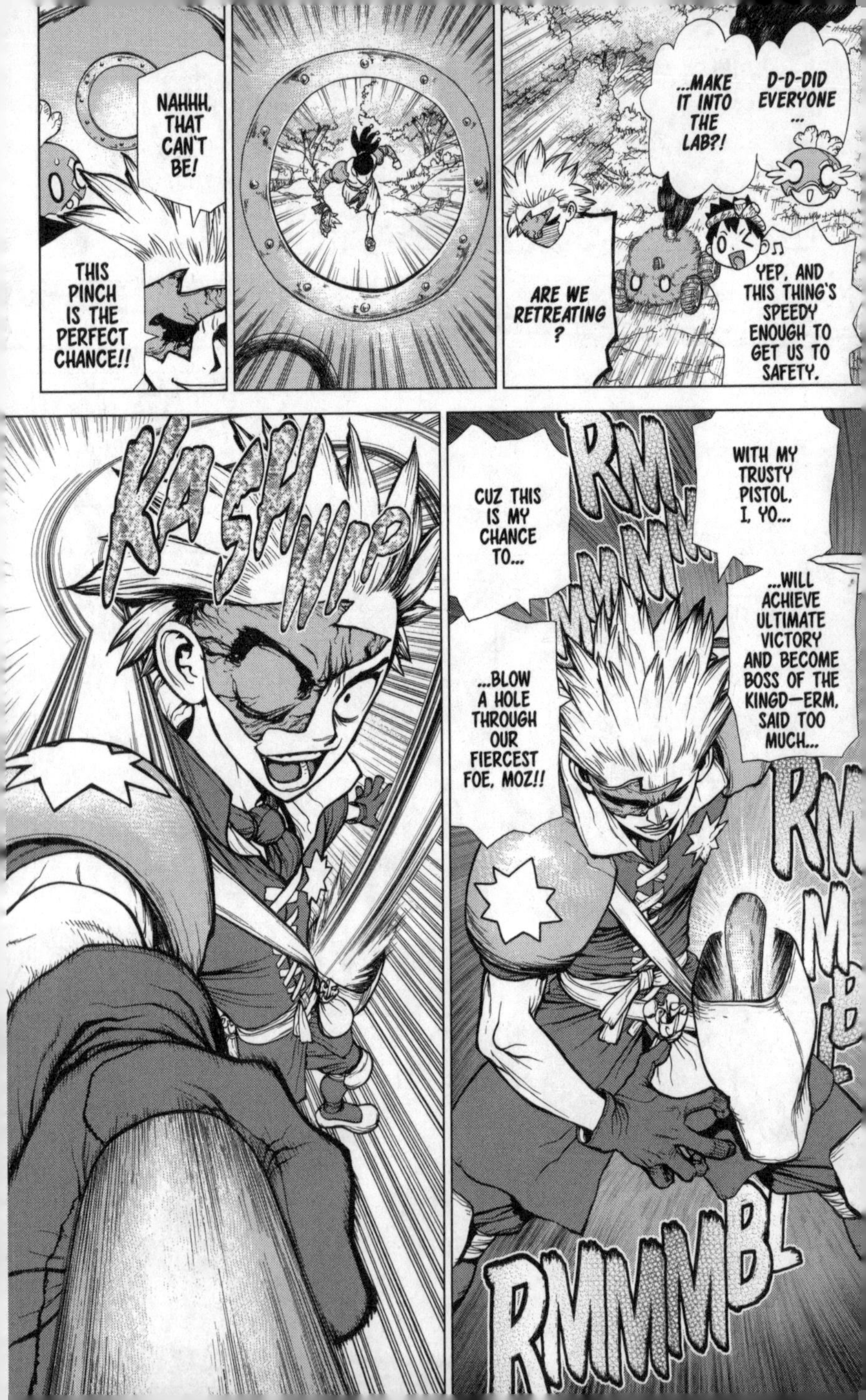
D-D-DID EVERYONE ...
...MAKE IT INTO THE LAB?!
YEP, AND THIS THING'S SPEEDY ENOUGH TO GET US TO SAFETY.
ARE WE RETREATING ?
NAHHH, THAT CAN'T BE!
THIS PINCH IS THE PERFECT CHANCE!!
RMMMM
WITH MY TRUSTY PISTOL, I, YO...
...WILL ACHIEVE ULTIMATE VICTORY AND BECOME BOSS OF THE KINGD—ERM, SAID TOO MUCH...
CUZ THIS IS MY CHANCE TO...
...BLOW A HOLE THROUGH OUR FIERCEST FOE, MOZ!!
RMMMBL
KASHWIP

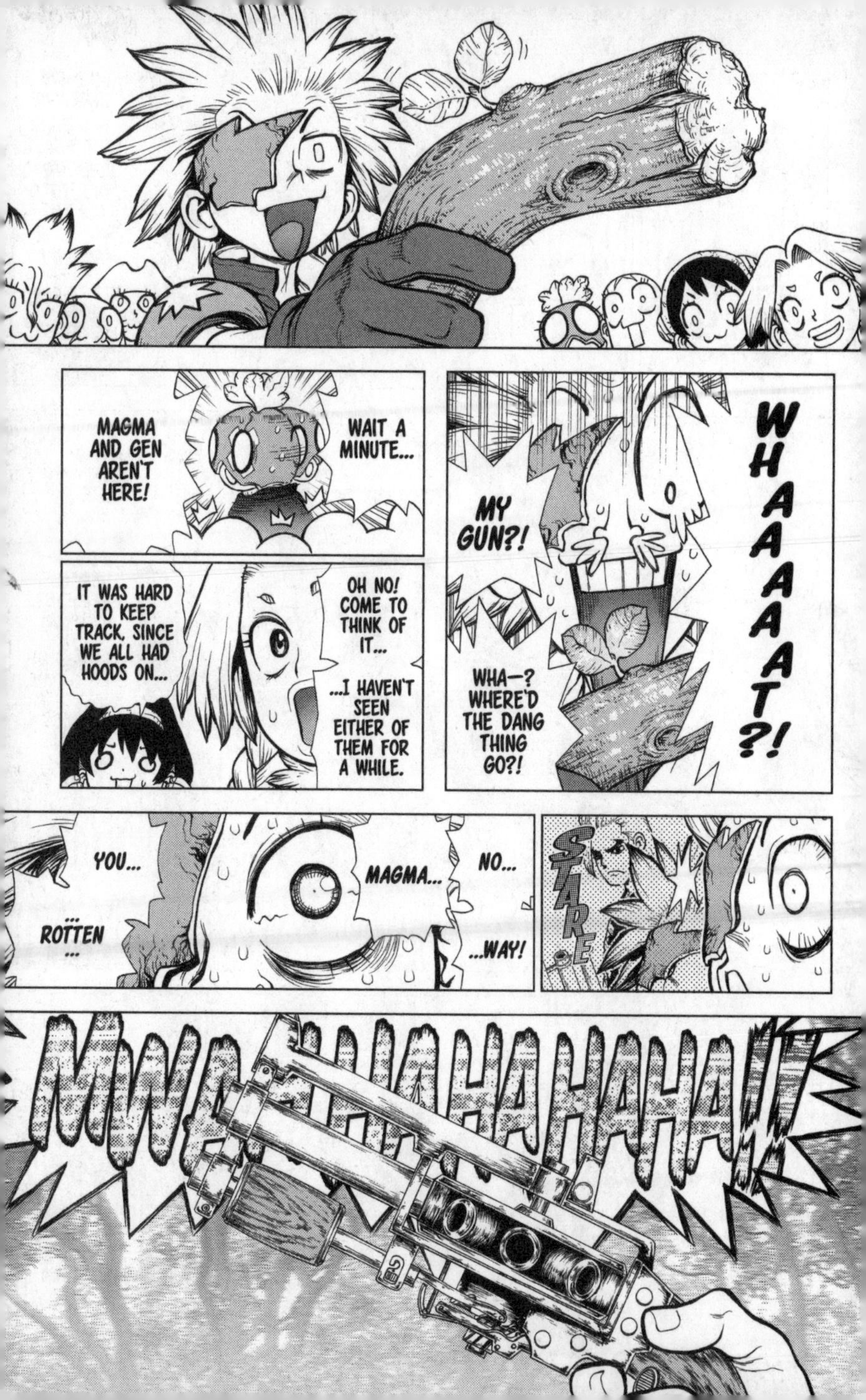
WHAAAAAAT?!
MY GUN?!
WHA—? WHERE'D THE DANG THING GO?!
WAIT A MINUTE...
MAGMA AND GEN AREN'T HERE!
OH NO! COME TO THINK OF IT...
...I HAVEN'T SEEN EITHER OF THEM FOR A WHILE.
IT WAS HARD TO KEEP TRACK, SINCE WE ALL HAD HOODS ON...
STARE
NO...
...WAY!
MAGMA...
YOU...
...ROTTEN...
MWAHAHAHAHA!!

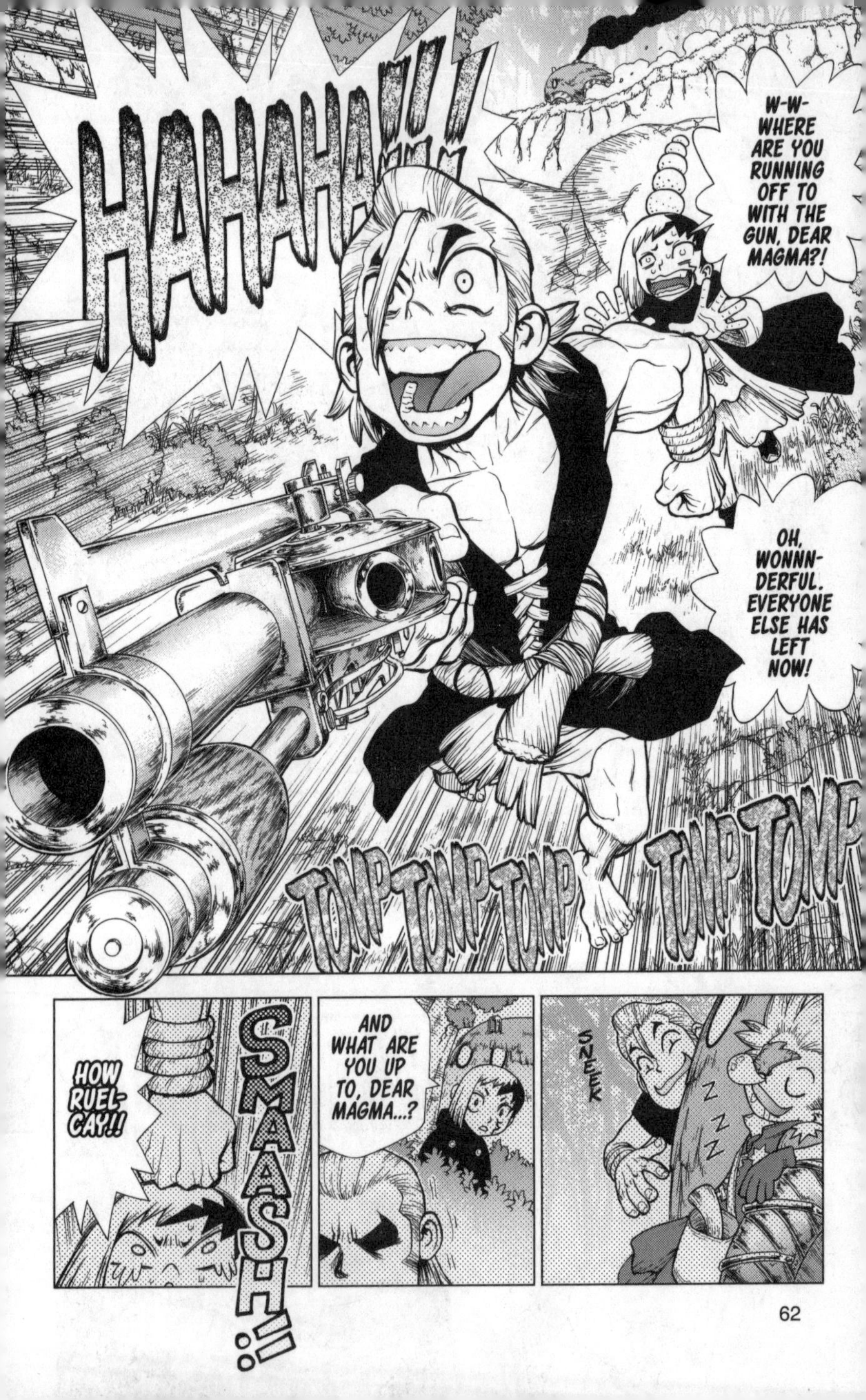
HAHAHA!!!
W-W-WHERE ARE YOU RUNNING OFF TO WITH THE GUN, DEAR MAGMA?!
OH, WONNN-DERFUL. EVERYONE ELSE HAS LEFT NOW!
TOMP TOMP
TOMP TOMP TOMP
SNEEK
Z Z Z
AND WHAT ARE YOU UP TO, DEAR MAGMA...?
SMAASH!!
HOW RUEL-CAY!!

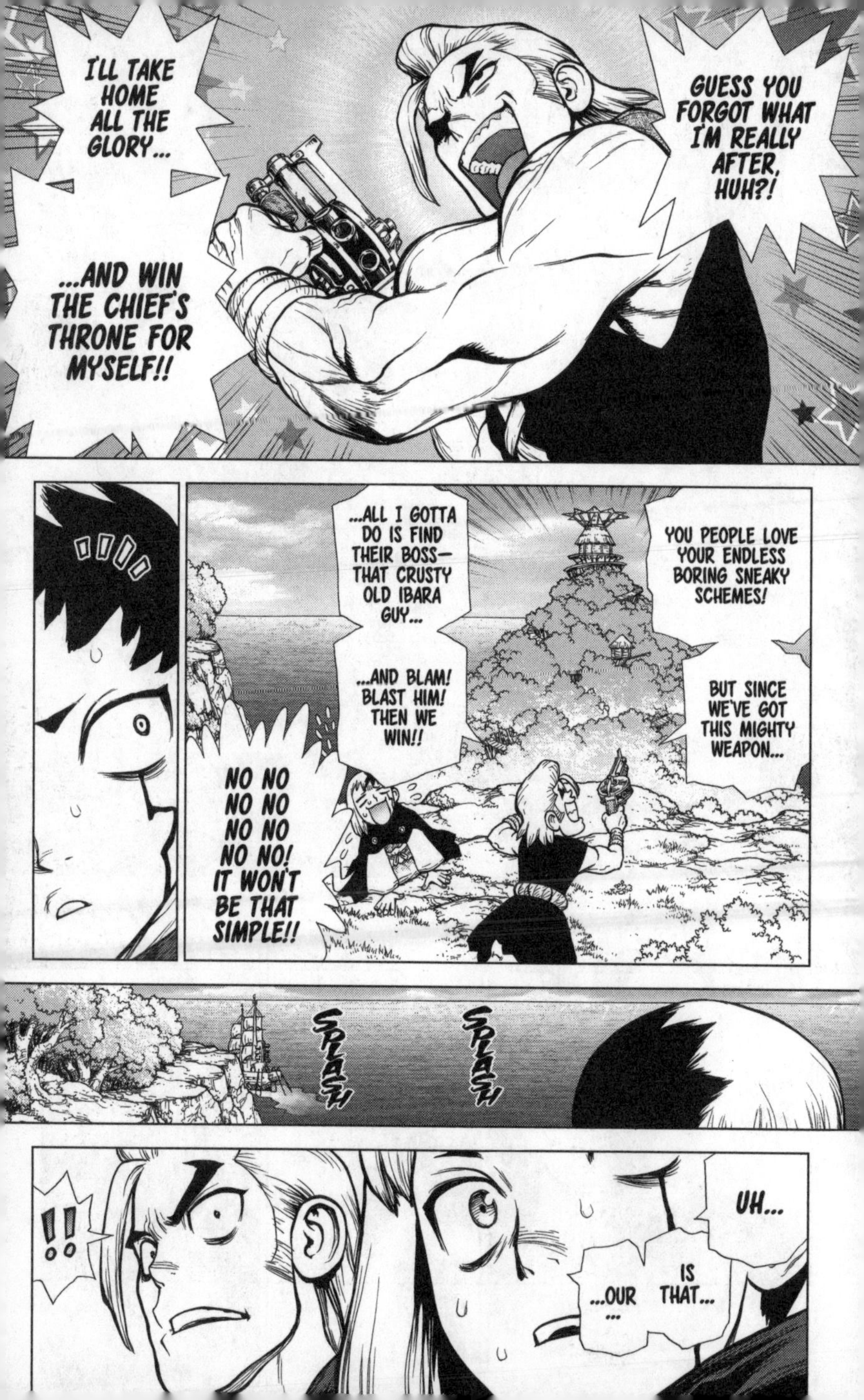
GUESS YOU FORGOT WHAT I'M REALLY AFTER, HUH?!
I'LL TAKE HOME ALL THE GLORY...
...AND WIN THE CHIEF'S THRONE FOR MYSELF!!
YOU PEOPLE LOVE YOUR ENDLESS BORING SNEAKY SCHEMES!
BUT SINCE WE'VE GOT THIS MIGHTY WEAPON...
...ALL I GOTTA DO IS FIND THEIR BOSS—THAT CRUSTY OLD IBARA GUY...
...AND BLAM! BLAST HIM! THEN WE WIN!!
NO NO NO NO NO NO NO NO! IT WON'T BE THAT SIMPLE!!
SPLASH
SPLASH
UH...
IS THAT...
...OUR ...
!!

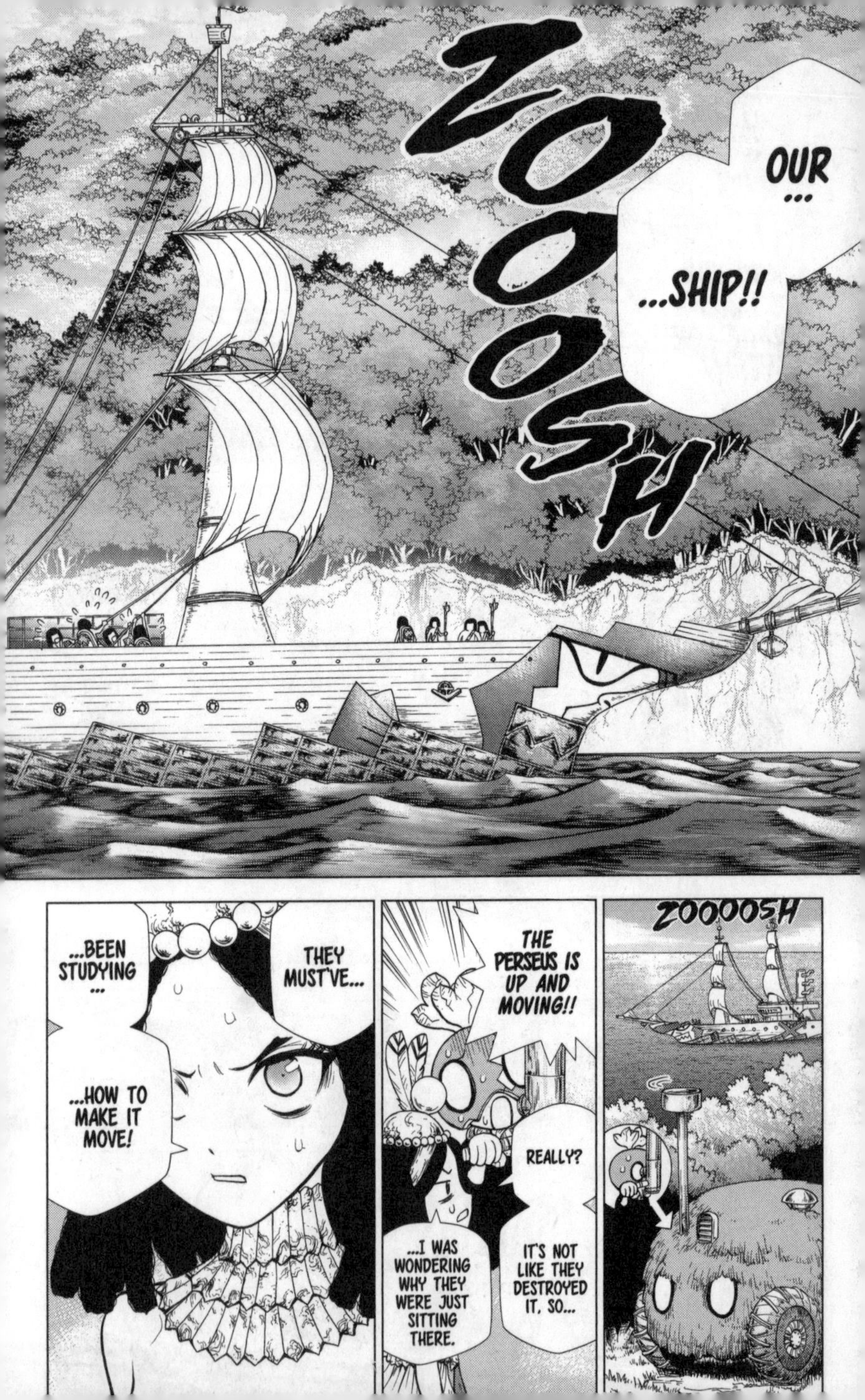
ZOOOSH
OUR...
...SHIP!!
ZOOOOSH
THE PERSEUS IS UP AND MOVING!!
REALLY?
IT'S NOT LIKE THEY DESTROYED IT, SO...
...I WAS WONDERING WHY THEY WERE JUST SITTING THERE.
THEY MUST'VE...
...BEEN STUDYING...
...HOW TO MAKE IT MOVE!

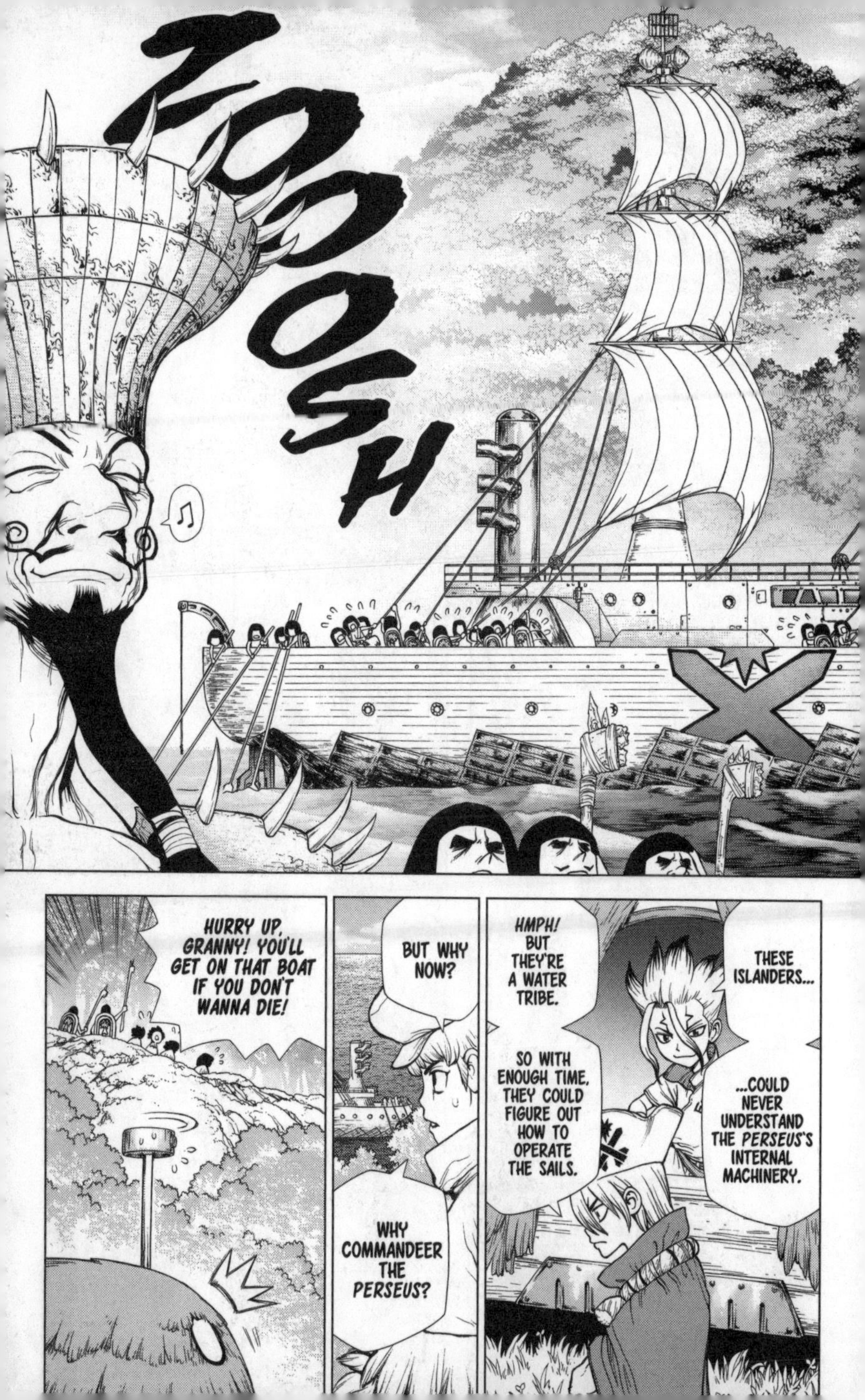
ZOOOSH
♪
THESE ISLANDERS...
...COULD NEVER UNDERSTAND THE *PERSEUS*'S INTERNAL MACHINERY.
HMPH! BUT THEY'RE A WATER TRIBE.
SO WITH ENOUGH TIME, THEY COULD FIGURE OUT HOW TO OPERATE THE SAILS.
BUT WHY NOW?
WHY COMMANDEER THE *PERSEUS*?
HURRY UP, GRANNY! YOU'LL GET ON THAT BOAT IF YOU DON'T WANNA DIE!

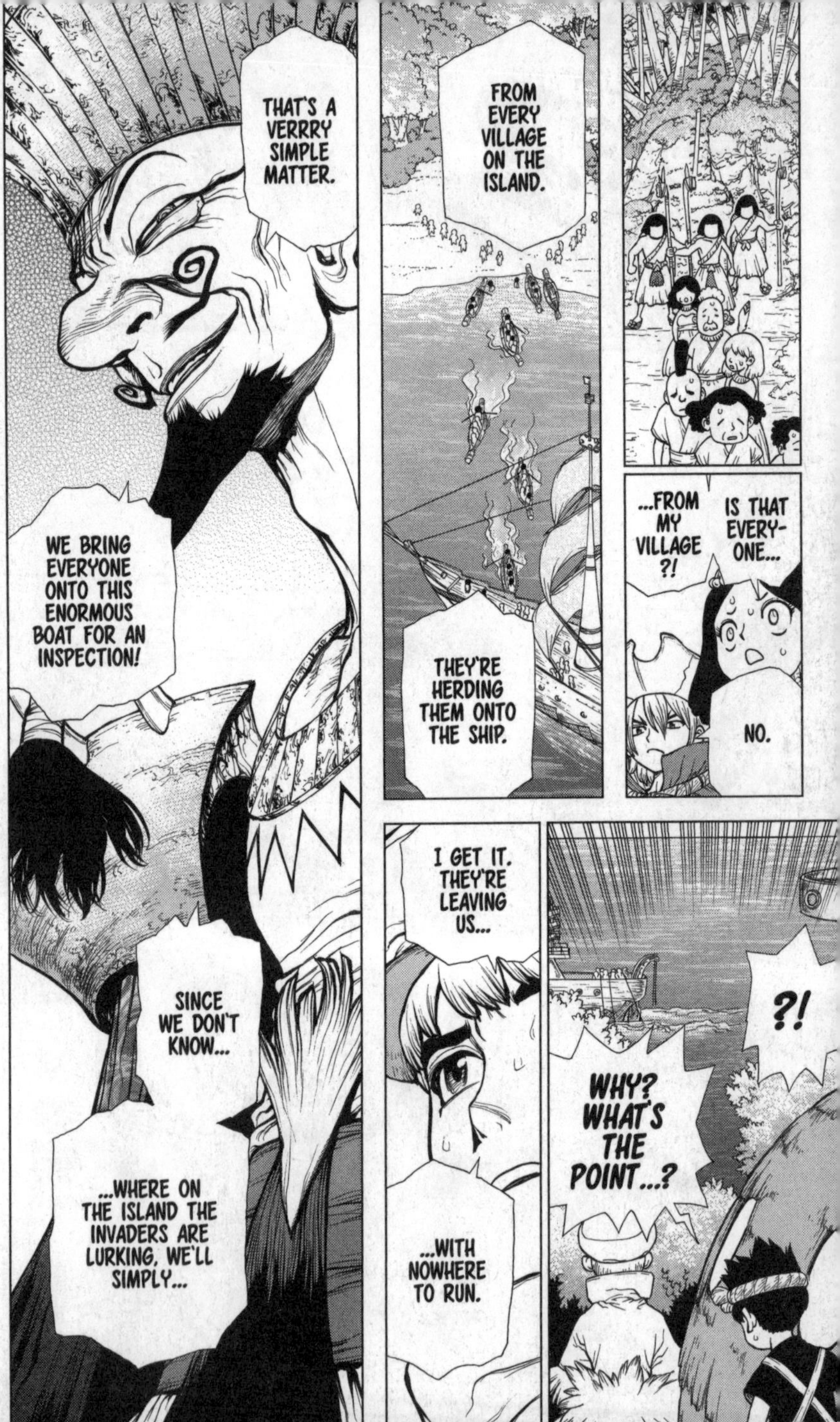
IS THAT EVERYONE...
...FROM MY VILLAGE?!
NO.
FROM EVERY VILLAGE ON THE ISLAND.
THEY'RE HERDING THEM ONTO THE SHIP.
?!
WHY? WHAT'S THE POINT...?
I GET IT. THEY'RE LEAVING US...
...WITH NOWHERE TO RUN.
THAT'S A VERRRY SIMPLE MATTER.
WE BRING EVERYONE ONTO THIS ENORMOUS BOAT FOR AN INSPECTION!
SINCE WE DON'T KNOW...
...WHERE ON THE ISLAND THE INVADERS ARE LURKING, WE'LL SIMPLY...

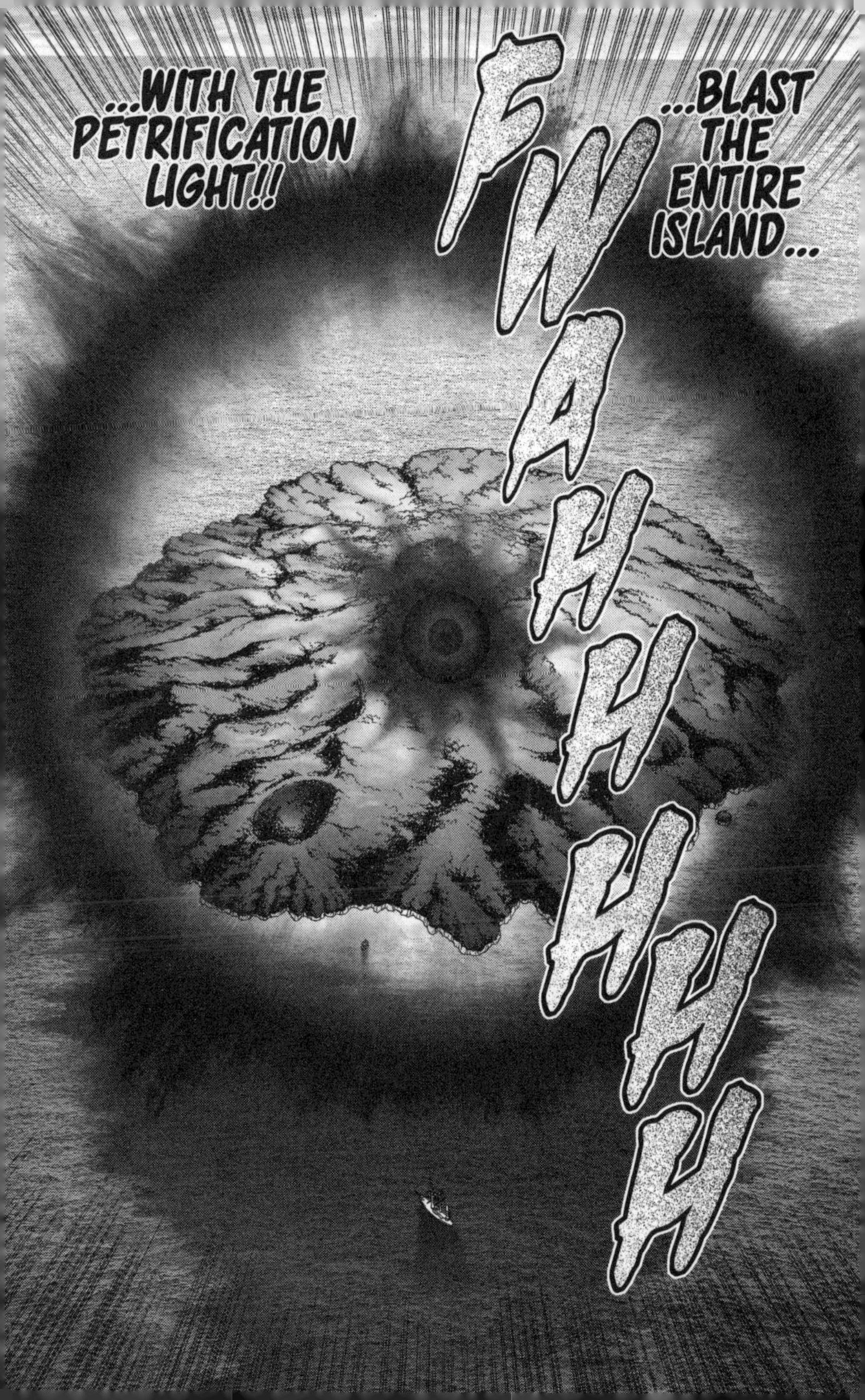
...BLAST THE ENTIRE ISLAND...
...WITH THE PETRIFICATION LIGHT!!
FWAHHHHH

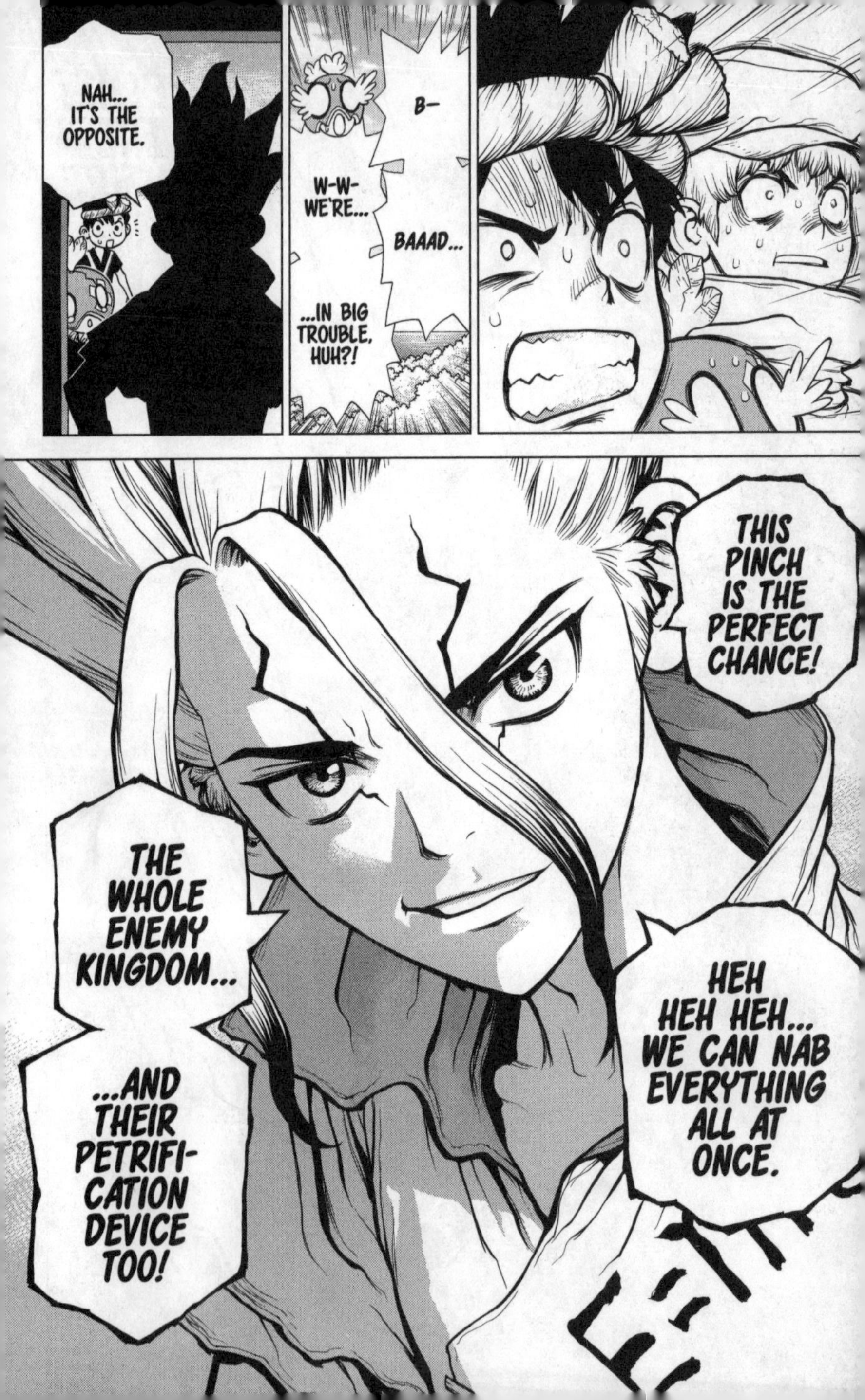
B-
W-W-WE'RE...
BAAAD...
...IN BIG TROUBLE, HUH?!
NAH... IT'S THE OPPOSITE.
THIS PINCH IS THE PERFECT CHANCE!
HEH HEH HEH... WE CAN NAB EVERYTHING ALL AT ONCE.
THE WHOLE ENEMY KINGDOM...
...AND THEIR PETRIFI-CATION DEVICE TOO!

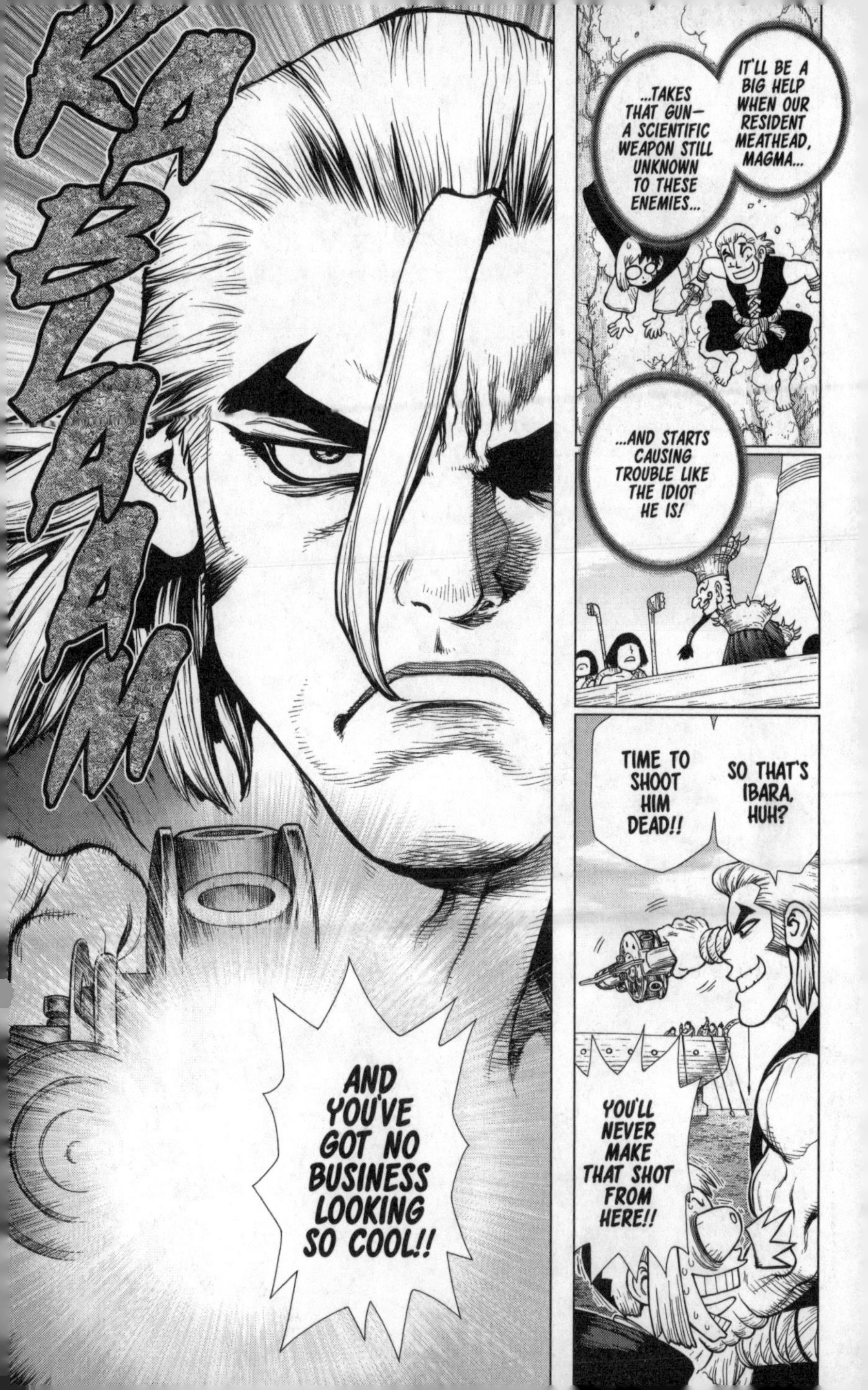
IT'LL BE A BIG HELP WHEN OUR RESIDENT MEATHEAD, MAGMA...
...TAKES THAT GUN— A SCIENTIFIC WEAPON STILL UNKNOWN TO THESE ENEMIES...
...AND STARTS CAUSING TROUBLE LIKE THE IDIOT HE IS!
SO THAT'S IBARA, HUH?
TIME TO SHOOT HIM DEAD!!
YOU'LL NEVER MAKE THAT SHOT FROM HERE!!
KABLAAM!!
AND YOU'VE GOT NO BUSINESS LOOKING SO COOL!!

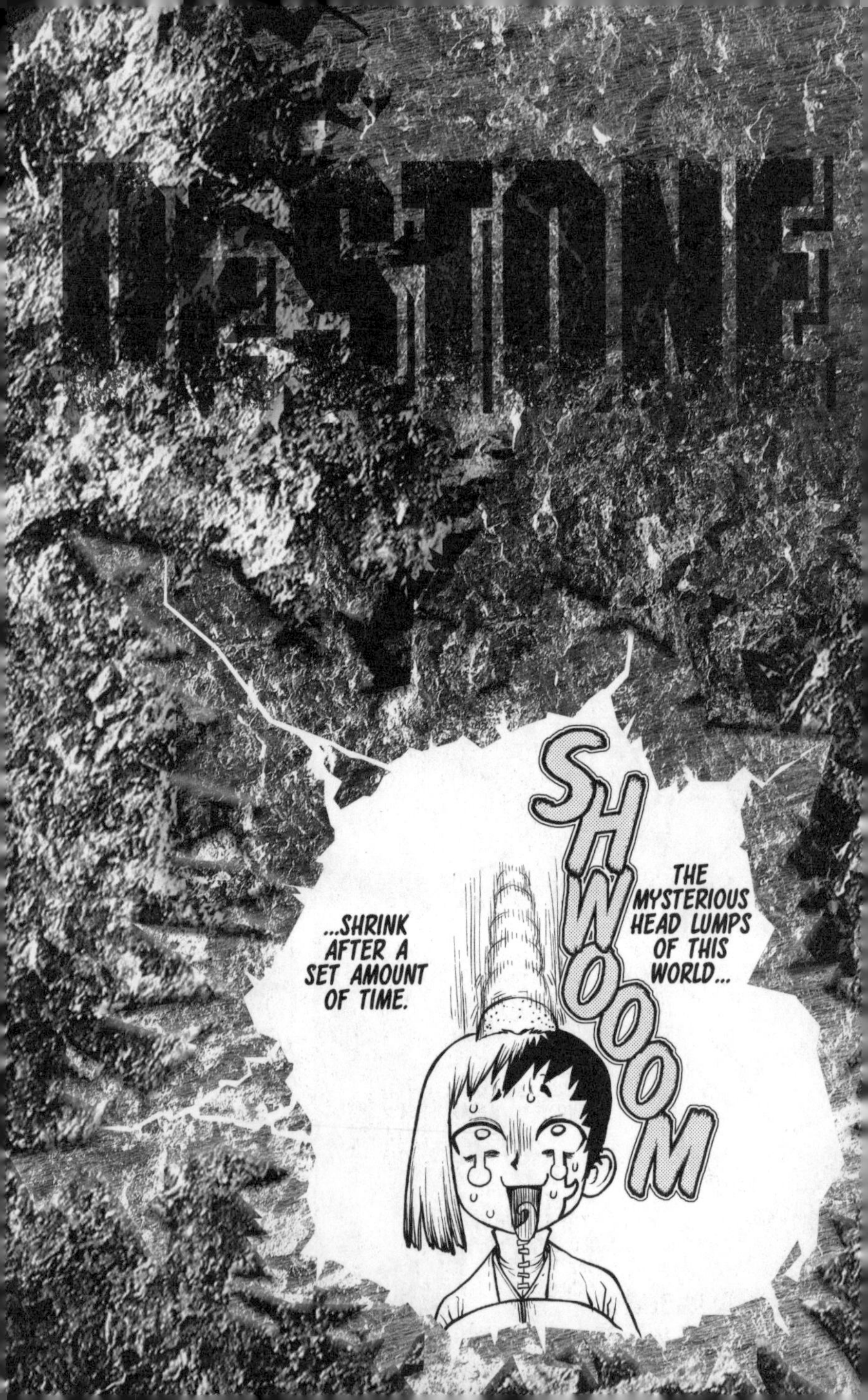
THE MYSTERIOUS HEAD LUMPS OF THIS WORLD...
SHWOOOOM
...SHRINK AFTER A SET AMOUNT OF TIME.

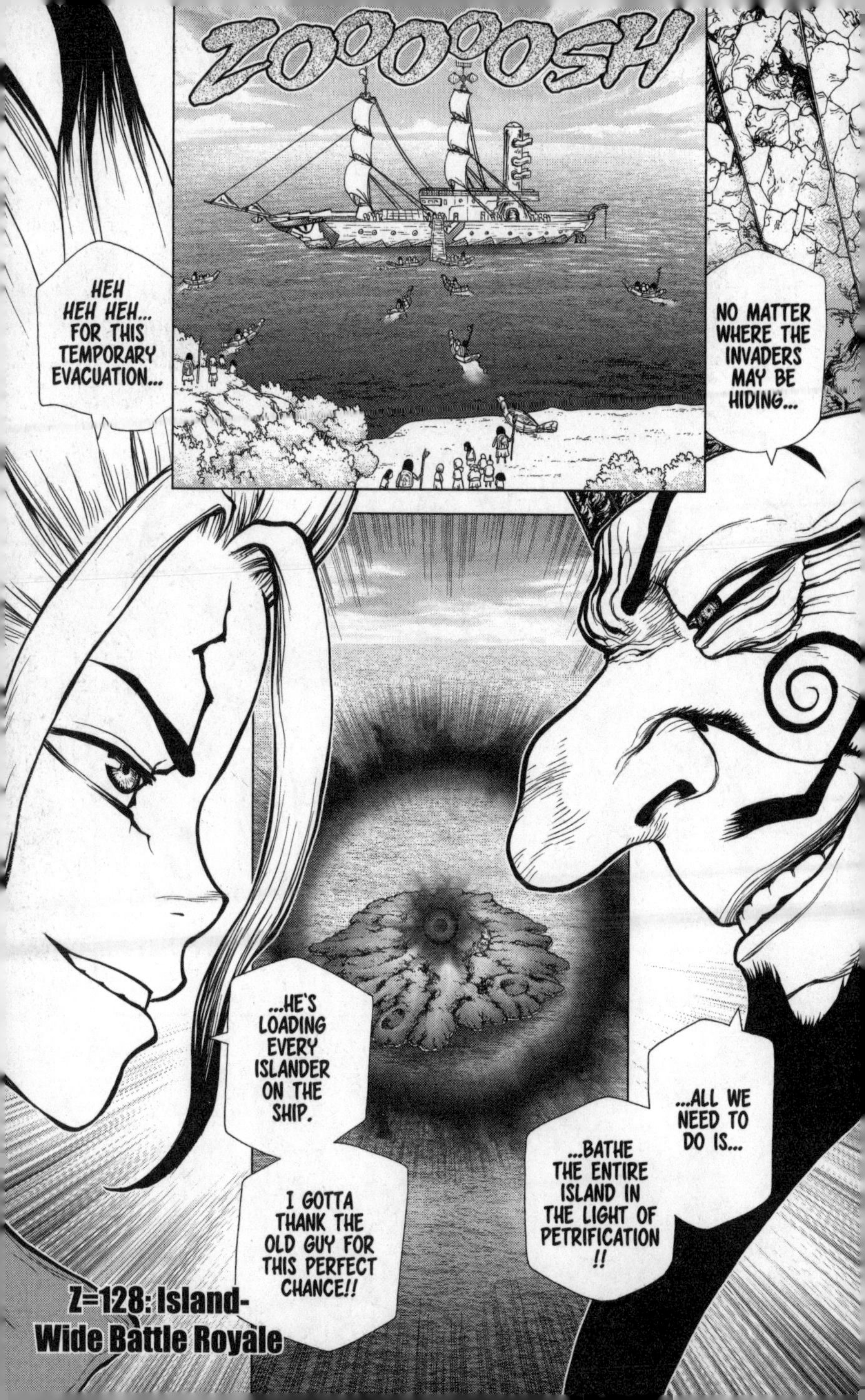
ZOOOOOSH
NO MATTER WHERE THE INVADERS MAY BE HIDING...
HEH HEH HEH... FOR THIS TEMPORARY EVACUATION...
...ALL WE NEED TO DO IS...
...BATHE THE ENTIRE ISLAND IN THE LIGHT OF PETRIFICATION!!
...HE'S LOADING EVERY ISLANDER ON THE SHIP.
I GOTTA THANK THE OLD GUY FOR THIS PERFECT CHANCE!!

## Z=128: Island-Wide Battle Royale

# Z=128: Island-Wide Battle Royale

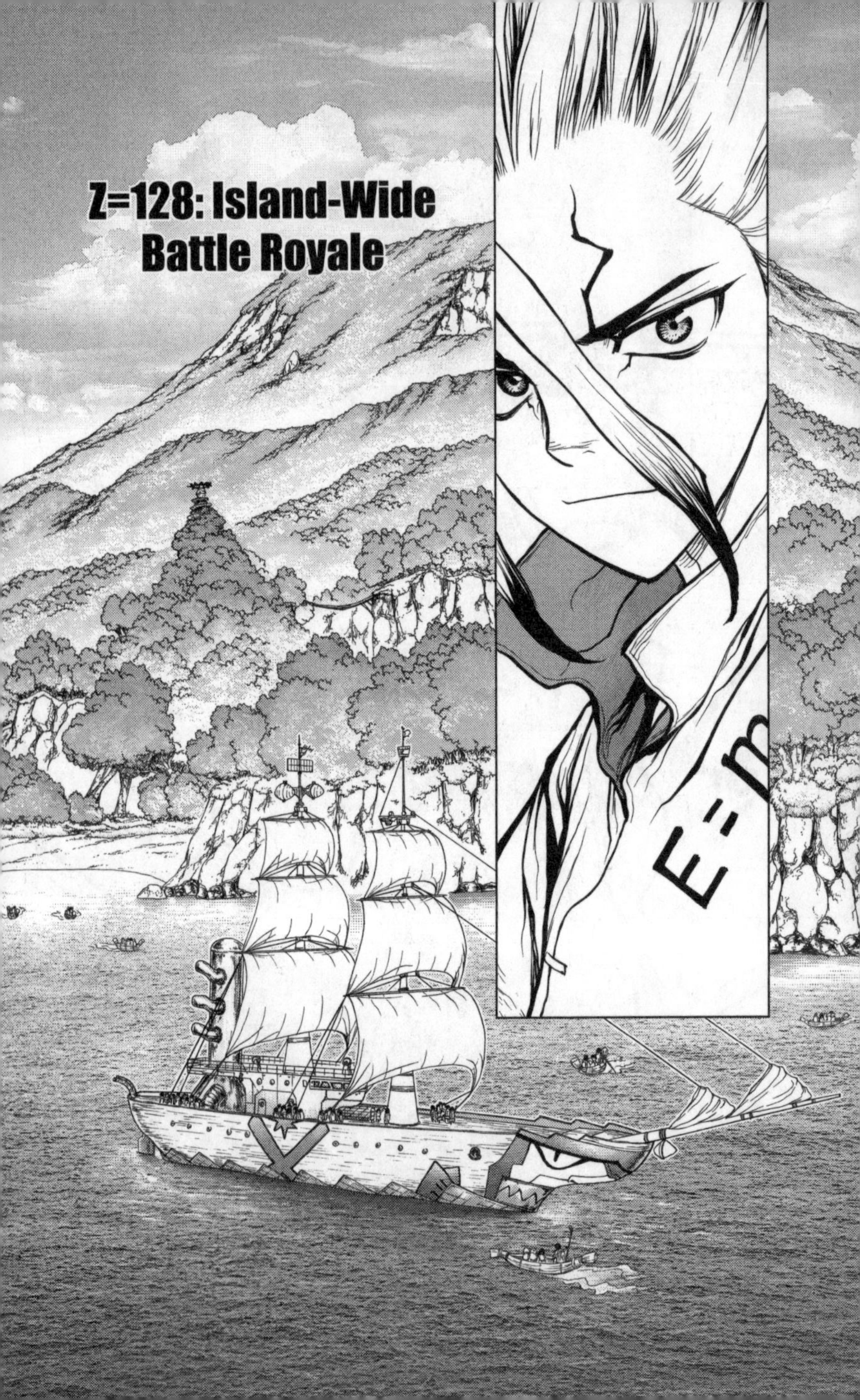
E=m

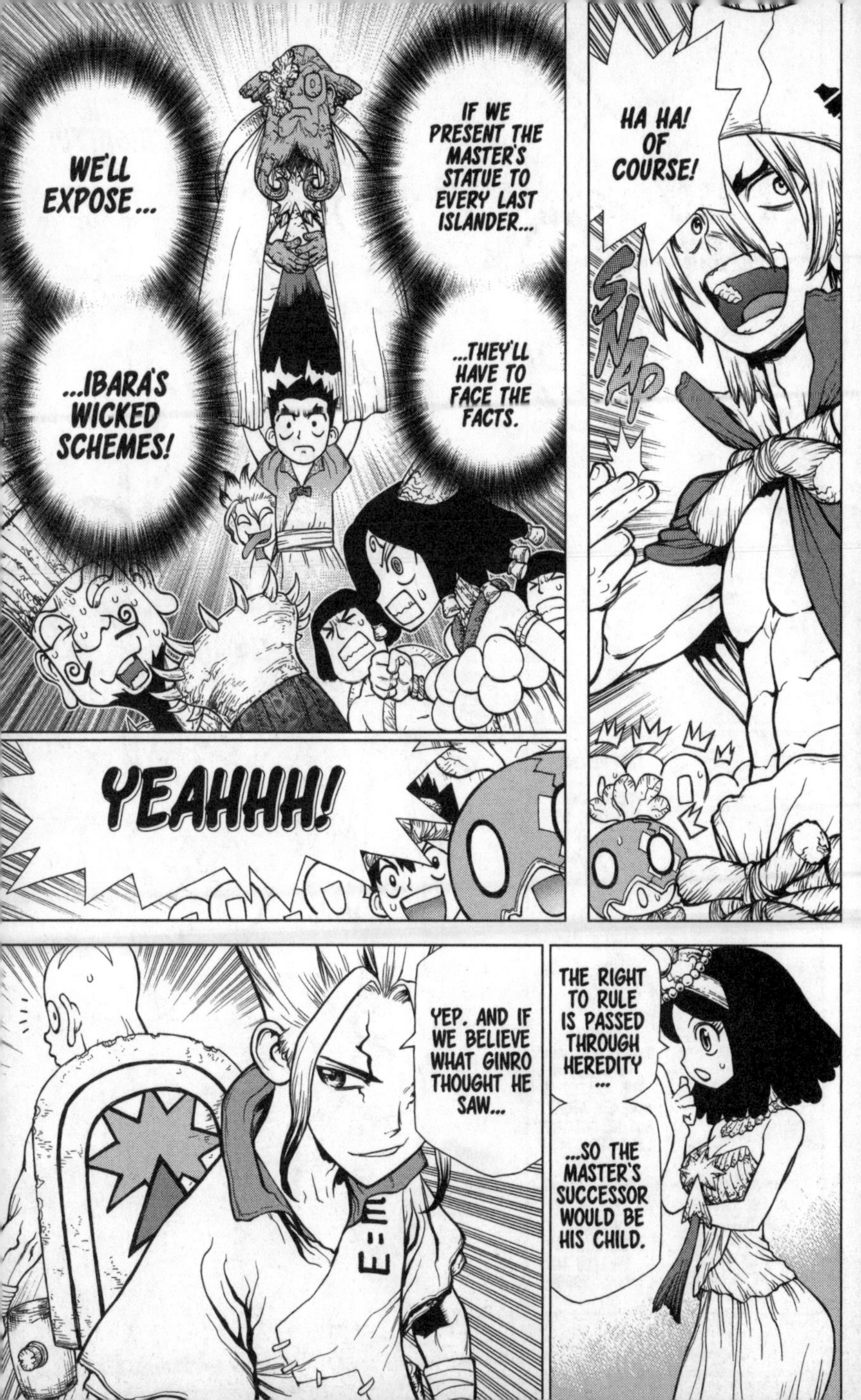

HA HA! OF COURSE!
SNAP
IF WE PRESENT THE MASTER'S STATUE TO EVERY LAST ISLANDER...
WE'LL EXPOSE...
...THEY'LL HAVE TO FACE THE FACTS.
...IBARA'S WICKED SCHEMES!
YEAHHH!
THE RIGHT TO RULE IS PASSED THROUGH HEREDITY...
...SO THE MASTER'S SUCCESSOR WOULD BE HIS CHILD.
YEP. AND IF WE BELIEVE WHAT GINRO THOUGHT HE SAW...

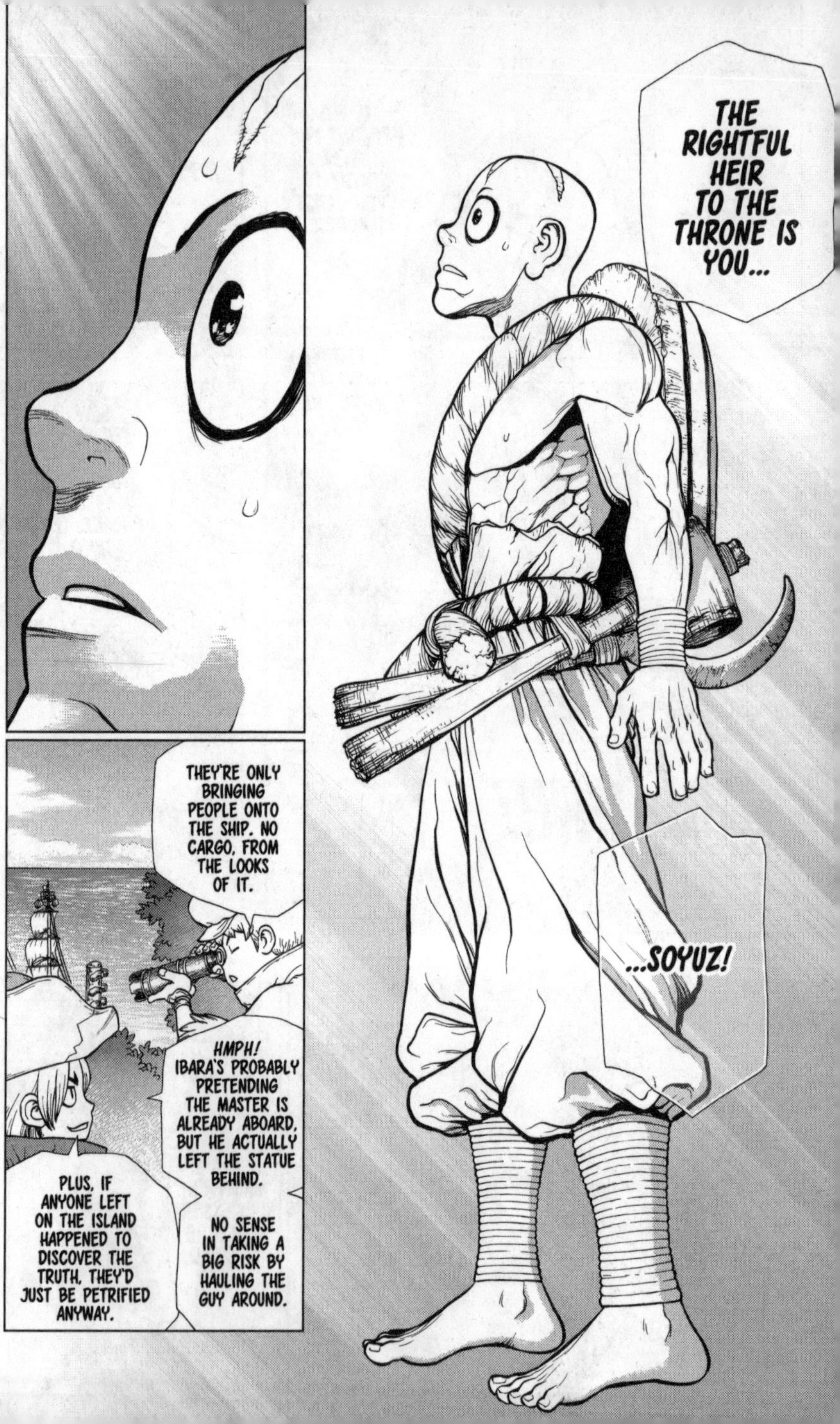
THE RIGHTFUL HEIR TO THE THRONE IS YOU...
...SOYUZ!
THEY'RE ONLY BRINGING PEOPLE ONTO THE SHIP. NO CARGO, FROM THE LOOKS OF IT.
HMPH! IBARA'S PROBABLY PRETENDING THE MASTER IS ALREADY ABOARD, BUT HE ACTUALLY LEFT THE STATUE BEHIND.
NO SENSE IN TAKING A BIG RISK BY HAULING THE GUY AROUND.
PLUS, IF ANYONE LEFT ON THE ISLAND HAPPENED TO DISCOVER THE TRUTH, THEY'D JUST BE PETRIFIED ANYWAY.

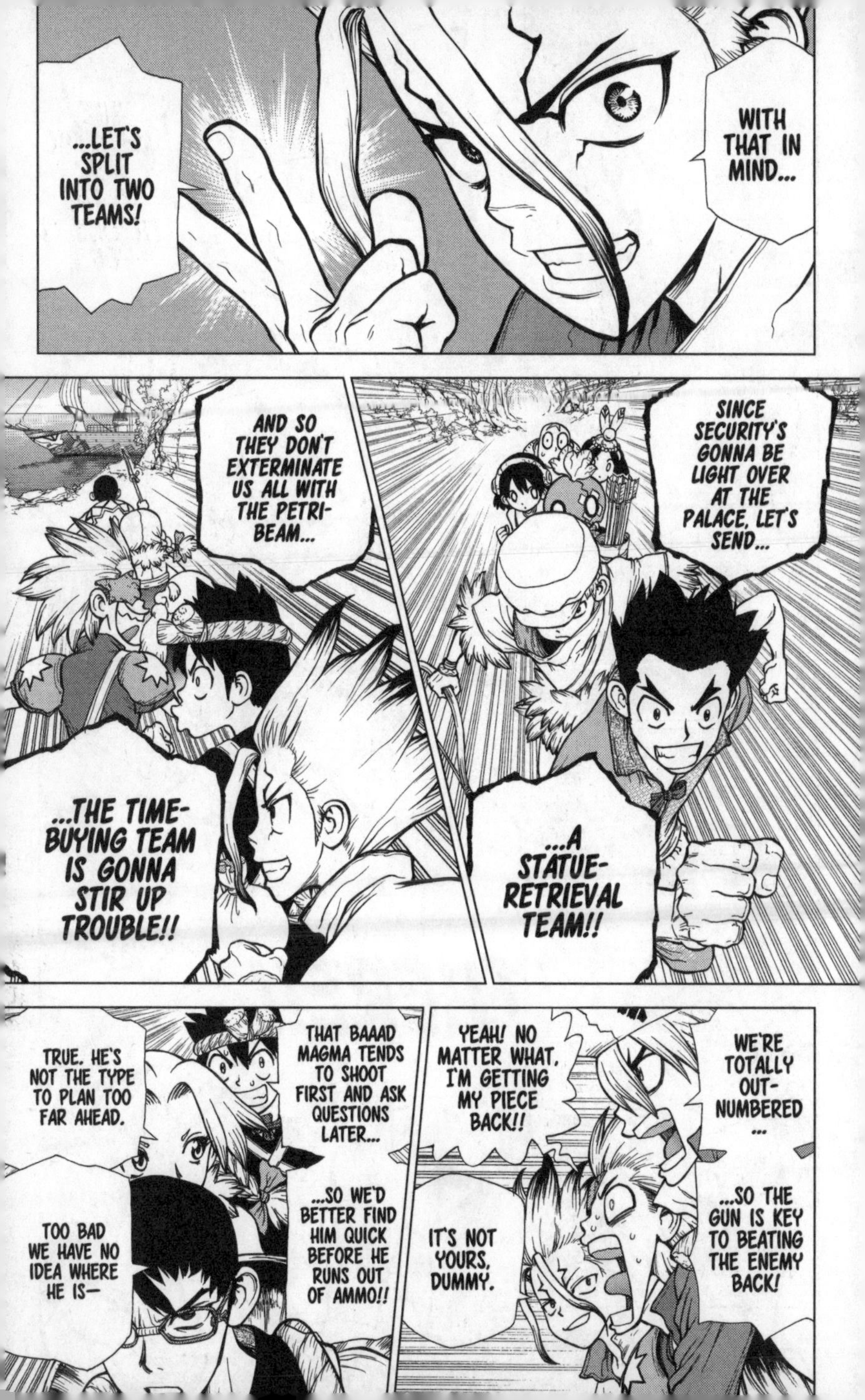
WITH THAT IN MIND...
...LET'S SPLIT INTO TWO TEAMS!
SINCE SECURITY'S GONNA BE LIGHT OVER AT THE PALACE, LET'S SEND...
...A STATUE-RETRIEVAL TEAM!!
AND SO THEY DON'T EXTERMINATE US ALL WITH THE PETRI-BEAM...
...THE TIME-BUYING TEAM IS GONNA STIR UP TROUBLE!!
WE'RE TOTALLY OUT-NUMBERED...
...SO THE GUN IS KEY TO BEATING THE ENEMY BACK!
YEAH! NO MATTER WHAT, I'M GETTING MY PIECE BACK!!
IT'S NOT YOURS, DUMMY.
THAT BAAAD MAGMA TENDS TO SHOOT FIRST AND ASK QUESTIONS LATER...
...SO WE'D BETTER FIND HIM QUICK BEFORE HE RUNS OUT OF AMMO!!
TRUE. HE'S NOT THE TYPE TO PLAN TOO FAR AHEAD.
TOO BAD WE HAVE NO IDEA WHERE HE IS—

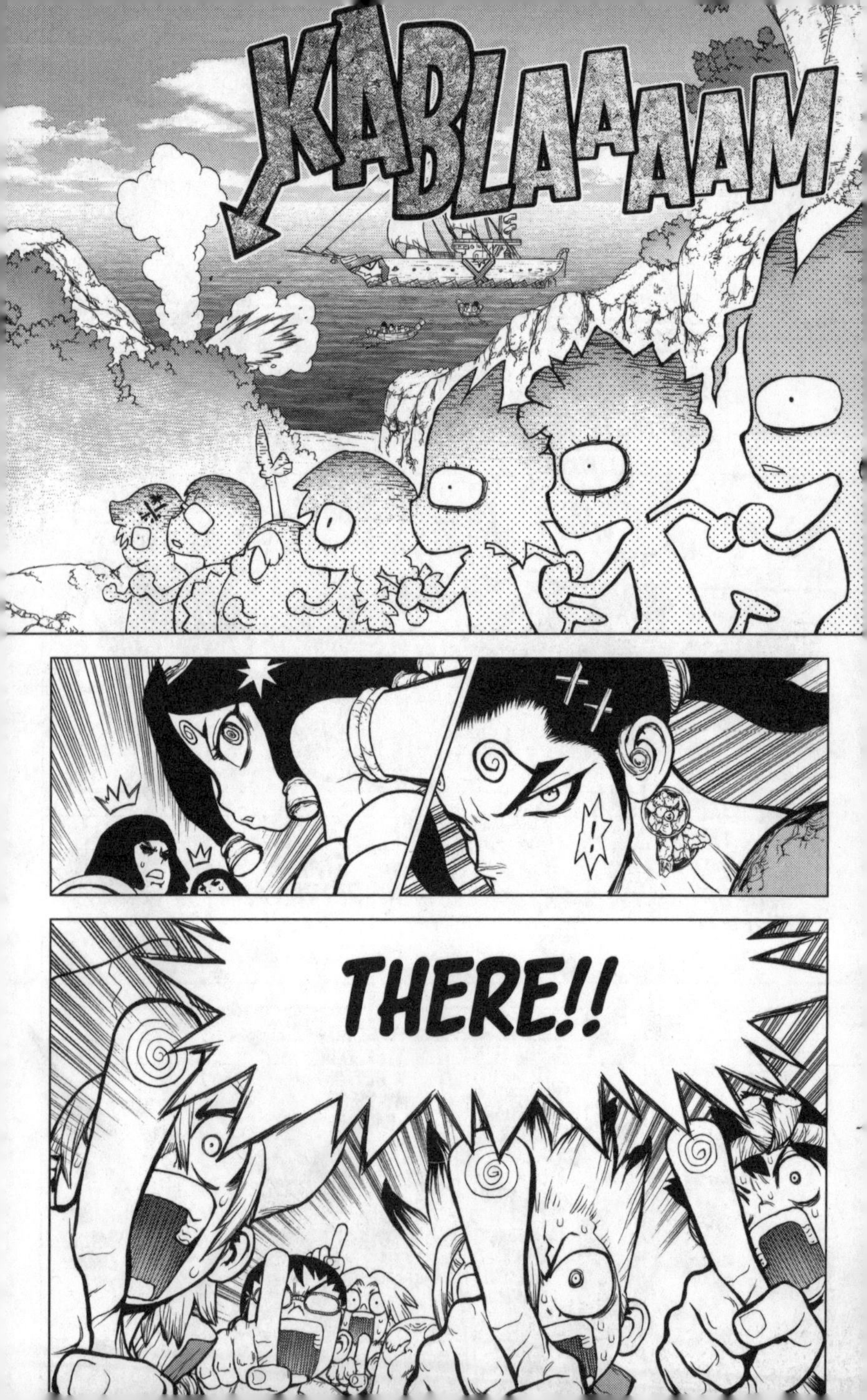
KABLAAAAAM
THERE!!

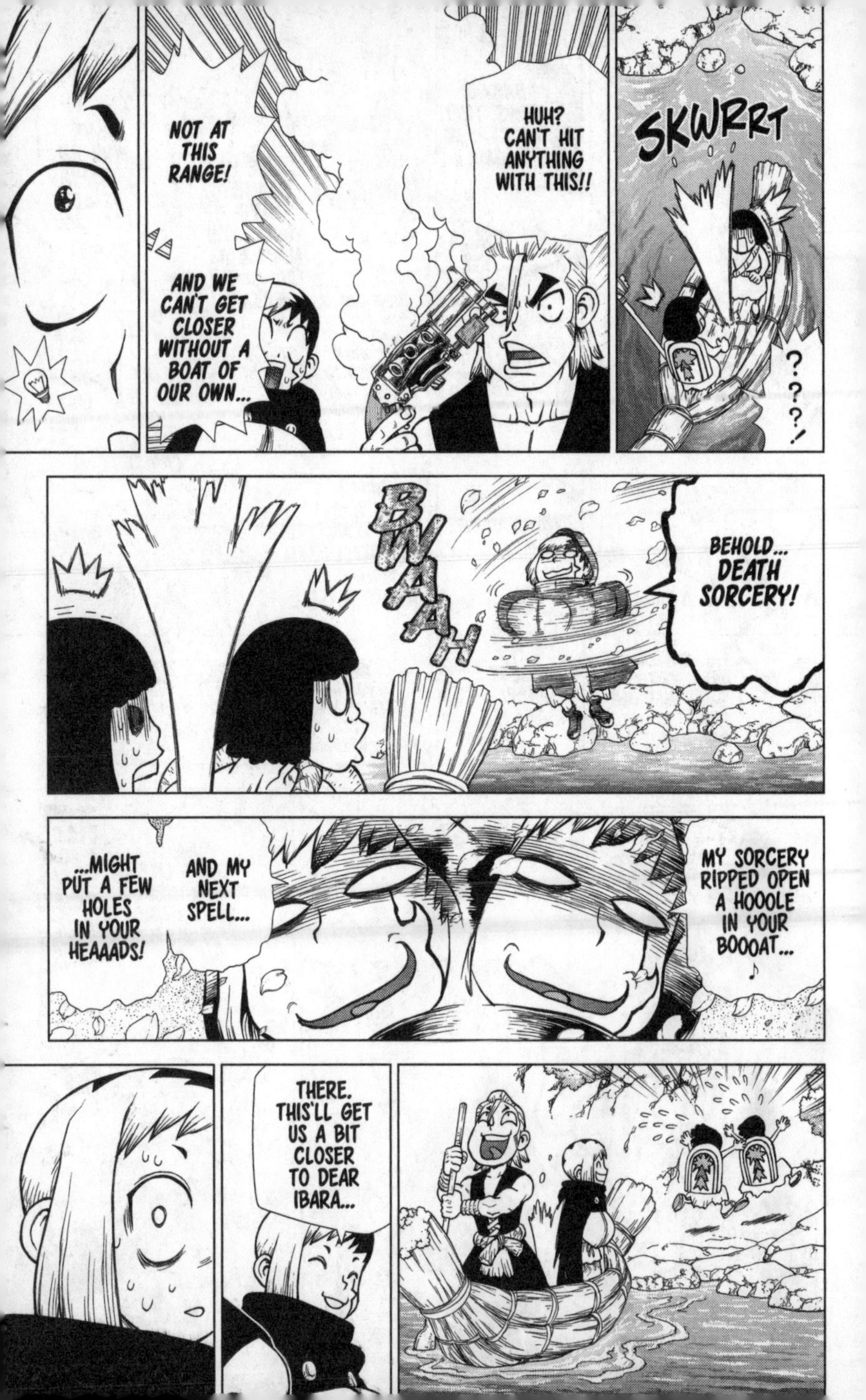
SKWRRT
???!
HUH? CAN'T HIT ANYTHING WITH THIS!!
NOT AT THIS RANGE!
AND WE CAN'T GET CLOSER WITHOUT A BOAT OF OUR OWN...
BEHOLD... DEATH SORCERY!
BWAAH
MY SORCERY RIPPED OPEN A HOOOLE IN YOUR BOOOAT... ♪
AND MY NEXT SPELL...
...MIGHT PUT A FEW HOLES IN YOUR HEAAADS!
THERE. THIS'LL GET US A BIT CLOSER TO DEAR IBARA...

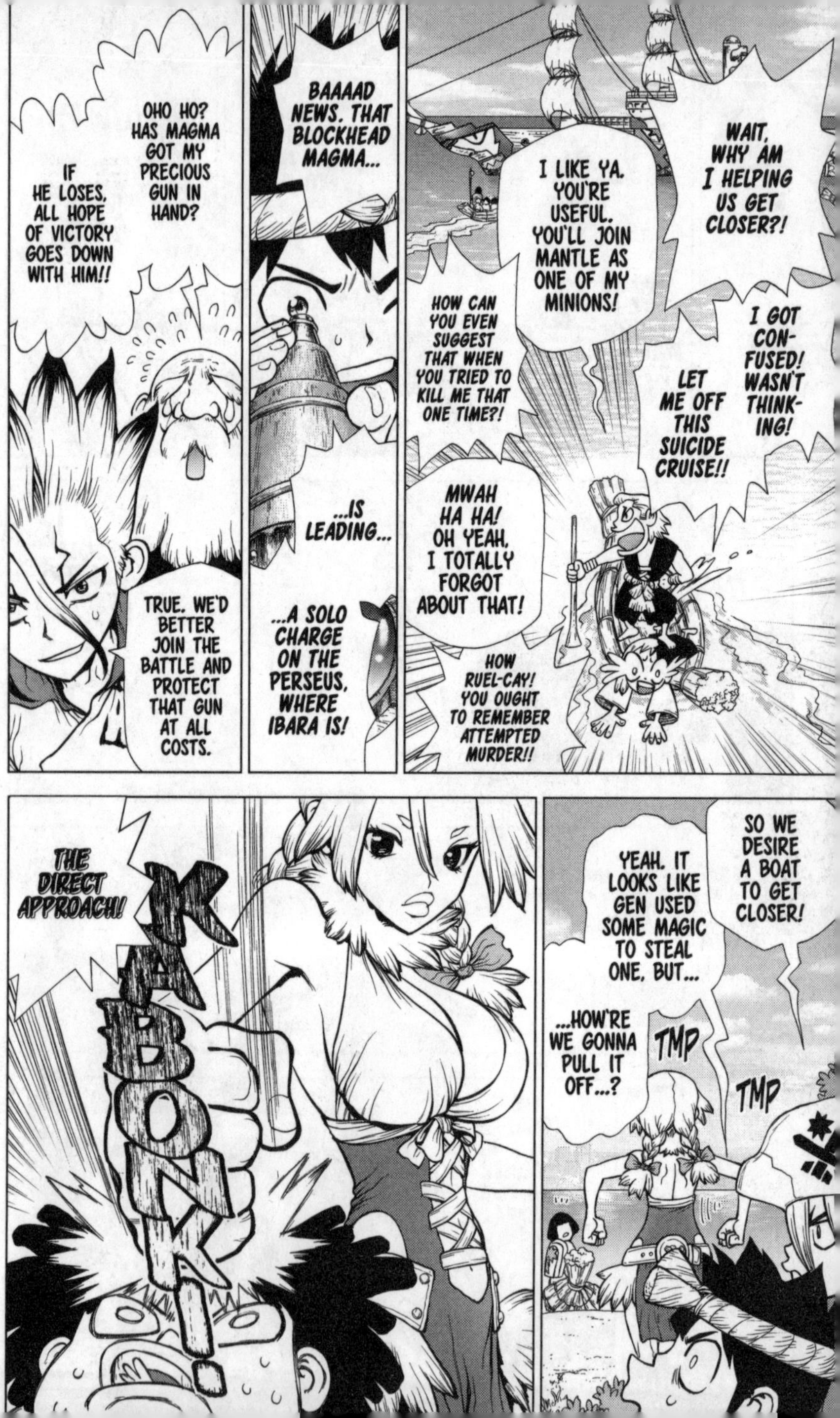

WAIT, WHY AM I HELPING US GET CLOSER?!
I LIKE YA. YOU'RE USEFUL. YOU'LL JOIN MANTLE AS ONE OF MY MINIONS!
I GOT CONFUSED! WASN'T THINKING!
LET ME OFF THIS SUICIDE CRUISE!!
HOW CAN YOU EVEN SUGGEST THAT WHEN YOU TRIED TO KILL ME THAT ONE TIME?!
MWAH HA HA! OH YEAH, I TOTALLY FORGOT ABOUT THAT!
HOW RUEL-CAY! YOU OUGHT TO REMEMBER ATTEMPTED MURDER!!
BAAAAD NEWS. THAT BLOCKHEAD MAGMA...
...IS LEADING...
...A SOLO CHARGE ON THE PERSEUS, WHERE IBARA IS!
OHO HO? HAS MAGMA GOT MY PRECIOUS GUN IN HAND?
IF HE LOSES, ALL HOPE OF VICTORY GOES DOWN WITH HIM!!
TRUE. WE'D BETTER JOIN THE BATTLE AND PROTECT THAT GUN AT ALL COSTS.
SO WE DESIRE A BOAT TO GET CLOSER!
YEAH. IT LOOKS LIKE GEN USED SOME MAGIC TO STEAL ONE, BUT...
TMP
TMP
...HOW'RE WE GONNA PULL IT OFF...?
THE DIRECT APPROACH!
KABONK!

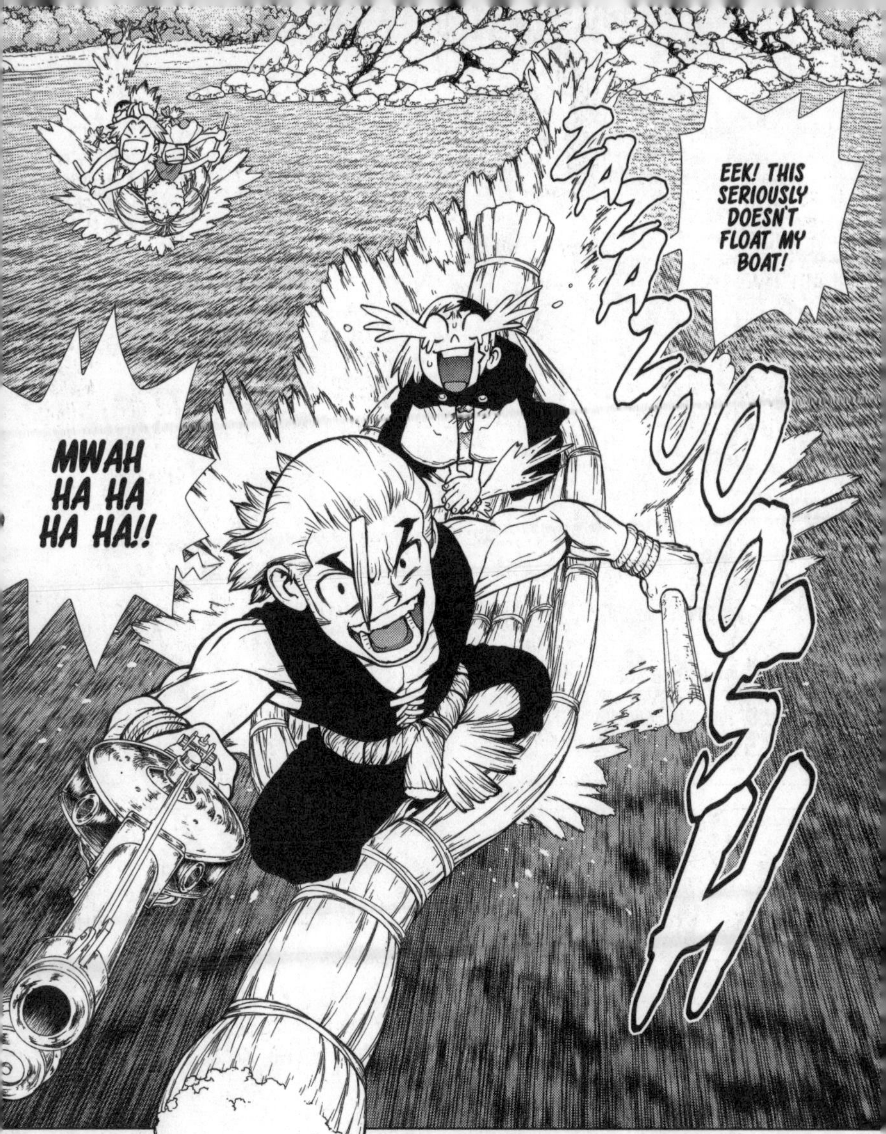
EEK! THIS SERIOUSLY DOESN'T FLOAT MY BOAT!
ZAZAZOOOOSH
MWAH HA HA HA HA!!
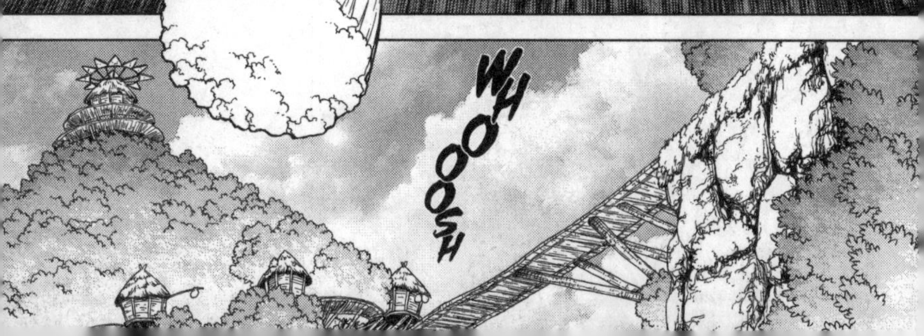
WHOOOOSH

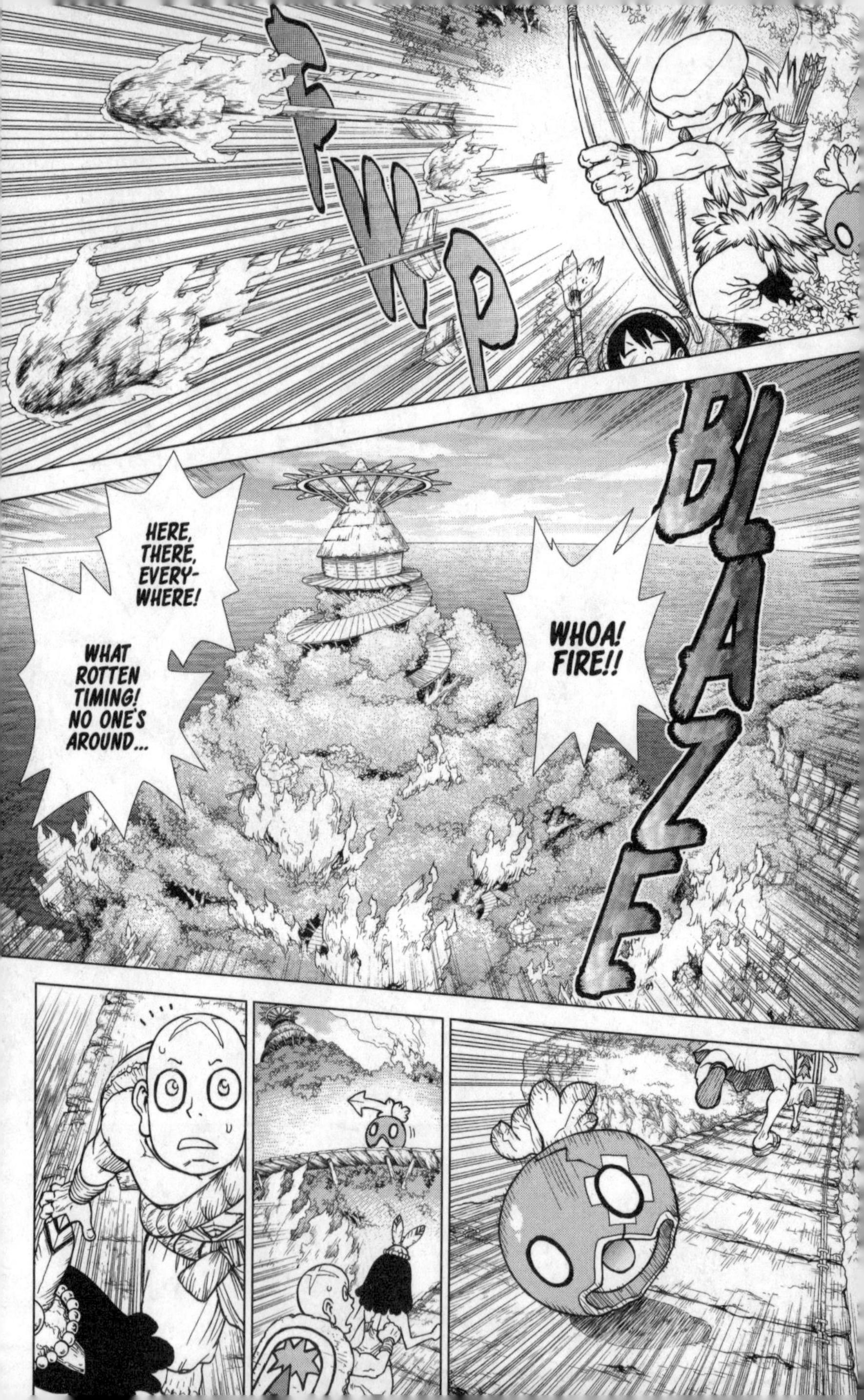
FWIP
BLAZE
WHOA! FIRE!!
HERE, THERE, EVERYWHERE!
WHAT ROTTEN TIMING! NO ONE'S AROUND...

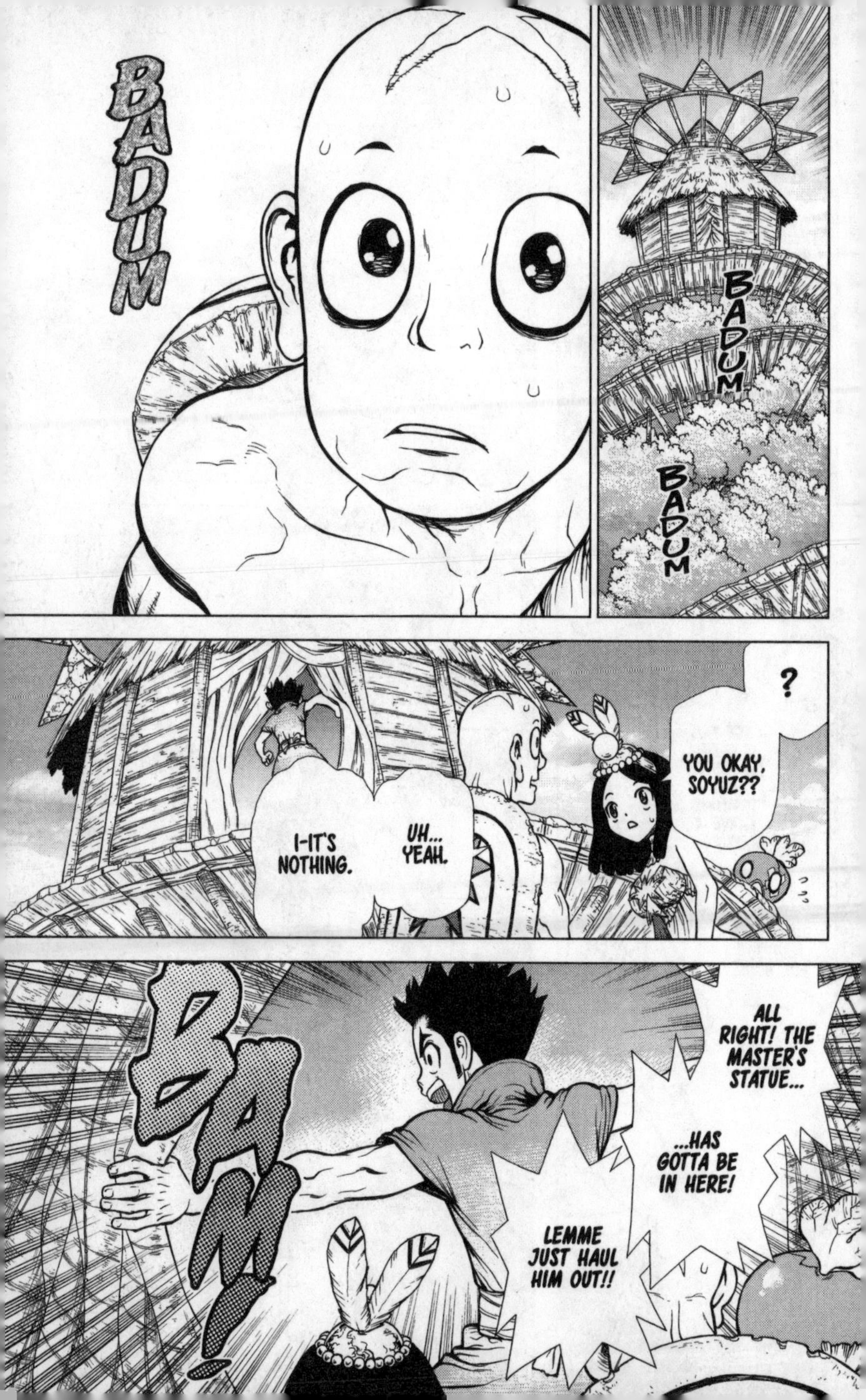
BADUM
BADUM
BADUM
?
YOU OKAY, SOYUZ??
UH... YEAH.
I-IT'S NOTHING.
ALL RIGHT! THE MASTER'S STATUE...
...HAS GOTTA BE IN HERE!
LEMME JUST HAUL HIM OUT!!
BAM

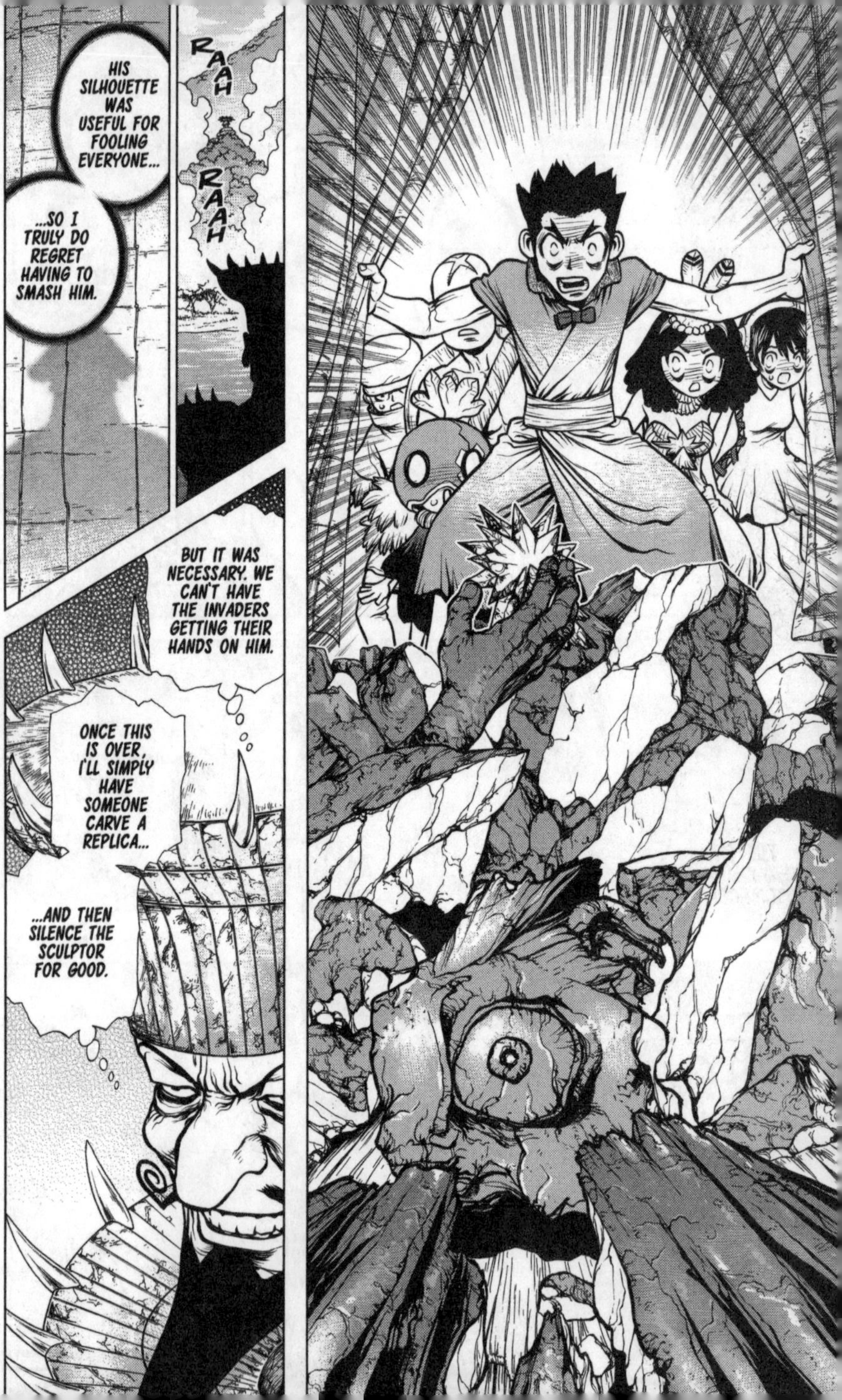
RAAH
RAAH
HIS SILHOUETTE WAS USEFUL FOR FOOLING EVERYONE...
...SO I TRULY DO REGRET HAVING TO SMASH HIM.
BUT IT WAS NECESSARY. WE CAN'T HAVE THE INVADERS GETTING THEIR HANDS ON HIM.
ONCE THIS IS OVER, I'LL SIMPLY HAVE SOMEONE CARVE A REPLICA...
...AND THEN SILENCE THE SCULPTOR FOR GOOD.

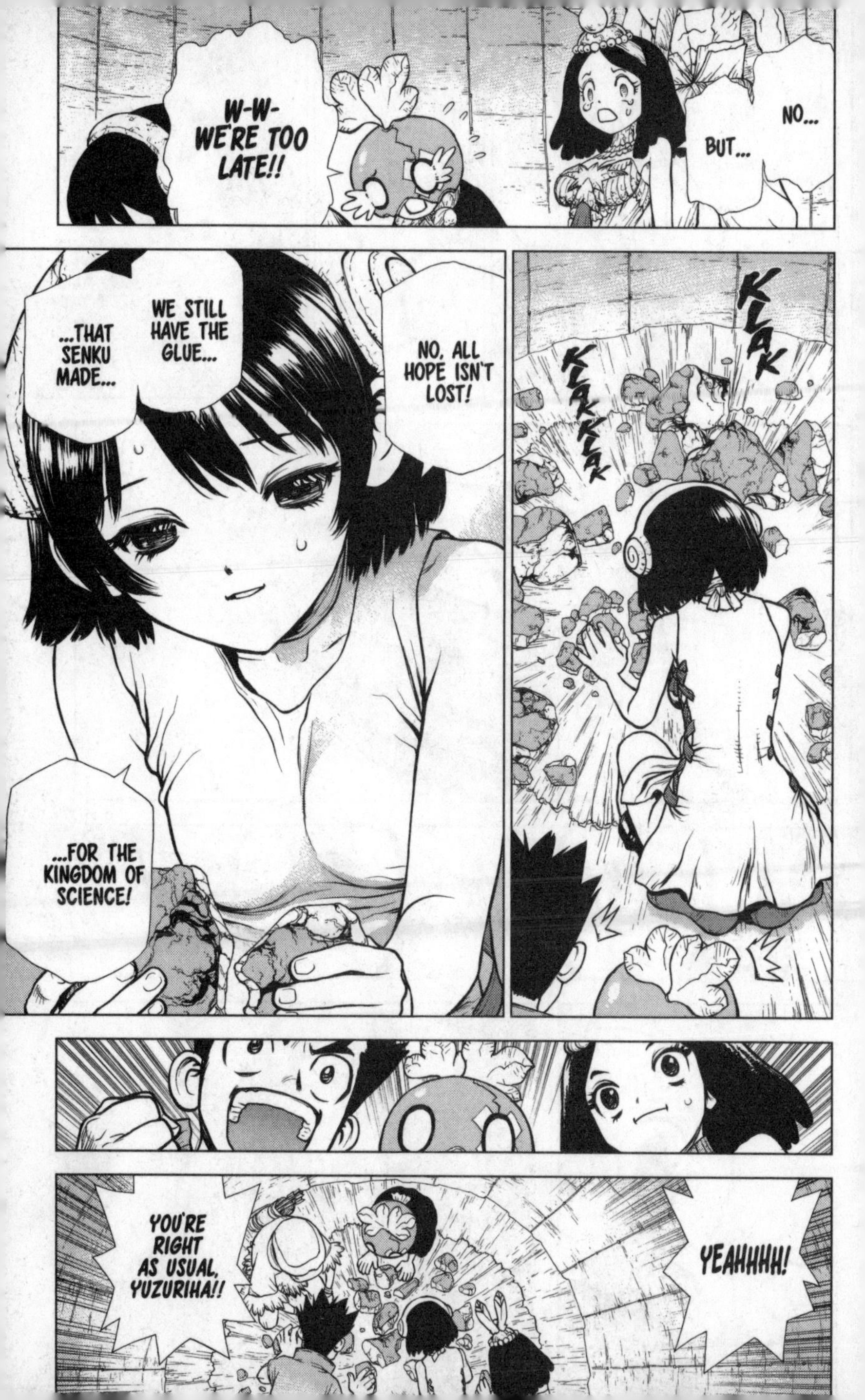
NO...
BUT...
W-W-WE'RE TOO LATE!!
KLAK
KLAKKLAK
NO, ALL HOPE ISN'T LOST!
WE STILL HAVE THE GLUE...
...THAT SENKU MADE...
...FOR THE KINGDOM OF SCIENCE!
YEAHHHH!
YOU'RE RIGHT AS USUAL, YUZURIHA!!

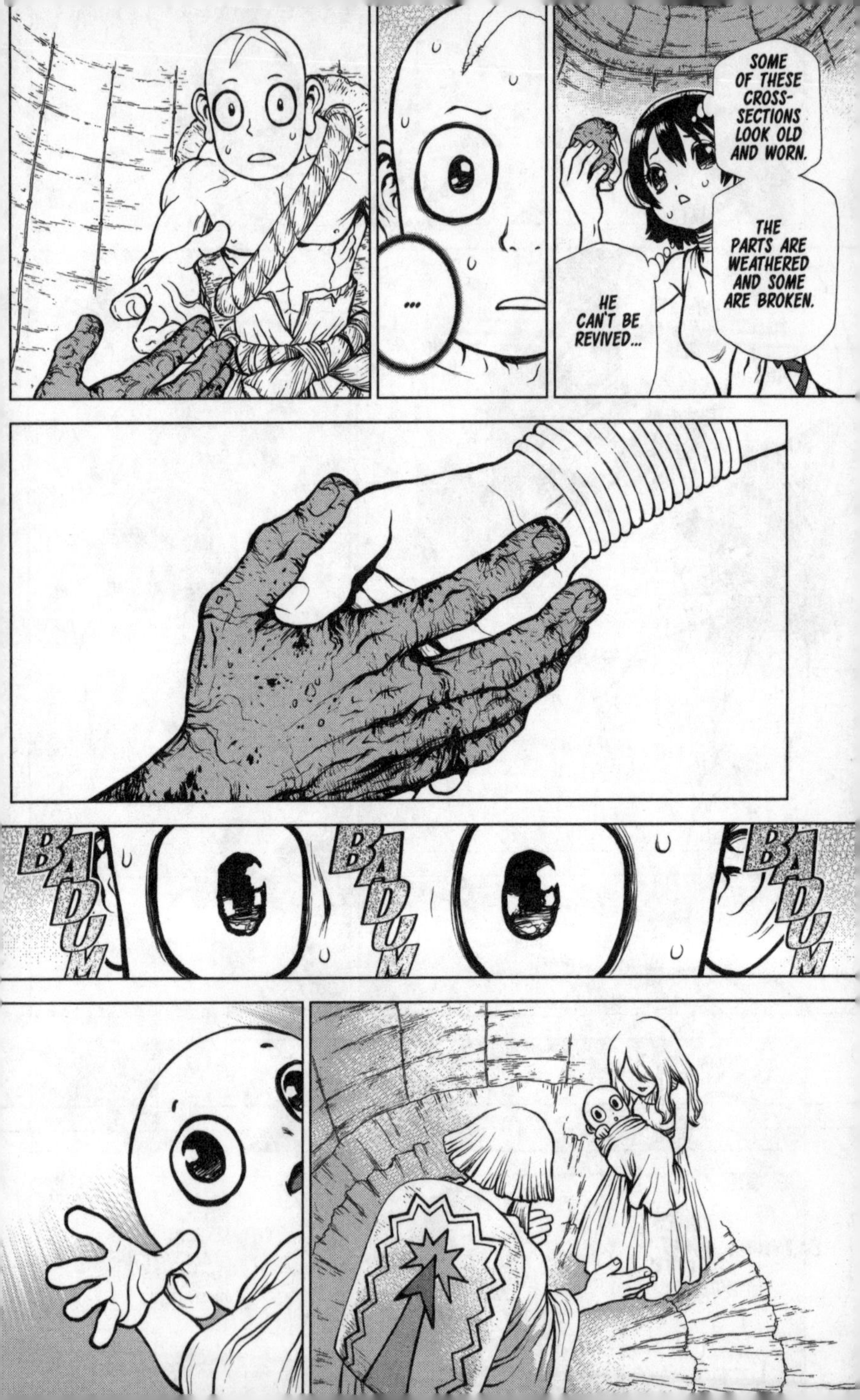
SOME OF THESE CROSS-SECTIONS LOOK OLD AND WORN.
THE PARTS ARE WEATHERED AND SOME ARE BROKEN.
HE CAN'T BE REVIVED...
...
BADUM
BADUM
BADUM

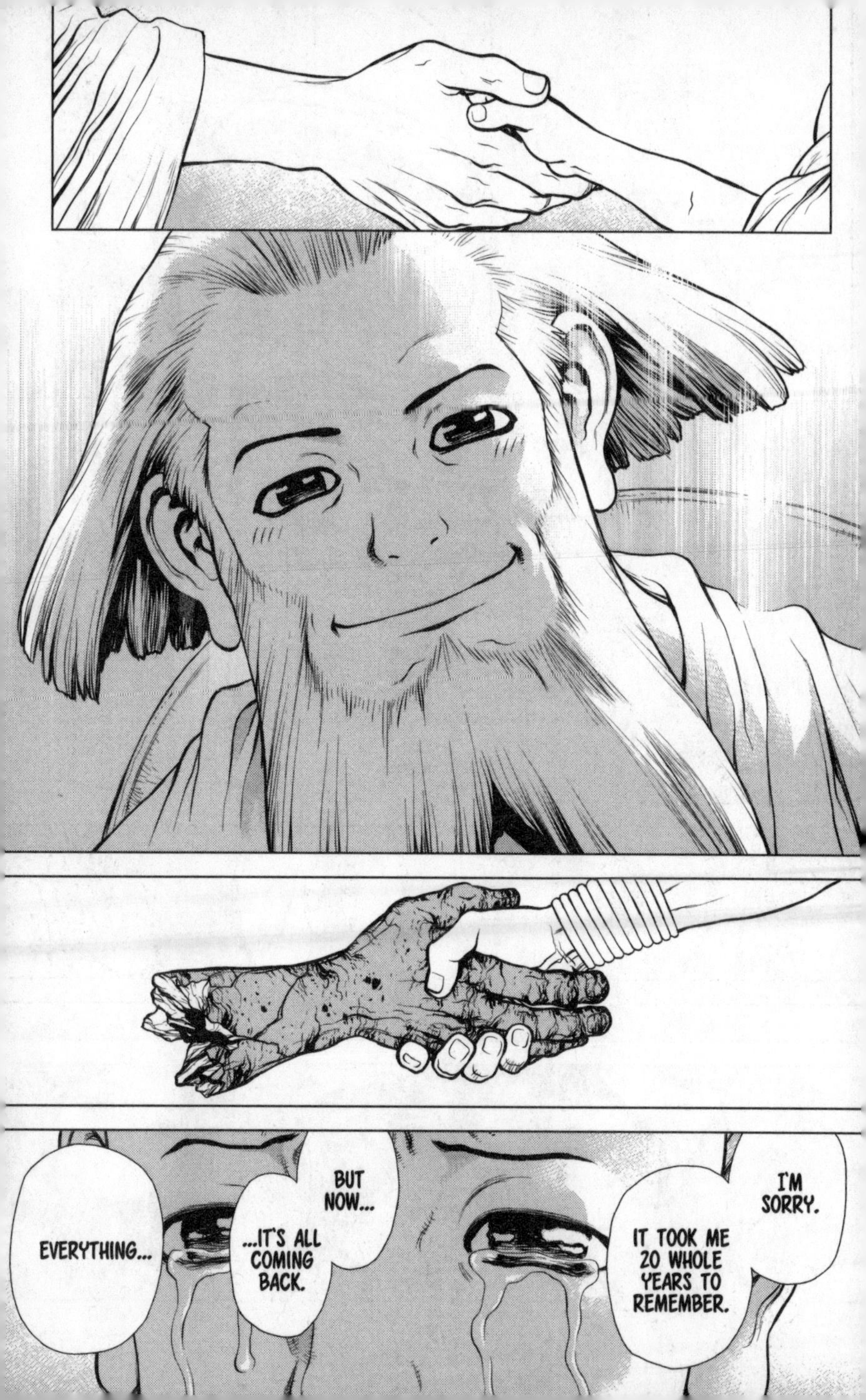
I'M SORRY.
IT TOOK ME 20 WHOLE YEARS TO REMEMBER.
BUT NOW...
...IT'S ALL COMING BACK.
EVERYTHING...

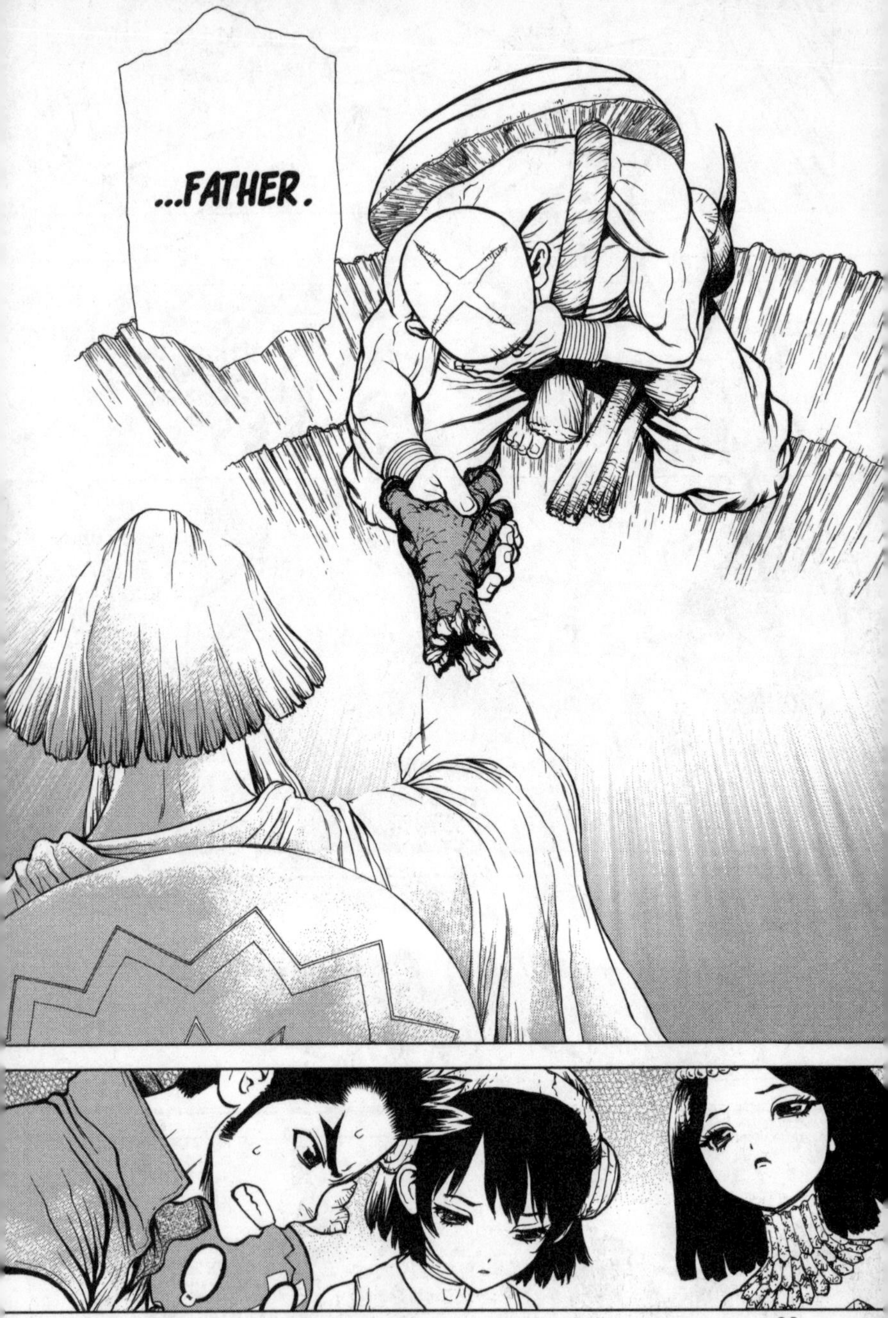
...FATHER.

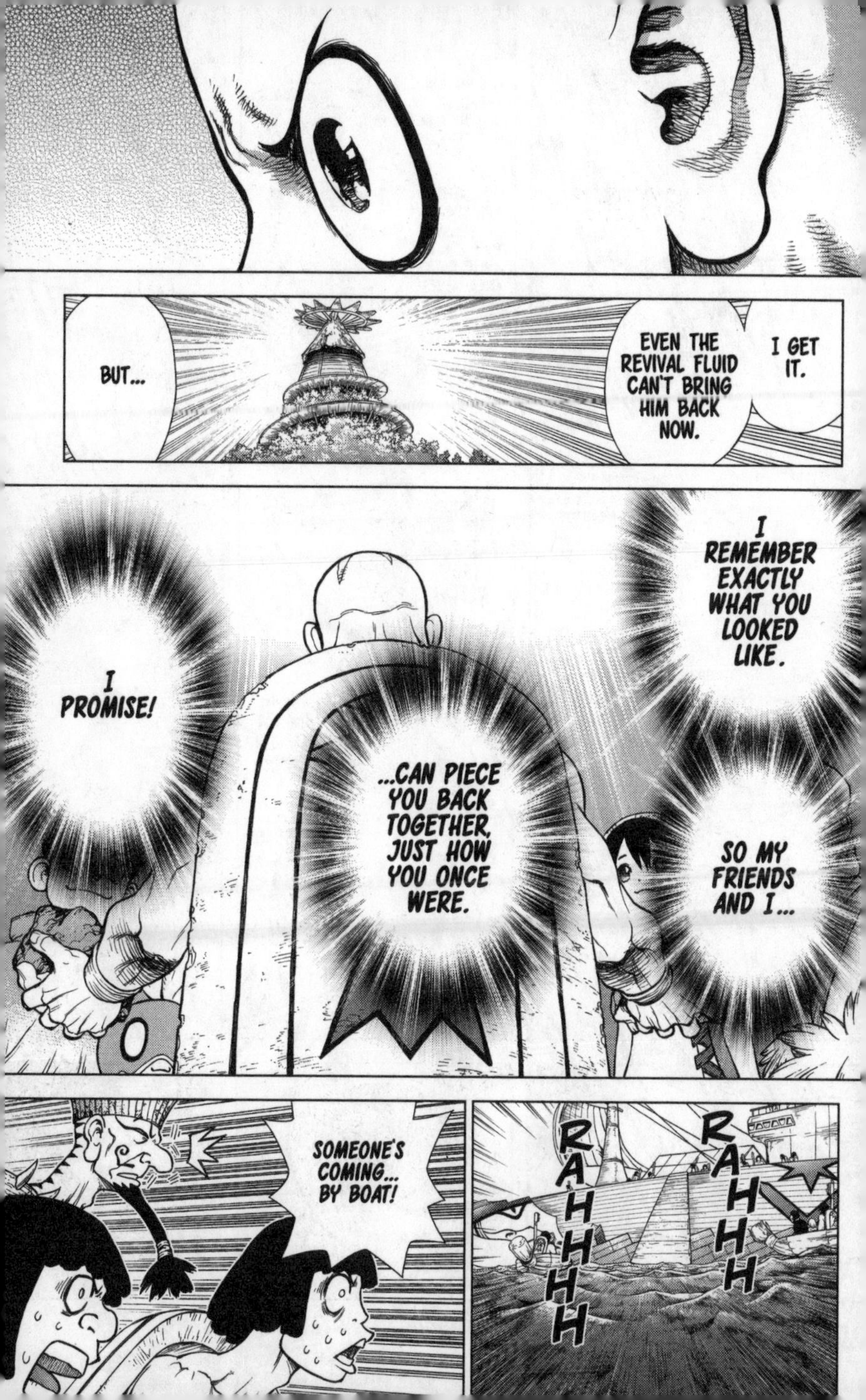
I GET IT.
EVEN THE REVIVAL FLUID CAN'T BRING HIM BACK NOW.
BUT...
I REMEMBER EXACTLY WHAT YOU LOOKED LIKE.
SO MY FRIENDS AND I...
...CAN PIECE YOU BACK TOGETHER, JUST HOW YOU ONCE WERE.
I PROMISE!
RAHHH
RAHHHH
SOMEONE'S COMING... BY BOAT!

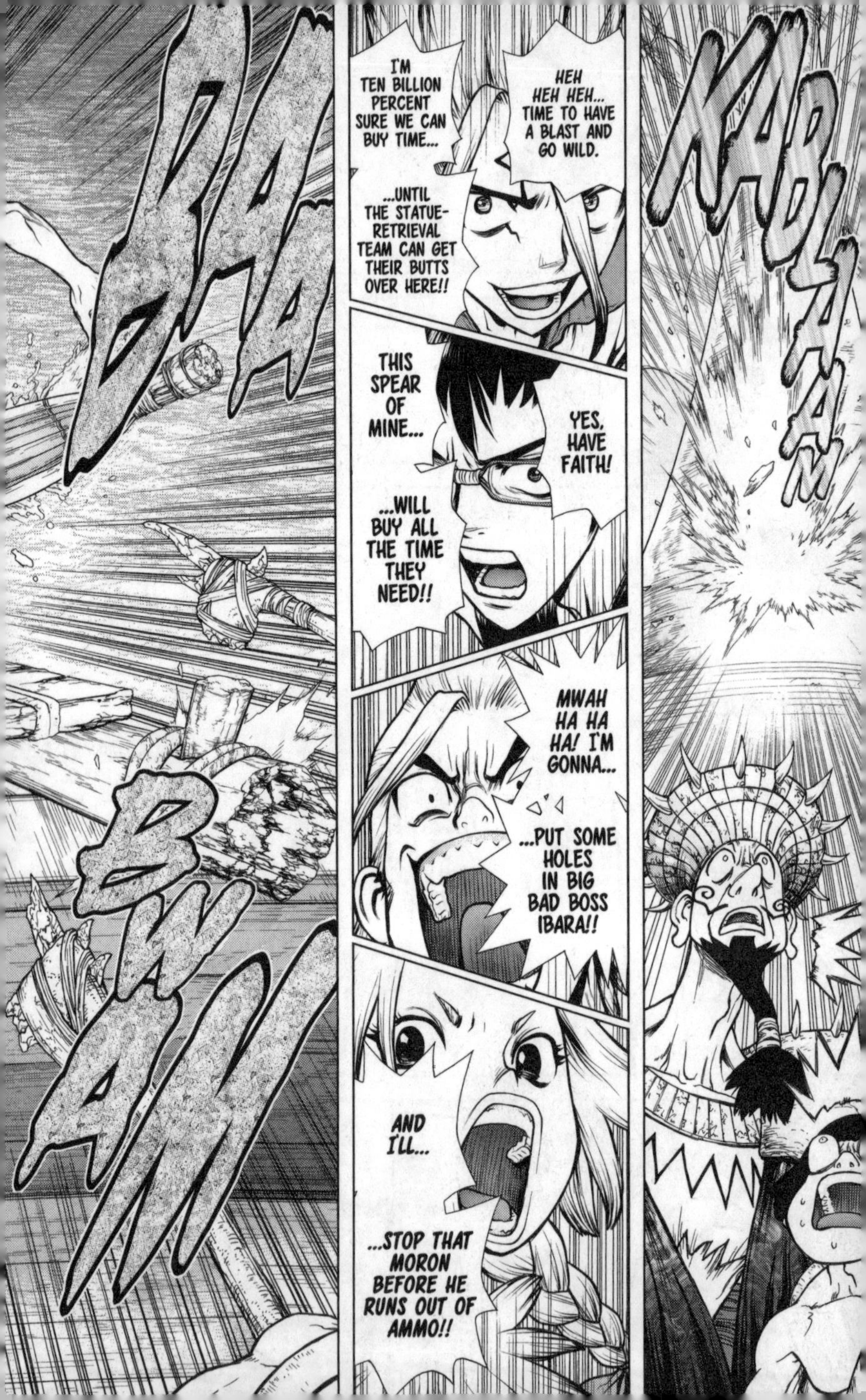
KABLAAM
I'M TEN BILLION PERCENT SURE WE CAN BUY TIME...
HEH HEH HEH... TIME TO HAVE A BLAST AND GO WILD.
...UNTIL THE STATUE-RETRIEVAL TEAM CAN GET THEIR BUTTS OVER HERE!!
THIS SPEAR OF MINE...
YES, HAVE FAITH!
...WILL BUY ALL THE TIME THEY NEED!!
MWAH HA HA HA! I'M GONNA...
...PUT SOME HOLES IN BIG BAD BOSS IBARA!!
AND I'LL...
...STOP THAT MORON BEFORE HE RUNS OUT OF AMMO!!

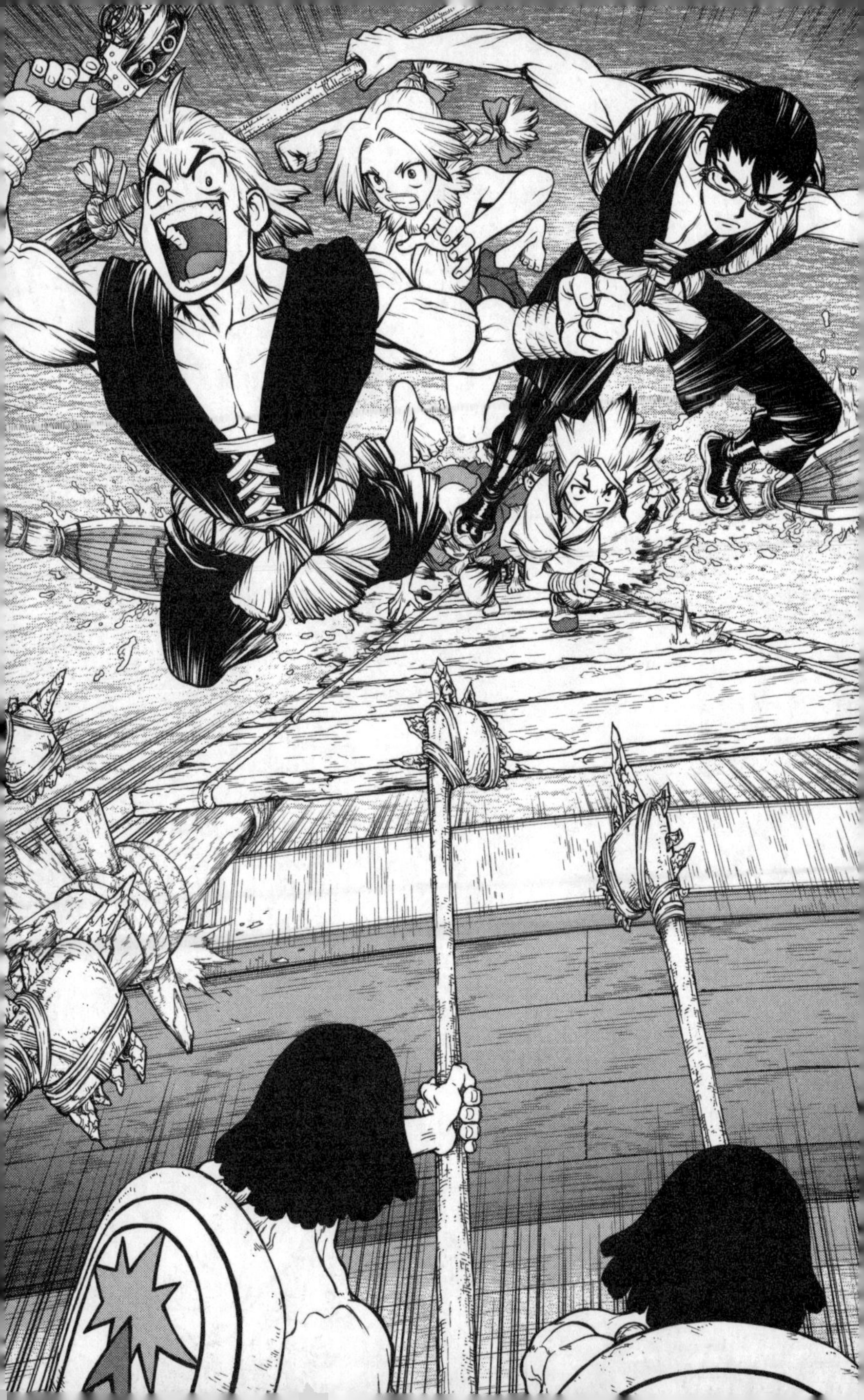

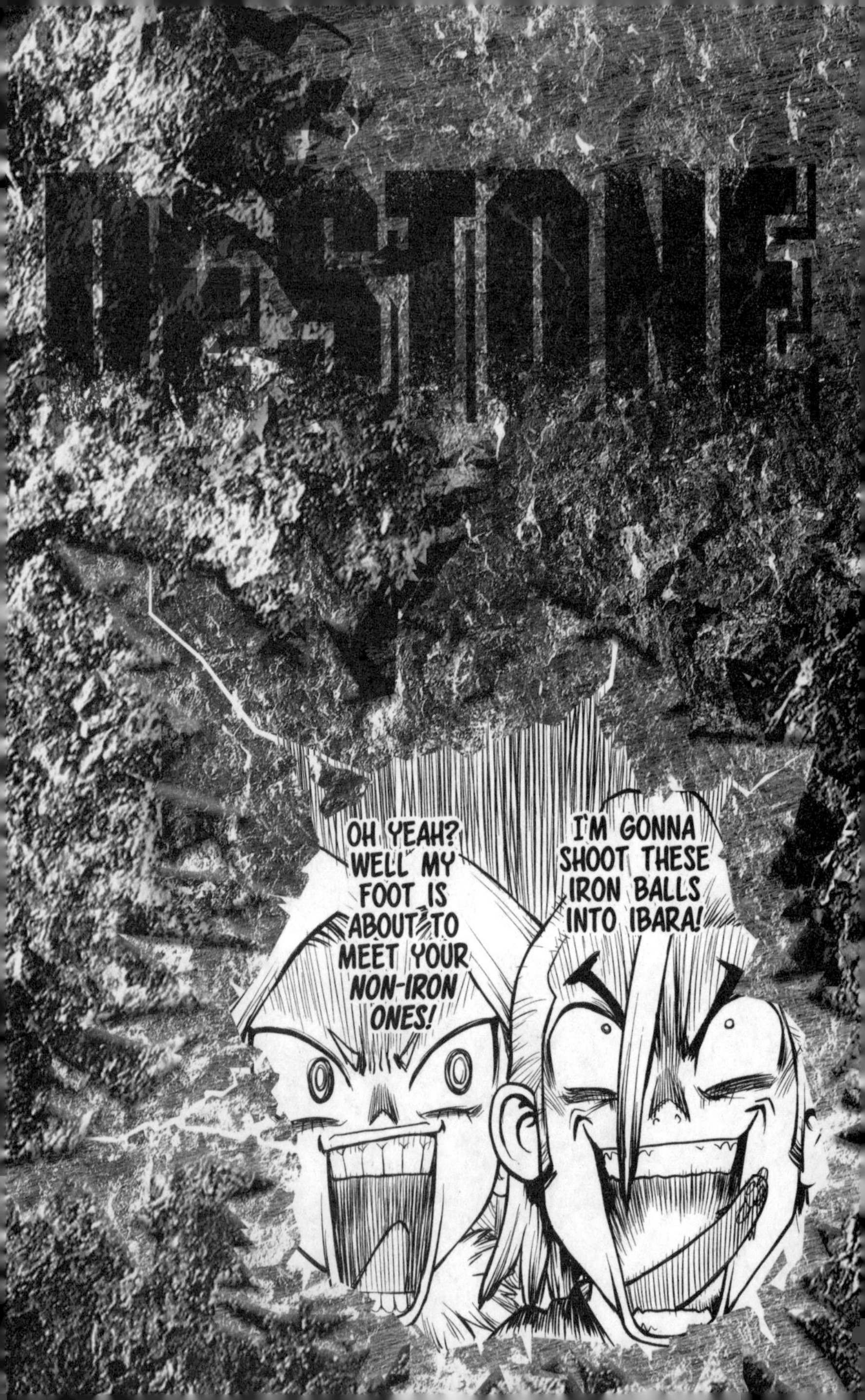
DR.STONE
I'M GONNA SHOOT THESE IRON BALLS INTO IBARA!
OH YEAH? WELL MY FOOT IS ABOUT TO MEET YOUR NON-IRON ONES!

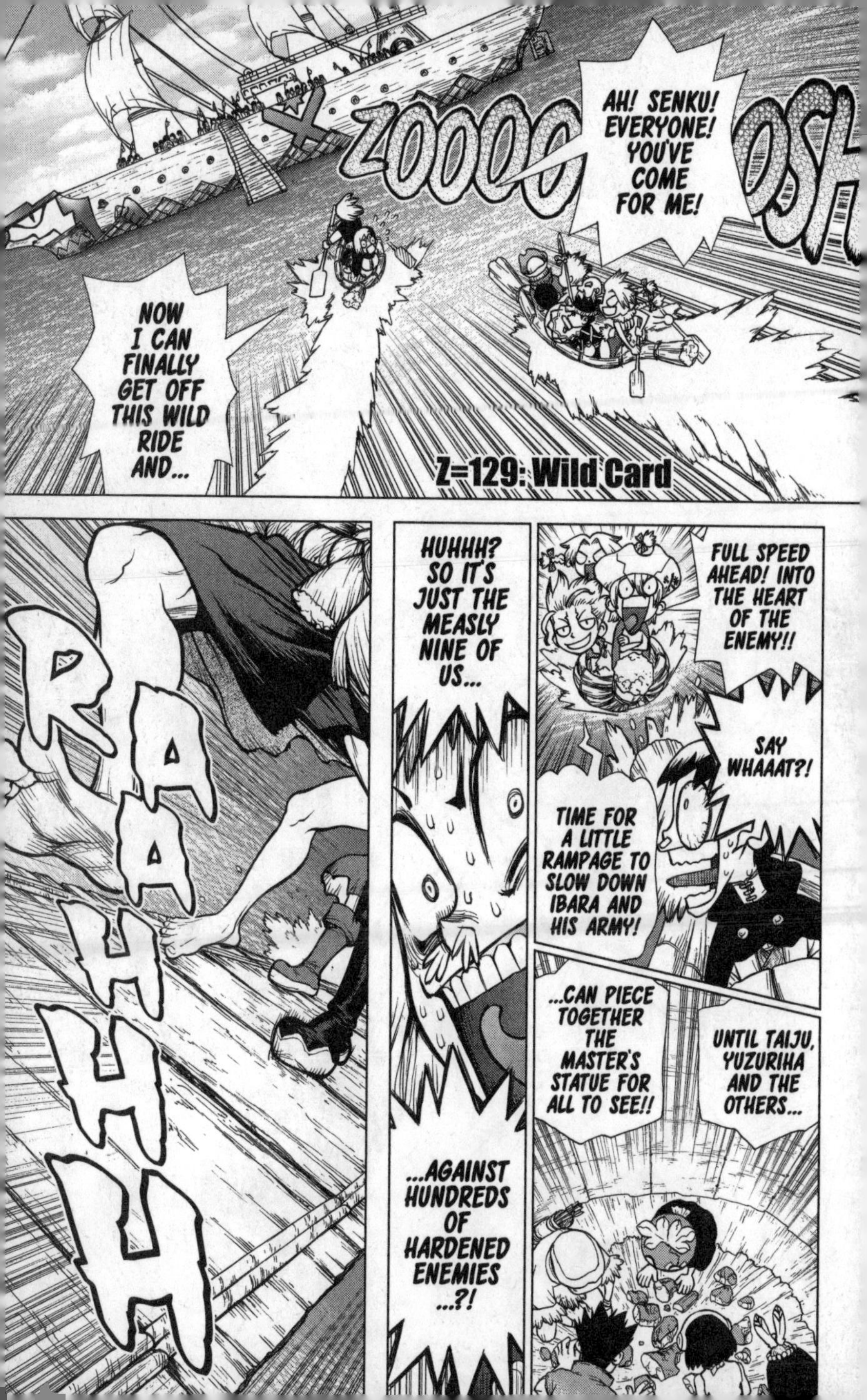
AH! SENKU! EVERYONE! YOU'VE COME FOR ME!
ZOOOOOOSH
NOW I CAN FINALLY GET OFF THIS WILD RIDE AND...
Z=129: Wild Card
FULL SPEED AHEAD! INTO THE HEART OF THE ENEMY!!
SAY WHAAAT?!
TIME FOR A LITTLE RAMPAGE TO SLOW DOWN IBARA AND HIS ARMY!
UNTIL TAIJU, YUZURIHA AND THE OTHERS...
...CAN PIECE TOGETHER THE MASTER'S STATUE FOR ALL TO SEE!!
HUHHH? SO IT'S JUST THE MEASLY NINE OF US...
...AGAINST HUNDREDS OF HARDENED ENEMIES...?!
RAAHHHH

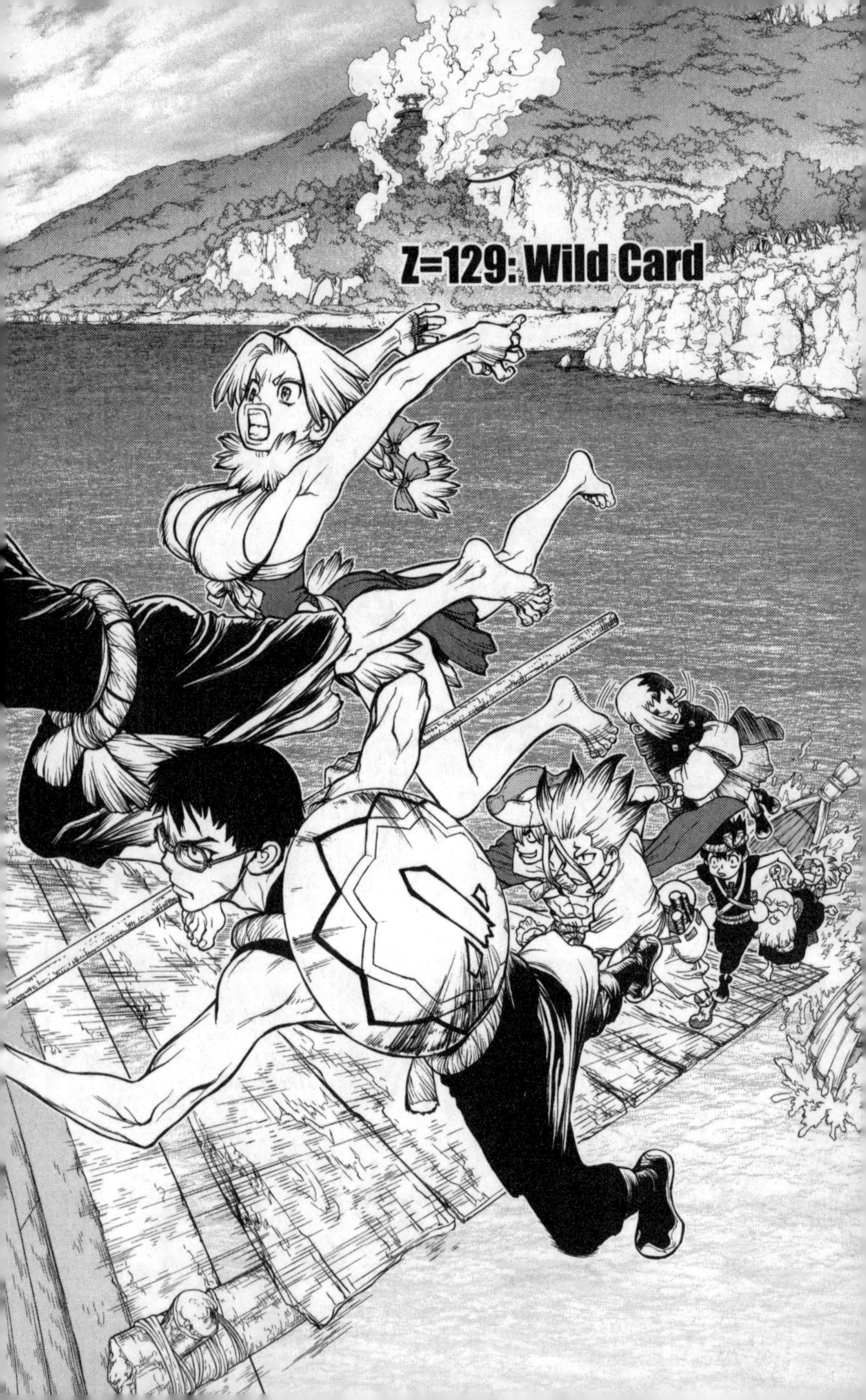
Z=129: Wild Card

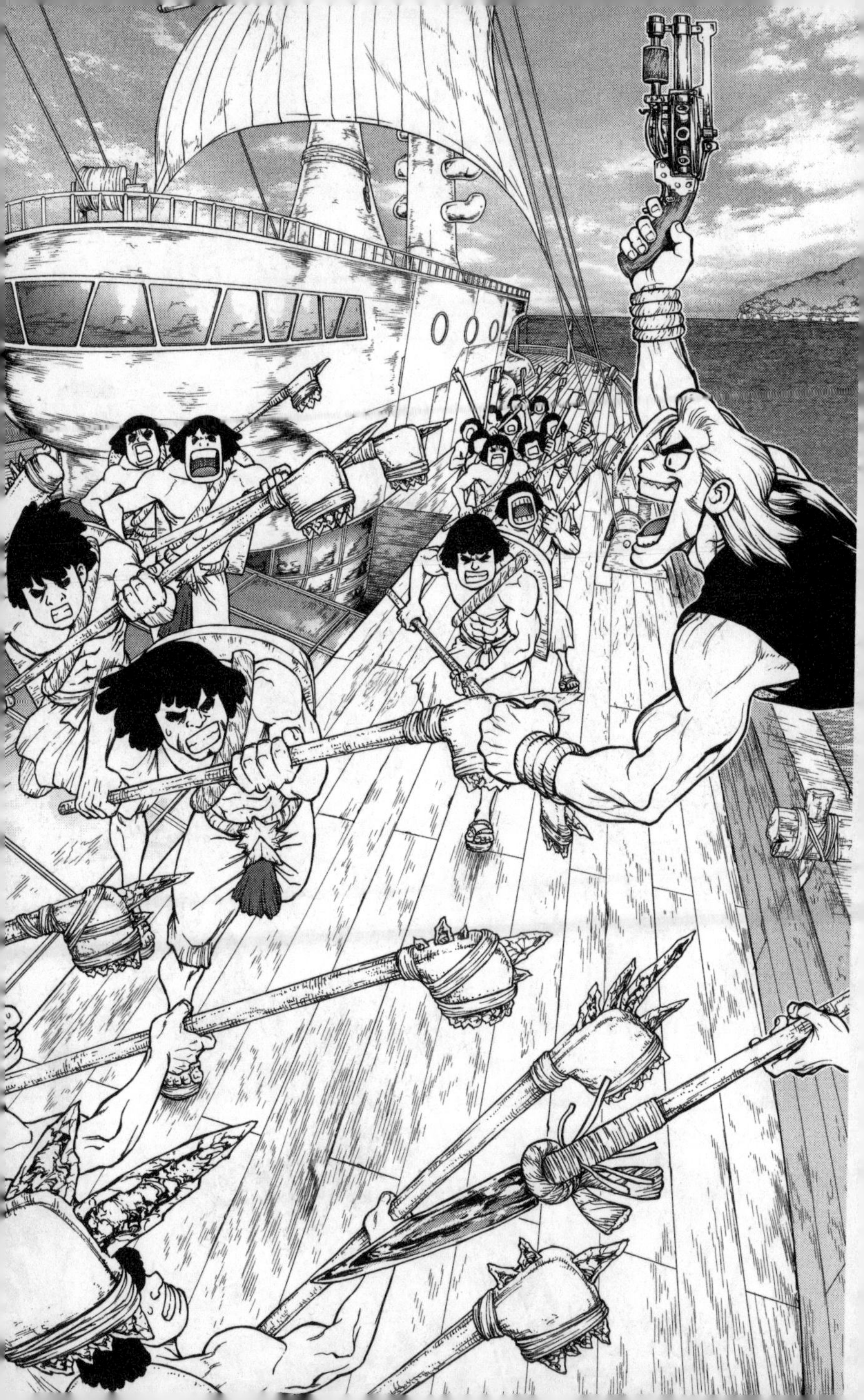

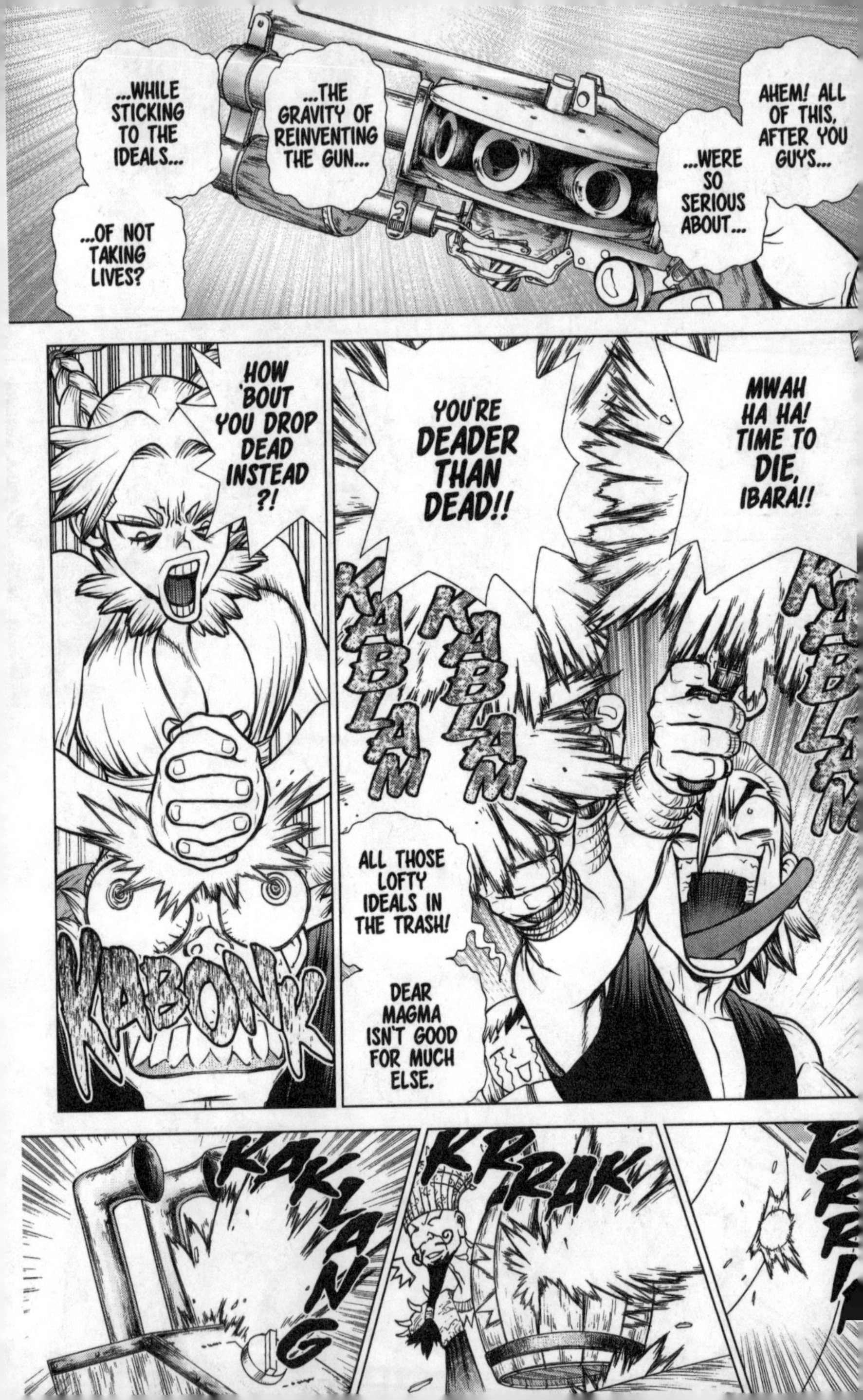
AHEM! ALL OF THIS, AFTER YOU GUYS...
...WERE SO SERIOUS ABOUT...
...THE GRAVITY OF REINVENTING THE GUN...
...WHILE STICKING TO THE IDEALS...
...OF NOT TAKING LIVES?
MWAH HA HA! TIME TO DIE, IBARA!!
YOU'RE DEADER THAN DEAD!!
KABLAM
KABLAM
KABLAM
ALL THOSE LOFTY IDEALS IN THE TRASH!
DEAR MAGMA ISN'T GOOD FOR MUCH ELSE.
HOW 'BOUT YOU DROP DEAD INSTEAD?!
KABONK
KRRAK!
KAKLANG

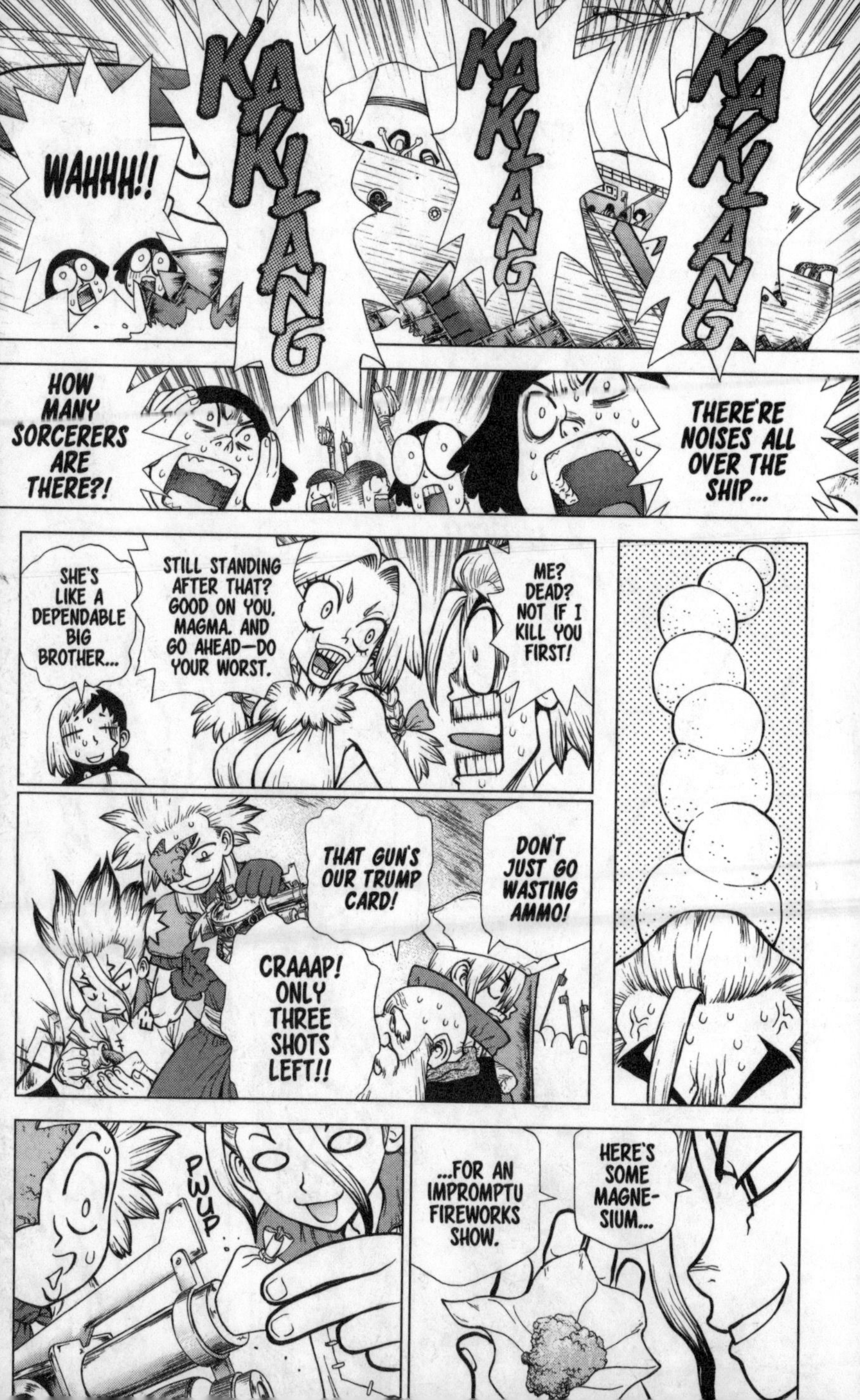
KAKLANG
KAKLANG
KAKLANG
WAHHH!!
THERE'RE NOISES ALL OVER THE SHIP...
HOW MANY SORCERERS ARE THERE?!
ME? DEAD? NOT IF I KILL YOU FIRST!
STILL STANDING AFTER THAT? GOOD ON YOU, MAGMA. AND GO AHEAD—DO YOUR WORST.
SHE'S LIKE A DEPENDABLE BIG BROTHER...
DON'T JUST GO WASTING AMMO!
THAT GUN'S OUR TRUMP CARD!
CRAAAP! ONLY THREE SHOTS LEFT!!
HERE'S SOME MAGNESIUM...
...FOR AN IMPROMPTU FIREWORKS SHOW.
PWUP

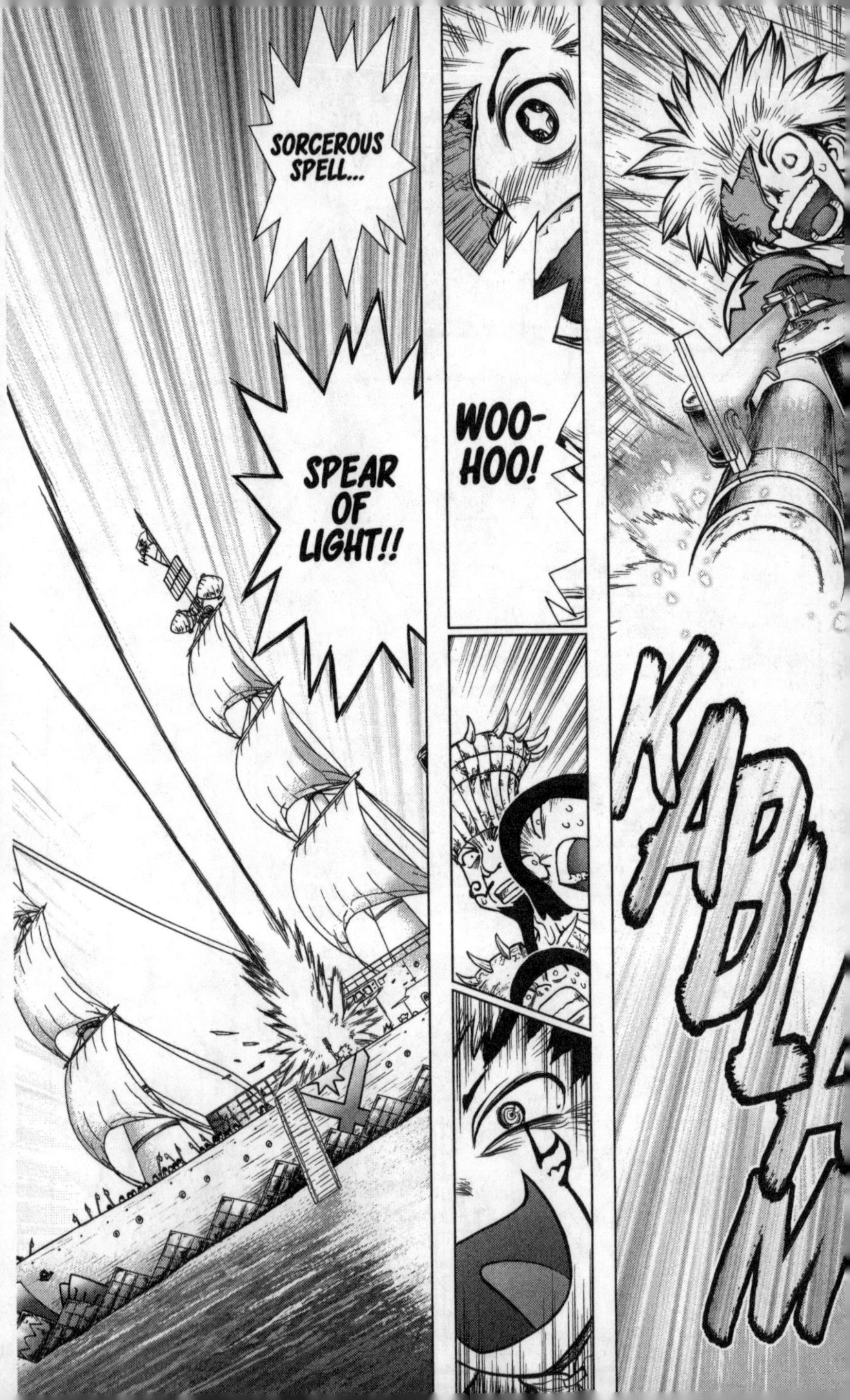
WOO-HOO!
SORCEROUS SPELL...
SPEAR OF LIGHT!!

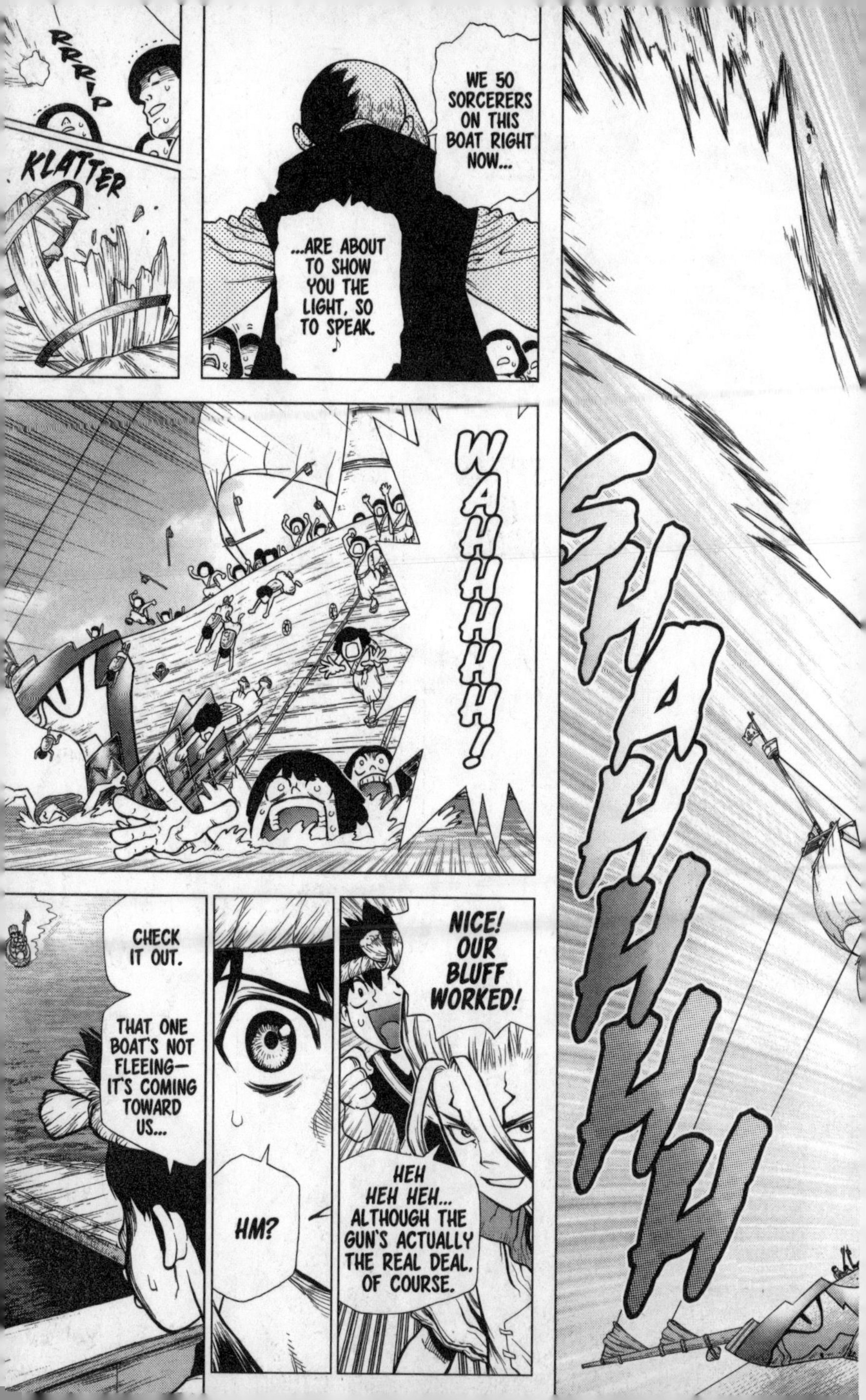
SHAHHHHH
WE 50 SORCERERS ON THIS BOAT RIGHT NOW...
...ARE ABOUT TO SHOW YOU THE LIGHT, SO TO SPEAK. ♪
RRRIP
KLATTER
WAHHHHHH!
NICE! OUR BLUFF WORKED!
HEH HEH HEH... ALTHOUGH THE GUN'S ACTUALLY THE REAL DEAL, OF COURSE.
HM?
CHECK IT OUT.
THAT ONE BOAT'S NOT FLEEING— IT'S COMING TOWARD US...

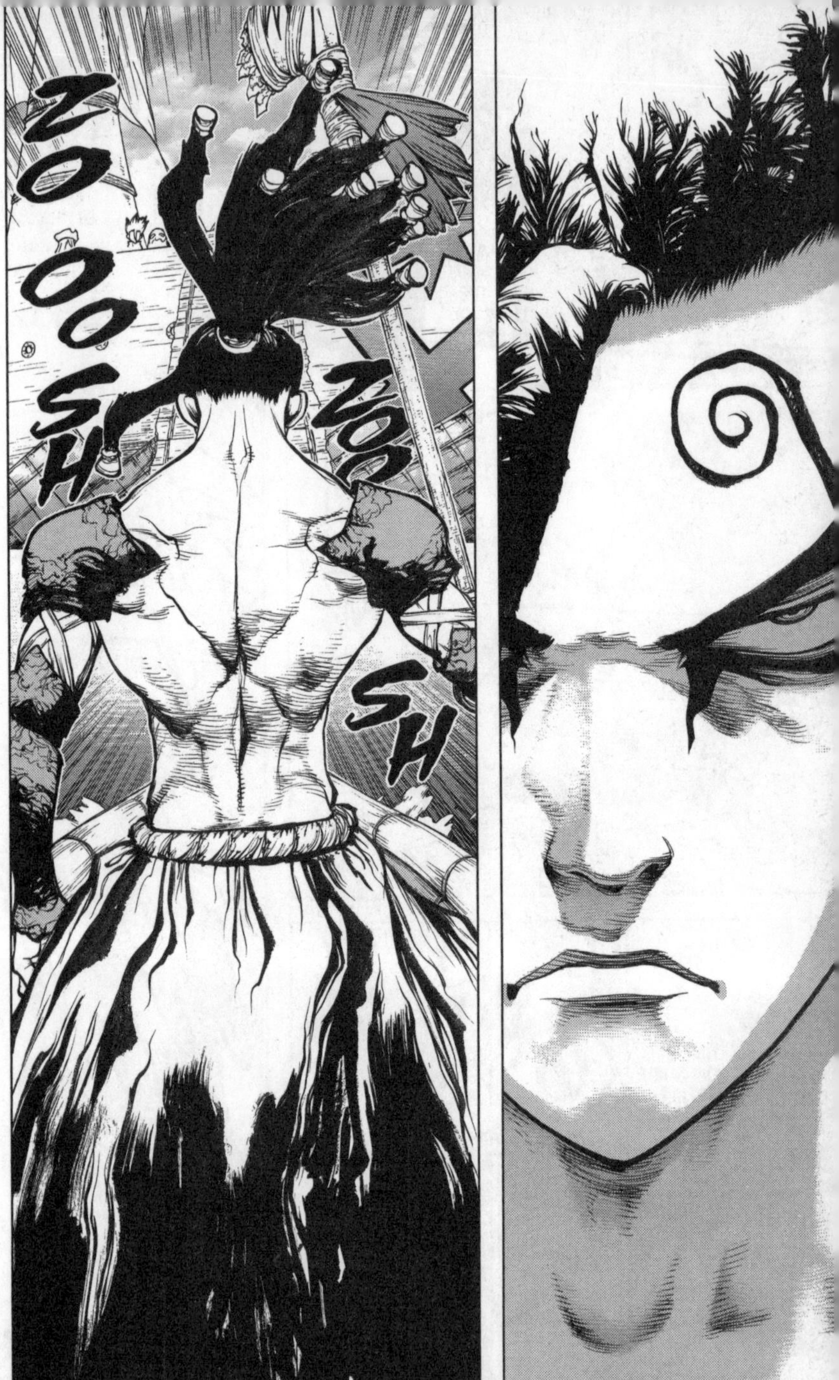
ZOOOSH
ZOOSH

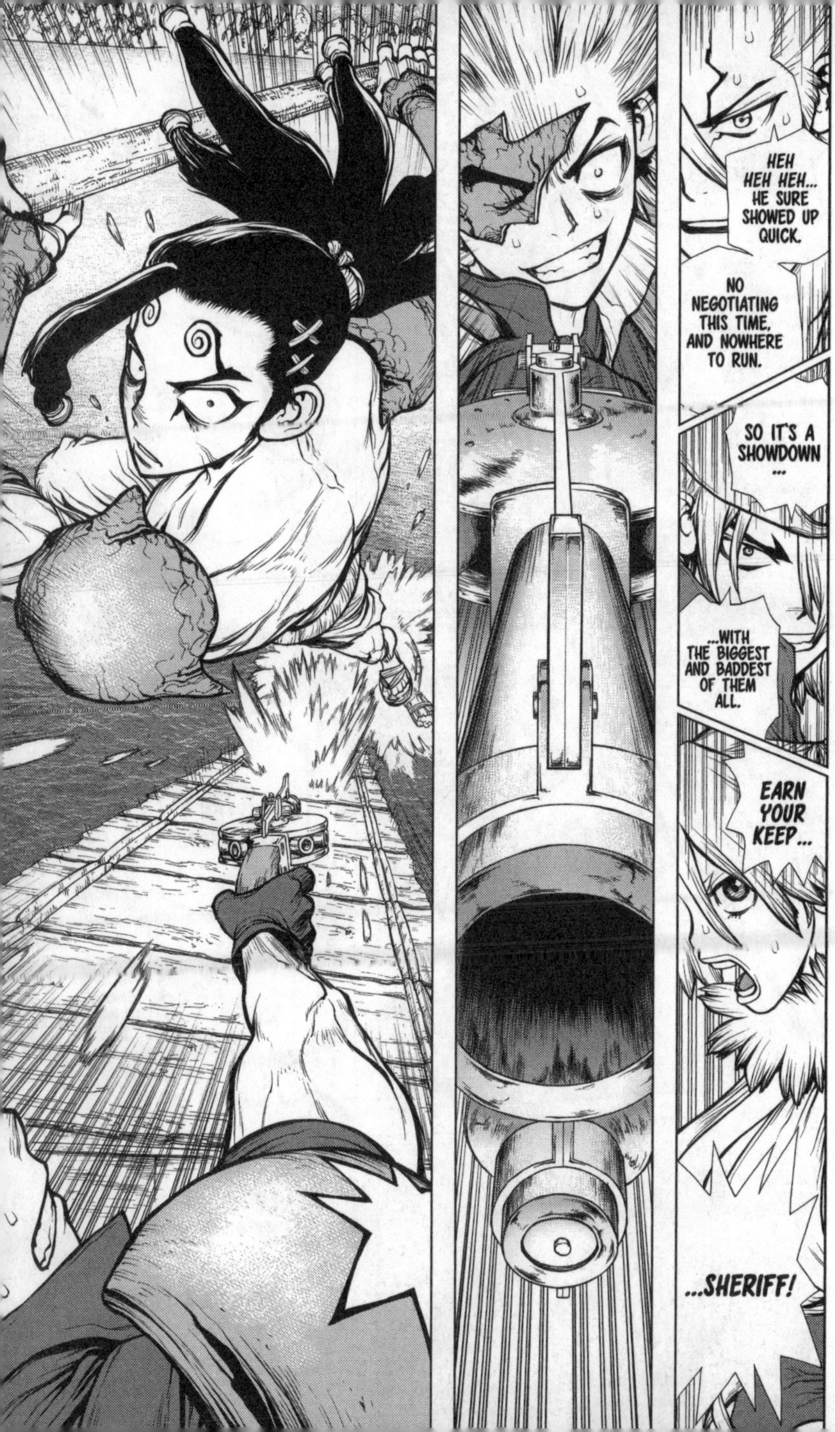
HEH HEH HEH... HE SURE SHOWED UP QUICK.
NO NEGOTIATING THIS TIME, AND NOWHERE TO RUN.
SO IT'S A SHOWDOWN ...
...WITH THE BIGGEST AND BADDEST OF THEM ALL.
EARN YOUR KEEP...
...SHERIFF!

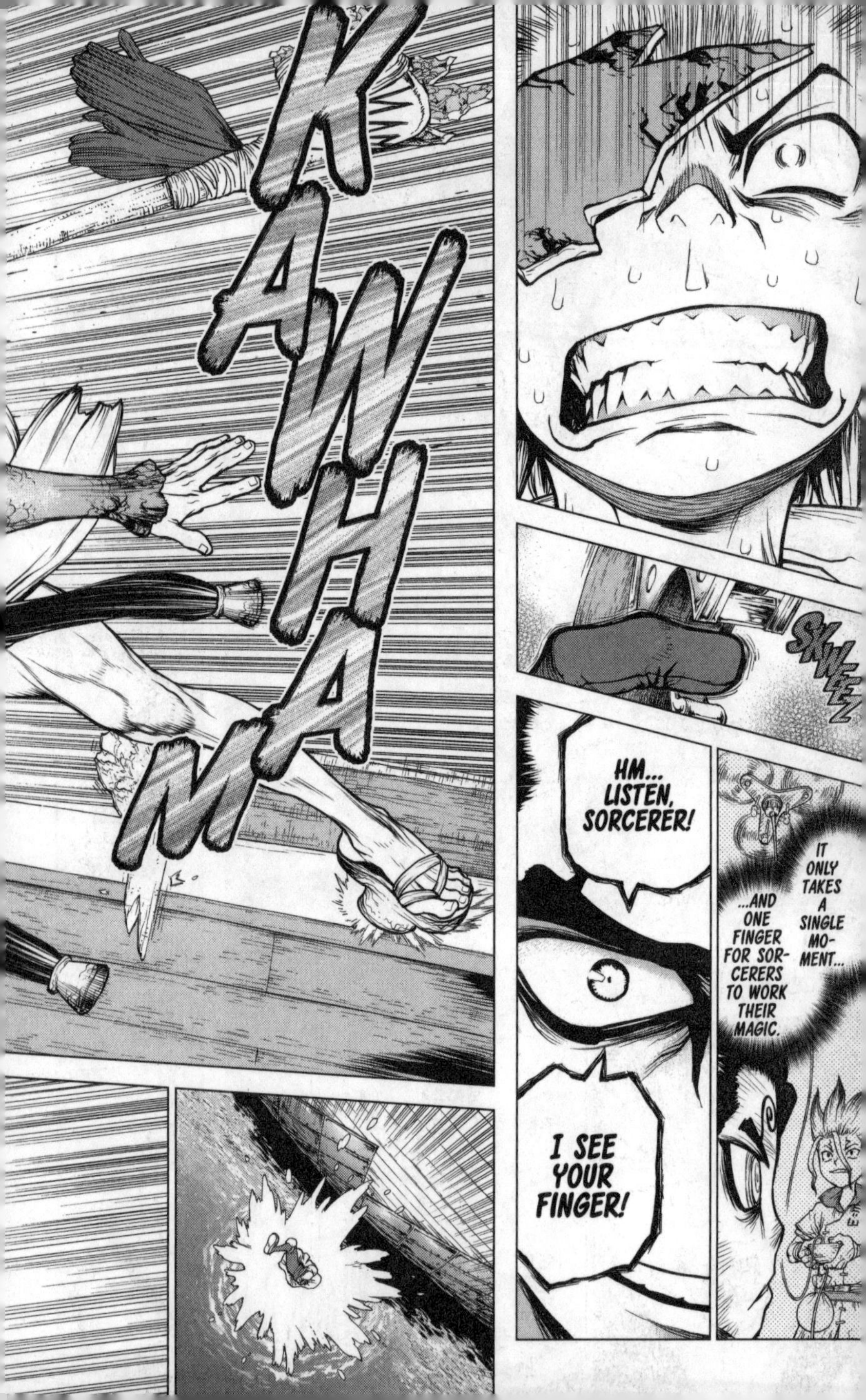

SKWEEZ
IT ONLY TAKES A SINGLE MOMENT...
...AND ONE FINGER FOR SORCERERS TO WORK THEIR MAGIC.
HM... LISTEN, SORCERER!
I SEE YOUR FINGER!
KAWHAM

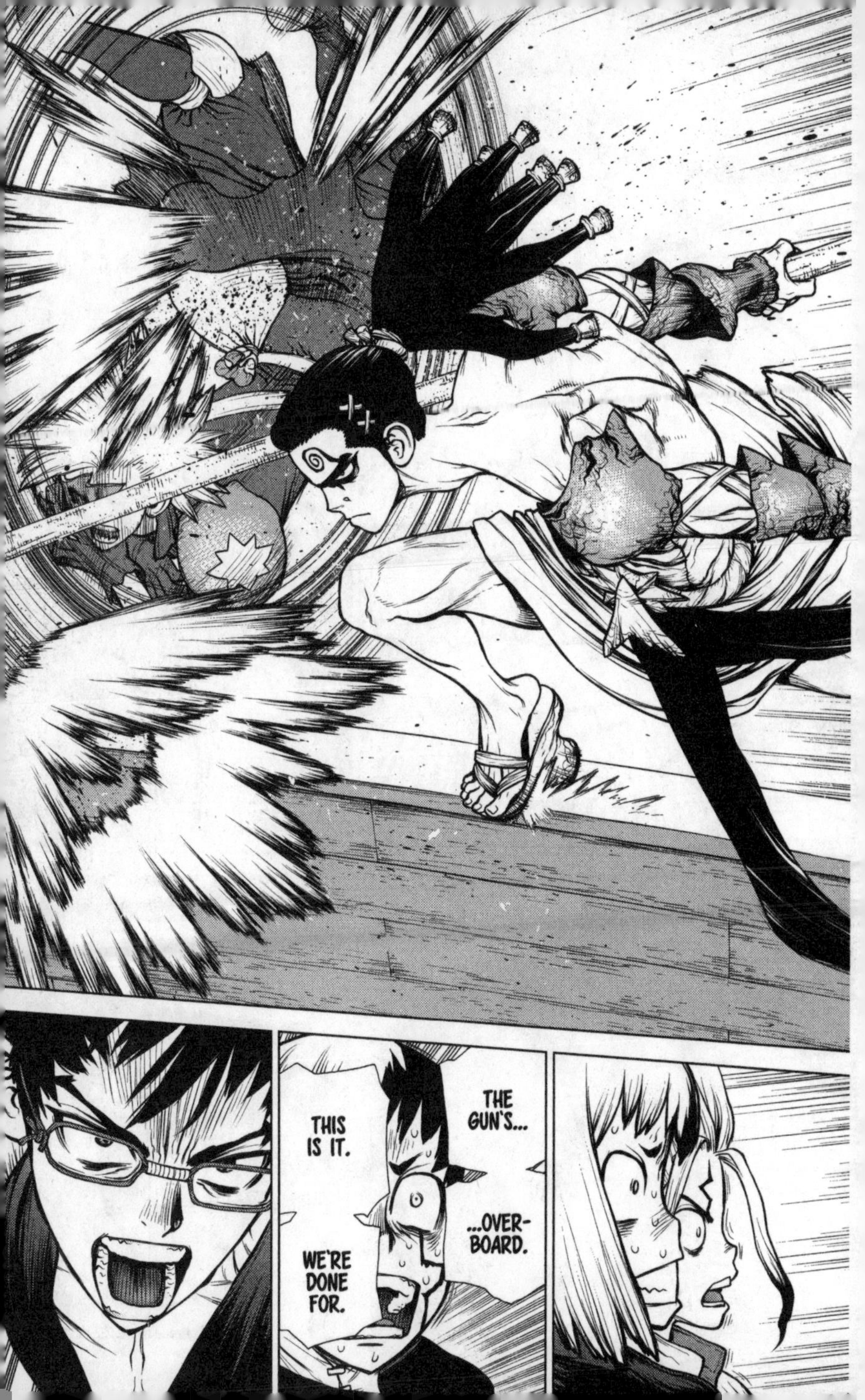
THE GUN'S...
THIS IS IT.
...OVER-BOARD.
WE'RE DONE FOR.

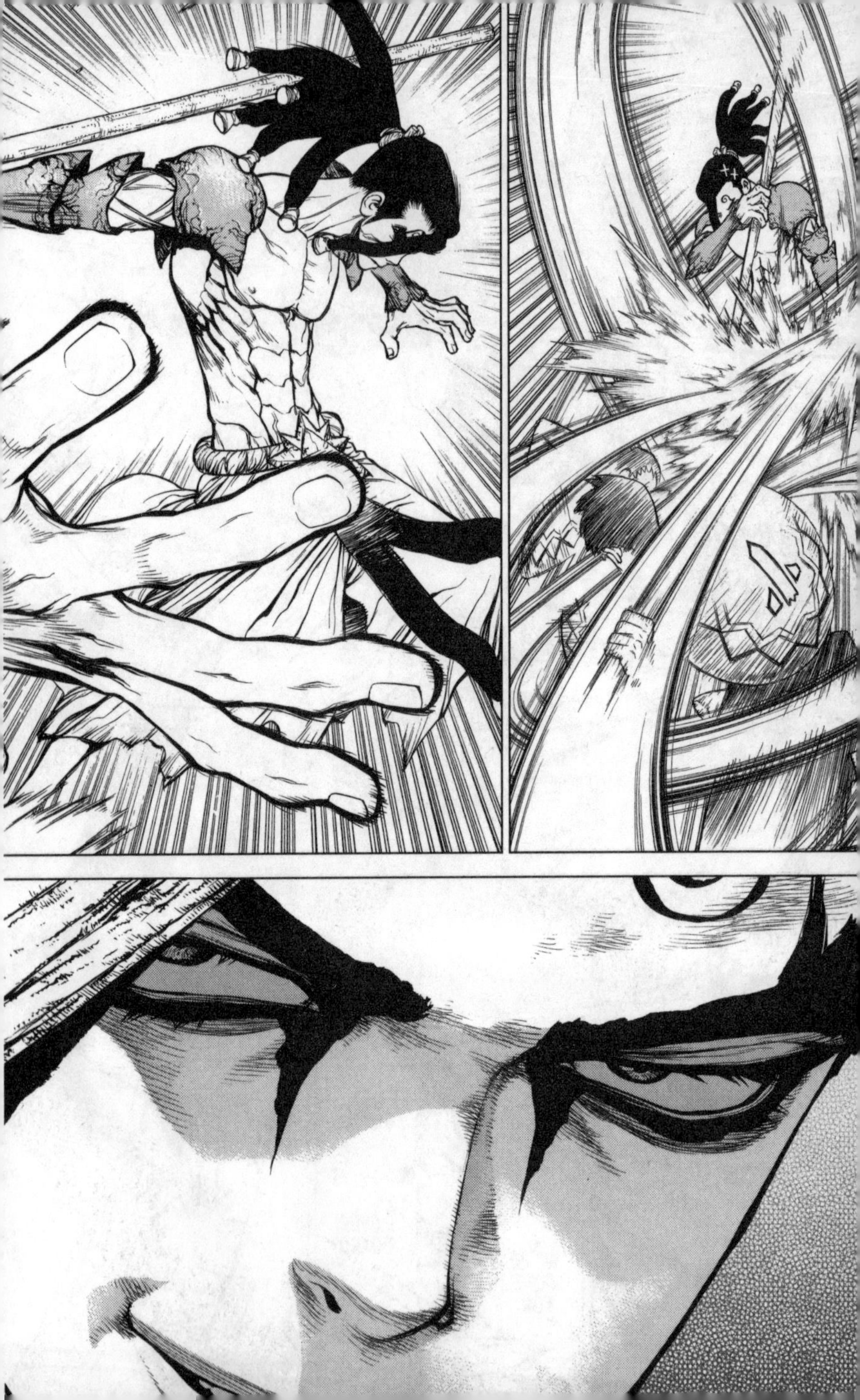

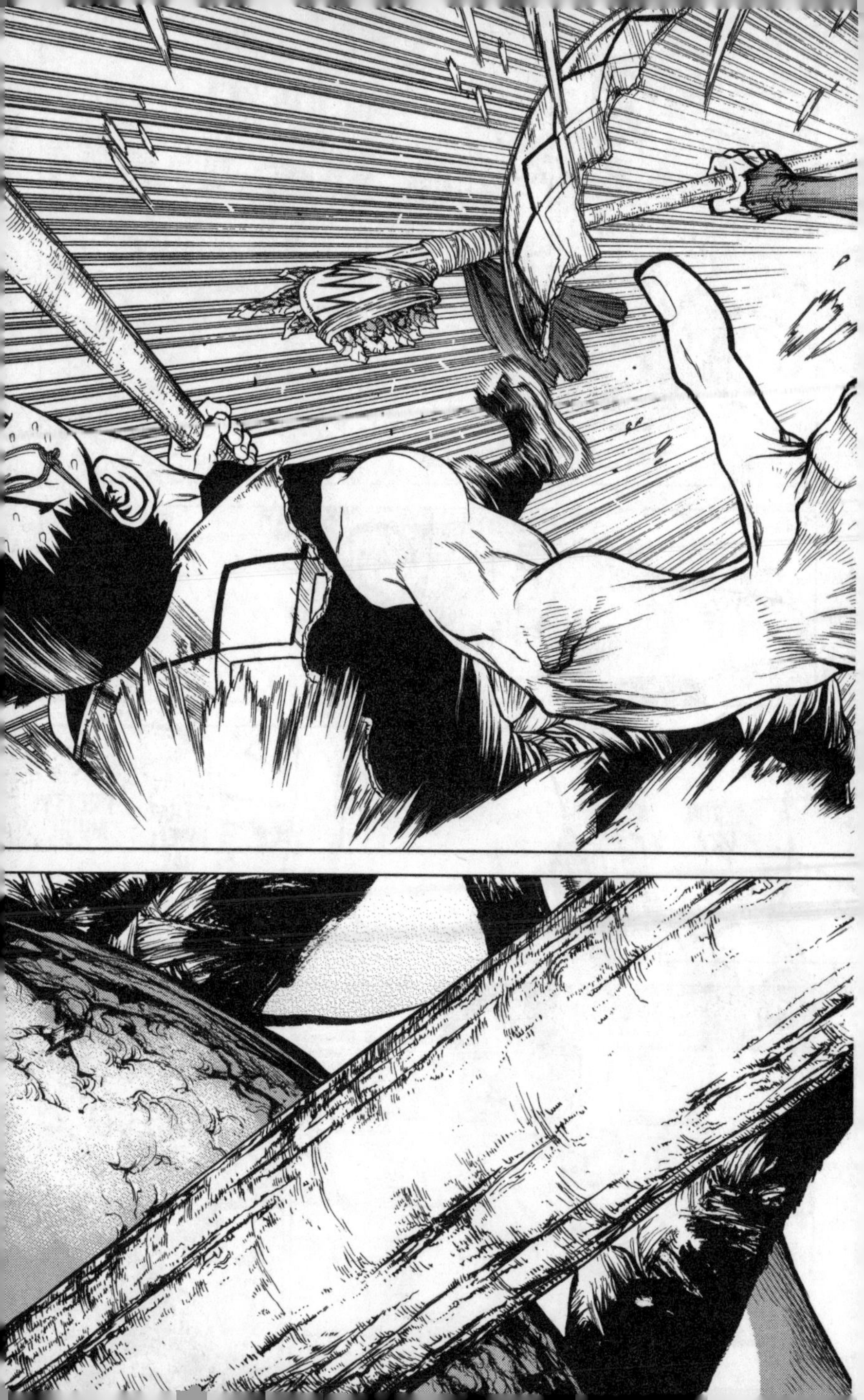

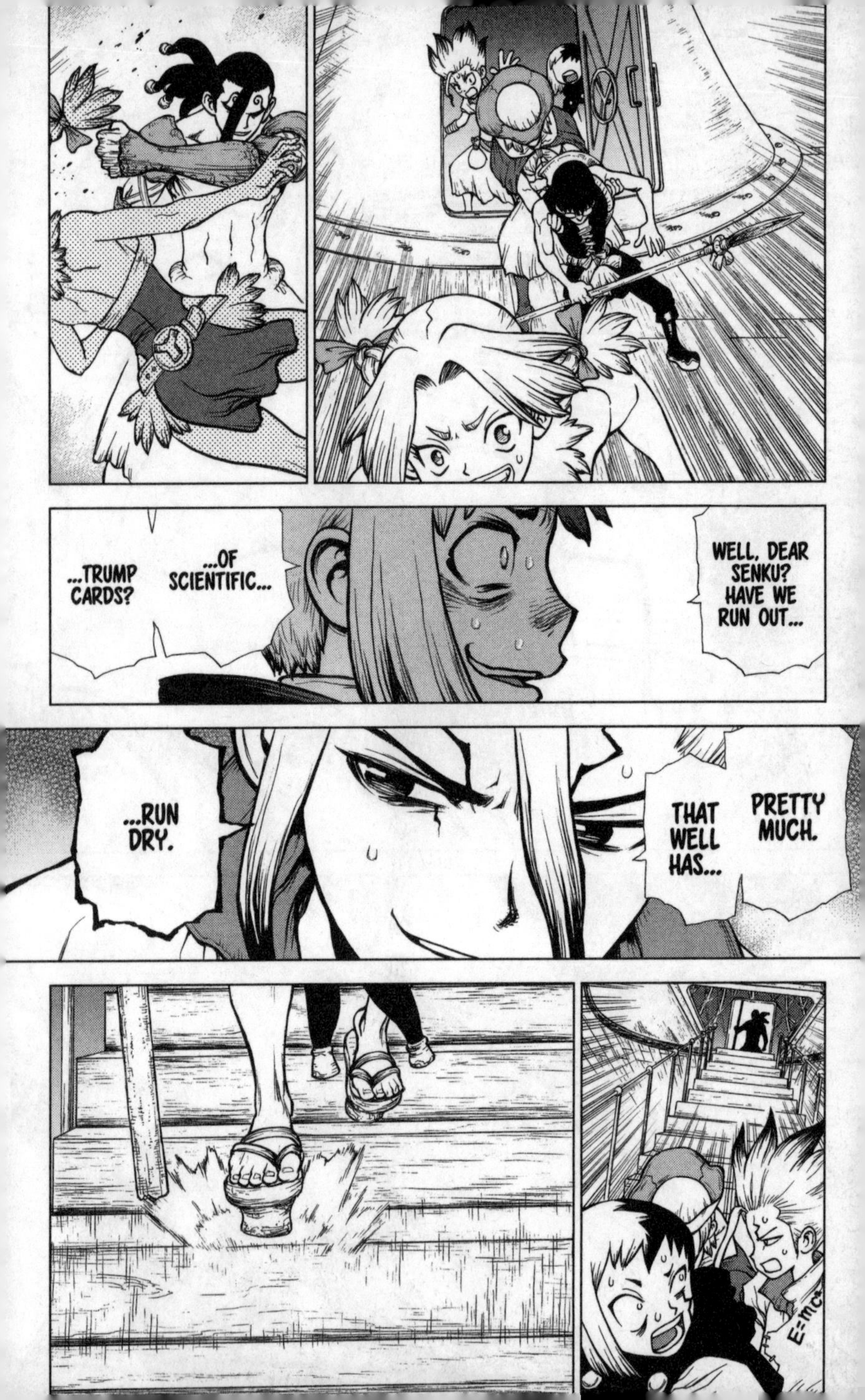
WELL, DEAR SENKU? HAVE WE RUN OUT...
...OF SCIENTIFIC...
...TRUMP CARDS?
PRETTY MUCH.
THAT WELL HAS...
...RUN DRY.

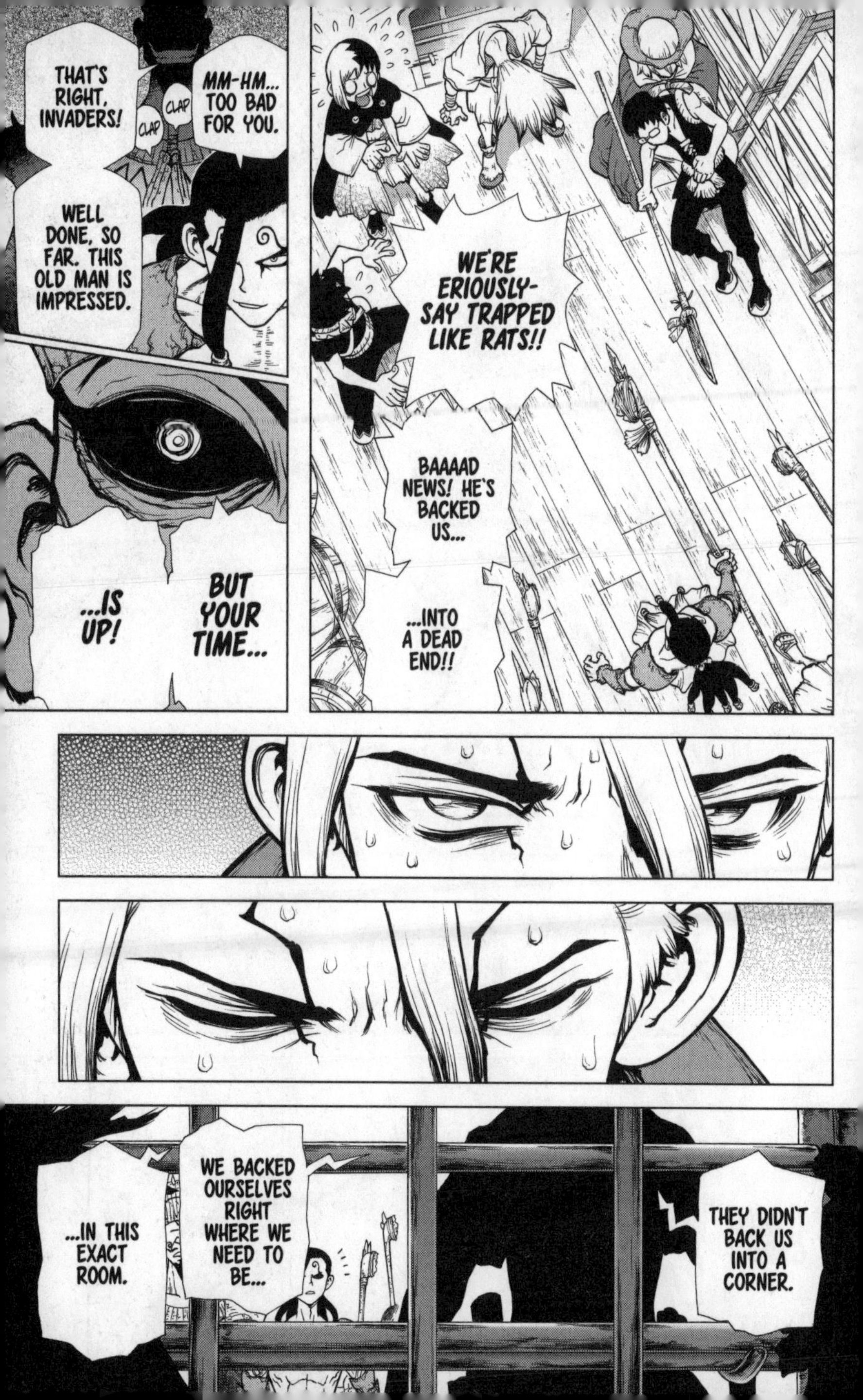
WE'RE ERIOUSLY-SAY TRAPPED LIKE RATS!!
BAAAAD NEWS! HE'S BACKED US...
...INTO A DEAD END!!
MM-HM... TOO BAD FOR YOU.
CLAP
CLAP
THAT'S RIGHT, INVADERS!
WELL DONE, SO FAR. THIS OLD MAN IS IMPRESSED.
BUT YOUR TIME...
...IS UP!
THEY DIDN'T BACK US INTO A CORNER.
WE BACKED OURSELVES RIGHT WHERE WE NEED TO BE...
...IN THIS EXACT ROOM.

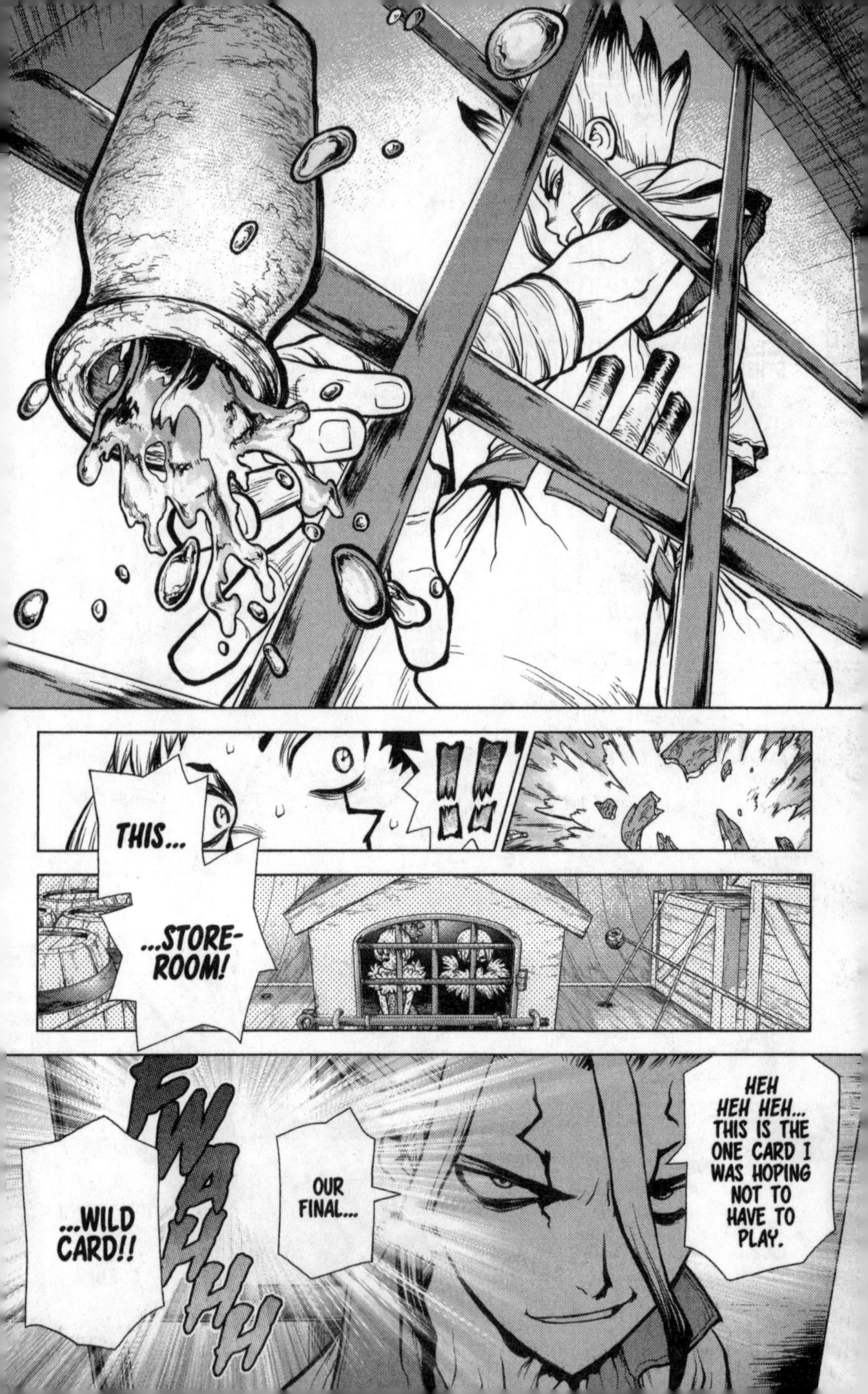
!!
THIS...
...STORE-ROOM!
HEH HEH HEH... THIS IS THE ONE CARD I WAS HOPING NOT TO HAVE TO PLAY.
OUR FINAL...
...WILD CARD!!
FWASHHH

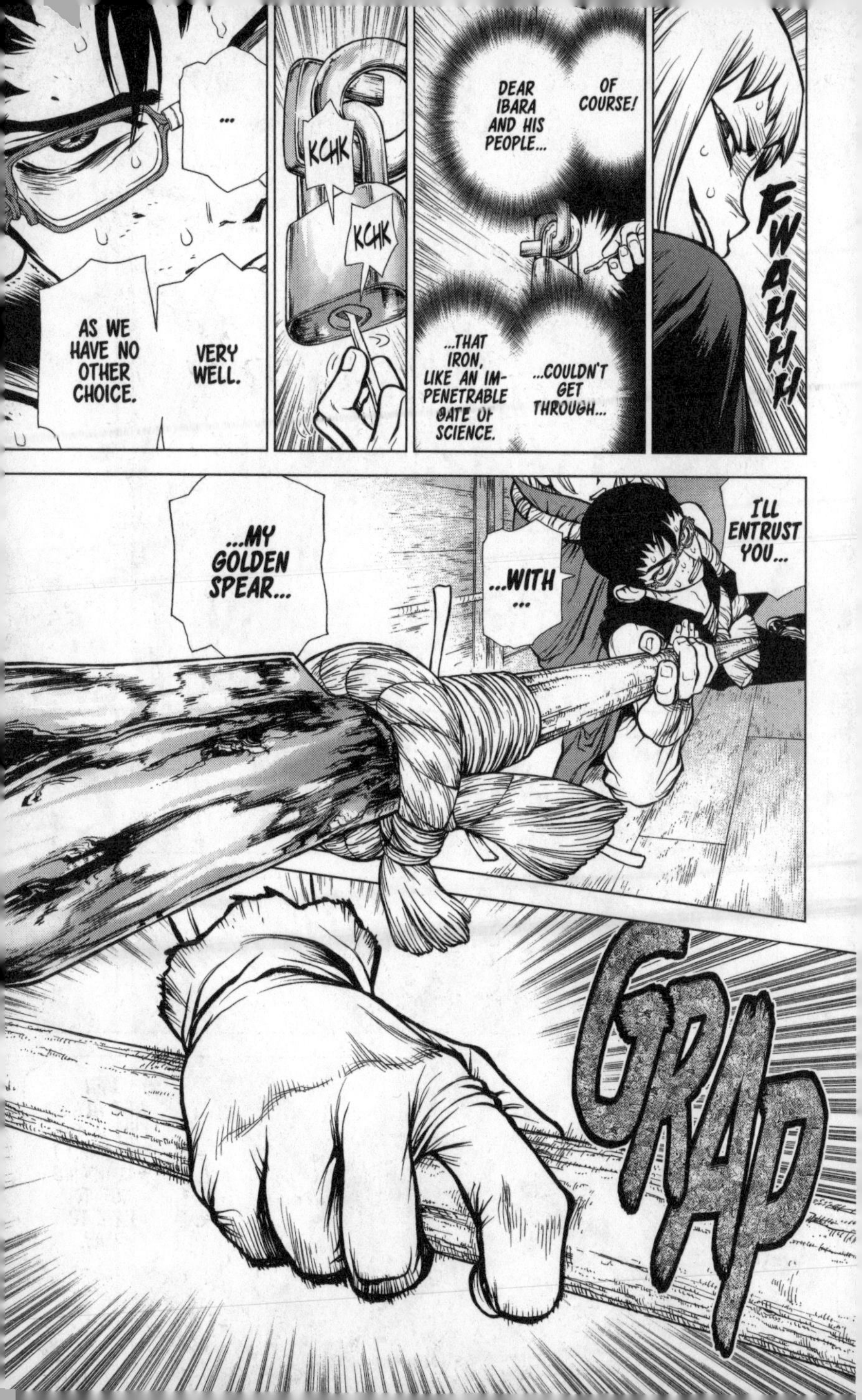
FWAHHH
OF COURSE!
DEAR IBARA AND HIS PEOPLE...
...COULDN'T GET THROUGH...
...THAT IRON, LIKE AN IMPENETRABLE GATE OF SCIENCE.
KCHK
KCHK
...
VERY WELL.
AS WE HAVE NO OTHER CHOICE.
I'LL ENTRUST YOU...
...WITH ...
...MY GOLDEN SPEAR...
GRAP

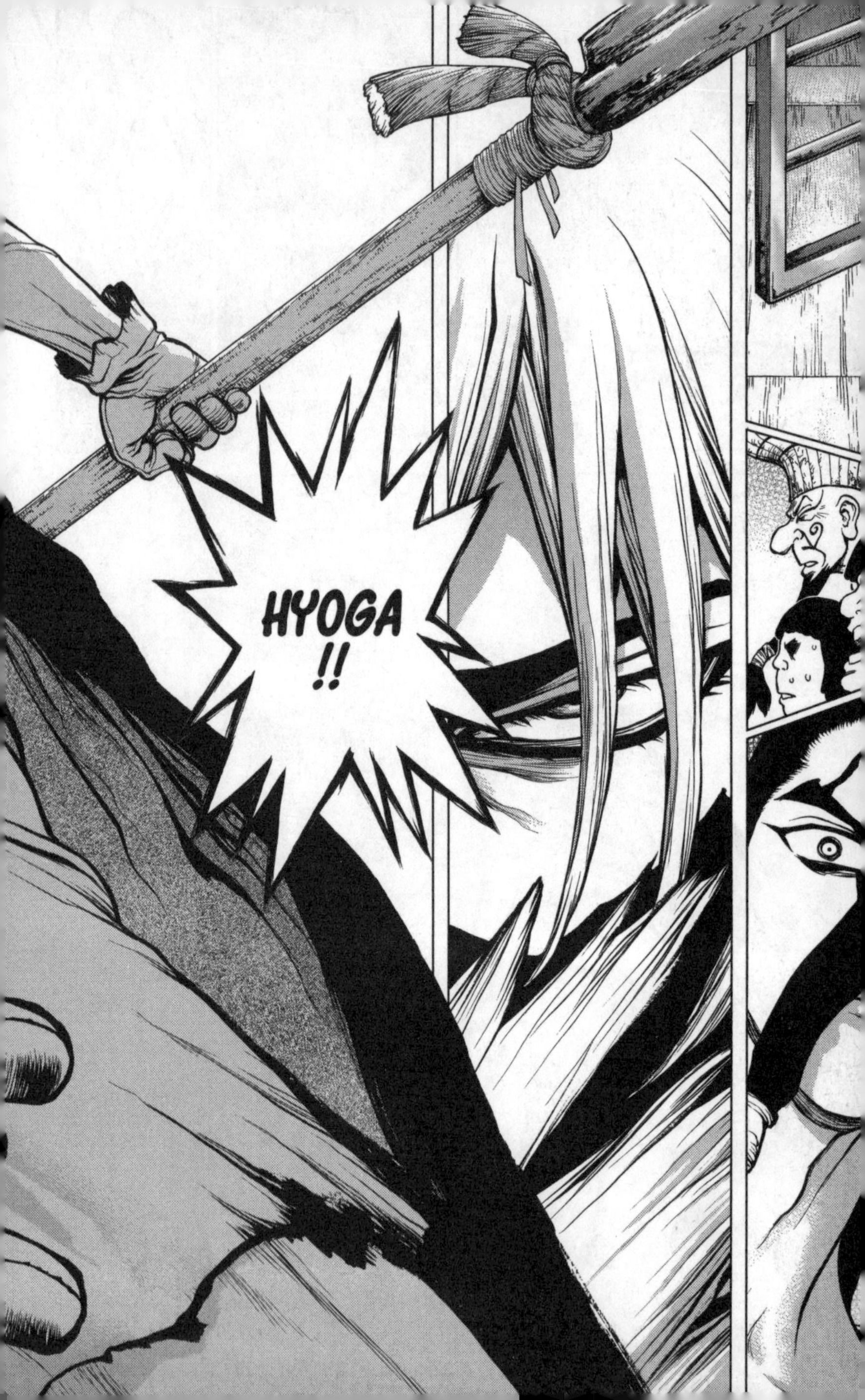
HYOGA !!

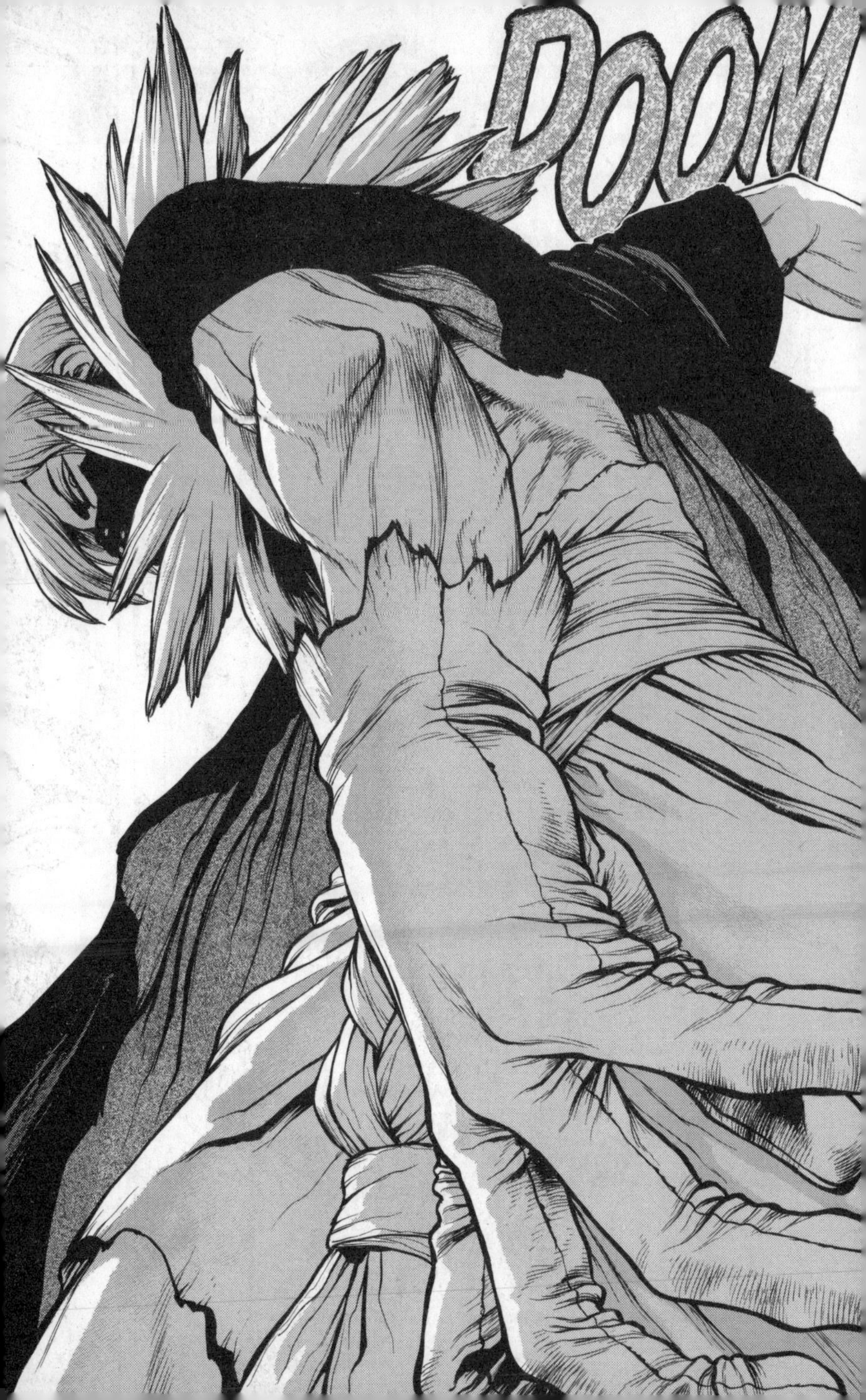
DOOM

## The Kingdom of Science's 8-Shot Repeating Firearm

## Ammo Usage

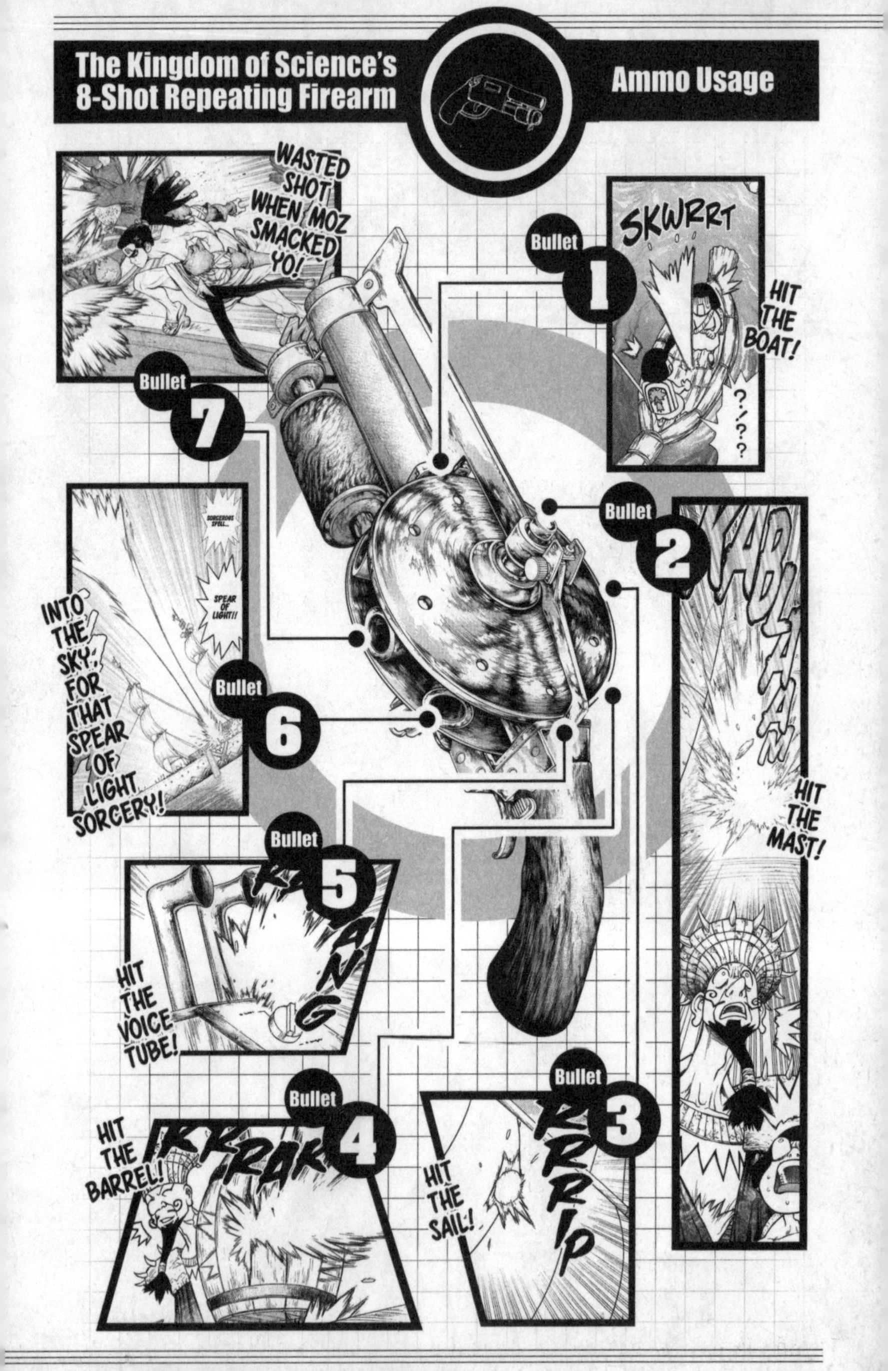
Bullet 1
SKWRRT
HIT THE BOAT!
?!??
Bullet 7
WASTED SHOT WHEN MOZ SMACKED YO!
Bullet 2
HIT THE MAST!
Bullet 6
SORCEROUS SPELL...
SPEAR OF LIGHT!!
INTO THE SKY, FOR THAT SPEAR OF LIGHT SORCERY!
Bullet 5
HIT THE VOICE TUBE!
Bullet 3
KRRRIP
HIT THE SAIL!
Bullet 4
KKRAK
HIT THE BARREL!

# Z=130: Devil's Choice

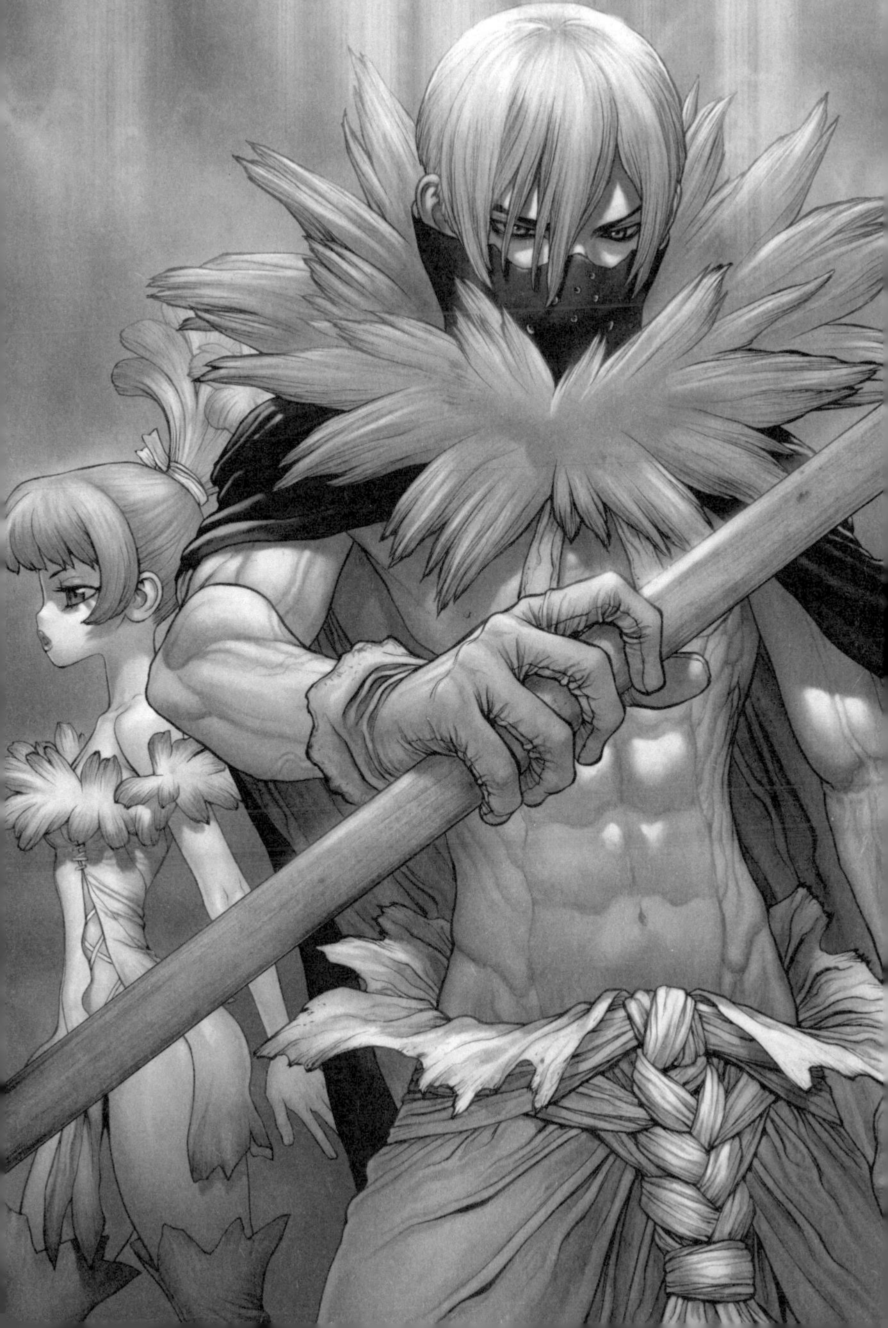

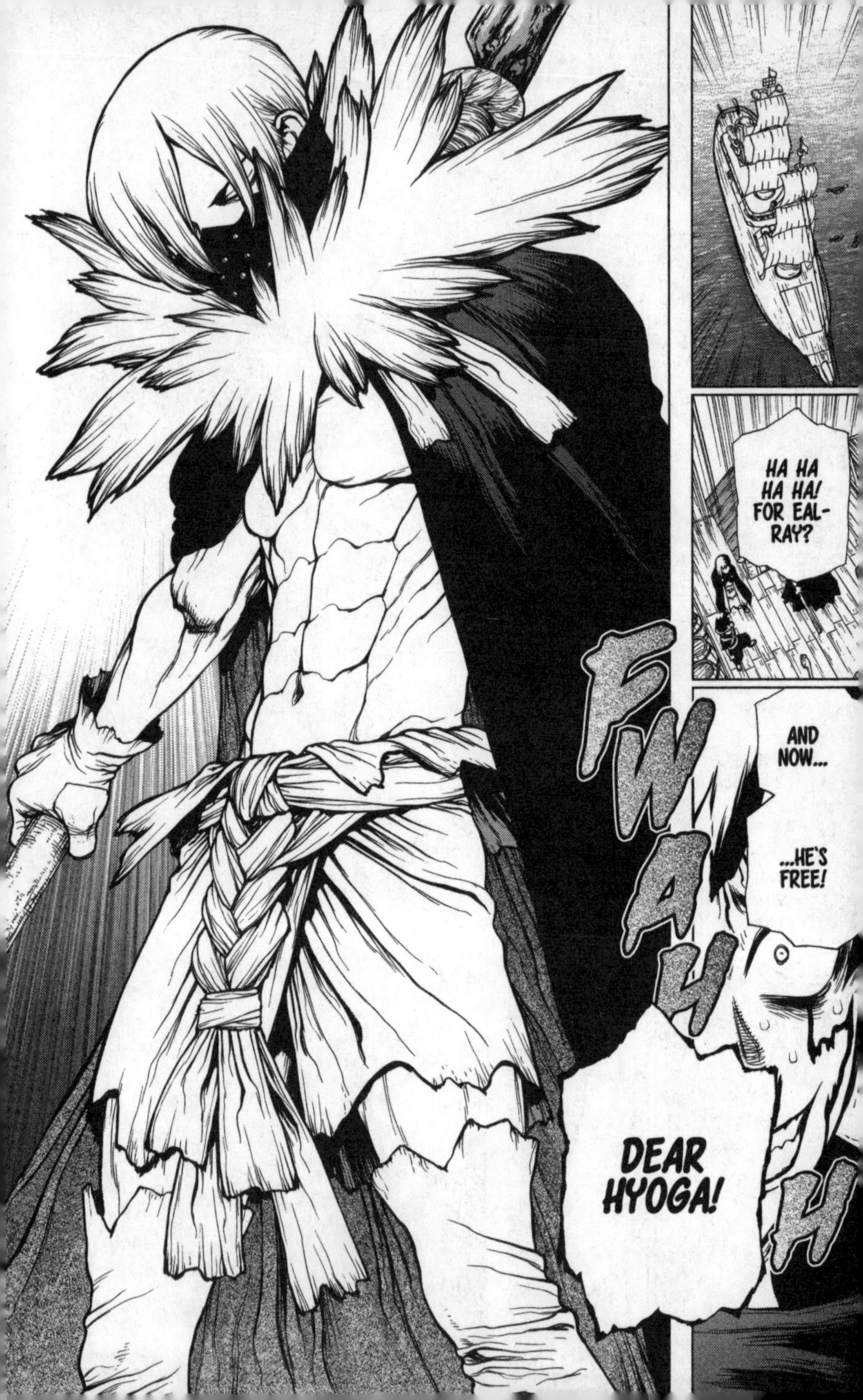
HA HA HA HA! FOR EAL-RAY?
AND NOW...
...HE'S FREE!
FWAHH
DEAR HYOGA!

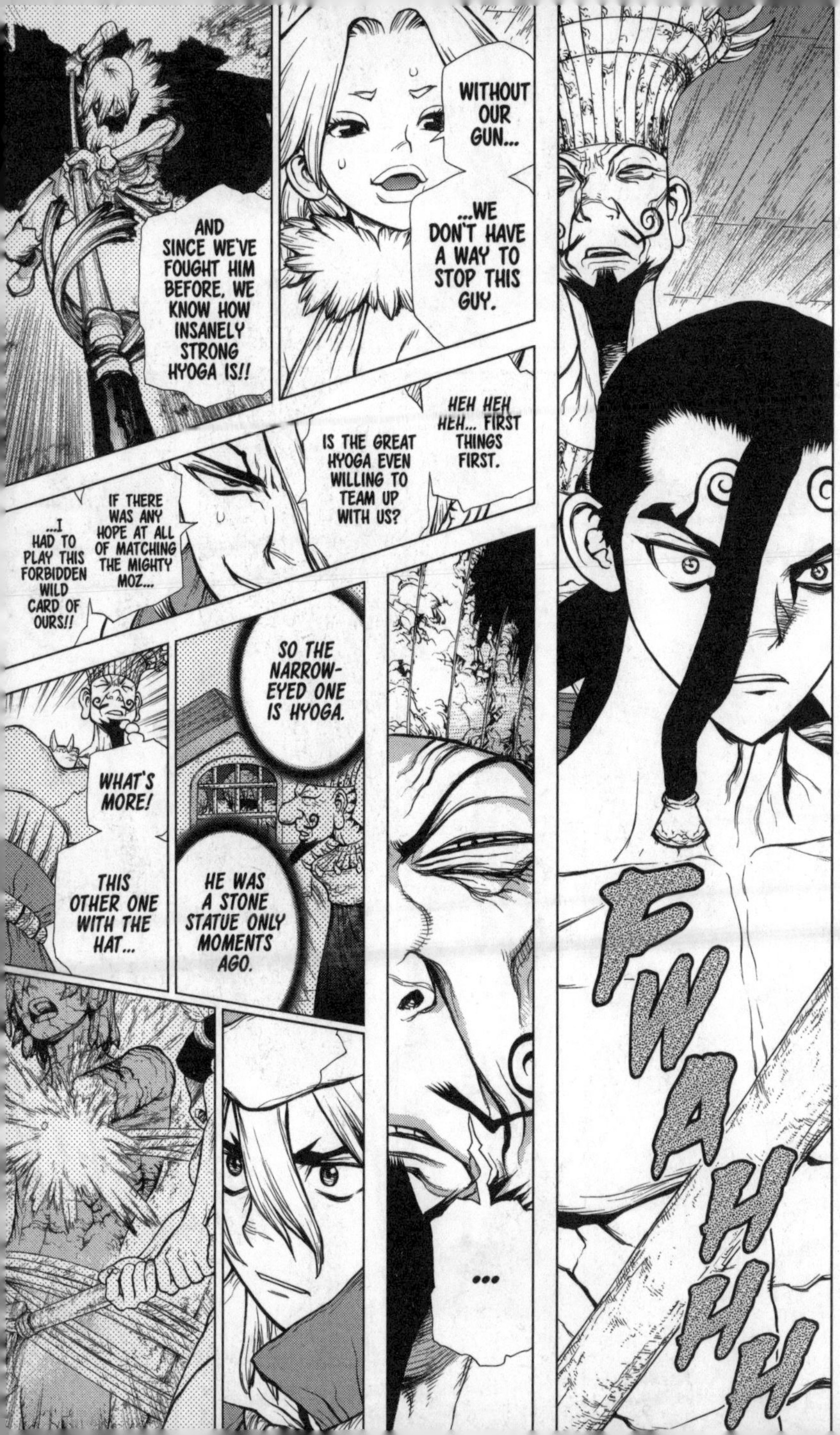
FWAHHH
WITHOUT OUR GUN...
...WE DON'T HAVE A WAY TO STOP THIS GUY.
AND SINCE WE'VE FOUGHT HIM BEFORE, WE KNOW HOW INSANELY STRONG HYOGA IS!!
HEH HEH HEH... FIRST THINGS FIRST.
IS THE GREAT HYOGA EVEN WILLING TO TEAM UP WITH US?
IF THERE WAS ANY HOPE AT ALL OF MATCHING THE MIGHTY MOZ...
...I HAD TO PLAY THIS FORBIDDEN WILD CARD OF OURS!!
...
SO THE NARROW-EYED ONE IS HYOGA.
HE WAS A STONE STATUE ONLY MOMENTS AGO.
WHAT'S MORE!
THIS OTHER ONE WITH THE HAT...

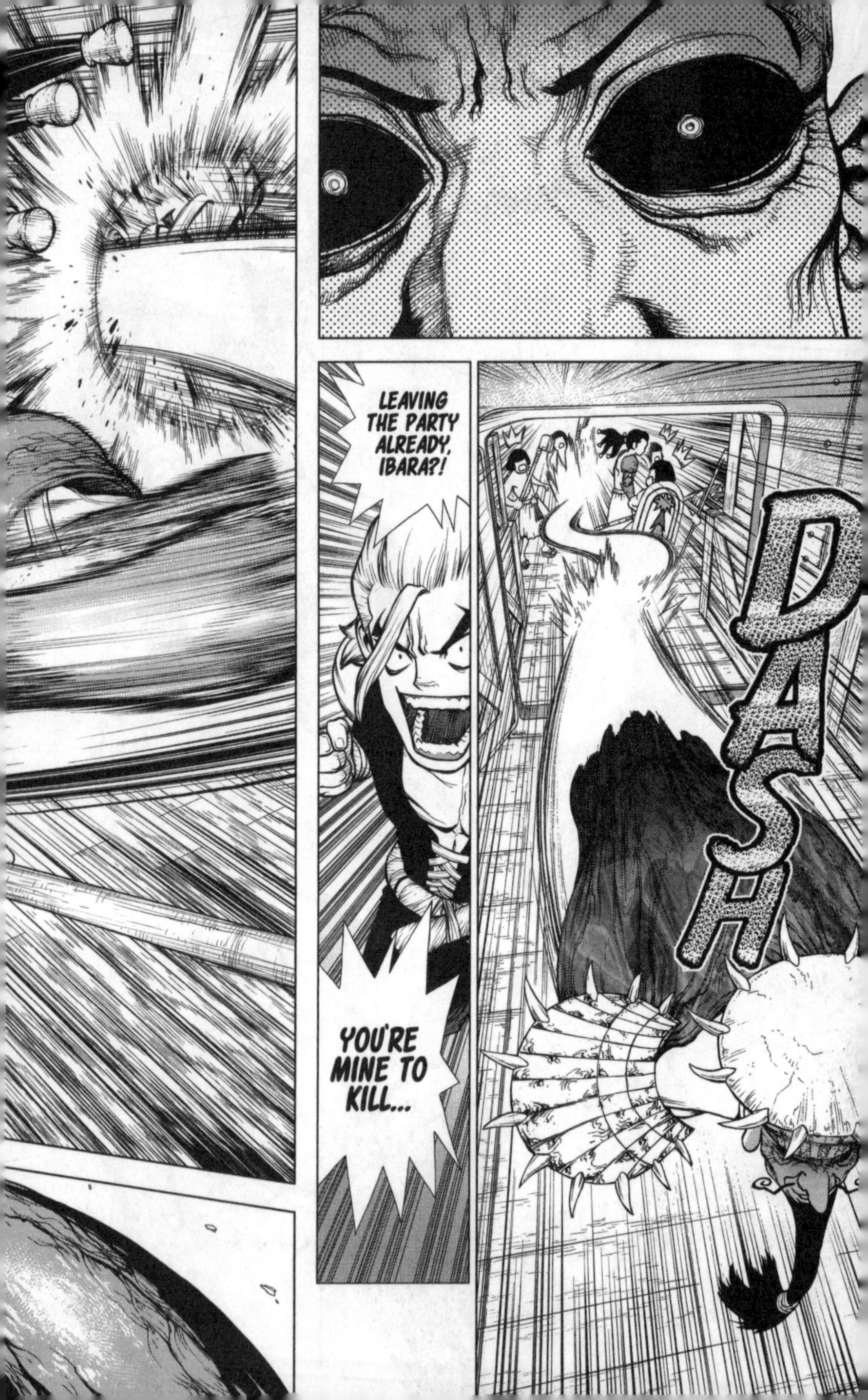
DASH
LEAVING THE PARTY ALREADY, IBARA?!
YOU'RE MINE TO KILL...

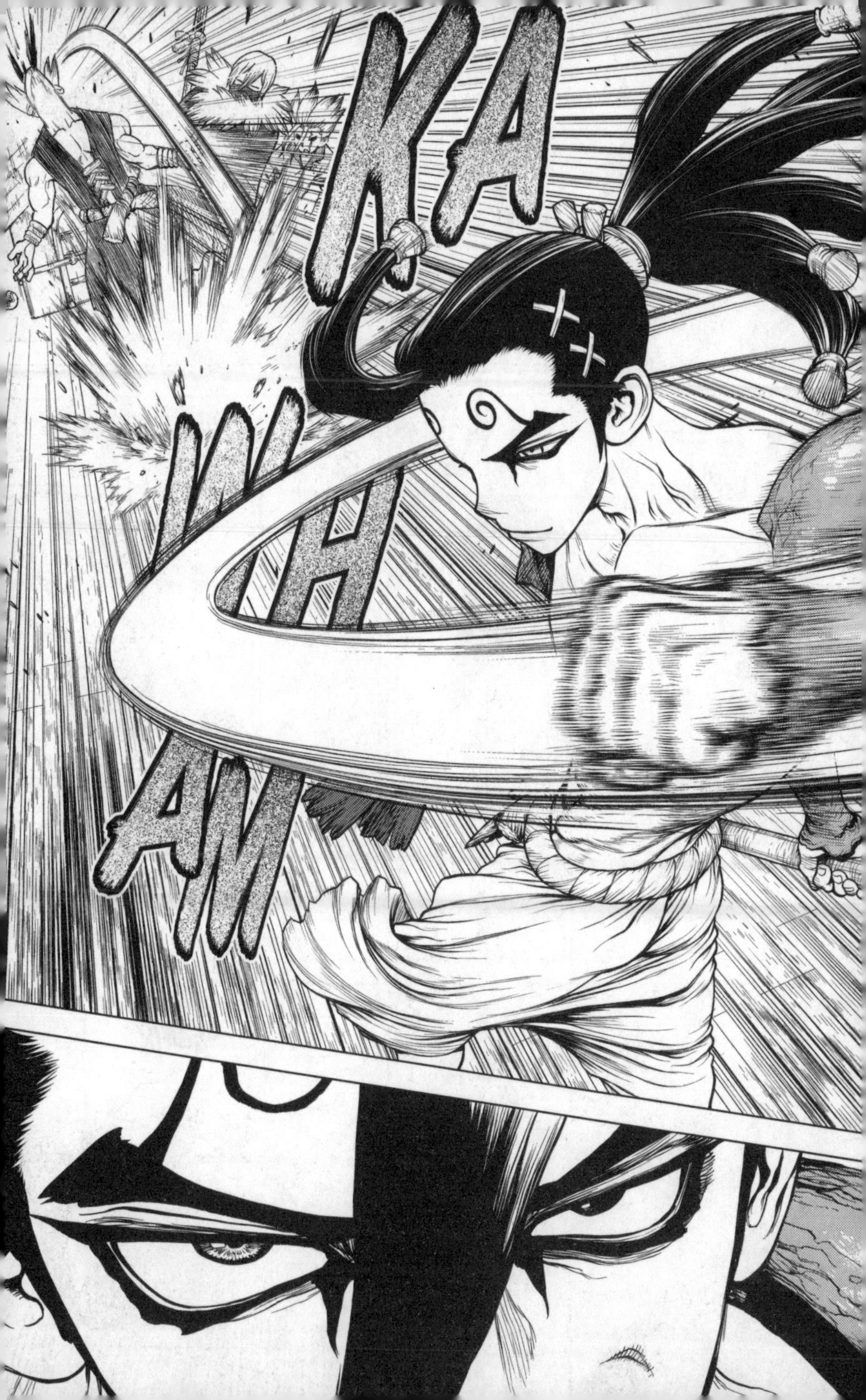
KAWHAM

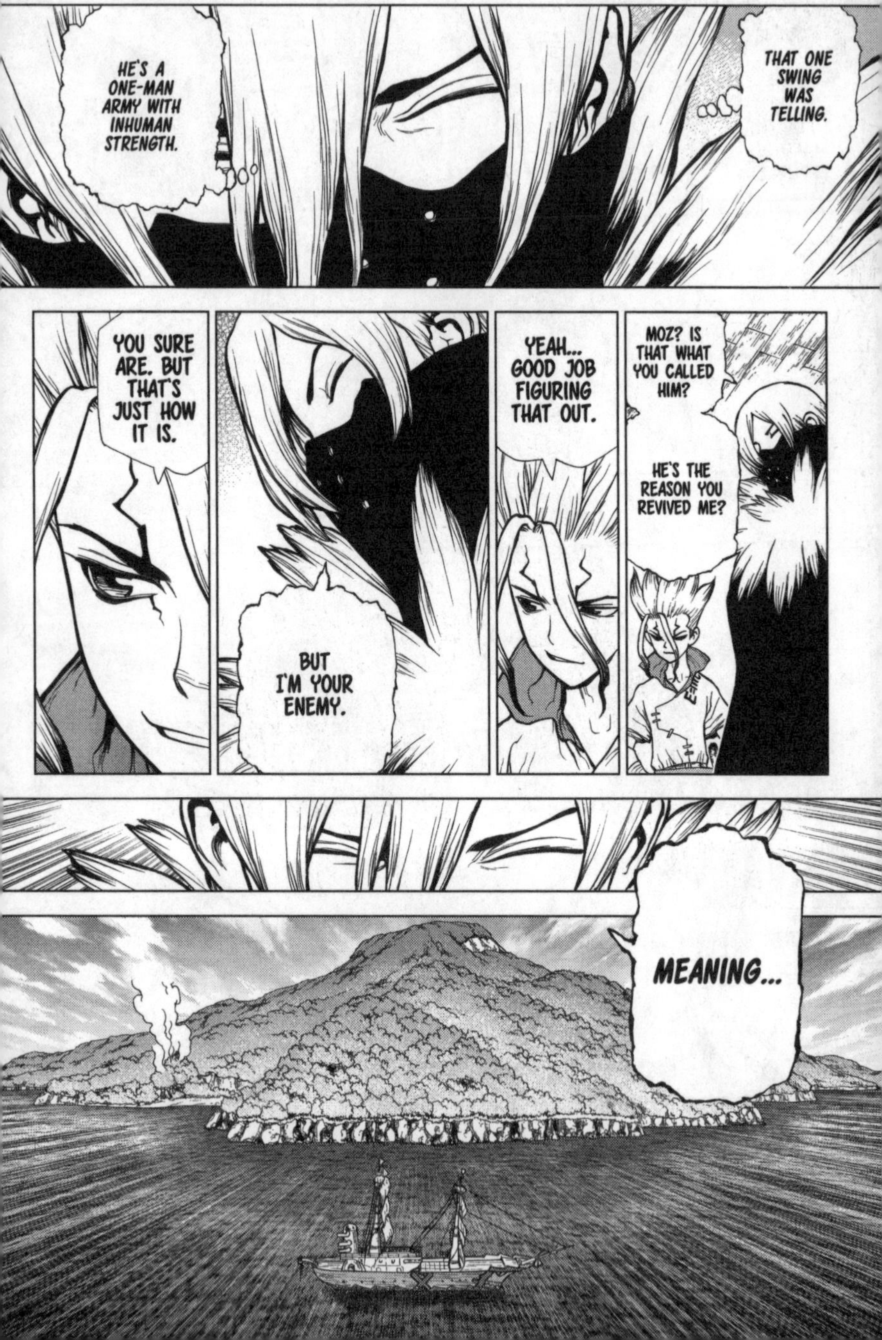
THAT ONE SWING WAS TELLING.
HE'S A ONE-MAN ARMY WITH INHUMAN STRENGTH.
MOZ? IS THAT WHAT YOU CALLED HIM?
HE'S THE REASON YOU REVIVED ME?
YEAH... GOOD JOB FIGURING THAT OUT.
BUT I'M YOUR ENEMY.
YOU SURE ARE. BUT THAT'S JUST HOW IT IS.
MEANING...

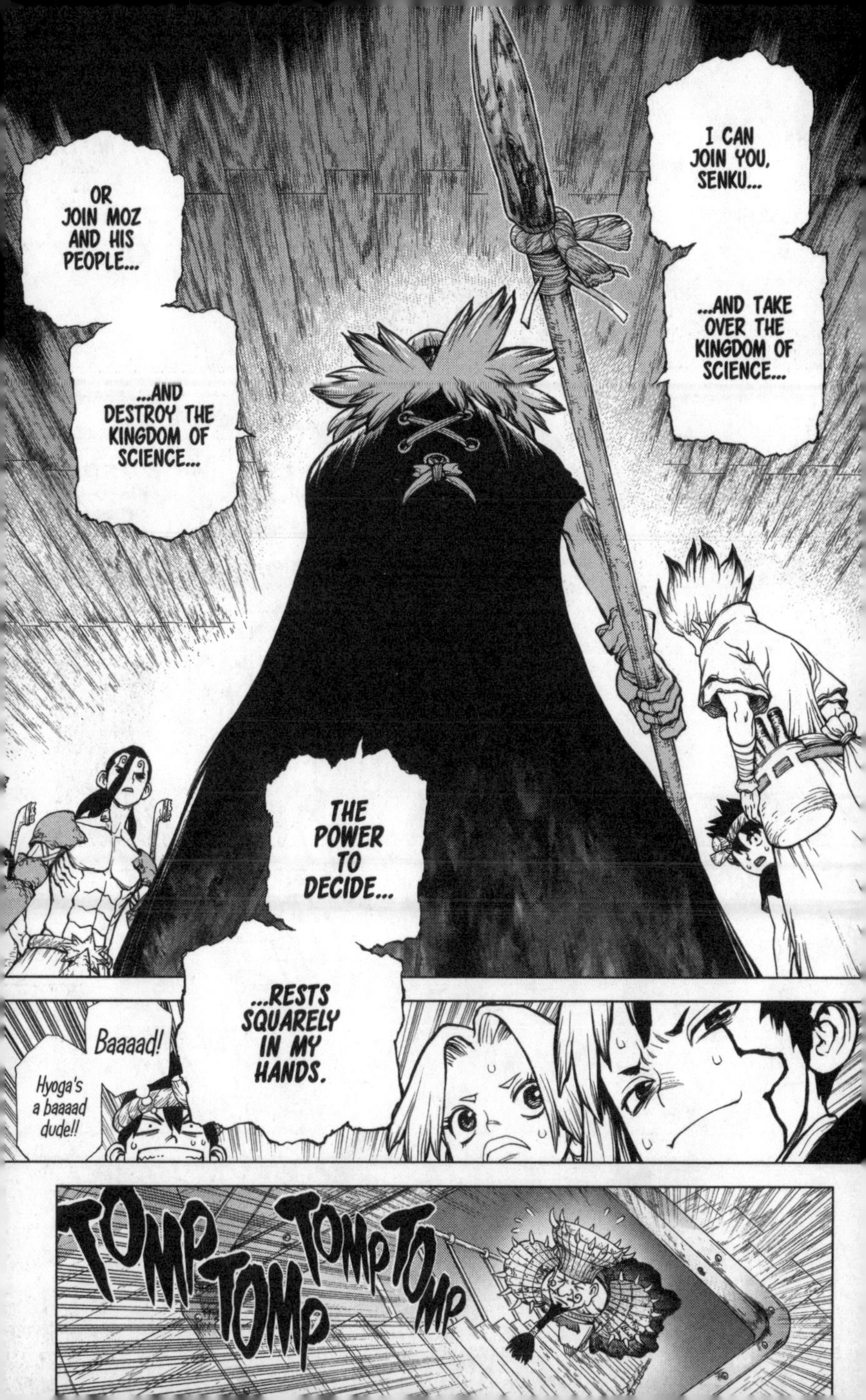
I CAN JOIN YOU, SENKU...
...AND TAKE OVER THE KINGDOM OF SCIENCE...
OR JOIN MOZ AND HIS PEOPLE...
...AND DESTROY THE KINGDOM OF SCIENCE...
THE POWER TO DECIDE...
...RESTS SQUARELY IN MY HANDS.
Baaaad!
Hyoga's a baaaad dude!!
TOMP TOMP
TOMP TOMP

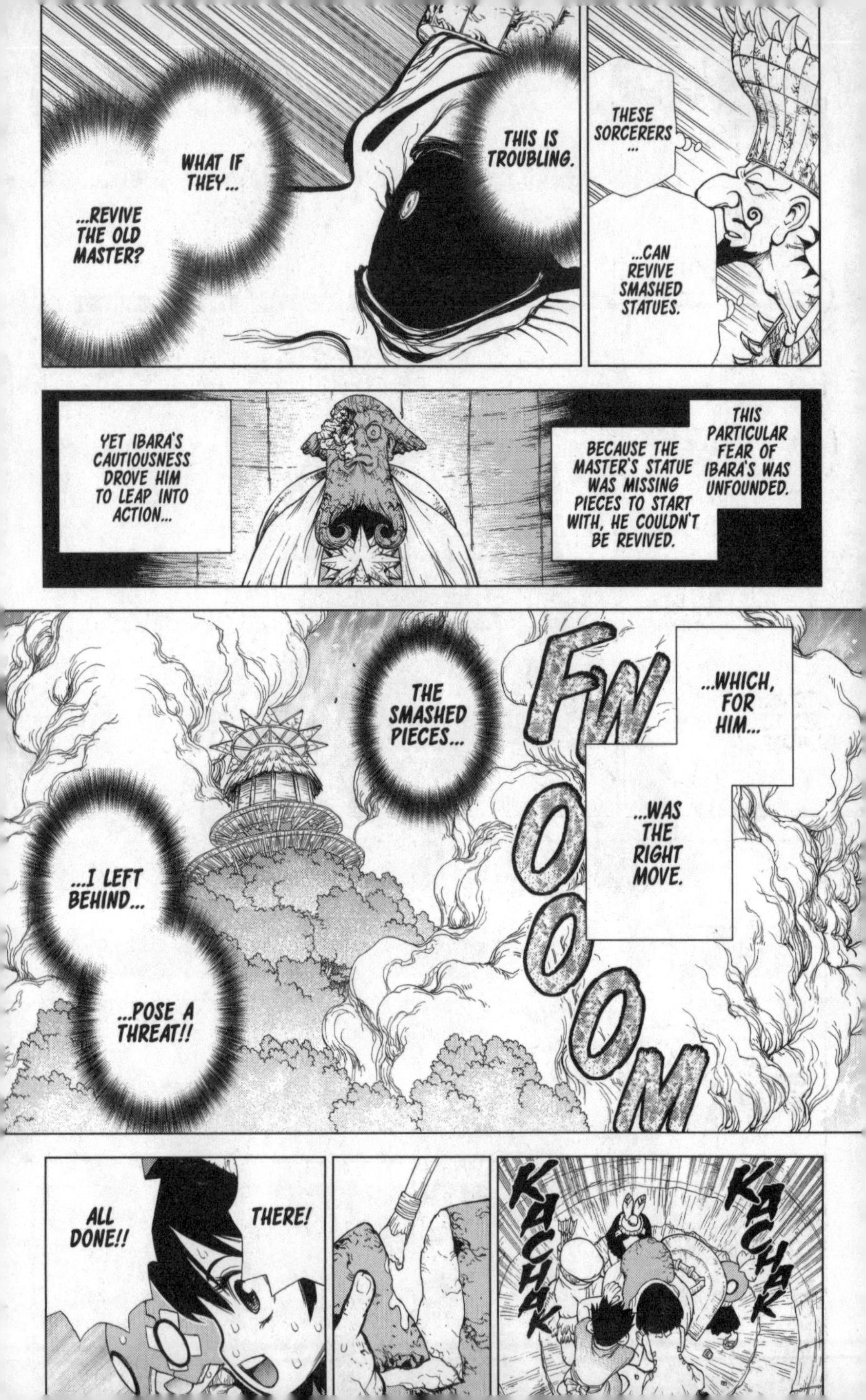
THESE SORCERERS...
...CAN REVIVE SMASHED STATUES.
THIS IS TROUBLING.
WHAT IF THEY...
...REVIVE THE OLD MASTER?
THIS PARTICULAR FEAR OF IBARA'S WAS UNFOUNDED.
BECAUSE THE MASTER'S STATUE WAS MISSING PIECES TO START WITH, HE COULDN'T BE REVIVED.
YET IBARA'S CAUTIOUSNESS DROVE HIM TO LEAP INTO ACTION...
...WHICH, FOR HIM...
...WAS THE RIGHT MOVE.
FWOOOOM
THE SMASHED PIECES...
...I LEFT BEHIND...
...POSE A THREAT!!
KACHAK
KACHAK
THERE!
ALL DONE!!

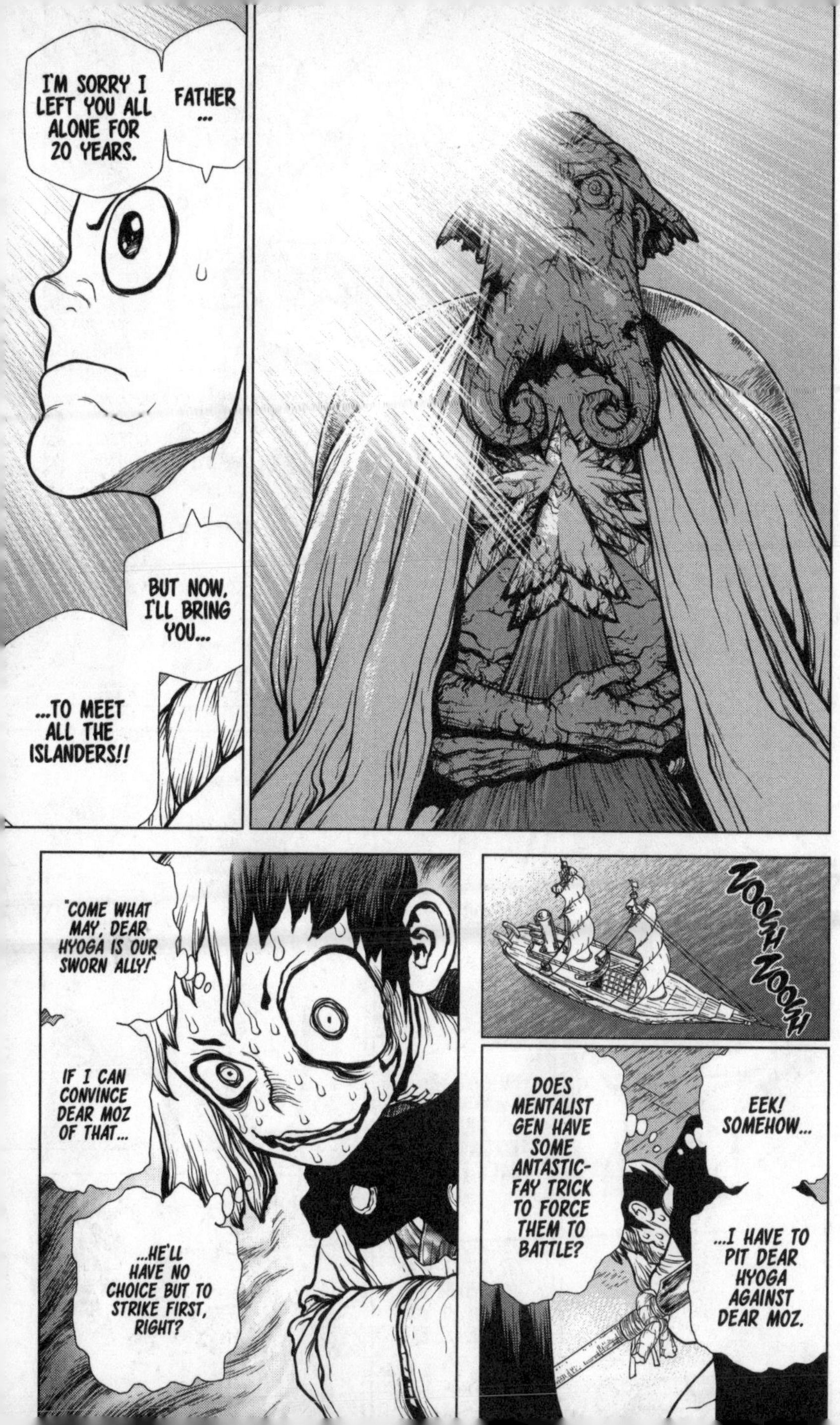
FATHER...
I'M SORRY I LEFT YOU ALL ALONE FOR 20 YEARS.
BUT NOW, I'LL BRING YOU...
...TO MEET ALL THE ISLANDERS!!
ZOOOH ZOOOH
EEK! SOMEHOW...
...I HAVE TO PIT DEAR HYOGA AGAINST DEAR MOZ.
DOES MENTALIST GEN HAVE SOME ANTASTIC-FAY TRICK TO FORCE THEM TO BATTLE?
"COME WHAT MAY, DEAR HYOGA IS OUR SWORN ALLY!"
IF I CAN CONVINCE DEAR MOZ OF THAT...
...HE'LL HAVE NO CHOICE BUT TO STRIKE FIRST, RIGHT?

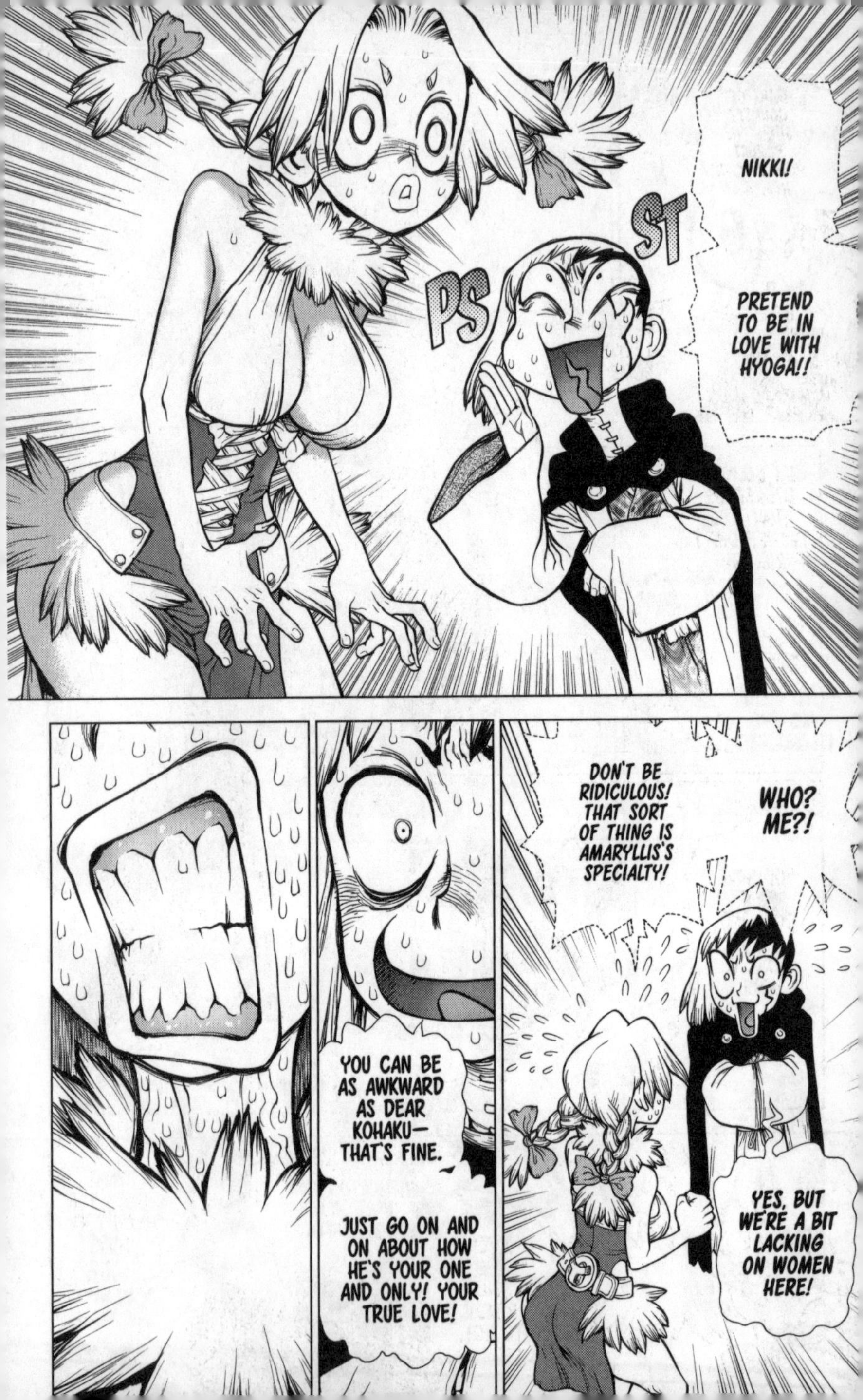
NIKKI!
PRETEND TO BE IN LOVE WITH HYOGA!!
PS ST
WHO? ME?!
DON'T BE RIDICULOUS! THAT SORT OF THING IS AMARYLLIS'S SPECIALTY!
YES, BUT WE'RE A BIT LACKING ON WOMEN HERE!
YOU CAN BE AS AWKWARD AS DEAR KOHAKU—THAT'S FINE.
JUST GO ON AND ON ABOUT HOW HE'S YOUR ONE AND ONLY! YOUR TRUE LOVE!

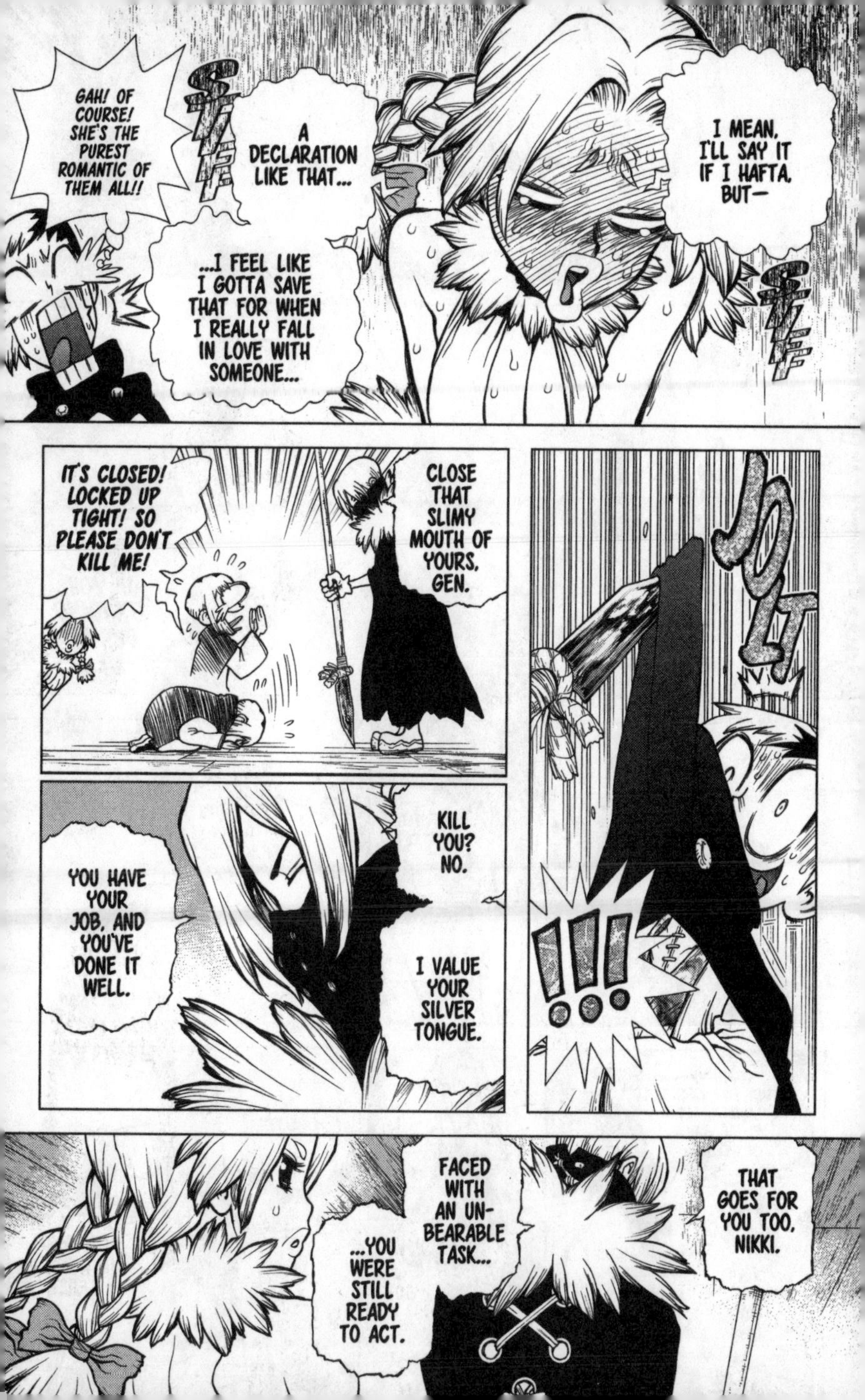
I MEAN, I'LL SAY IT IF I HAFTA, BUT—
STIFF
A DECLARATION LIKE THAT...
...I FEEL LIKE I GOTTA SAVE THAT FOR WHEN I REALLY FALL IN LOVE WITH SOMEONE...
STIFF
GAH! OF COURSE! SHE'S THE PUREST ROMANTIC OF THEM ALL!!
JOLT
!!!...
CLOSE THAT SLIMY MOUTH OF YOURS, GEN.
IT'S CLOSED! LOCKED UP TIGHT! SO PLEASE DON'T KILL ME!
KILL YOU? NO.
I VALUE YOUR SILVER TONGUE.
YOU HAVE YOUR JOB, AND YOU'VE DONE IT WELL.
THAT GOES FOR YOU TOO, NIKKI.
FACED WITH AN UN-BEARABLE TASK...
...YOU WERE STILL READY TO ACT.

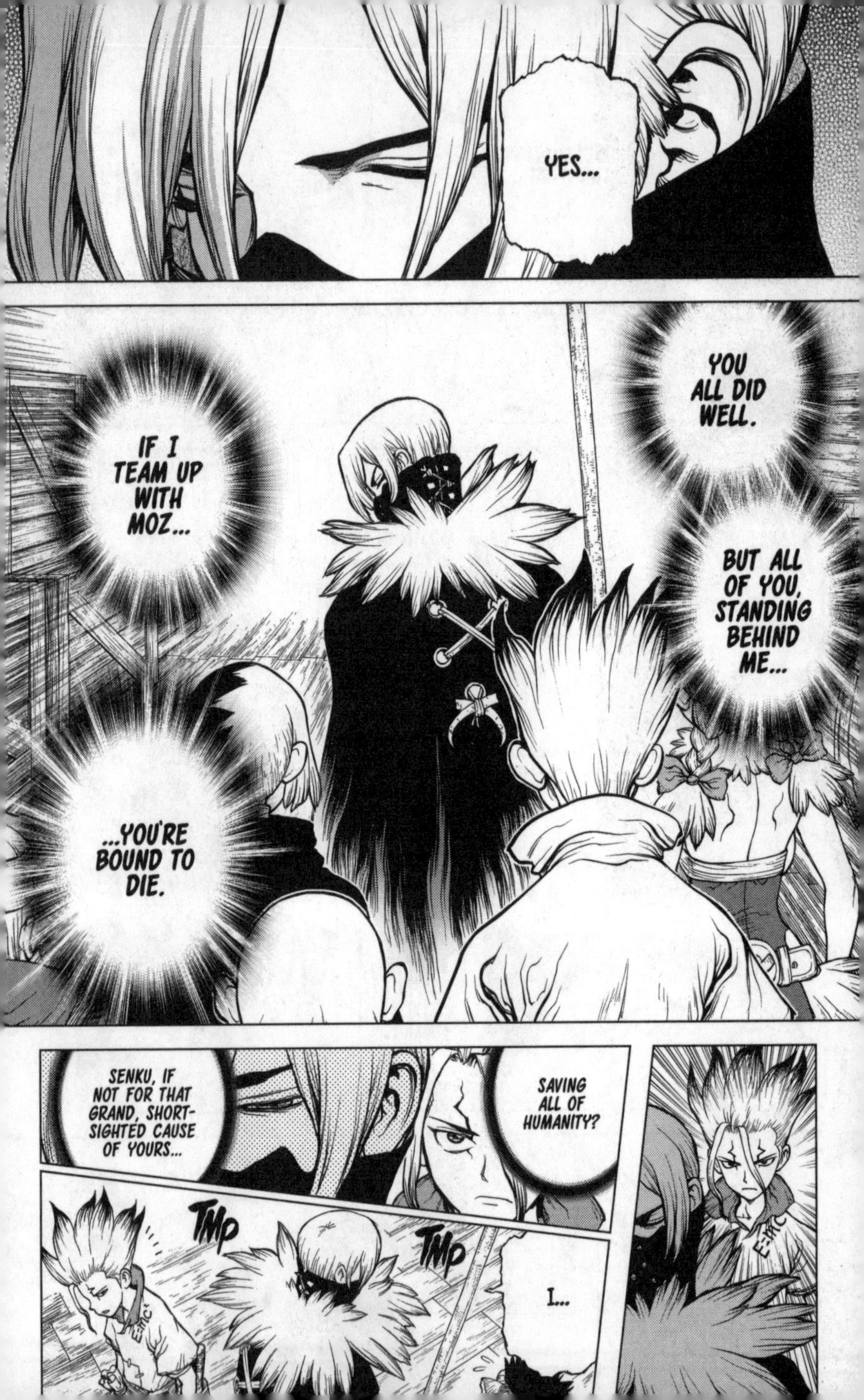
YES...
YOU ALL DID WELL.
BUT ALL OF YOU, STANDING BEHIND ME...
IF I TEAM UP WITH MOZ...
...YOU'RE BOUND TO DIE.
SAVING ALL OF HUMANITY?
SENKU, IF NOT FOR THAT GRAND, SHORT-SIGHTED CAUSE OF YOURS...
TMP
TMP
I...

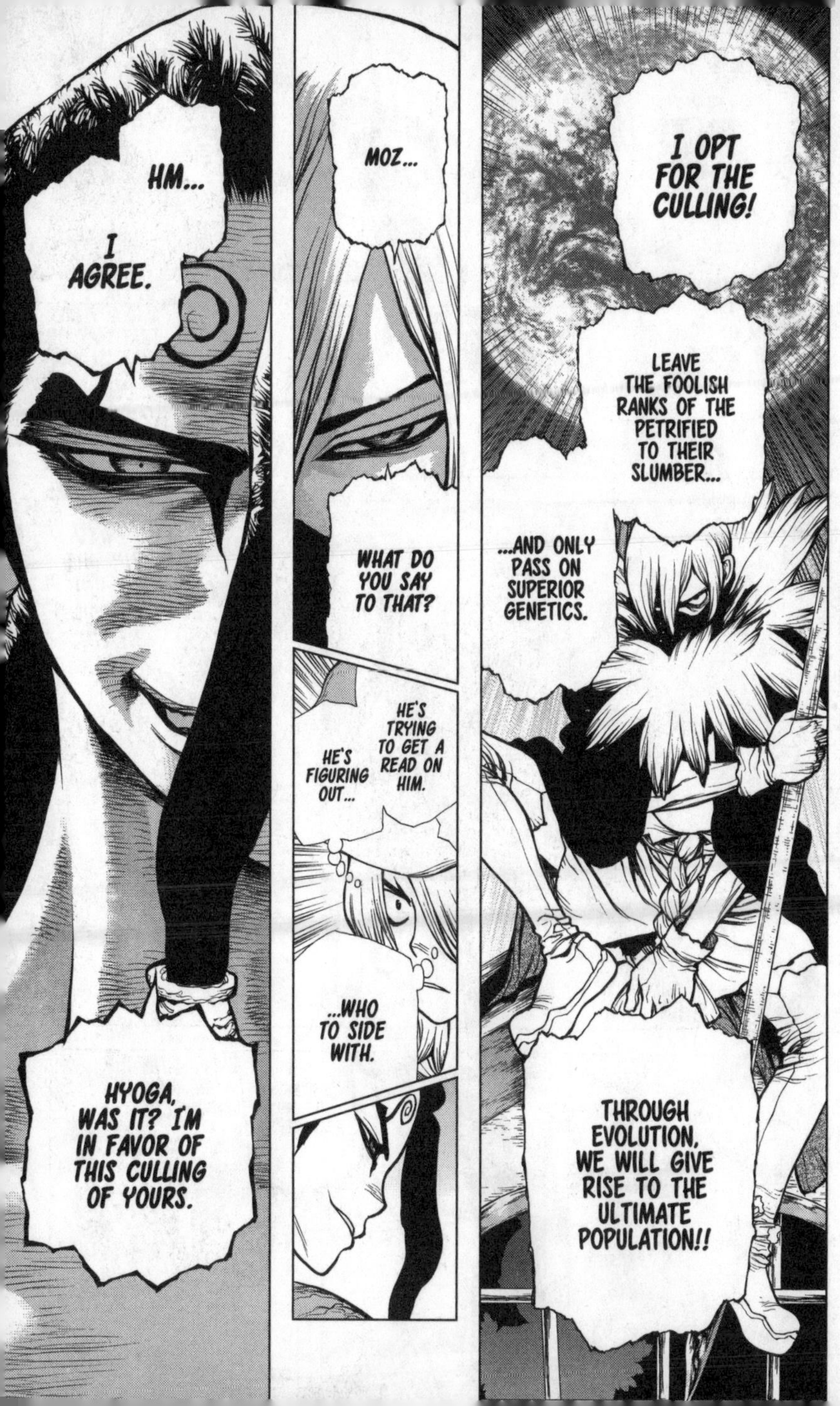
I OPT FOR THE CULLING!
LEAVE THE FOOLISH RANKS OF THE PETRIFIED TO THEIR SLUMBER...
...AND ONLY PASS ON SUPERIOR GENETICS.
THROUGH EVOLUTION, WE WILL GIVE RISE TO THE ULTIMATE POPULATION!!
MOZ...
WHAT DO YOU SAY TO THAT?
HE'S TRYING TO GET A READ ON HIM.
HE'S FIGURING OUT...
...WHO TO SIDE WITH.
HM...
I AGREE.
HYOGA, WAS IT? I'M IN FAVOR OF THIS CULLING OF YOURS.

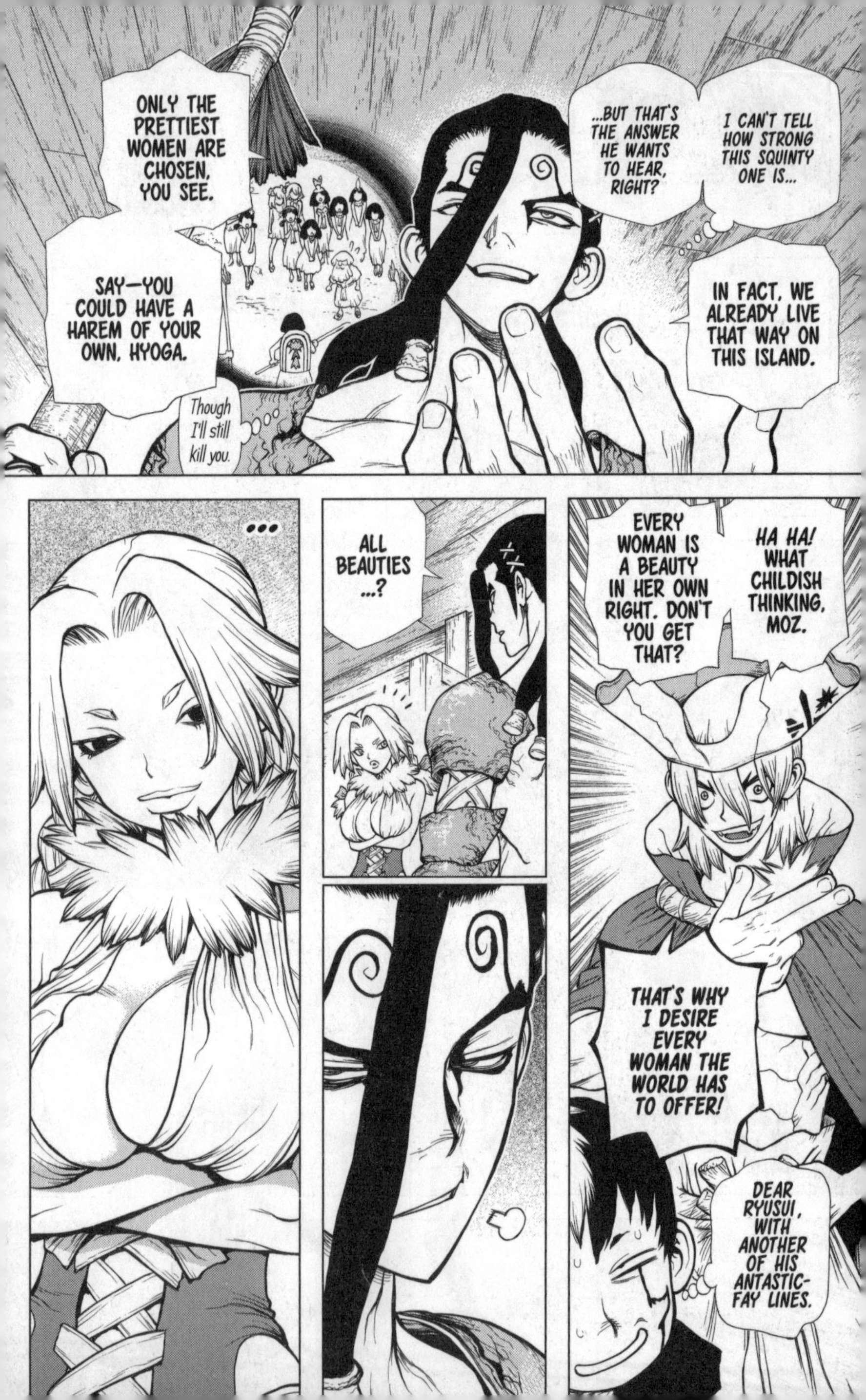
I CAN'T TELL HOW STRONG THIS SQUINTY ONE IS...
...BUT THAT'S THE ANSWER HE WANTS TO HEAR, RIGHT?
IN FACT, WE ALREADY LIVE THAT WAY ON THIS ISLAND.
ONLY THE PRETTIEST WOMEN ARE CHOSEN, YOU SEE.
SAY—YOU COULD HAVE A HAREM OF YOUR OWN, HYOGA.
Though I'll still kill you.
HA HA! WHAT CHILDISH THINKING, MOZ.
EVERY WOMAN IS A BEAUTY IN HER OWN RIGHT. DON'T YOU GET THAT?
THAT'S WHY I DESIRE EVERY WOMAN THE WORLD HAS TO OFFER!
DEAR RYUSUI, WITH ANOTHER OF HIS ANTASTIC-FAY LINES.
ALL BEAUTIES ...?
•••

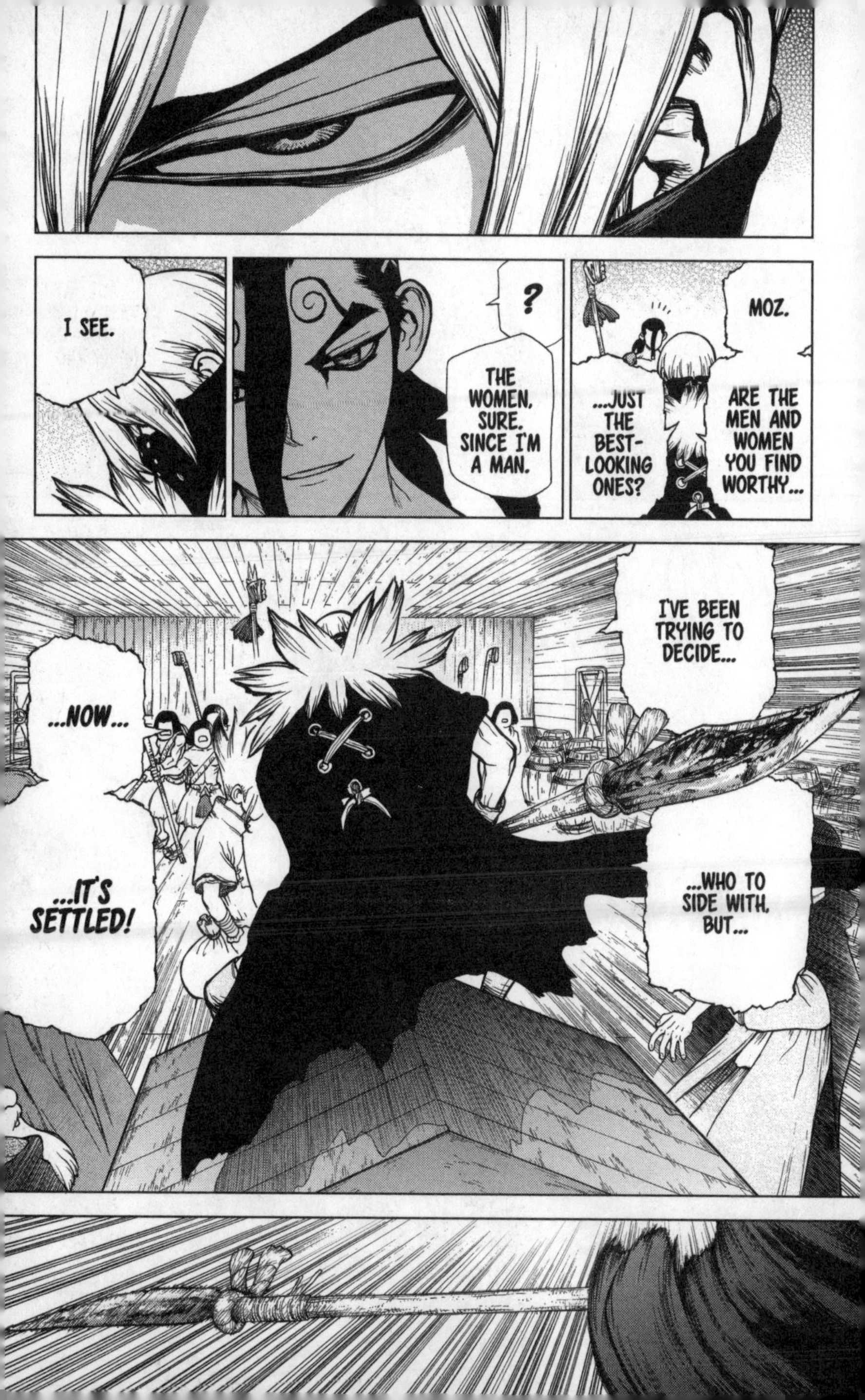
MOZ.
ARE THE MEN AND WOMEN YOU FIND WORTHY...
...JUST THE BEST-LOOKING ONES?
?
THE WOMEN, SURE. SINCE I'M A MAN.
I SEE.
I'VE BEEN TRYING TO DECIDE...
...WHO TO SIDE WITH, BUT...
...NOW...
...IT'S SETTLED!

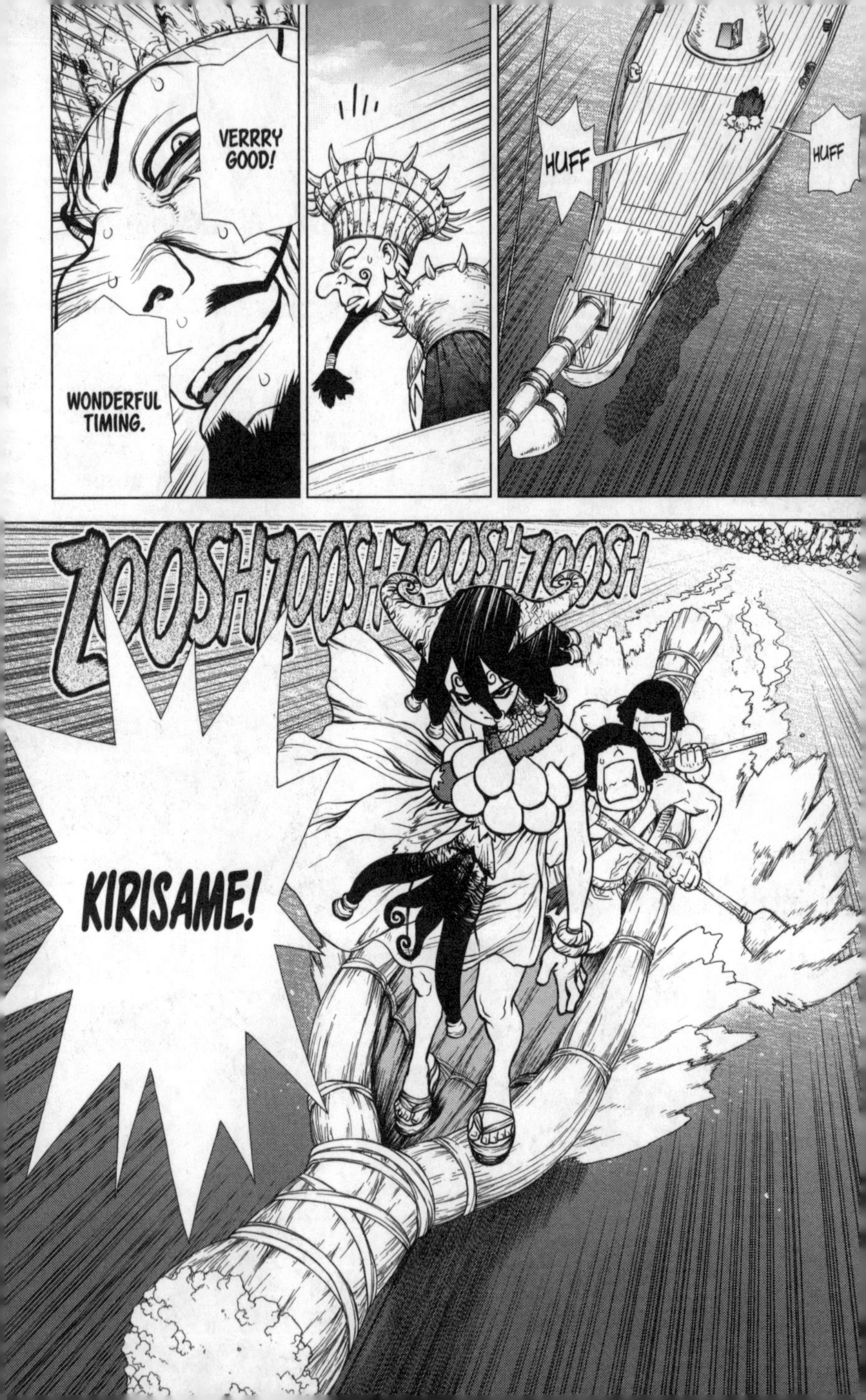
HUFF
HUFF
VERRRY GOOD!
WONDERFUL TIMING.
ZOOSH ZOOSH ZOOSH ZOOSH
KIRISAME!

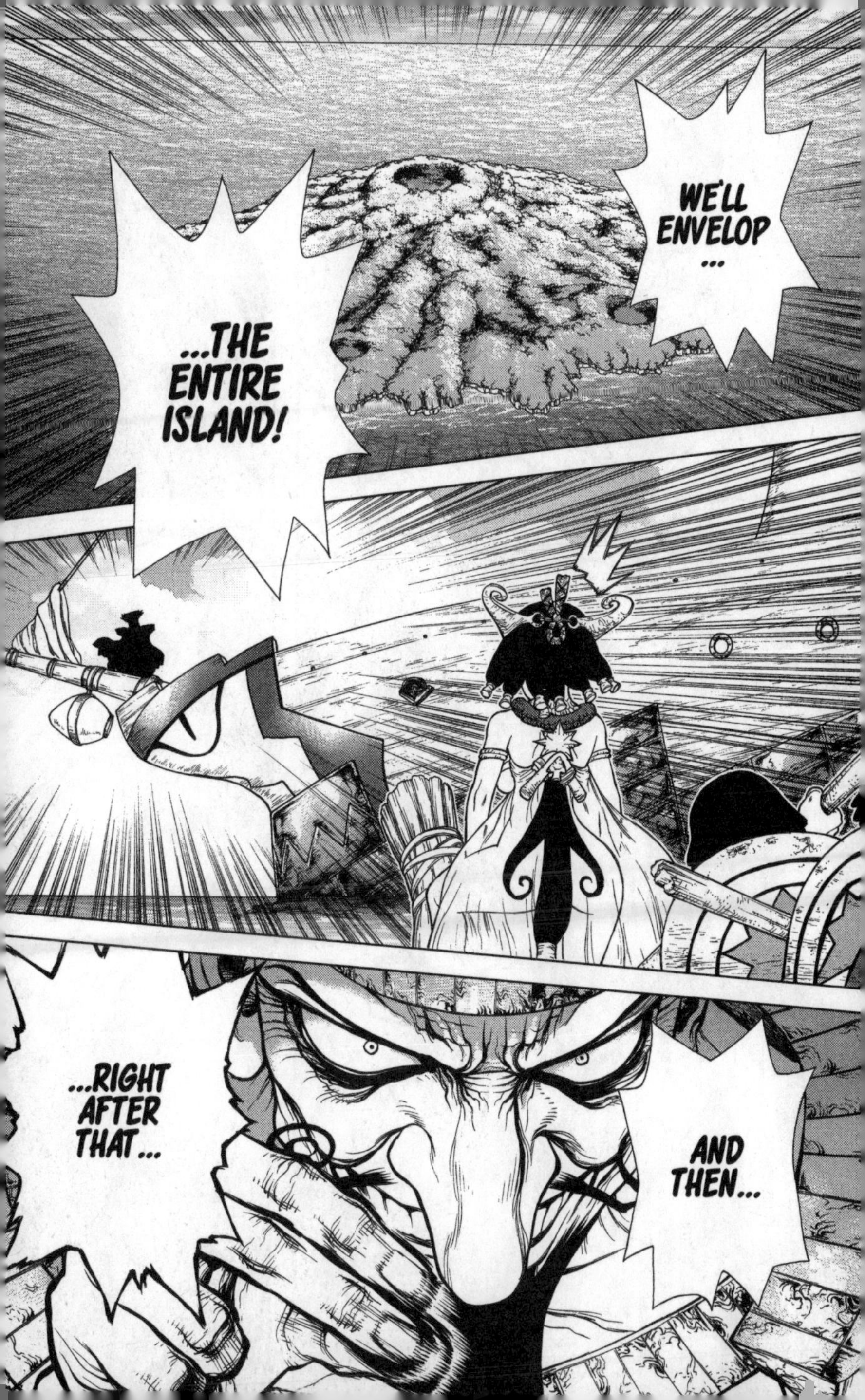
WE'LL ENVELOP ...
...THE ENTIRE ISLAND!
AND THEN...
...RIGHT AFTER THAT...

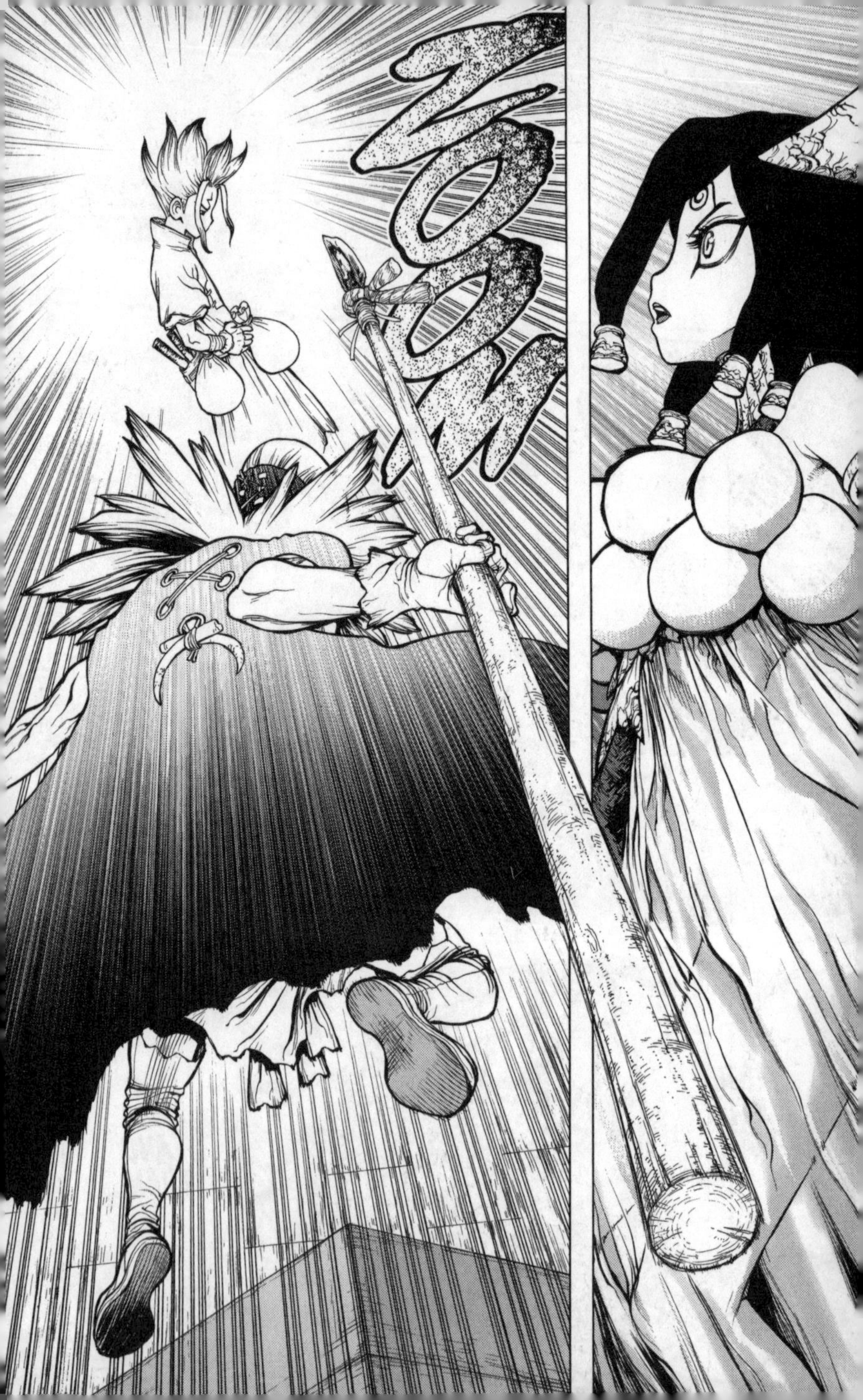
WOOM

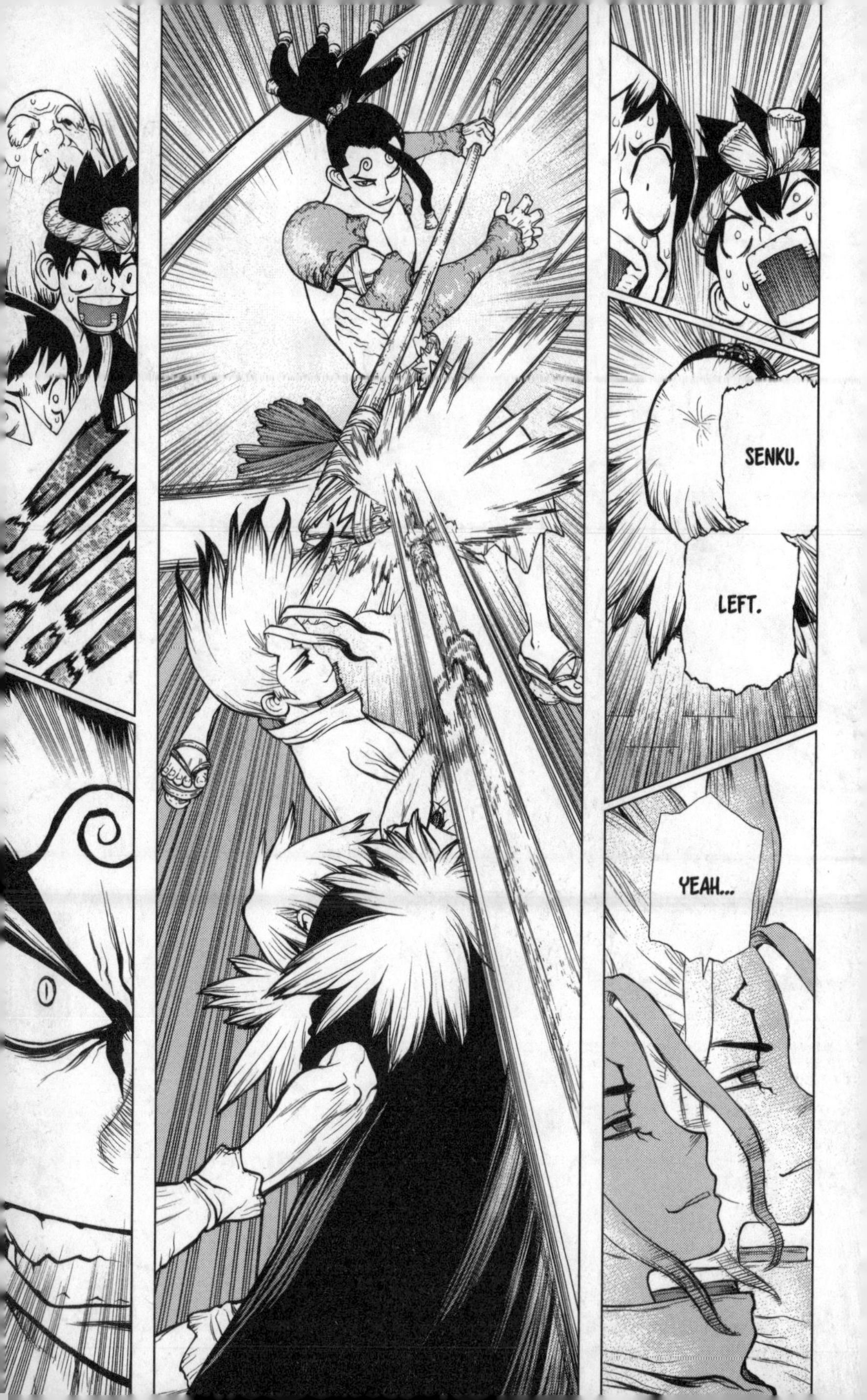
SENKU.
LEFT.
YEAH...

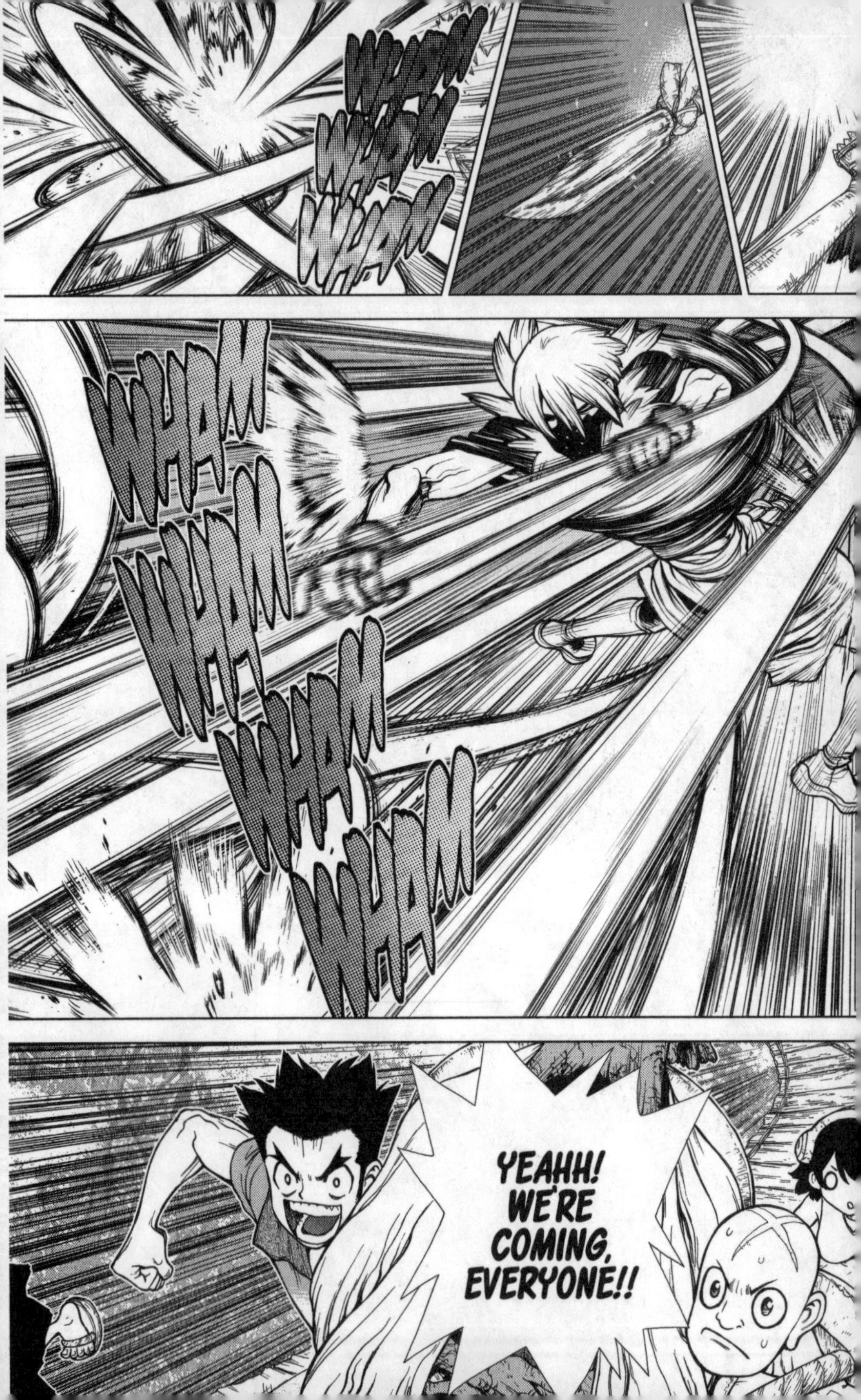
WHAM
WHAM
WHAM
WHAM
WHAM
WHAM
WHAM
WHAM
YEAHH! WE'RE COMING, EVERYONE!!

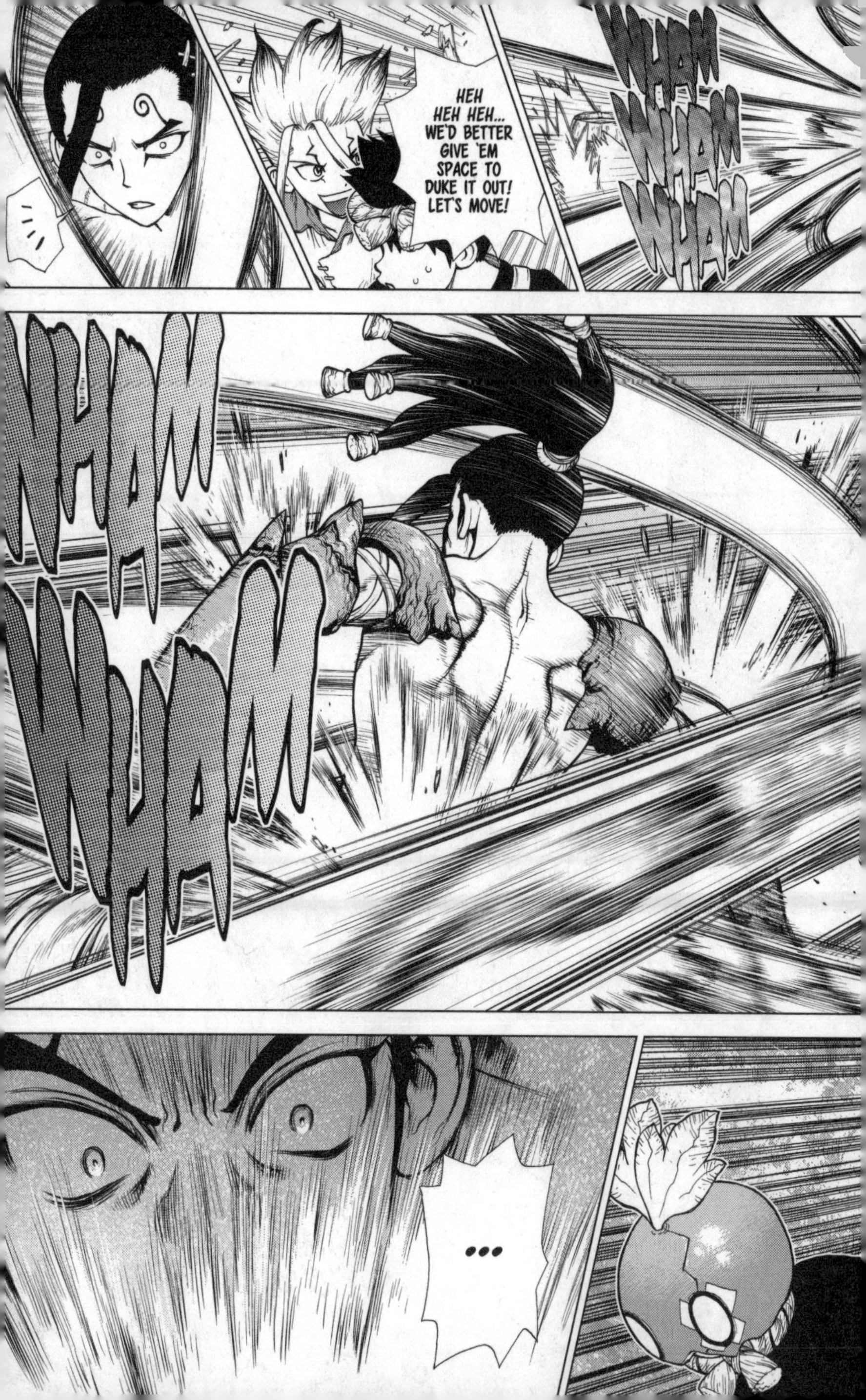
WHAM WHAM WHAM
HEH HEH HEH... WE'D BETTER GIVE 'EM SPACE TO DUKE IT OUT! LET'S MOVE!
WHAM WHAM
...

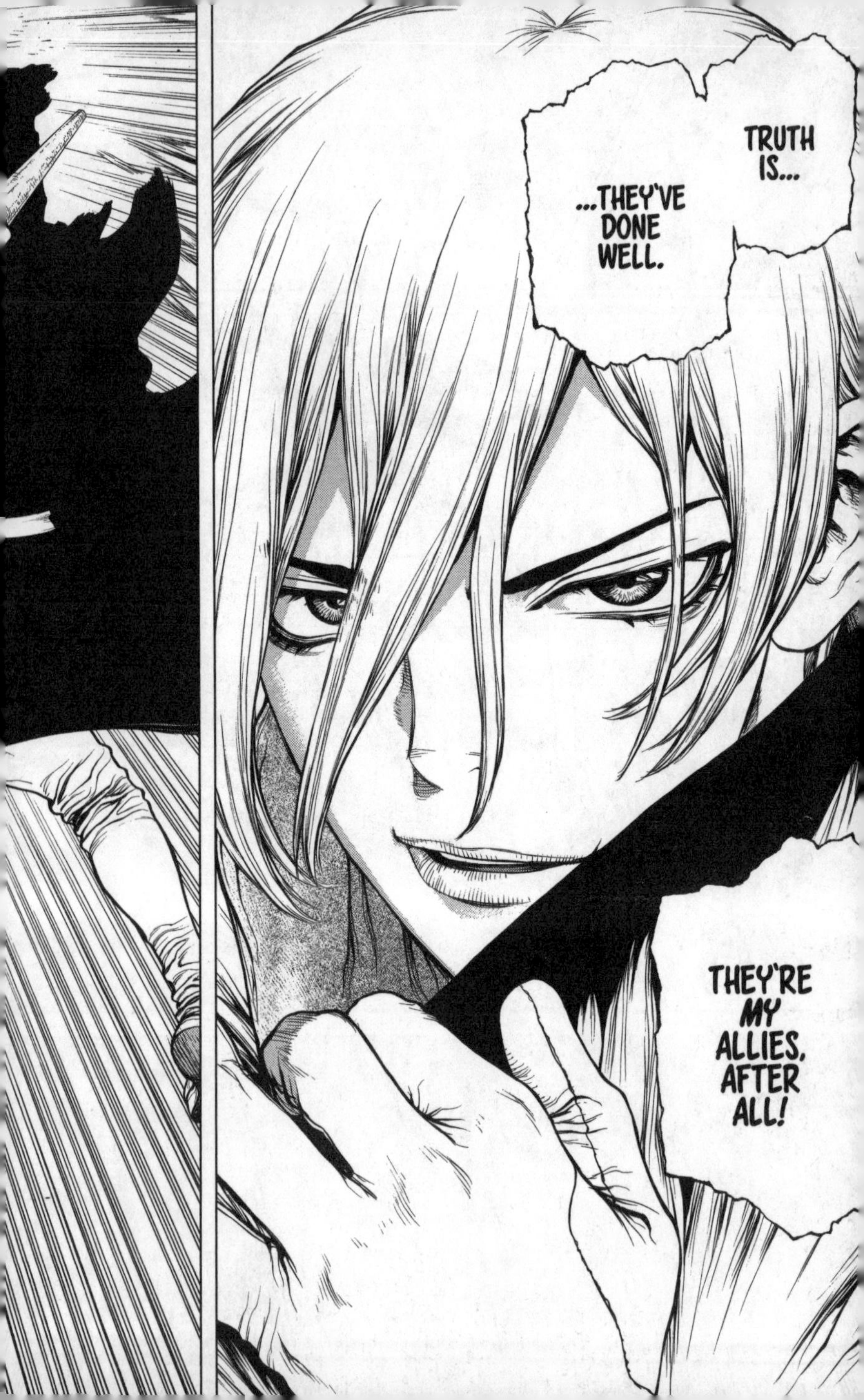
TRUTH IS...
...THEY'VE DONE WELL.
THEY'RE *MY* ALLIES, AFTER ALL!

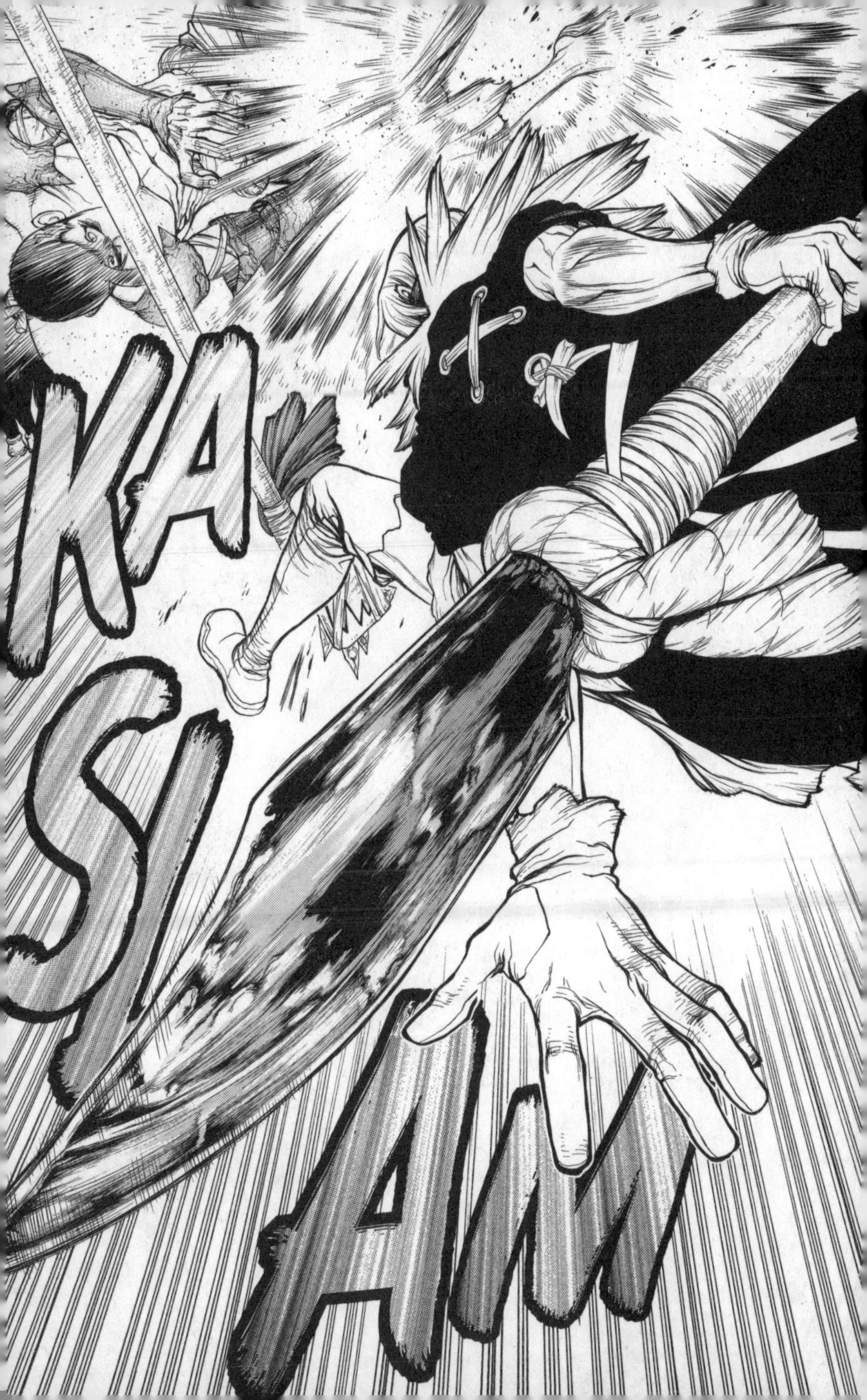
KA
SL
AM

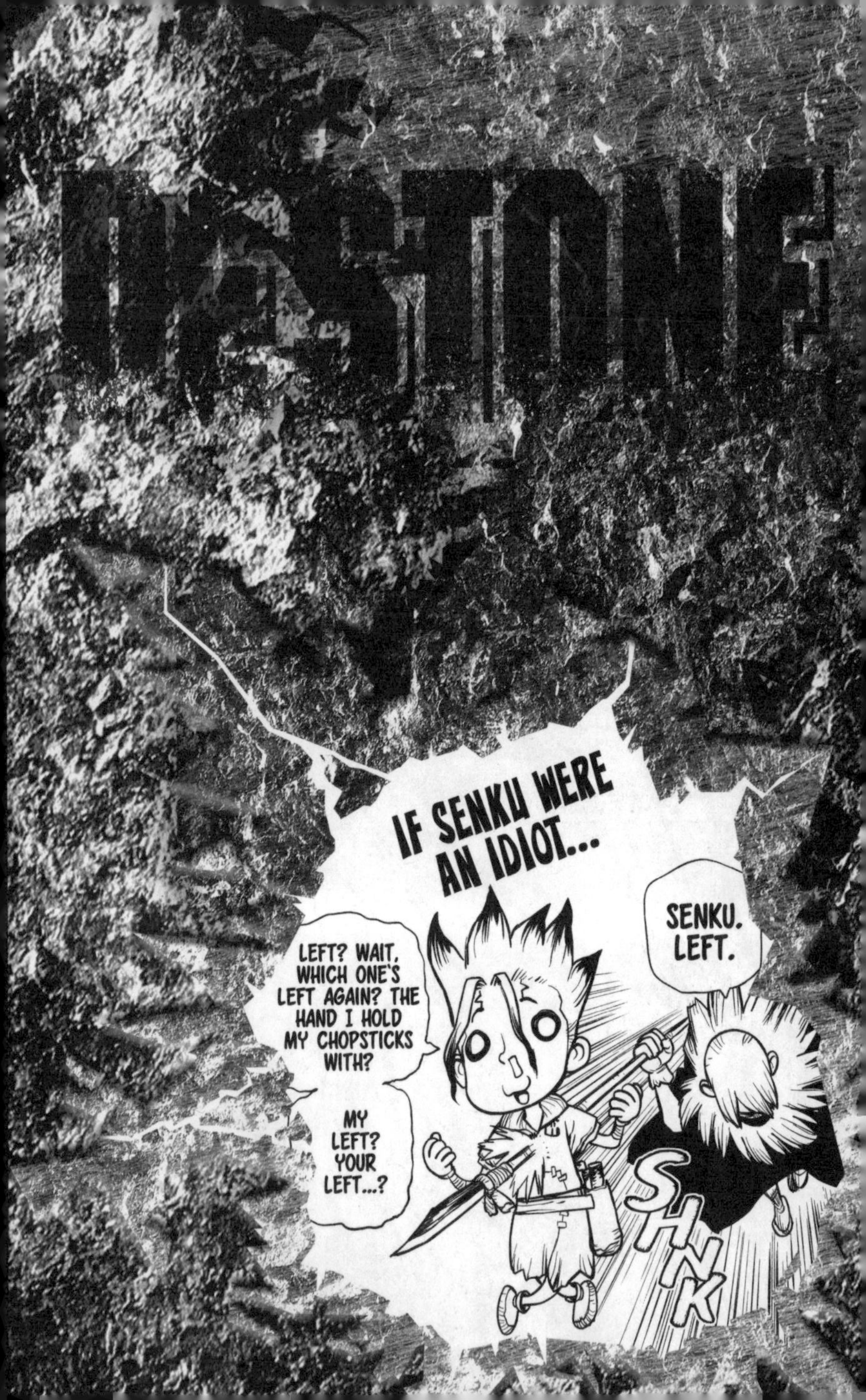
Dr.STONE
IF SENKU WERE AN IDIOT...
SENKU. LEFT.
SHNK
LEFT? WAIT, WHICH ONE'S LEFT AGAIN? THE HAND I HOLD MY CHOPSTICKS WITH?
MY LEFT? YOUR LEFT...?

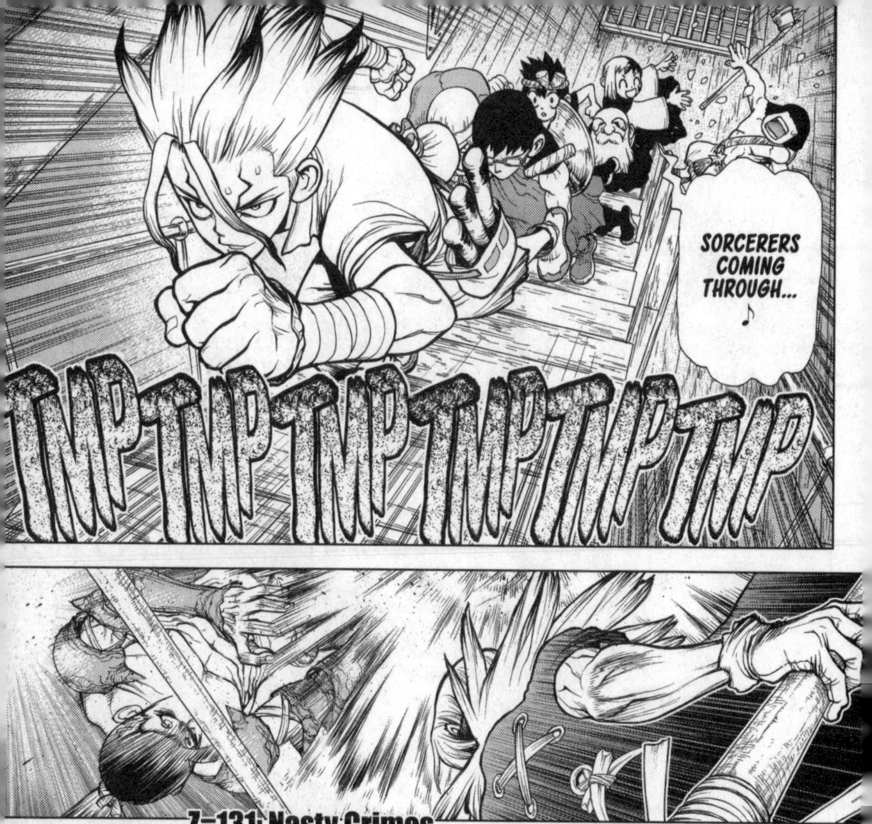
SORCERERS COMING THROUGH... ♪
TMP TMP TMP TMP TMP TMP TMP

## Z=131: Nasty Crimes

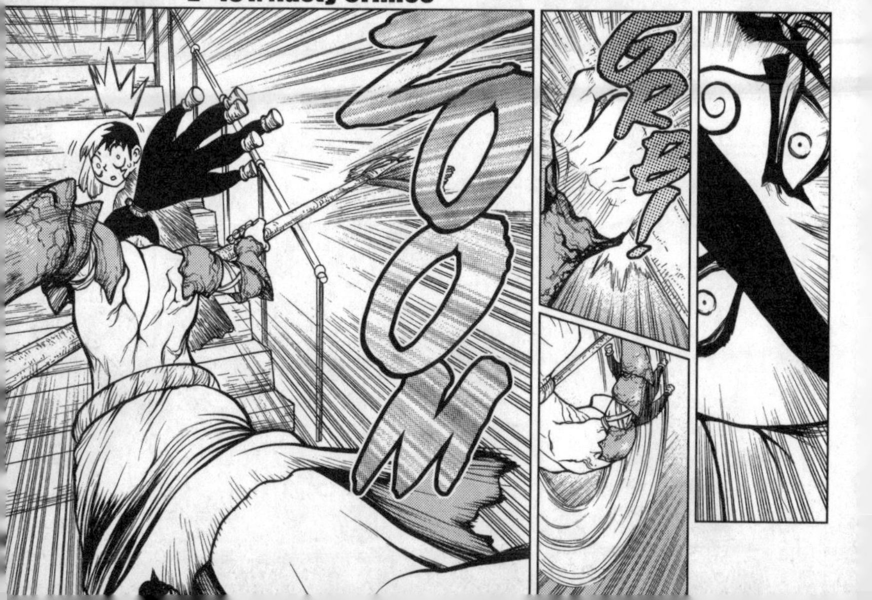
GRAB!
WOOM

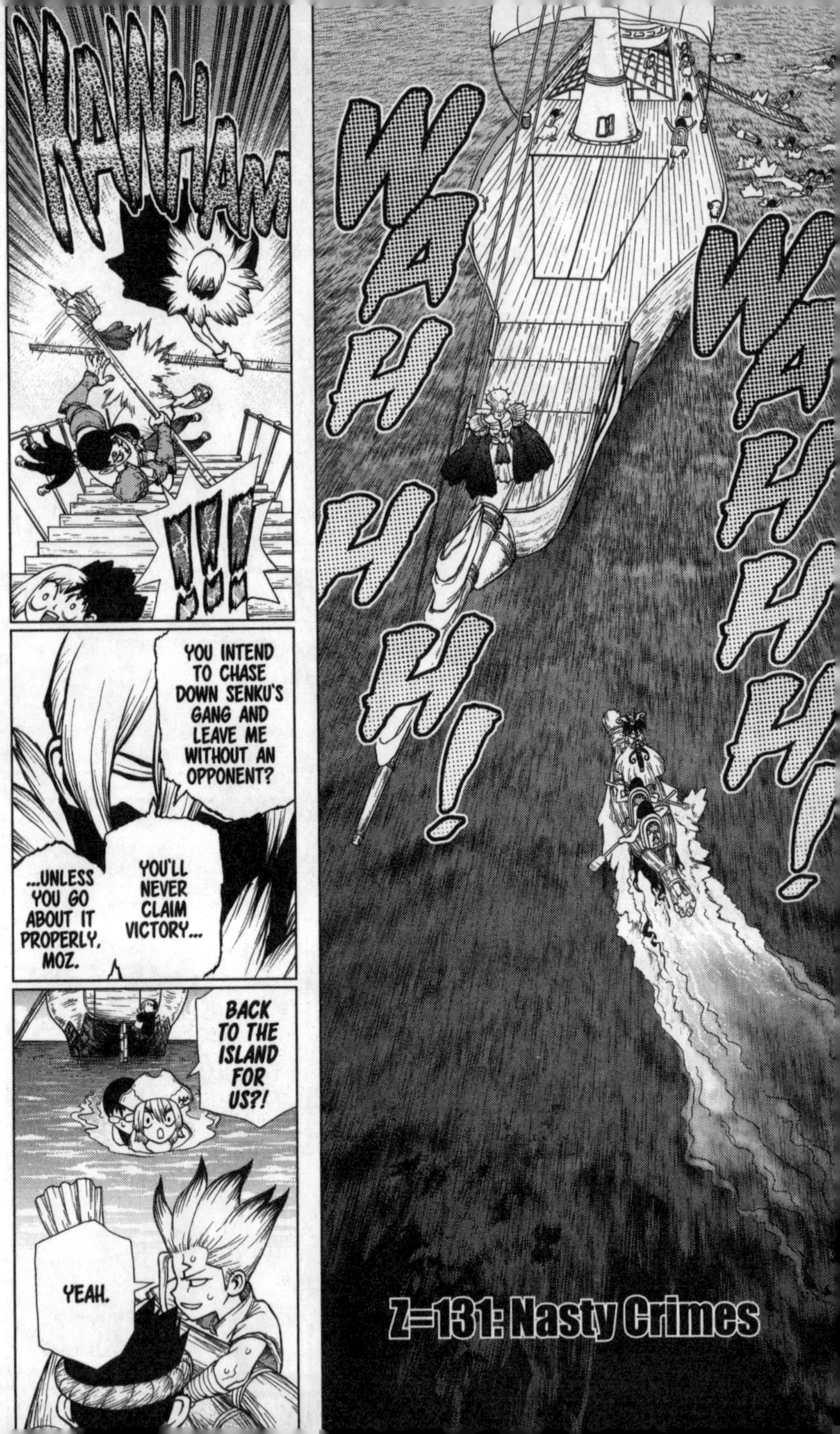
WAHHH!
WAHHH!
Z=131: Nasty Crimes
KAWHAM
!!!
YOU INTEND TO CHASE DOWN SENKU'S GANG AND LEAVE ME WITHOUT AN OPPONENT?
YOU'LL NEVER CLAIM VICTORY...
...UNLESS YOU GO ABOUT IT PROPERLY, MOZ.
BACK TO THE ISLAND FOR US?!
YEAH.

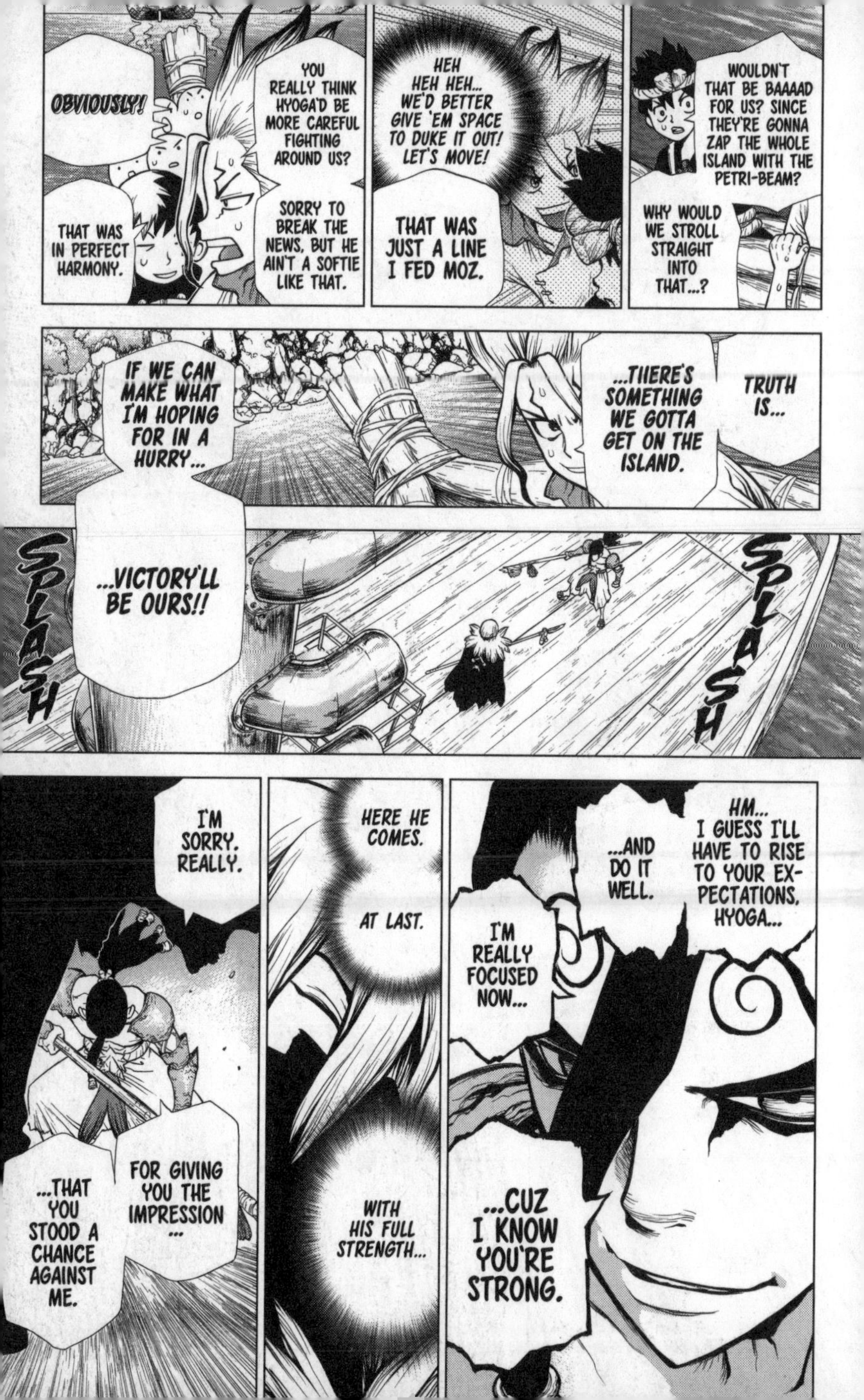
WOULDN'T THAT BE BAAAAD FOR US? SINCE THEY'RE GONNA ZAP THE WHOLE ISLAND WITH THE PETRI-BEAM?
WHY WOULD WE STROLL STRAIGHT INTO THAT...?
HEH HEH HEH... WE'D BETTER GIVE 'EM SPACE TO DUKE IT OUT! LET'S MOVE!
THAT WAS JUST A LINE I FED MOZ.
YOU REALLY THINK HYOGA'D BE MORE CAREFUL FIGHTING AROUND US?
OBVIOUSLY!
SORRY TO BREAK THE NEWS, BUT HE AIN'T A SOFTIE LIKE THAT.
THAT WAS IN PERFECT HARMONY.
TRUTH IS...
...THERE'S SOMETHING WE GOTTA GET ON THE ISLAND.
IF WE CAN MAKE WHAT I'M HOPING FOR IN A HURRY...
...VICTORY'LL BE OURS!!
SPLASH
SPLASH
HM... I GUESS I'LL HAVE TO RISE TO YOUR EX-PECTATIONS, HYOGA...
...AND DO IT WELL.
I'M REALLY FOCUSED NOW...
...CUZ I KNOW YOU'RE STRONG.
HERE HE COMES.
AT LAST.
WITH HIS FULL STRENGTH...
I'M SORRY. REALLY.
FOR GIVING YOU THE IMPRESSION...
...THAT YOU STOOD A CHANCE AGAINST ME.

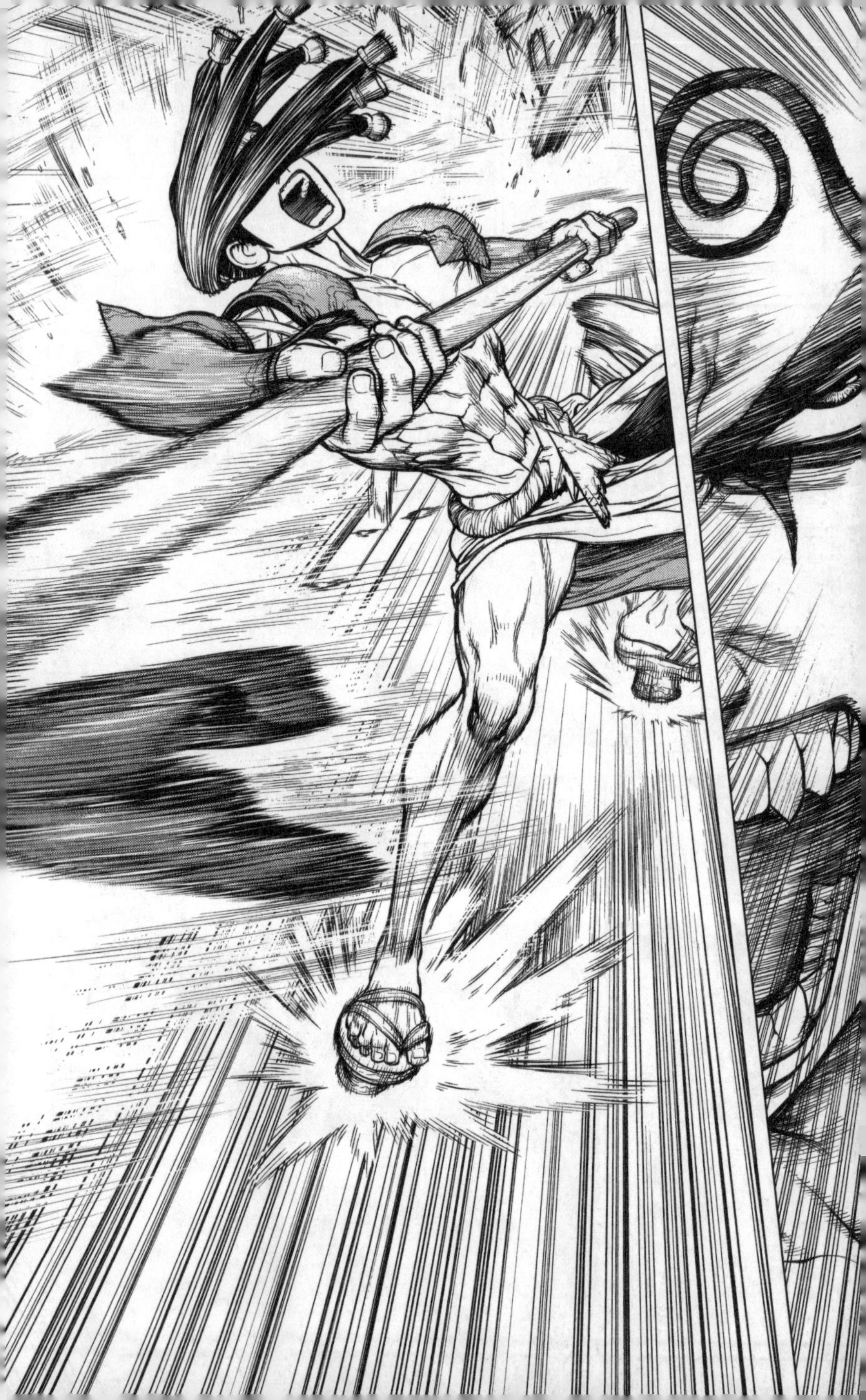

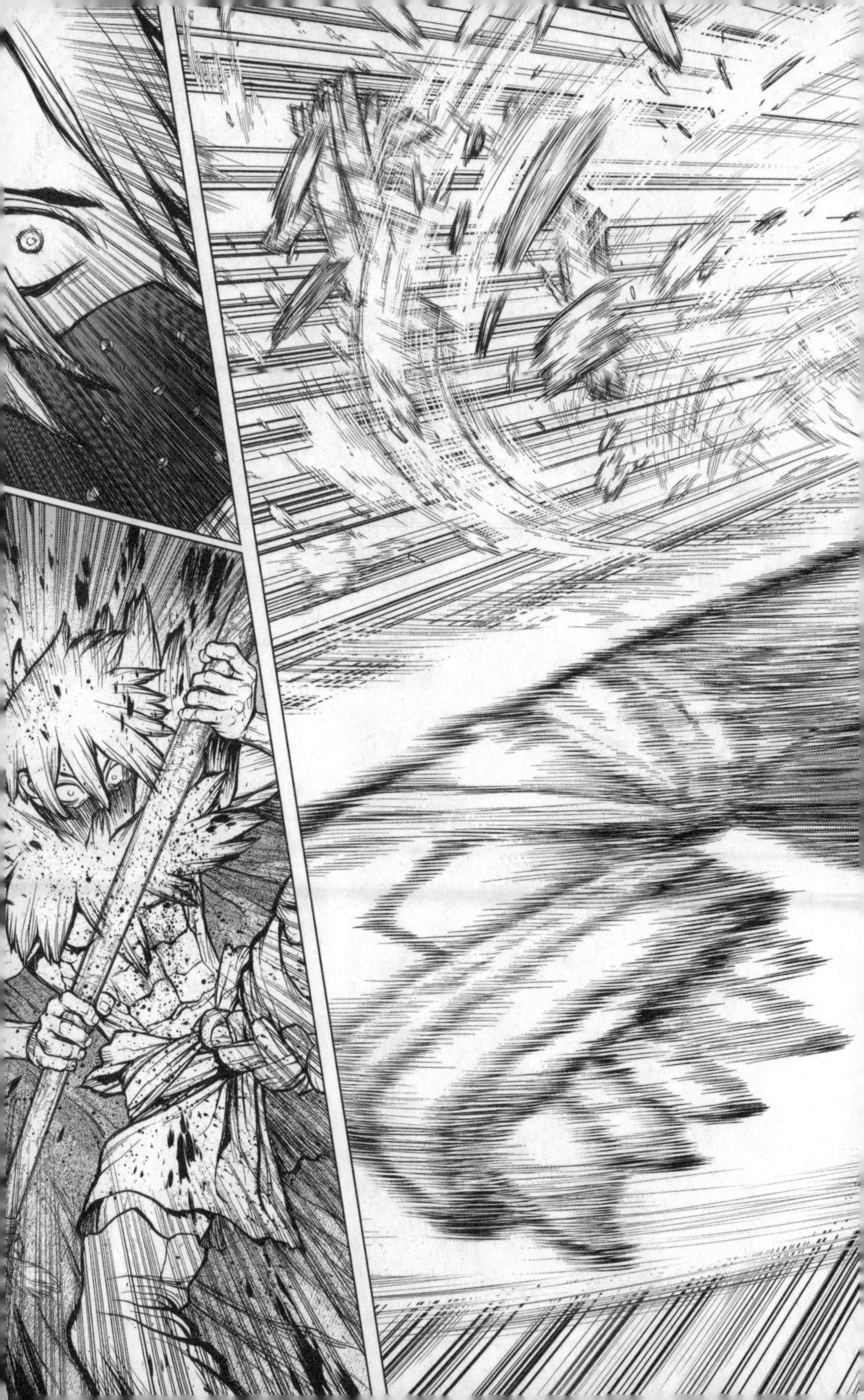

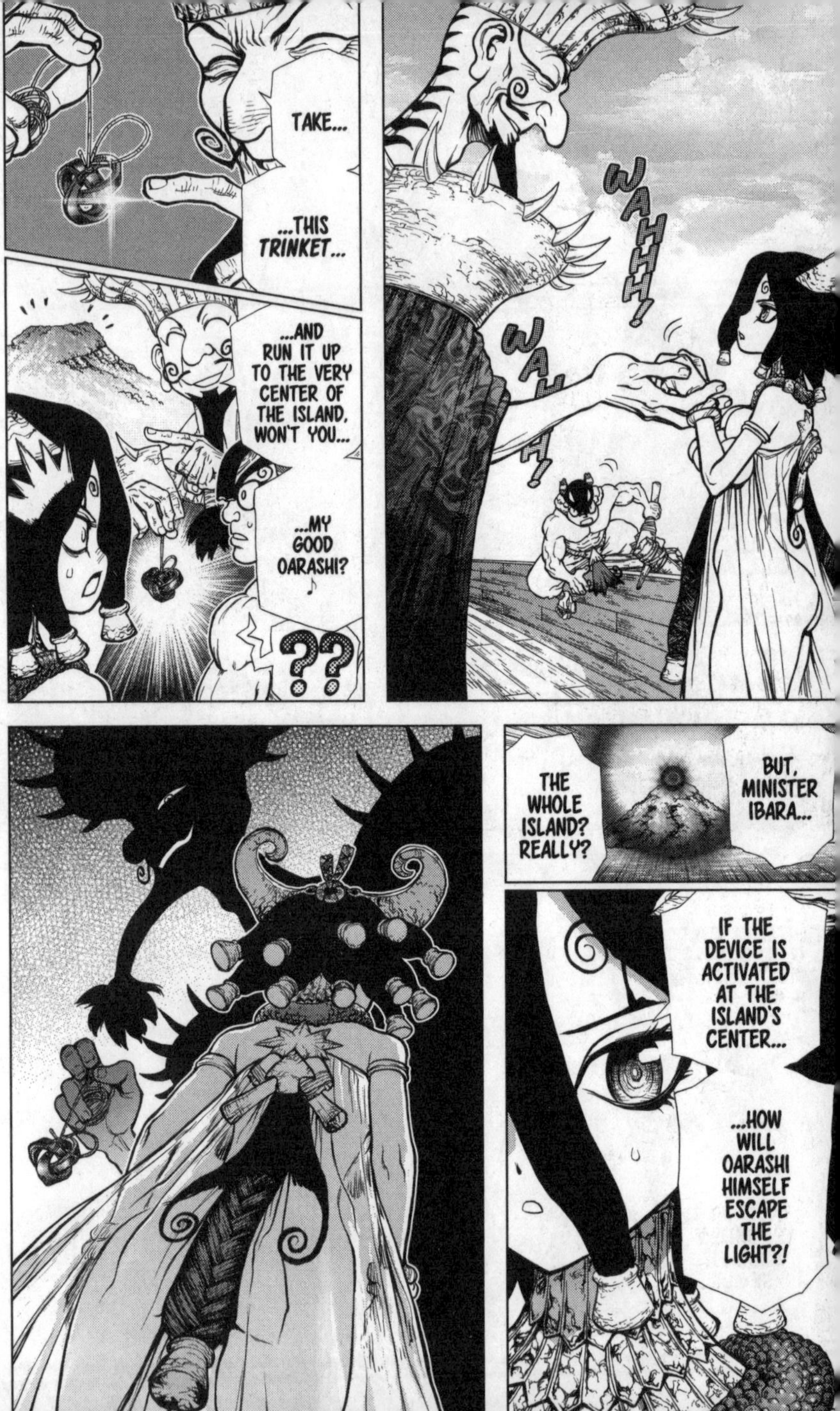

WAHHH!
WAHH!
TAKE...
...THIS TRINKET...
...AND RUN IT UP TO THE VERY CENTER OF THE ISLAND, WON'T YOU...
...MY GOOD OARASHI? ♪
??
BUT, MINISTER IBARA...
THE WHOLE ISLAND? REALLY?
IF THE DEVICE IS ACTIVATED AT THE ISLAND'S CENTER...
...HOW WILL OARASHI HIMSELF ESCAPE THE LIGHT?!

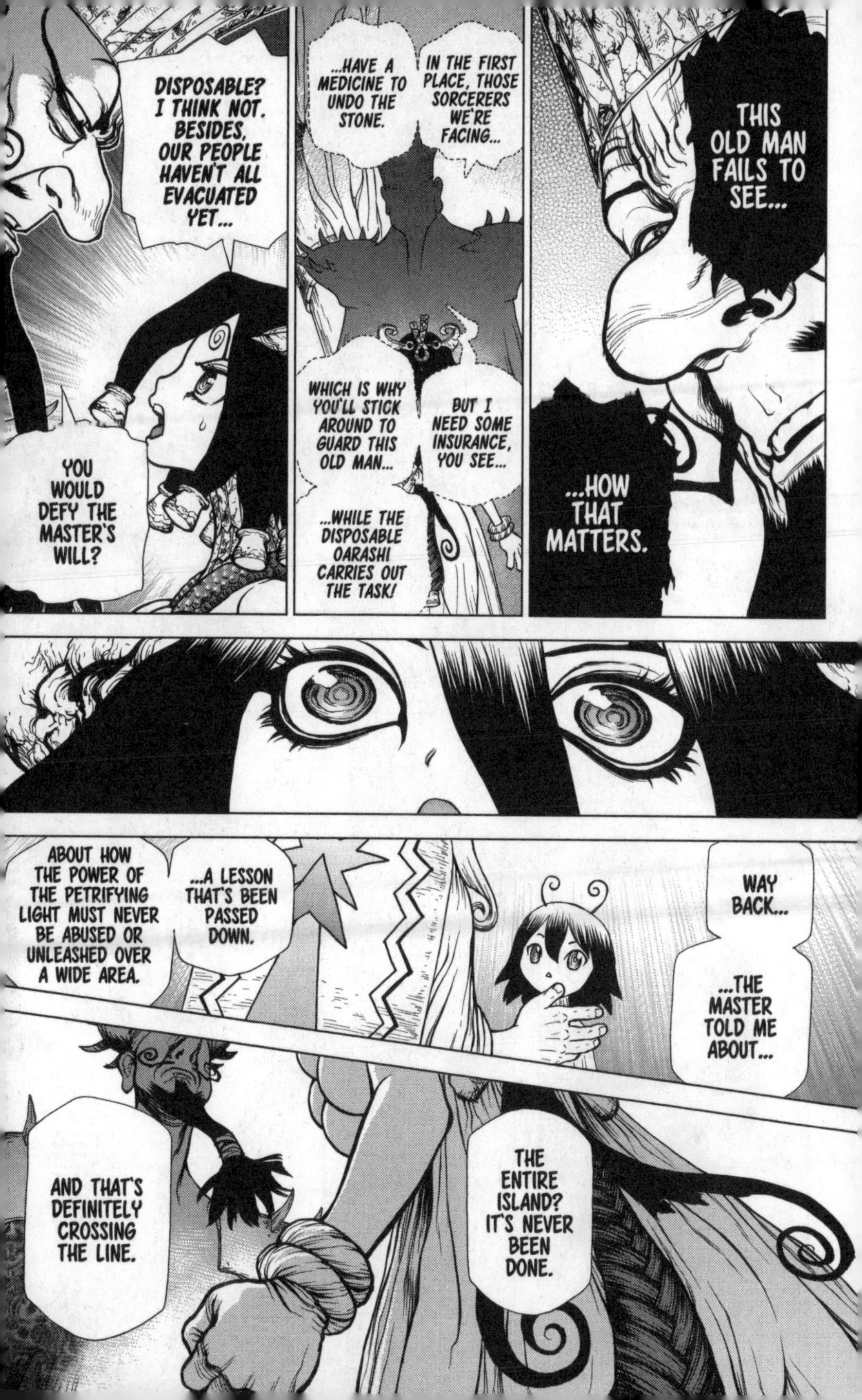
THIS OLD MAN FAILS TO SEE...
...HOW THAT MATTERS.
IN THE FIRST PLACE, THOSE SORCERERS WE'RE FACING...
...HAVE A MEDICINE TO UNDO THE STONE.
BUT I NEED SOME INSURANCE, YOU SEE...
WHICH IS WHY YOU'LL STICK AROUND TO GUARD THIS OLD MAN...
...WHILE THE DISPOSABLE OARASHI CARRIES OUT THE TASK!
DISPOSABLE? I THINK NOT. BESIDES, OUR PEOPLE HAVEN'T ALL EVACUATED YET...
YOU WOULD DEFY THE MASTER'S WILL?
WAY BACK...
...THE MASTER TOLD ME ABOUT...
...A LESSON THAT'S BEEN PASSED DOWN.
ABOUT HOW THE POWER OF THE PETRIFYING LIGHT MUST NEVER BE ABUSED OR UNLEASHED OVER A WIDE AREA.
THE ENTIRE ISLAND? IT'S NEVER BEEN DONE.
AND THAT'S DEFINITELY CROSSING THE LINE.

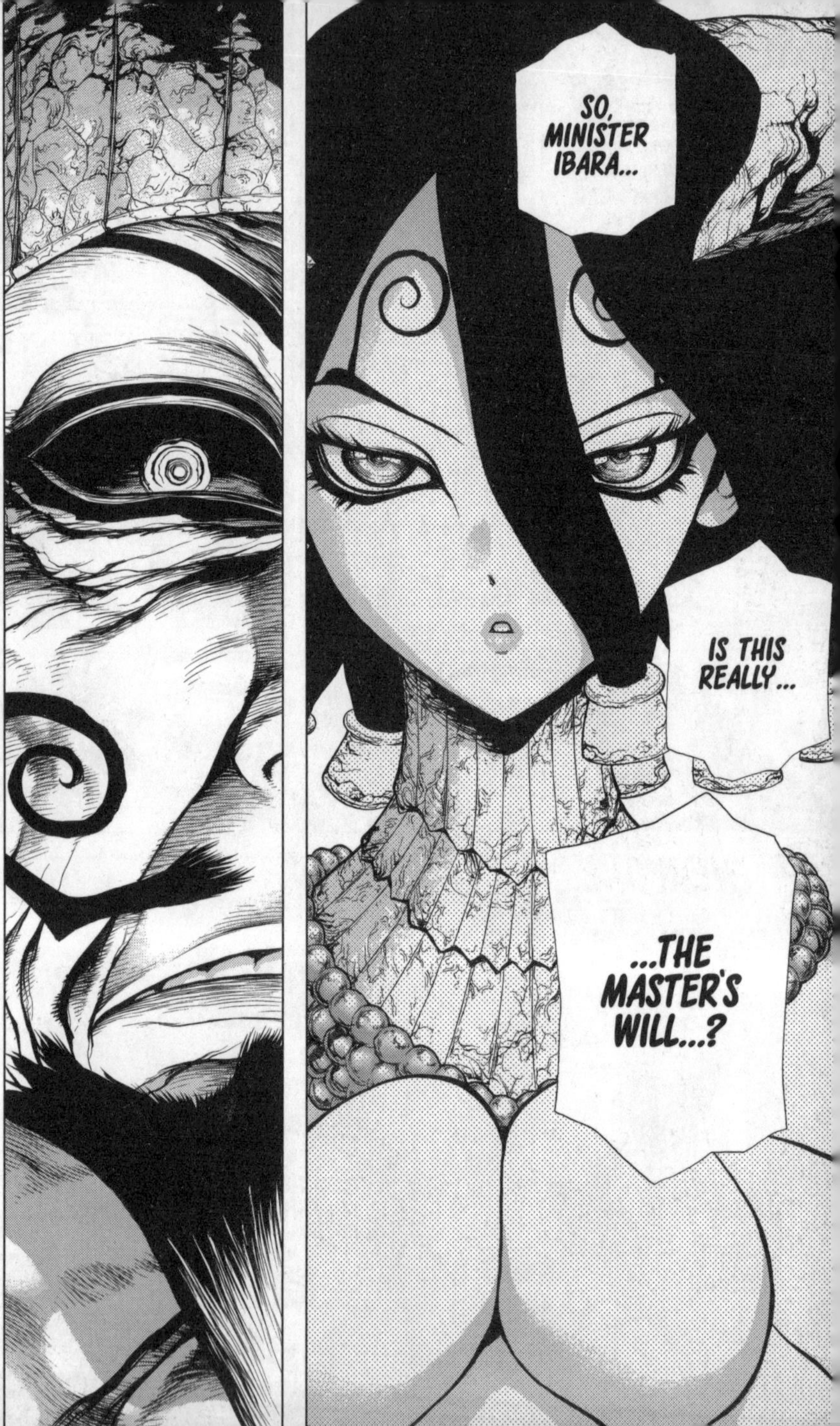
SO, MINISTER IBARA...
IS THIS REALLY...
...THE MASTER'S WILL...?

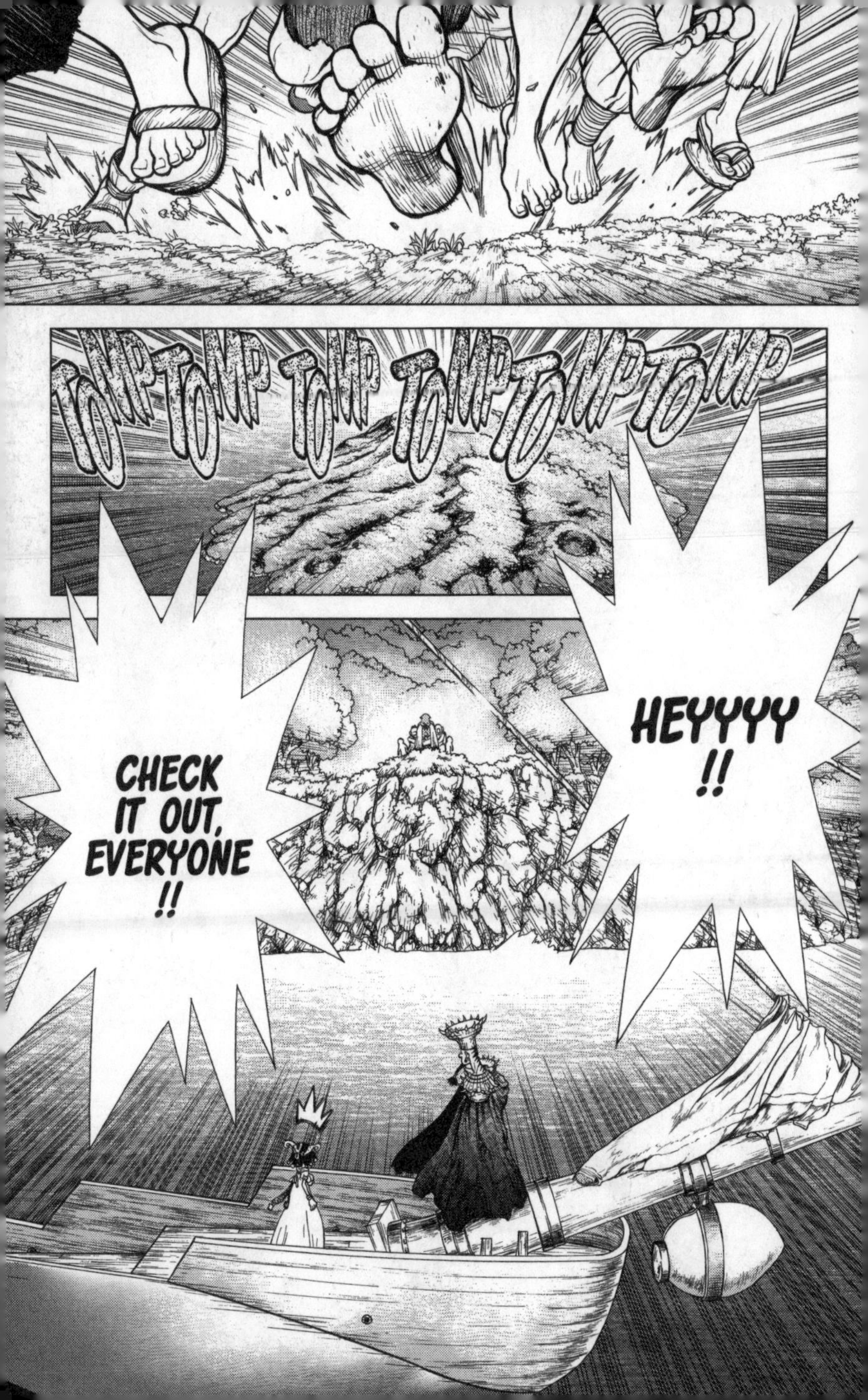
TOMP TOMP TOMP TOMP TOMP TOMP
HEYYYY!!
CHECK IT OUT, EVERYONE!!

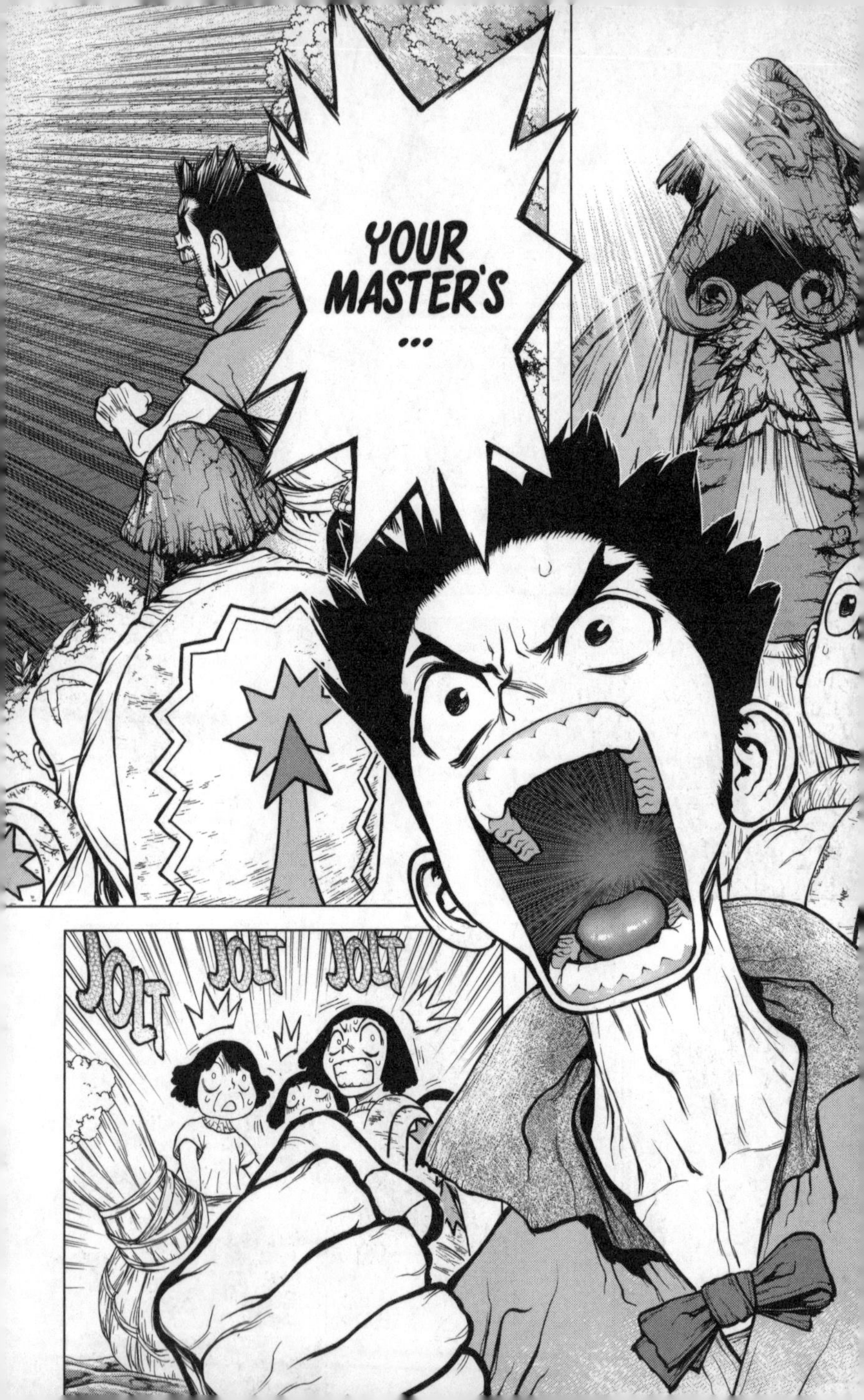
YOUR MASTER'S ...
JOLT JOLT JOLT

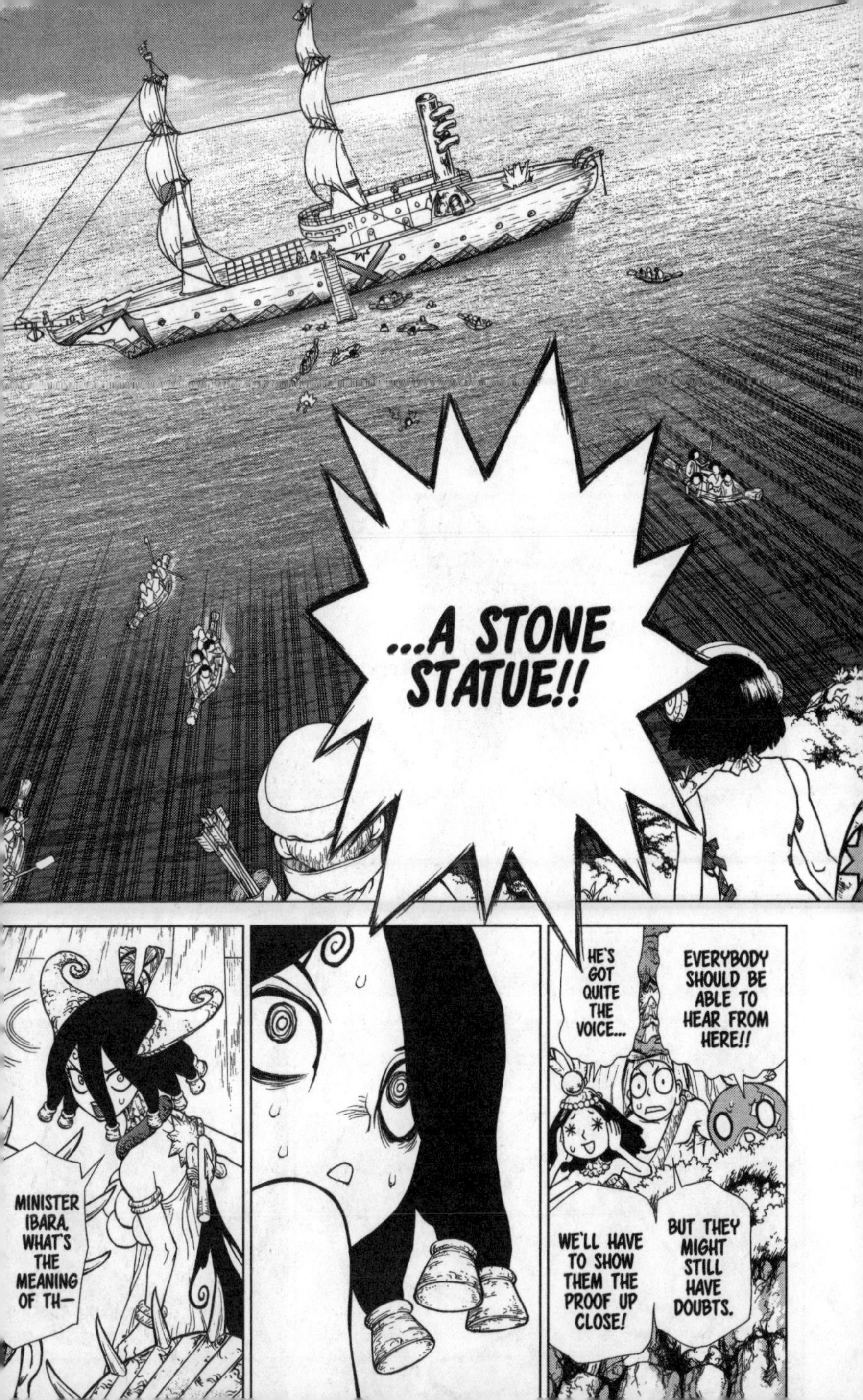
...A STONE STATUE!!
EVERYBODY SHOULD BE ABLE TO HEAR FROM HERE!!
HE'S GOT QUITE THE VOICE...
BUT THEY MIGHT STILL HAVE DOUBTS.
WE'LL HAVE TO SHOW THEM THE PROOF UP CLOSE!
MINISTER IBARA, WHAT'S THE MEANING OF TH—

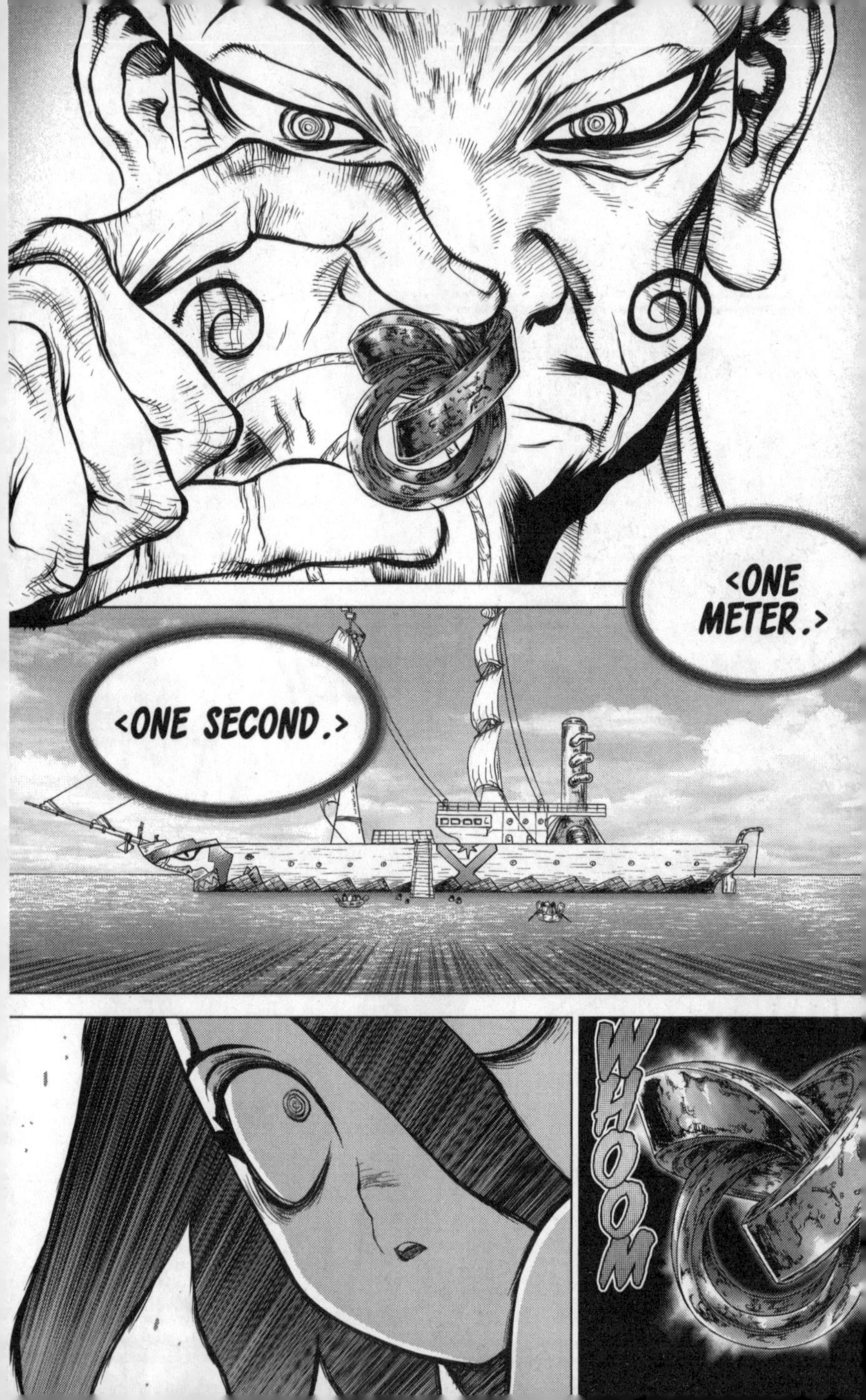
<ONE METER.>
<ONE SECOND.>
WHOOM

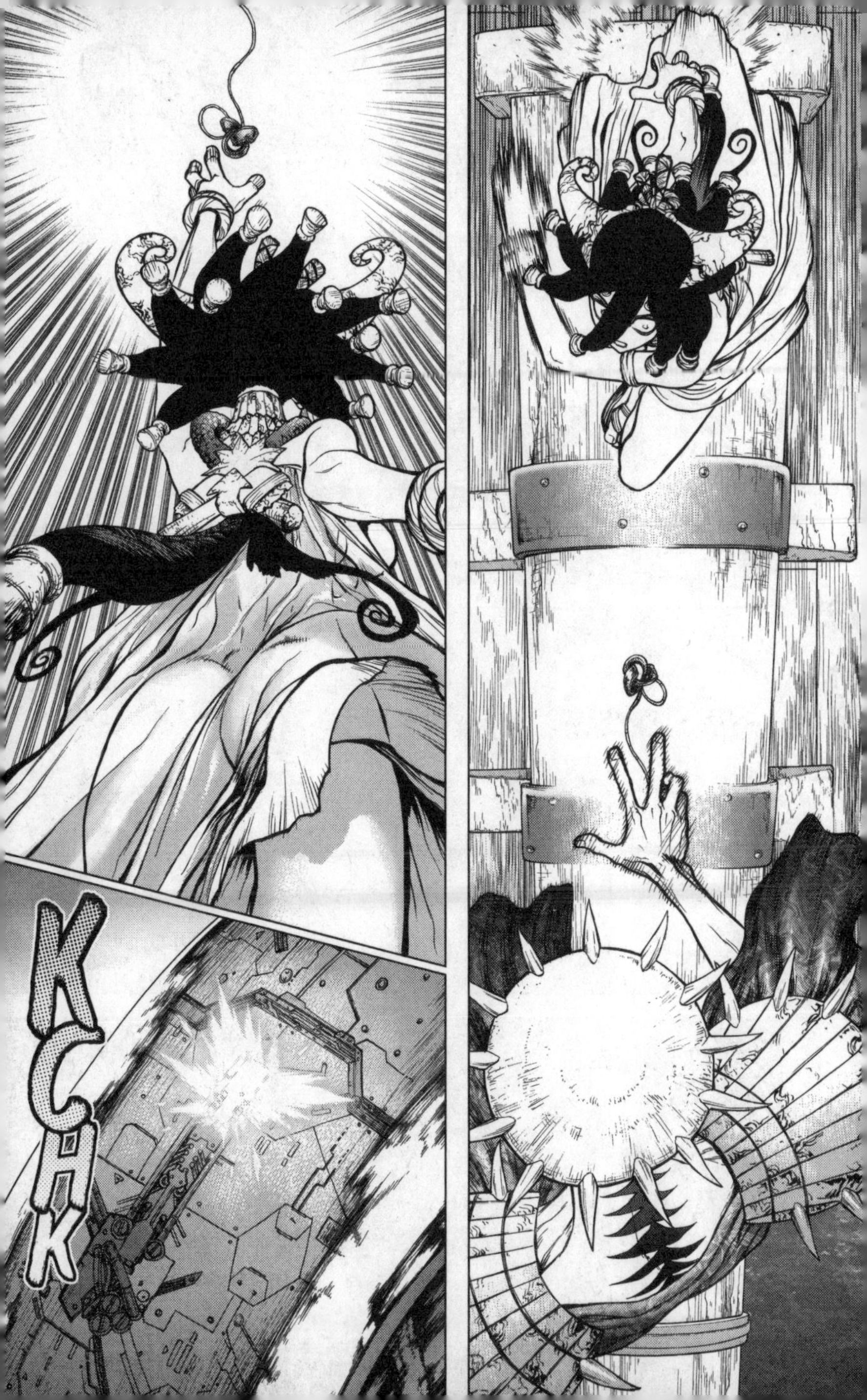
KCHK

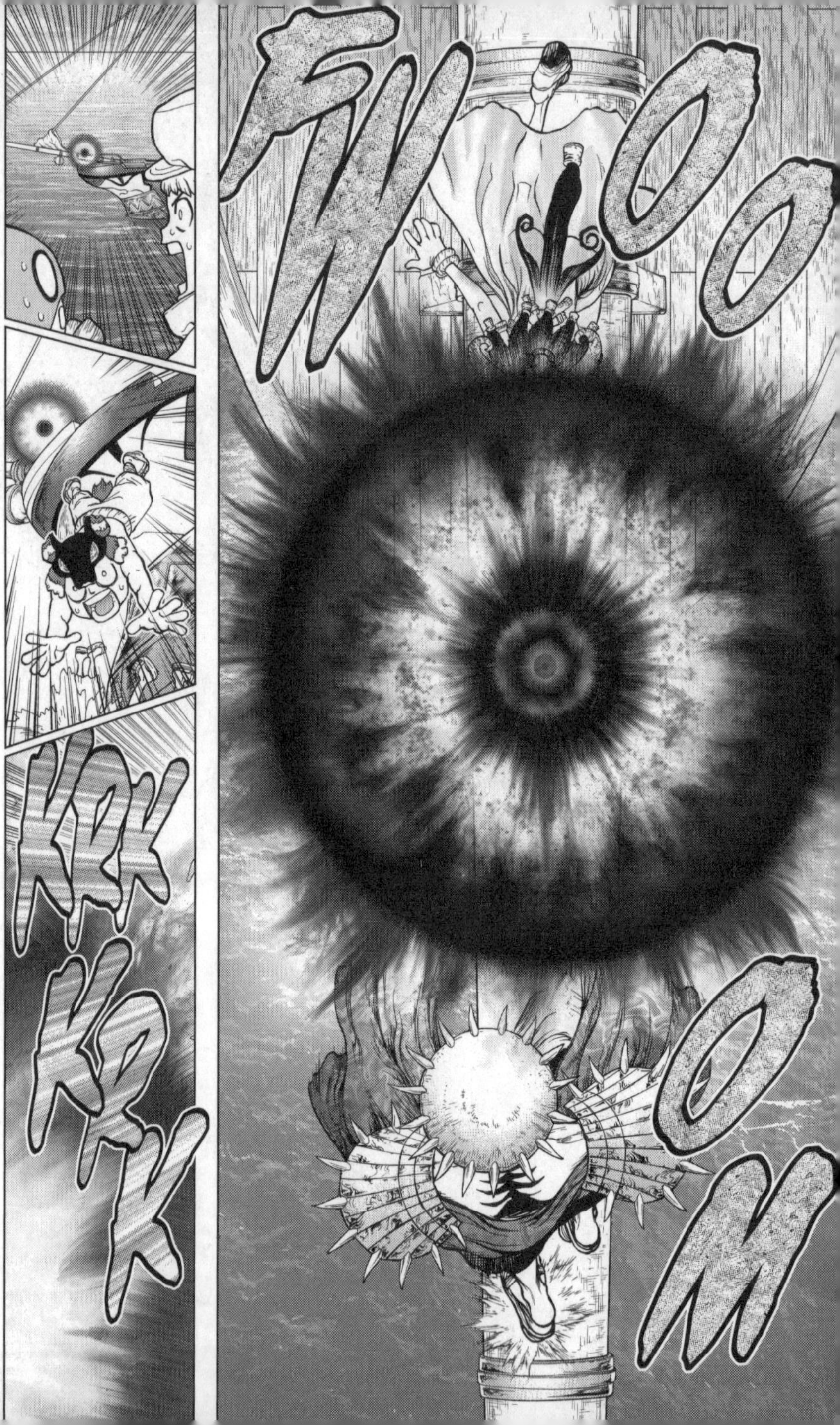
FWOOOOOM
KRK KRK

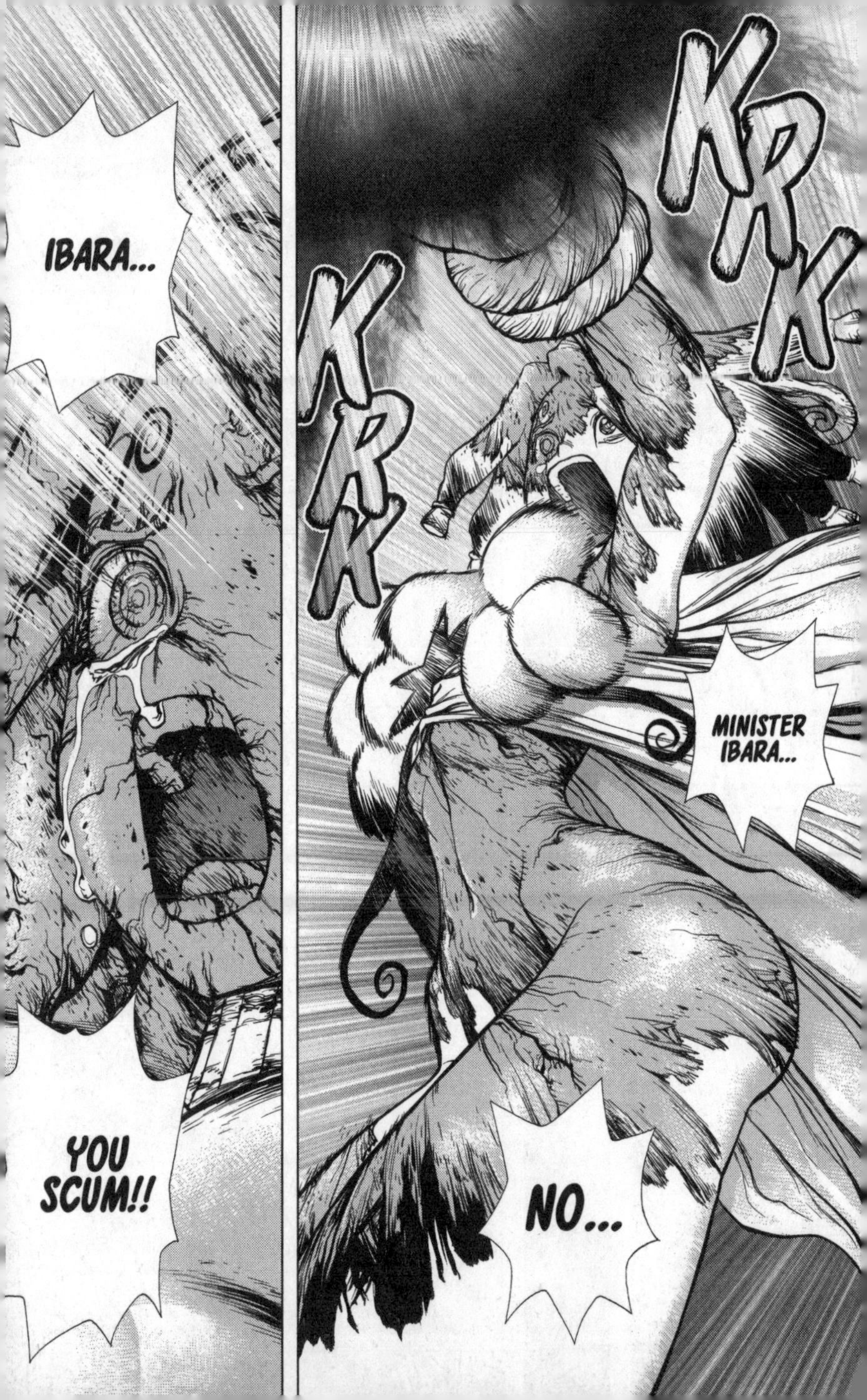
KRKK
KRKK
MINISTER IBARA...
NO...
IBARA...
YOU SCUM!!

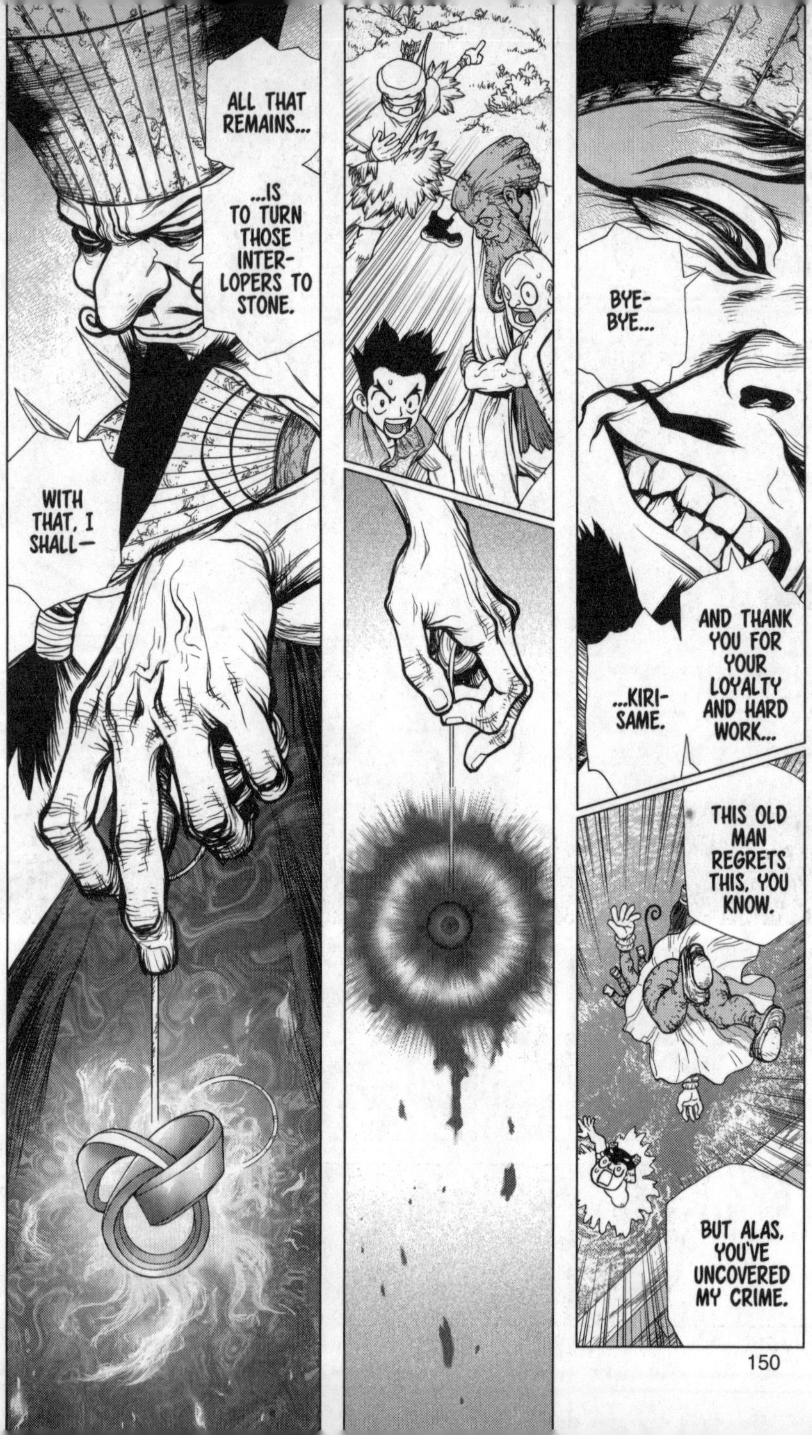
BYE-BYE...
AND THANK YOU FOR YOUR LOYALTY AND HARD WORK...
...KIRI-SAME.
THIS OLD MAN REGRETS THIS, YOU KNOW.
BUT ALAS, YOU'VE UNCOVERED MY CRIME.
ALL THAT REMAINS...
...IS TO TURN THOSE INTER-LOPERS TO STONE.
WITH THAT, I SHALL—

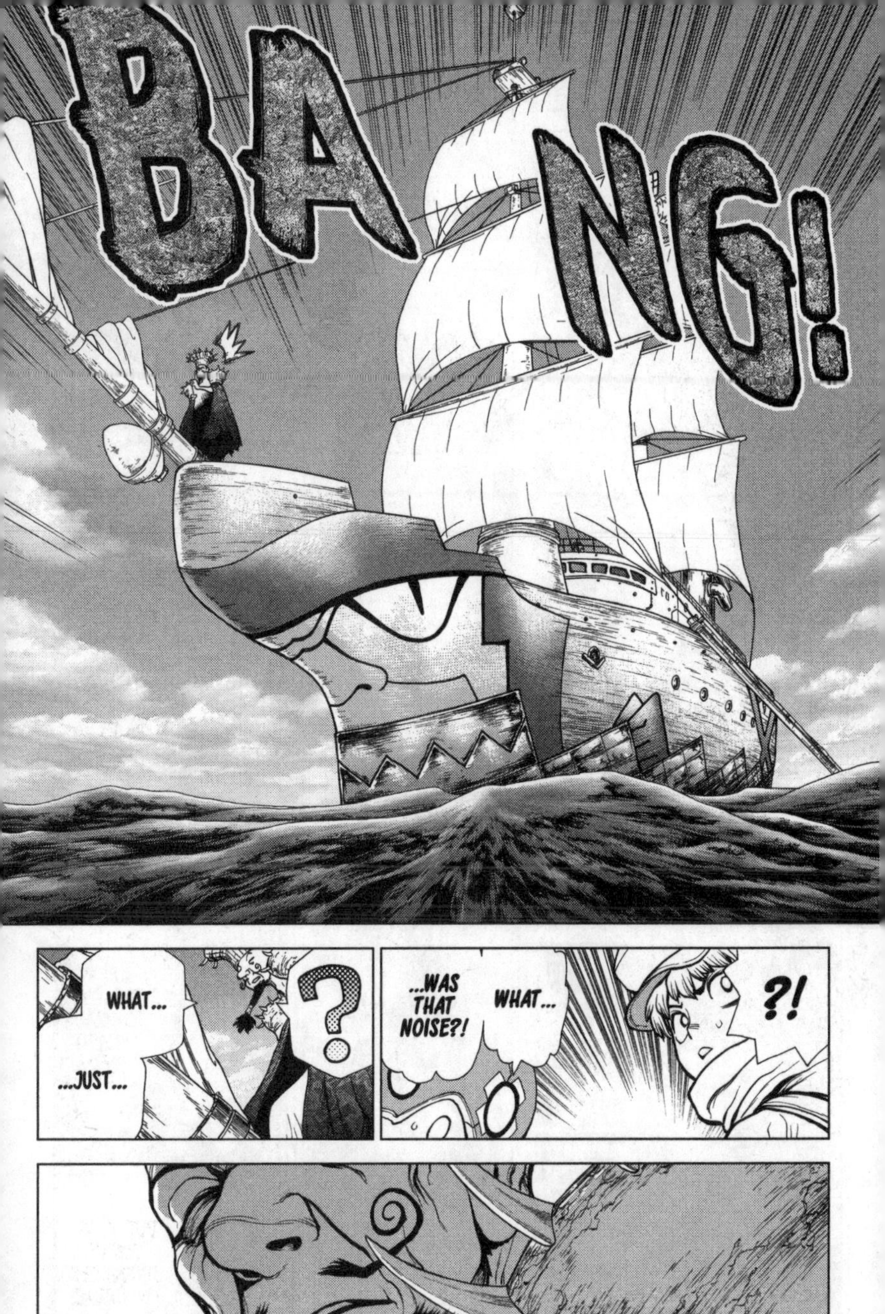
BANG!
WHAT...
...WAS THAT NOISE?!
?!
WHAT...
...JUST...
?

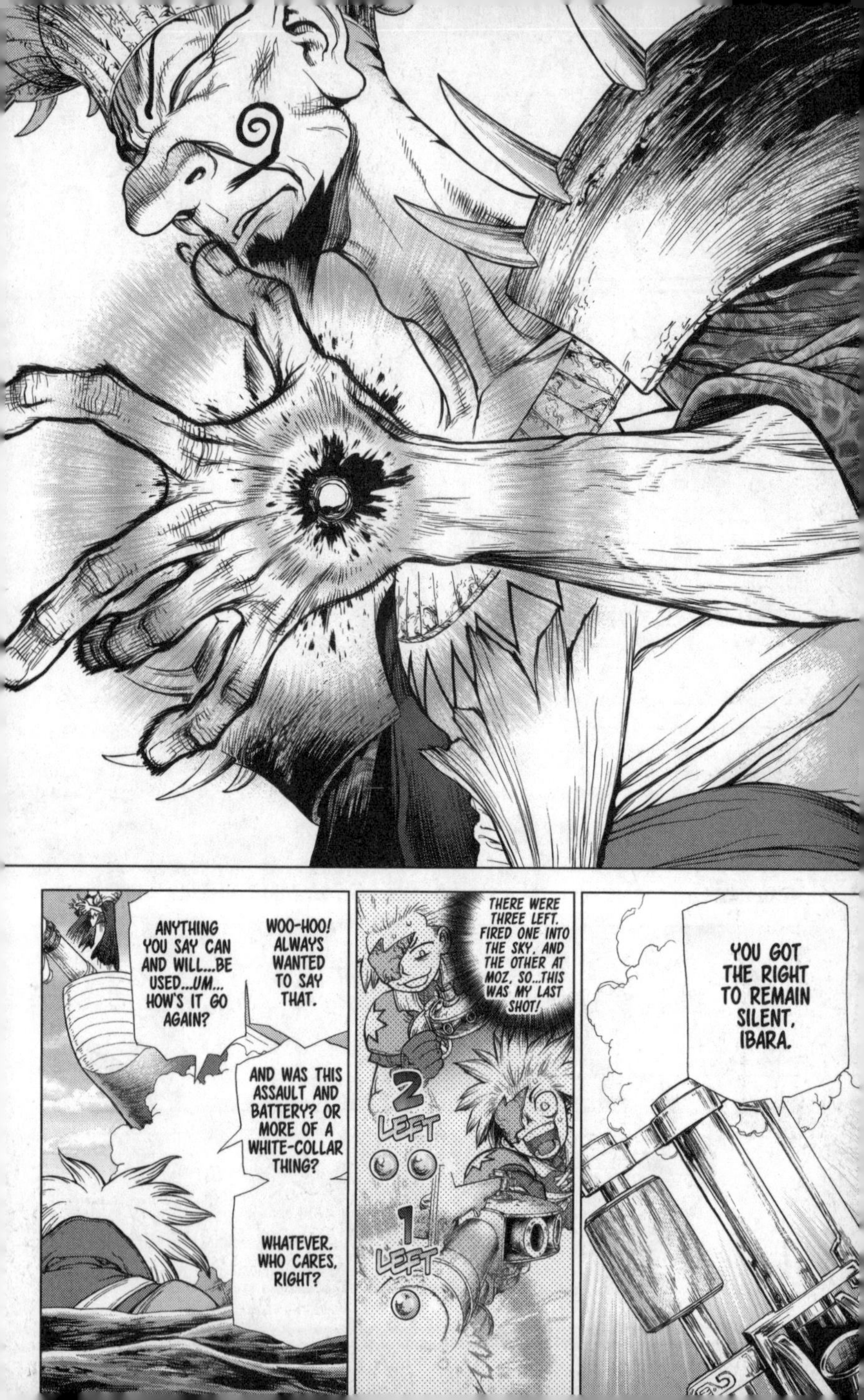
YOU GOT THE RIGHT TO REMAIN SILENT, IBARA.
THERE WERE THREE LEFT. FIRED ONE INTO THE SKY, AND THE OTHER AT MOZ, SO...THIS WAS MY LAST SHOT!
2 LEFT
1 LEFT
WOO-HOO! ALWAYS WANTED TO SAY THAT.
ANYTHING YOU SAY CAN AND WILL...BE USED...UM... HOW'S IT GO AGAIN?
AND WAS THIS ASSAULT AND BATTERY? OR MORE OF A WHITE-COLLAR THING?
WHATEVER. WHO CARES, RIGHT?

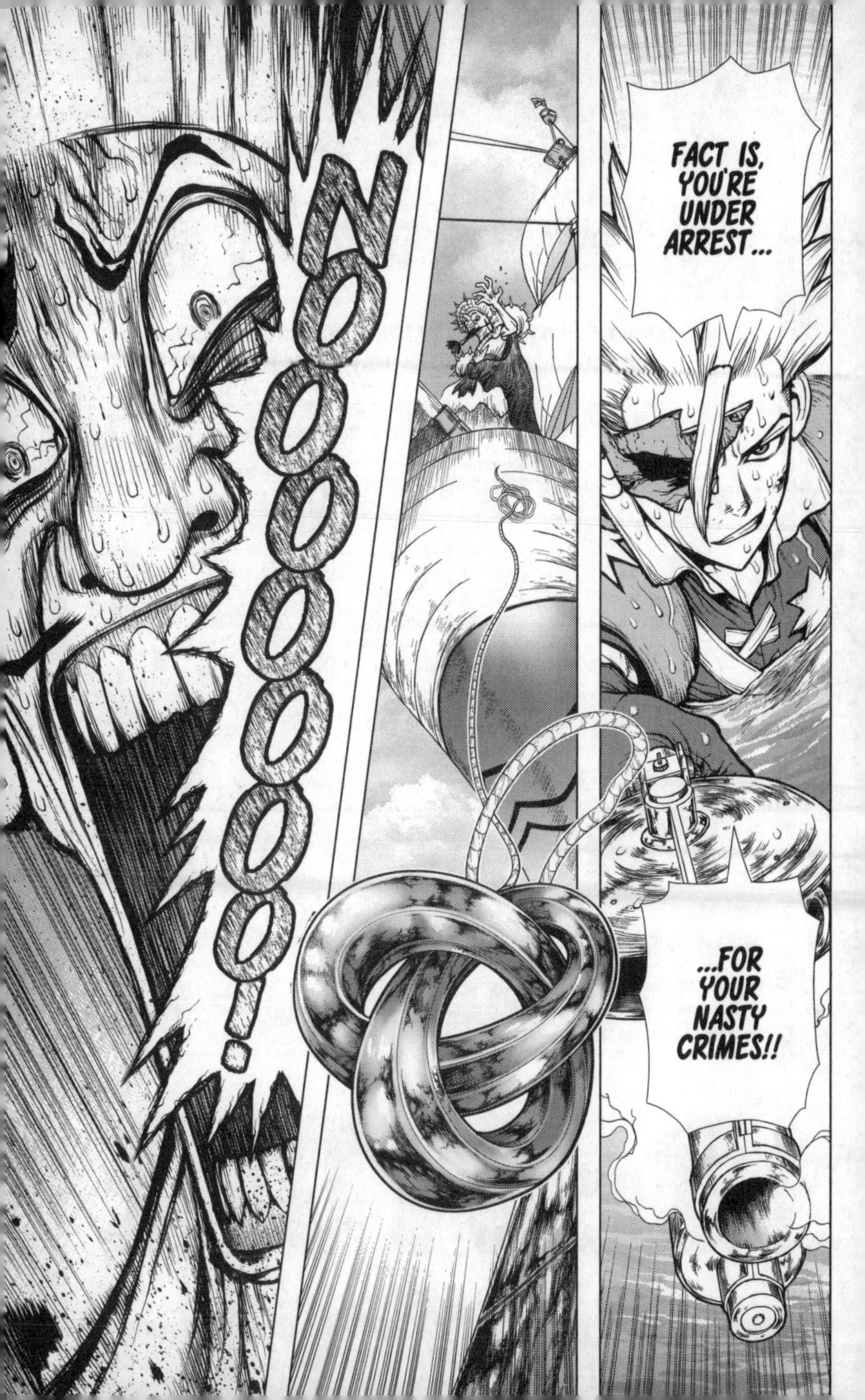
FACT IS, YOU'RE UNDER ARREST...
...FOR YOUR NASTY CRIMES!!
NOOOOOOOOOO!

# MECHA SENKU Q&A

**SEARCH**
Question Corner

Ibara has a type of girl he favors, but could Senku, Gen and Soyuz in drag have met his standards?

Kosei Omori from Iwate Prefecture **SEARCH**

**NOPE!!**

**HM? THE TWO ON THE RIGHT AREN'T BAD... WAIT. NOPE!!**

| Science Questions | How does one make gasoline out of plastic bottle caps? |
| Character Questions | If Taiju and Tsukasa really fought, who would win? |
| Questions That Aren't Really Questions | I wanna get petrified and challenge myself to count the seconds... |

Now accepting any and all queries! Submit ten billion questions to me!

My name is **MECHA SENKU!!**

**WHRRR KLANG**

# Dr. STONE

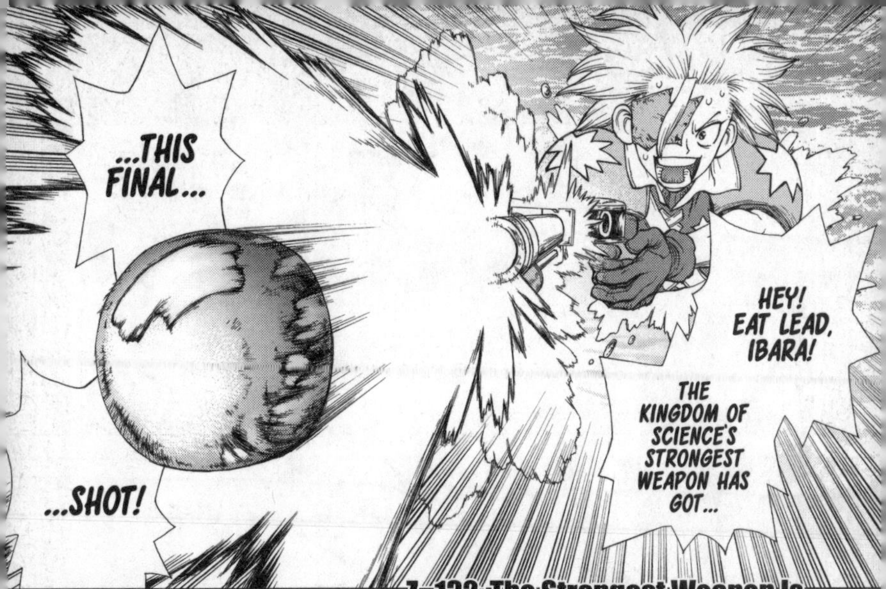
HEY! EAT LEAD, IBARA!
THE KINGDOM OF SCIENCE'S STRONGEST WEAPON HAS GOT...
...THIS FINAL...
...SHOT!

## Z=132: The Strongest Weapon Is...

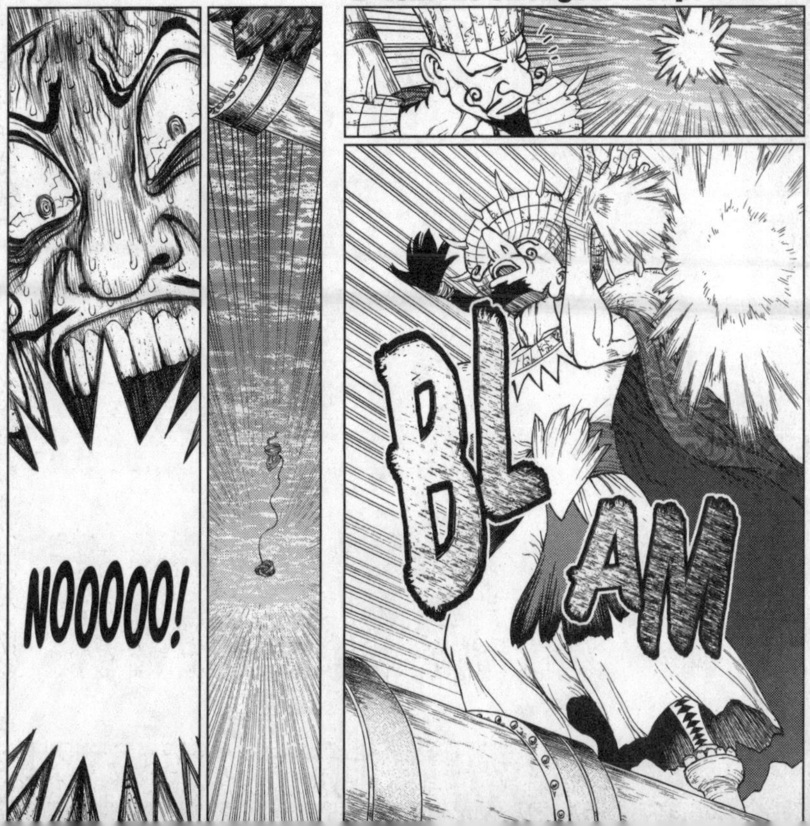
BLAM
NOOOOO!

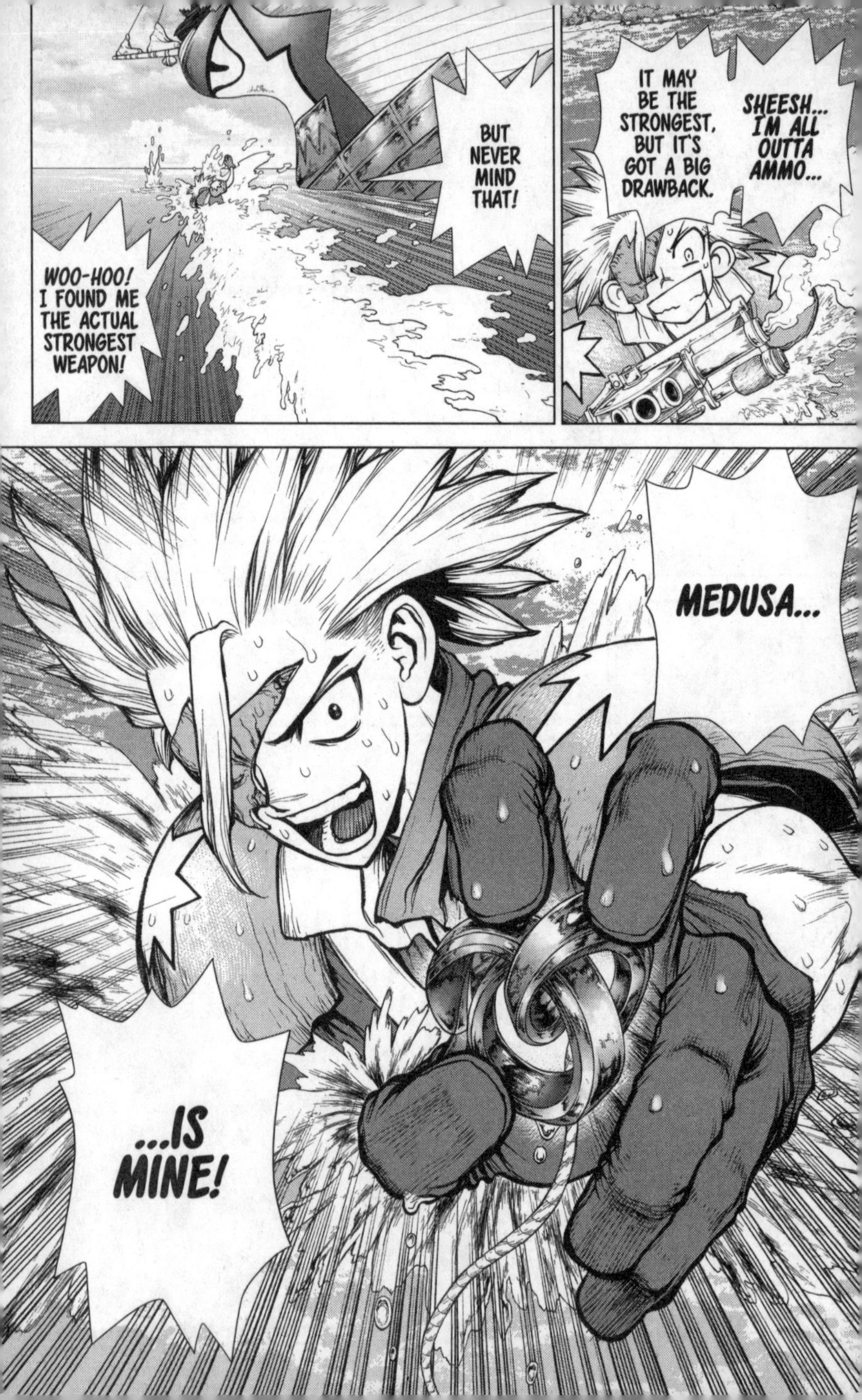
SHEESH... I'M ALL OUTTA AMMO...
IT MAY BE THE STRONGEST, BUT IT'S GOT A BIG DRAWBACK.
BUT NEVER MIND THAT!
WOO-HOO! I FOUND ME THE ACTUAL STRONGEST WEAPON!
MEDUSA...
...IS MINE!

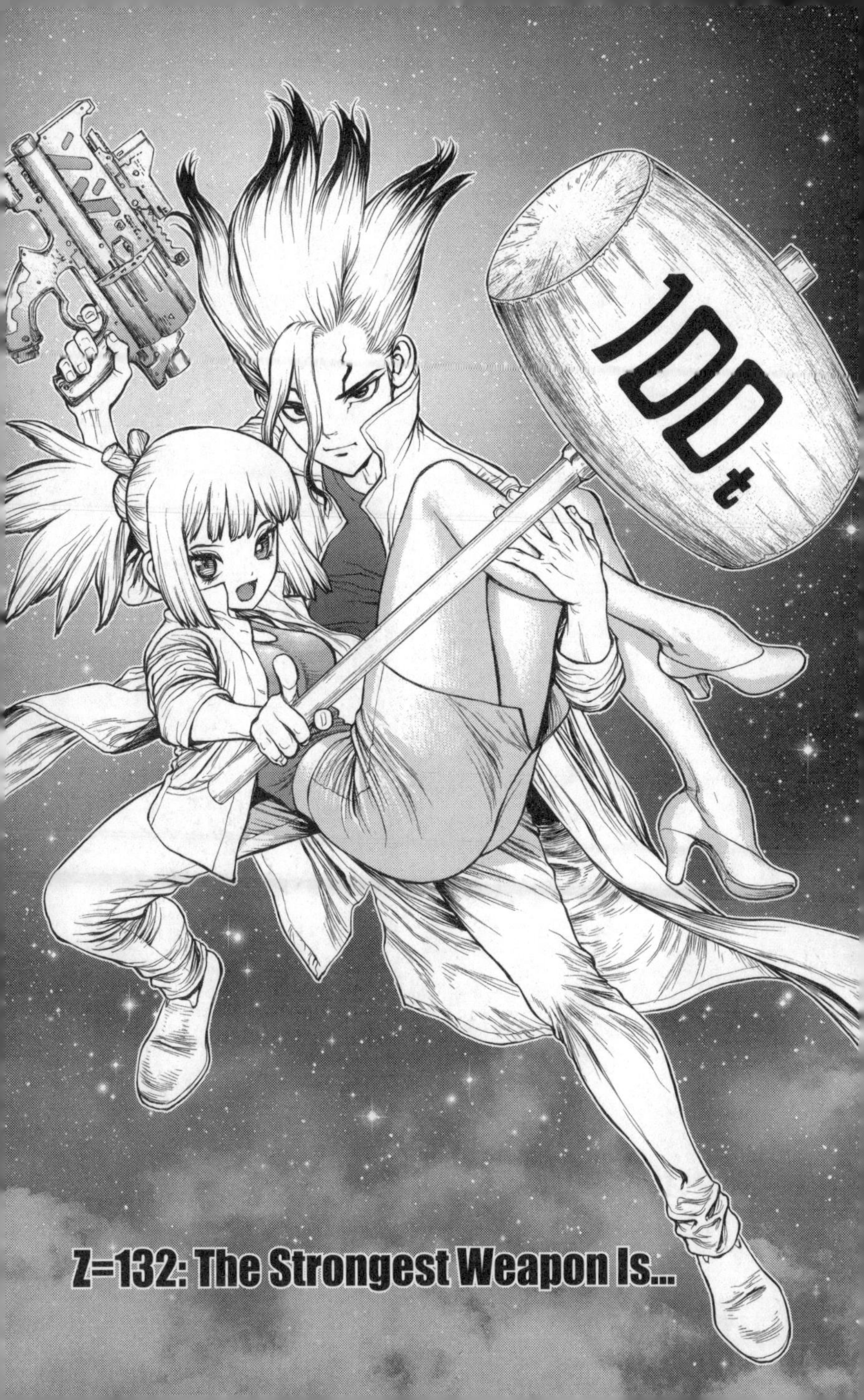
100t
Z=132: The Strongest Weapon Is...

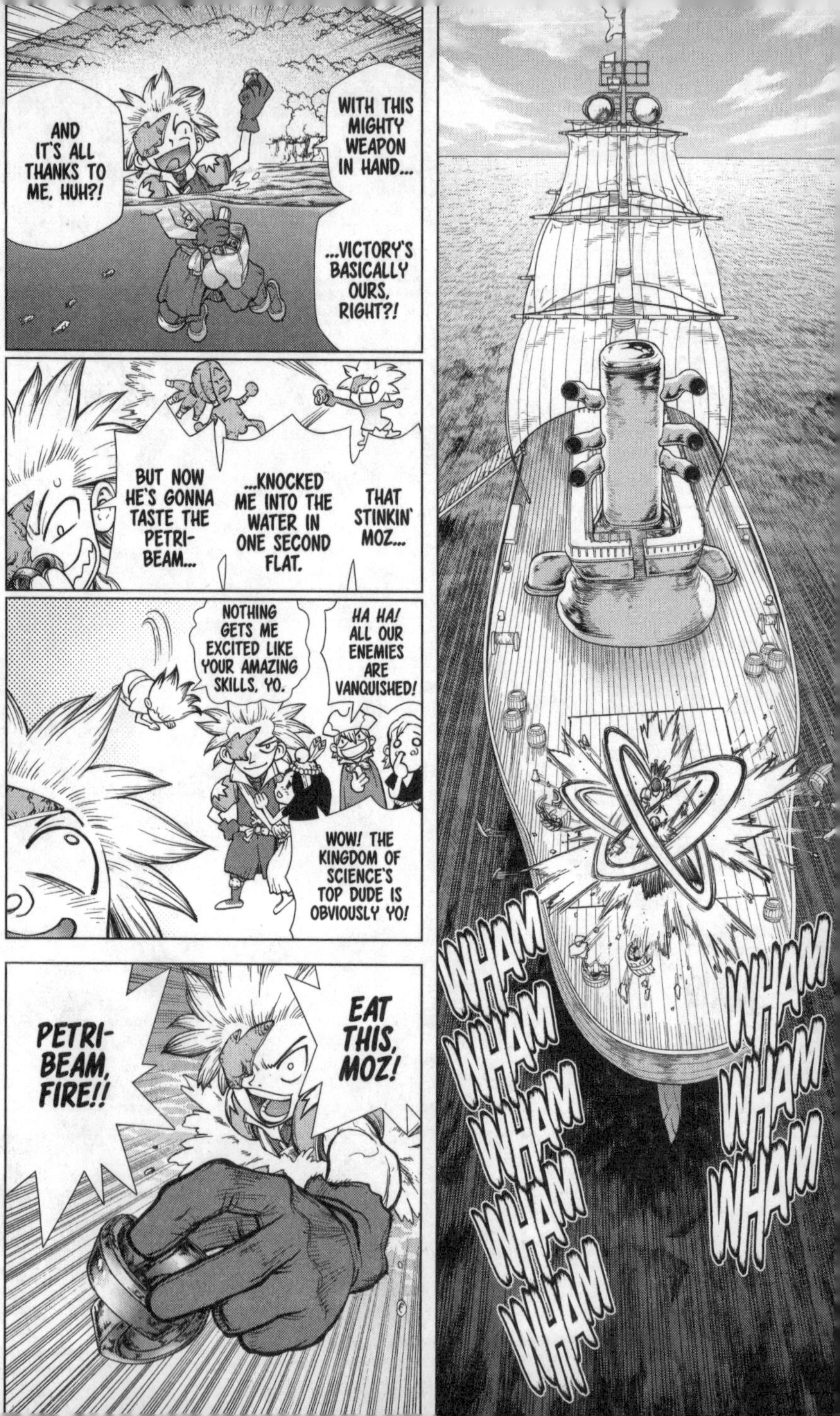
WHAM WHAM WHAM WHAM
WHAM WHAM WHAM WHAM WHAM WHAM
WITH THIS MIGHTY WEAPON IN HAND...
...VICTORY'S BASICALLY OURS, RIGHT?!
AND IT'S ALL THANKS TO ME, HUH?!
THAT STINKIN' MOZ...
...KNOCKED ME INTO THE WATER IN ONE SECOND FLAT.
BUT NOW HE'S GONNA TASTE THE PETRI-BEAM...
HA HA! ALL OUR ENEMIES ARE VANQUISHED!
NOTHING GETS ME EXCITED LIKE YOUR AMAZING SKILLS, YO.
WOW! THE KINGDOM OF SCIENCE'S TOP DUDE IS OBVIOUSLY YO!
EAT THIS, MOZ!
PETRI-BEAM, FIRE!!

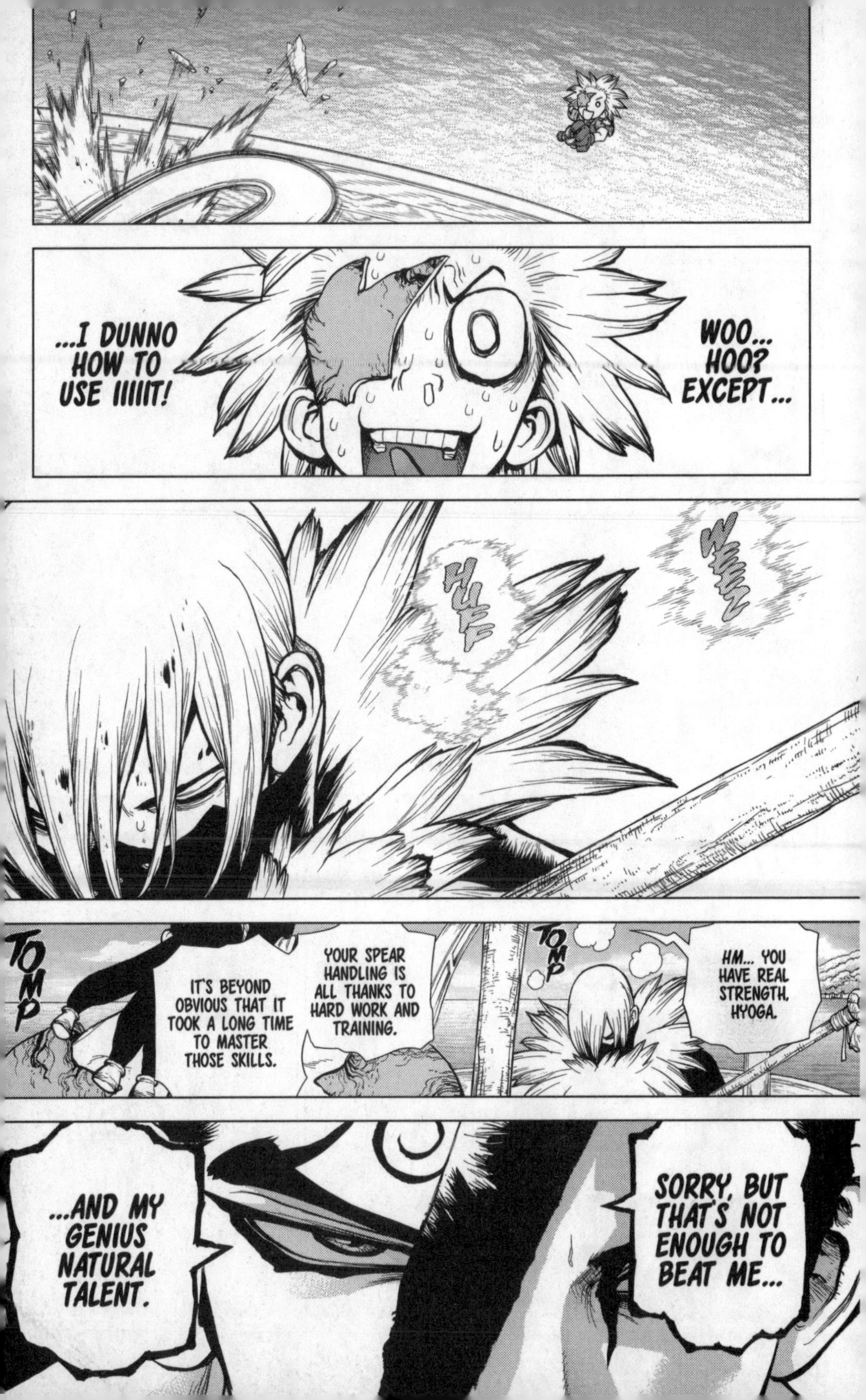
WOO... HOO? EXCEPT...
...I DUNNO HOW TO USE IIIIIIT!
WHEW
HUFF
HM... YOU HAVE REAL STRENGTH, HYOGA.
TOMP
YOUR SPEAR HANDLING IS ALL THANKS TO HARD WORK AND TRAINING.
IT'S BEYOND OBVIOUS THAT IT TOOK A LONG TIME TO MASTER THOSE SKILLS.
TOMP
SORRY, BUT THAT'S NOT ENOUGH TO BEAT ME...
...AND MY GENIUS NATURAL TALENT.

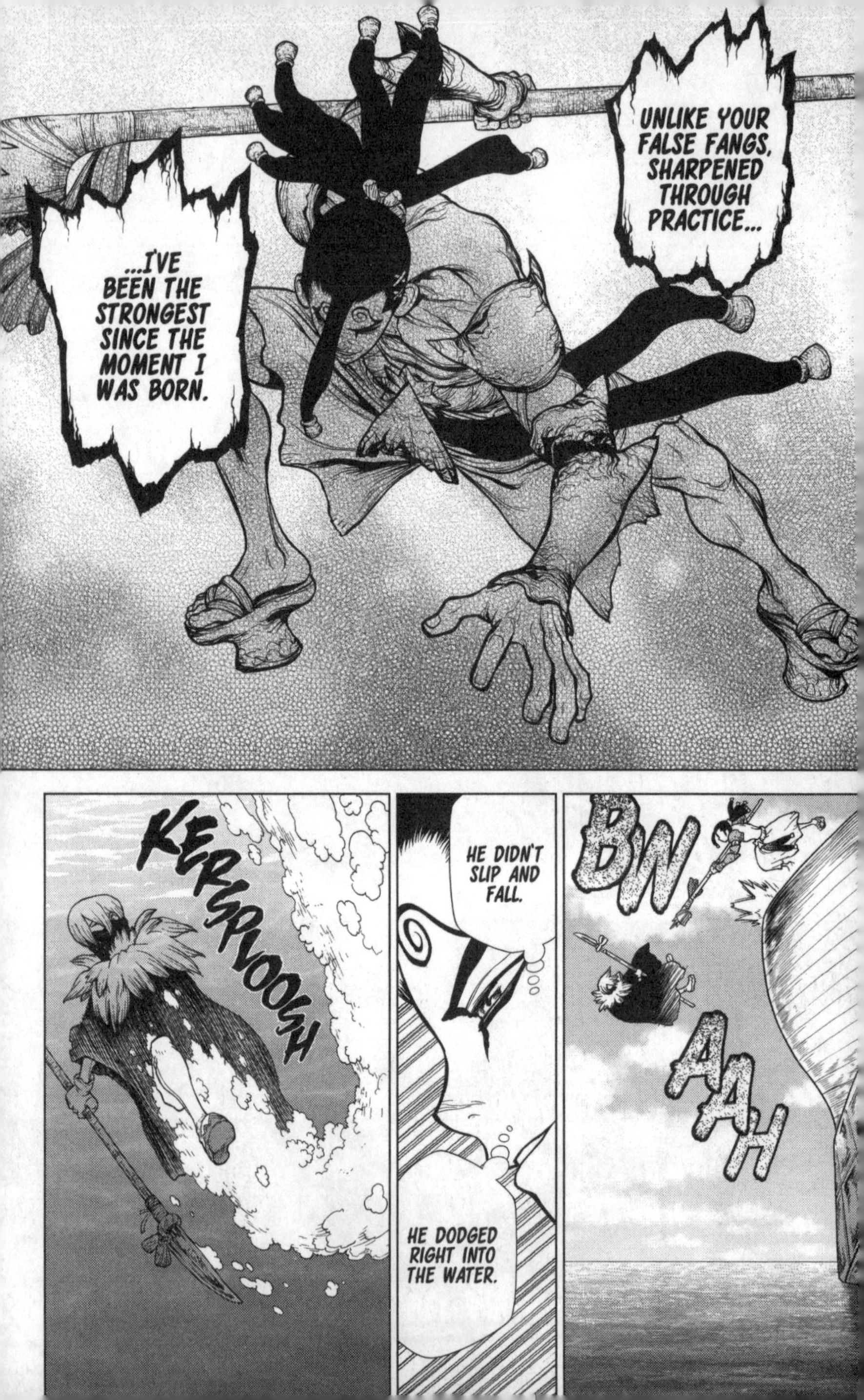
UNLIKE YOUR FALSE FANGS, SHARPENED THROUGH PRACTICE...
...I'VE BEEN THE STRONGEST SINCE THE MOMENT I WAS BORN.
BWAAH
HE DIDN'T SLIP AND FALL.
HE DODGED RIGHT INTO THE WATER.
KERSPLOOOSH

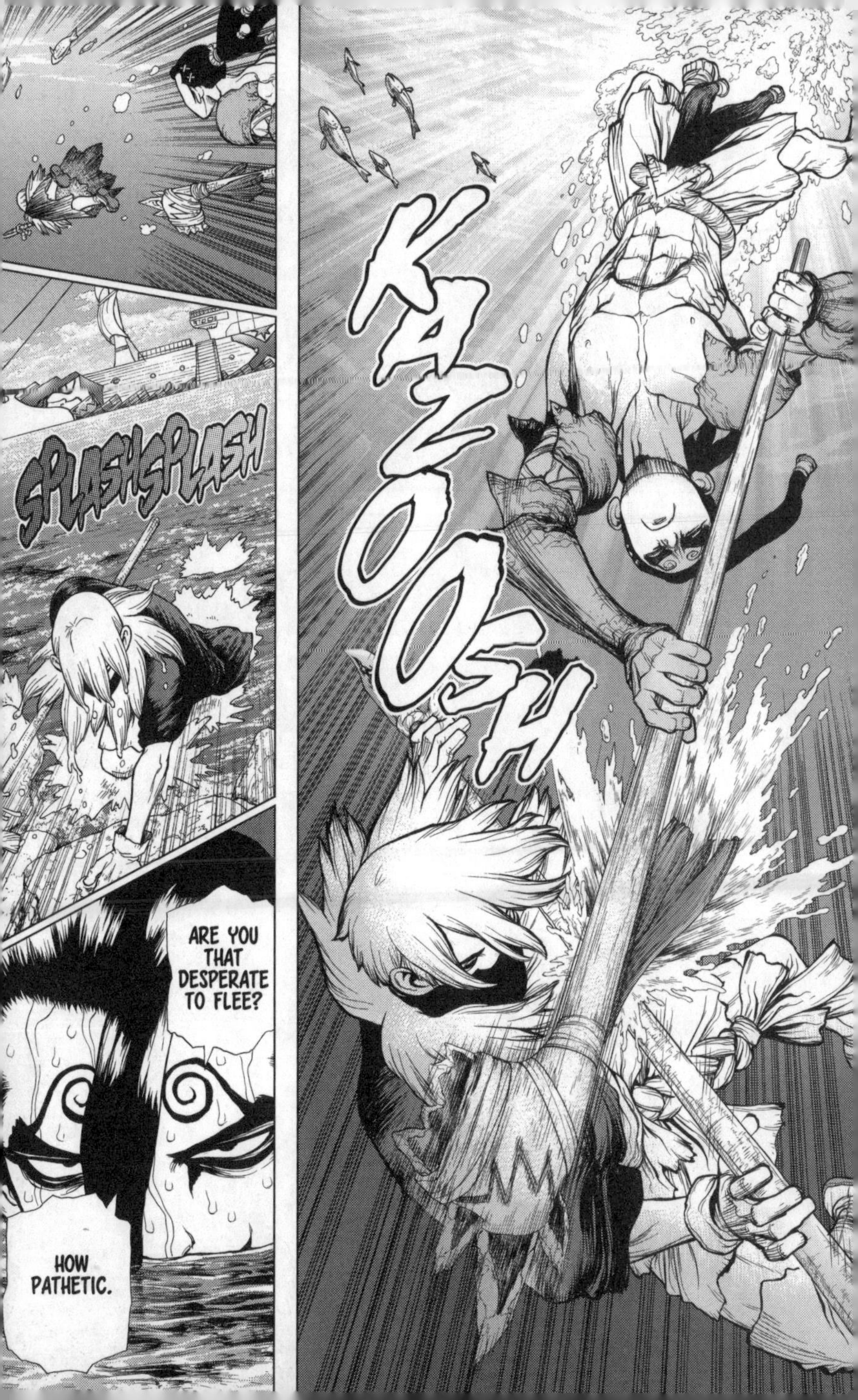
KAZOOSH
SPLASHSPLASH
ARE YOU THAT DESPERATE TO FLEE?
HOW PATHETIC.

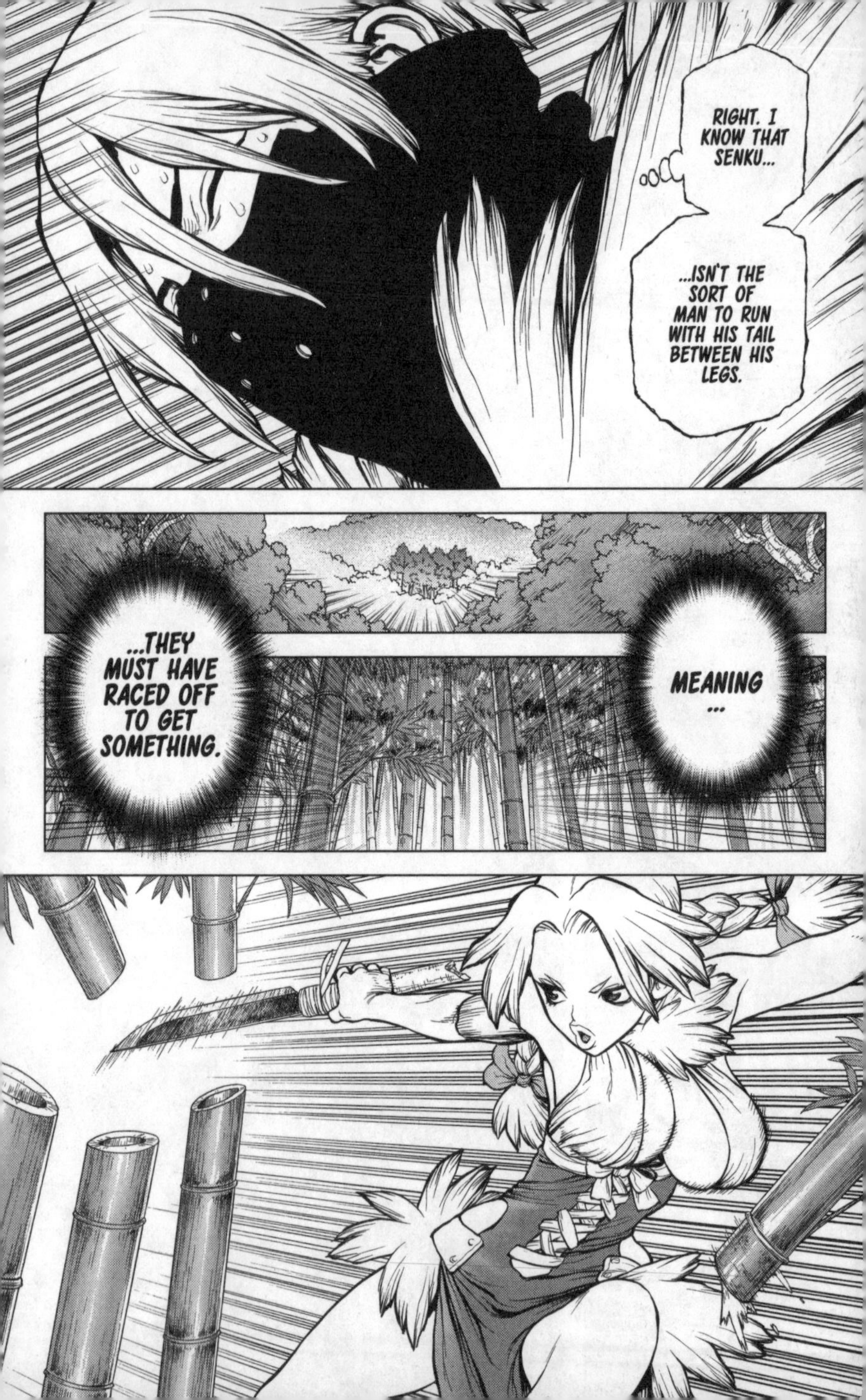
RIGHT. I KNOW THAT SENKU...
...ISN'T THE SORT OF MAN TO RUN WITH HIS TAIL BETWEEN HIS LEGS.
MEANING ...
...THEY MUST HAVE RACED OFF TO GET SOMETHING.

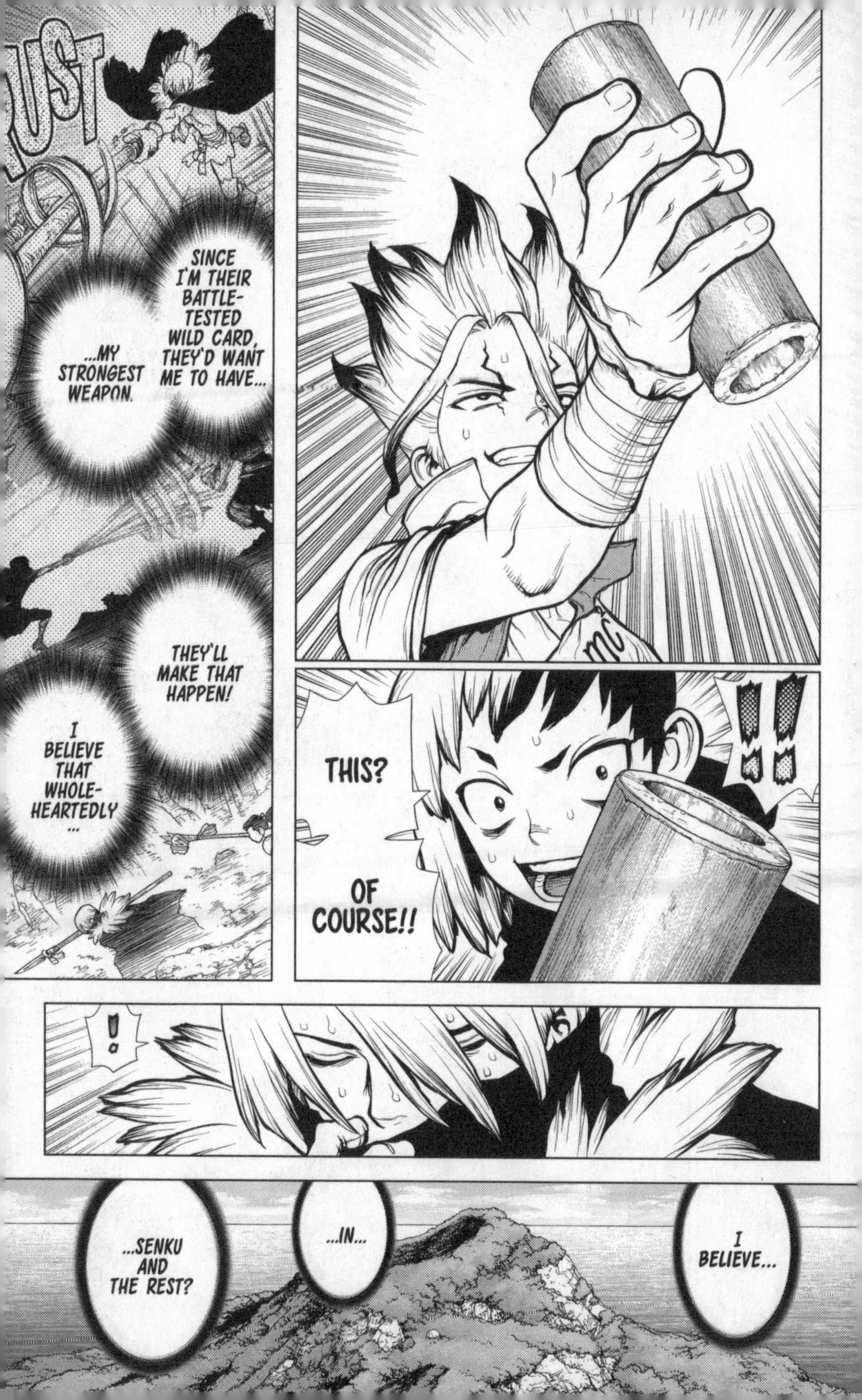

!!
THIS?
OF COURSE!!
RUST
SINCE I'M THEIR BATTLE-TESTED WILD CARD, THEY'D WANT ME TO HAVE...
...MY STRONGEST WEAPON.
THEY'LL MAKE THAT HAPPEN!
I BELIEVE THAT WHOLE-HEARTEDLY...
!
I BELIEVE...
...IN...
...SENKU AND THE REST?

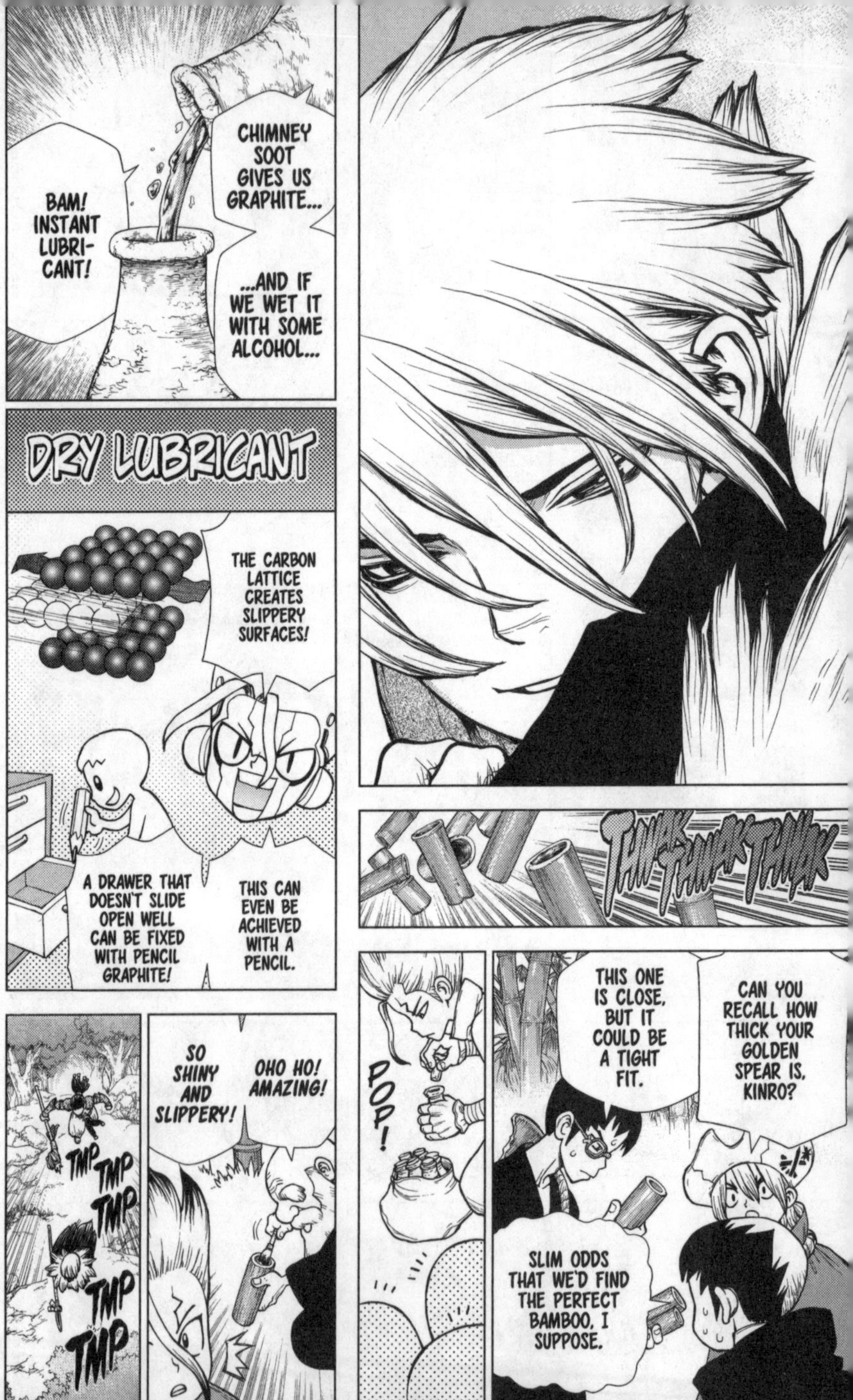
THWAK THWAK THWAK
CAN YOU RECALL HOW THICK YOUR GOLDEN SPEAR IS, KINRO?
THIS ONE IS CLOSE, BUT IT COULD BE A TIGHT FIT.
SLIM ODDS THAT WE'D FIND THE PERFECT BAMBOO, I SUPPOSE.
POP!
CHIMNEY SOOT GIVES US GRAPHITE...
...AND IF WE WET IT WITH SOME ALCOHOL...
BAM! INSTANT LUBRICANT!
DRY LUBRICANT
THE CARBON LATTICE CREATES SLIPPERY SURFACES!
THIS CAN EVEN BE ACHIEVED WITH A PENCIL.
A DRAWER THAT DOESN'T SLIDE OPEN WELL CAN BE FIXED WITH PENCIL GRAPHITE!
OHO HO! AMAZING!
SO SHINY AND SLIPPERY!
TMP TMP TMP TMP TMP

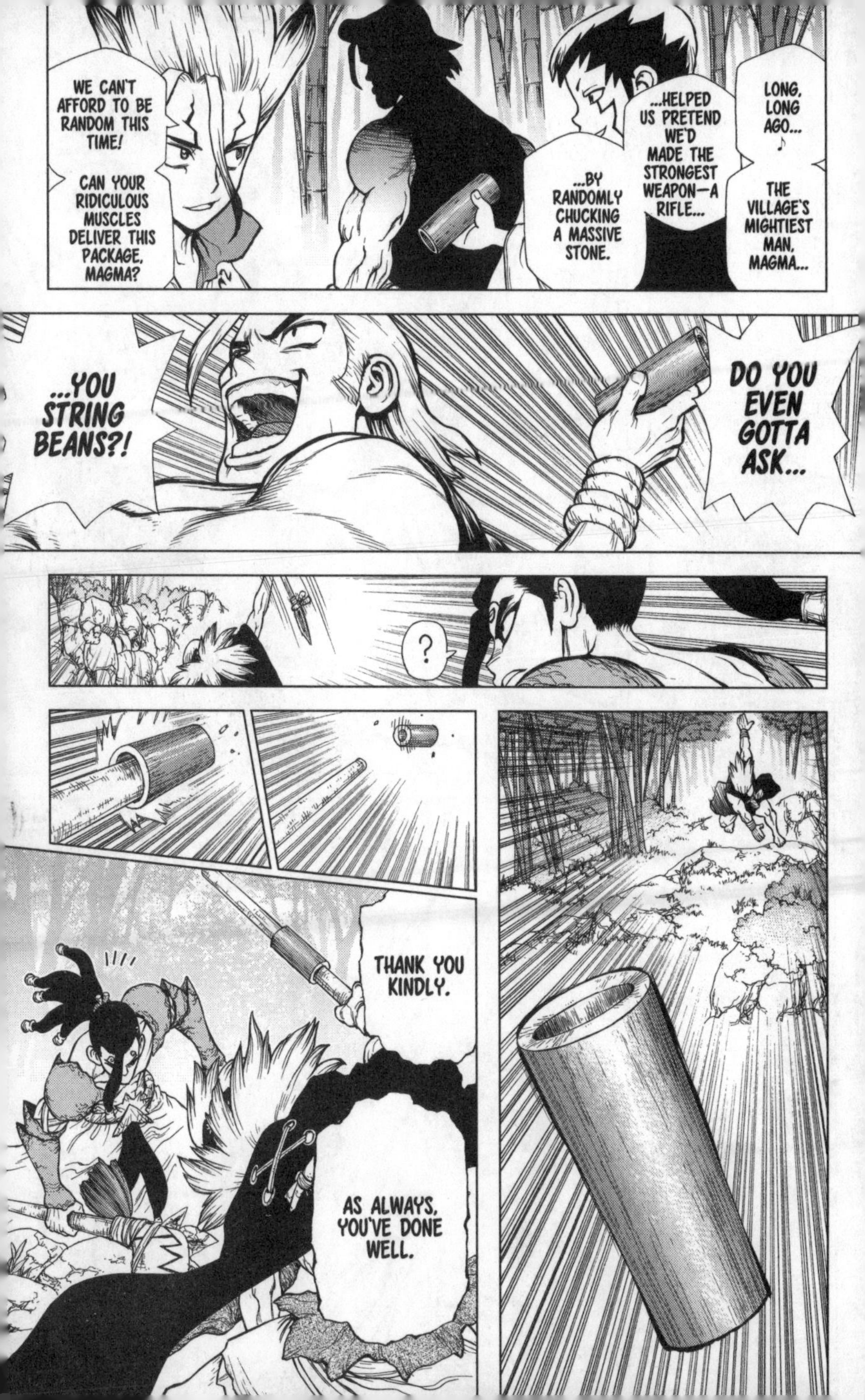
LONG, LONG AGO... ♪
THE VILLAGE'S MIGHTIEST MAN, MAGMA...
...HELPED US PRETEND WE'D MADE THE STRONGEST WEAPON—A RIFLE...
...BY RANDOMLY CHUCKING A MASSIVE STONE.
WE CAN'T AFFORD TO BE RANDOM THIS TIME!
CAN YOUR RIDICULOUS MUSCLES DELIVER THIS PACKAGE, MAGMA?
DO YOU EVEN GOTTA ASK...
...YOU STRING BEANS?!
?
THANK YOU KINDLY.
AS ALWAYS, YOU'VE DONE WELL.

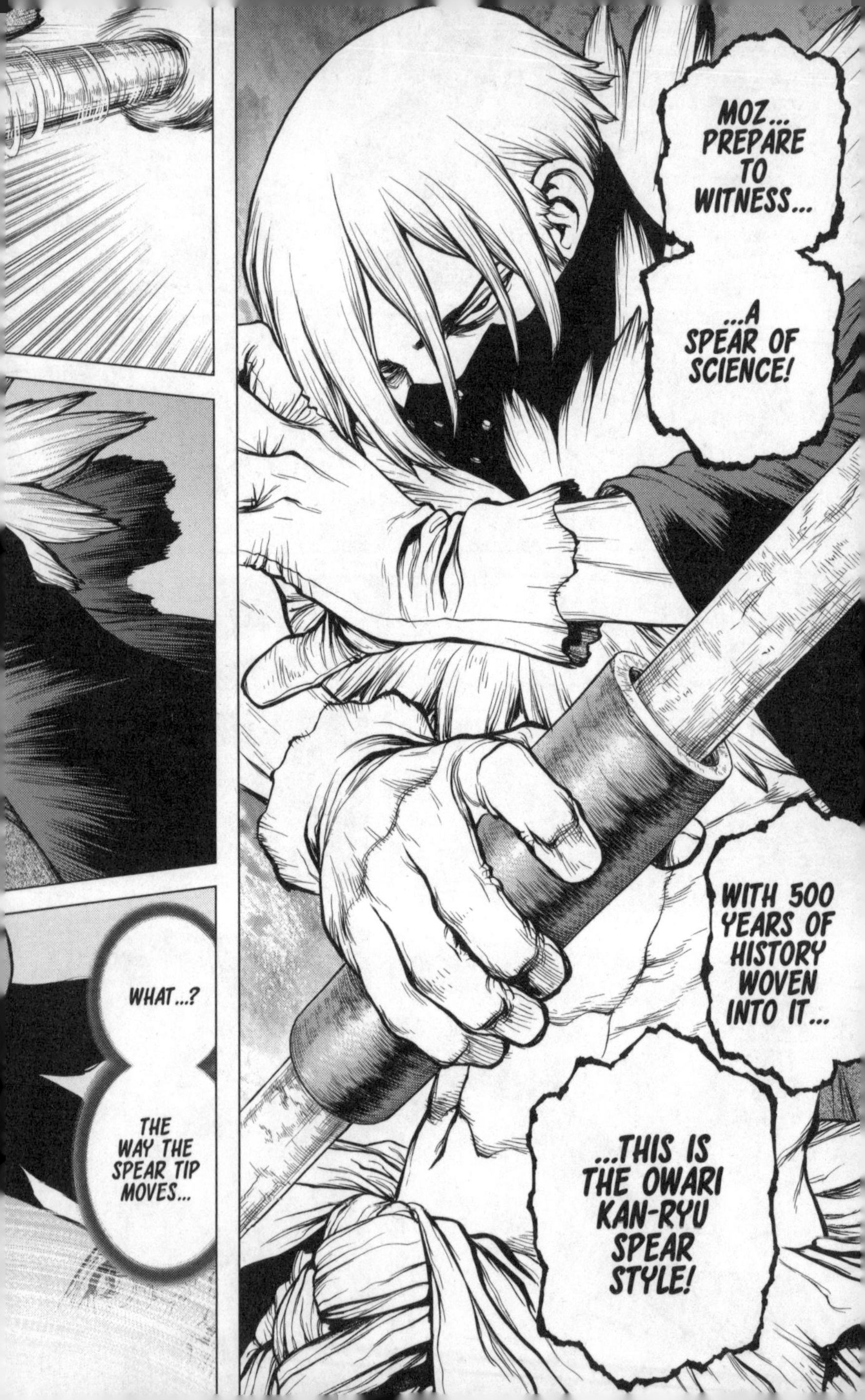
MOZ... PREPARE TO WITNESS...
...A SPEAR OF SCIENCE!
WITH 500 YEARS OF HISTORY WOVEN INTO IT...
...THIS IS THE OWARI KAN-RYU SPEAR STYLE!
WHAT...?
THE WAY THE SPEAR TIP MOVES...

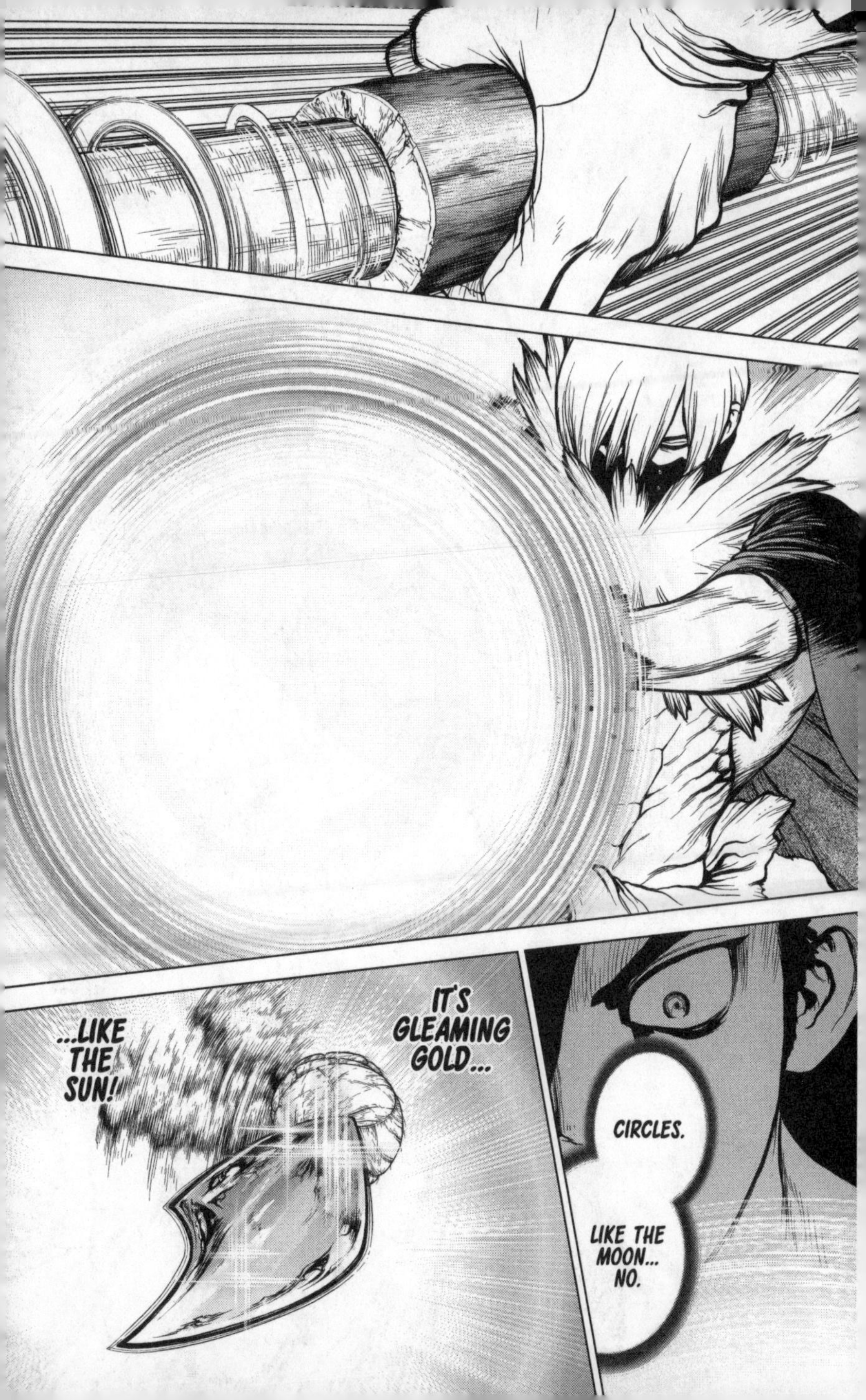
CIRCLES.
LIKE THE MOON... NO.
IT'S GLEAMING GOLD...
...LIKE THE SUN!

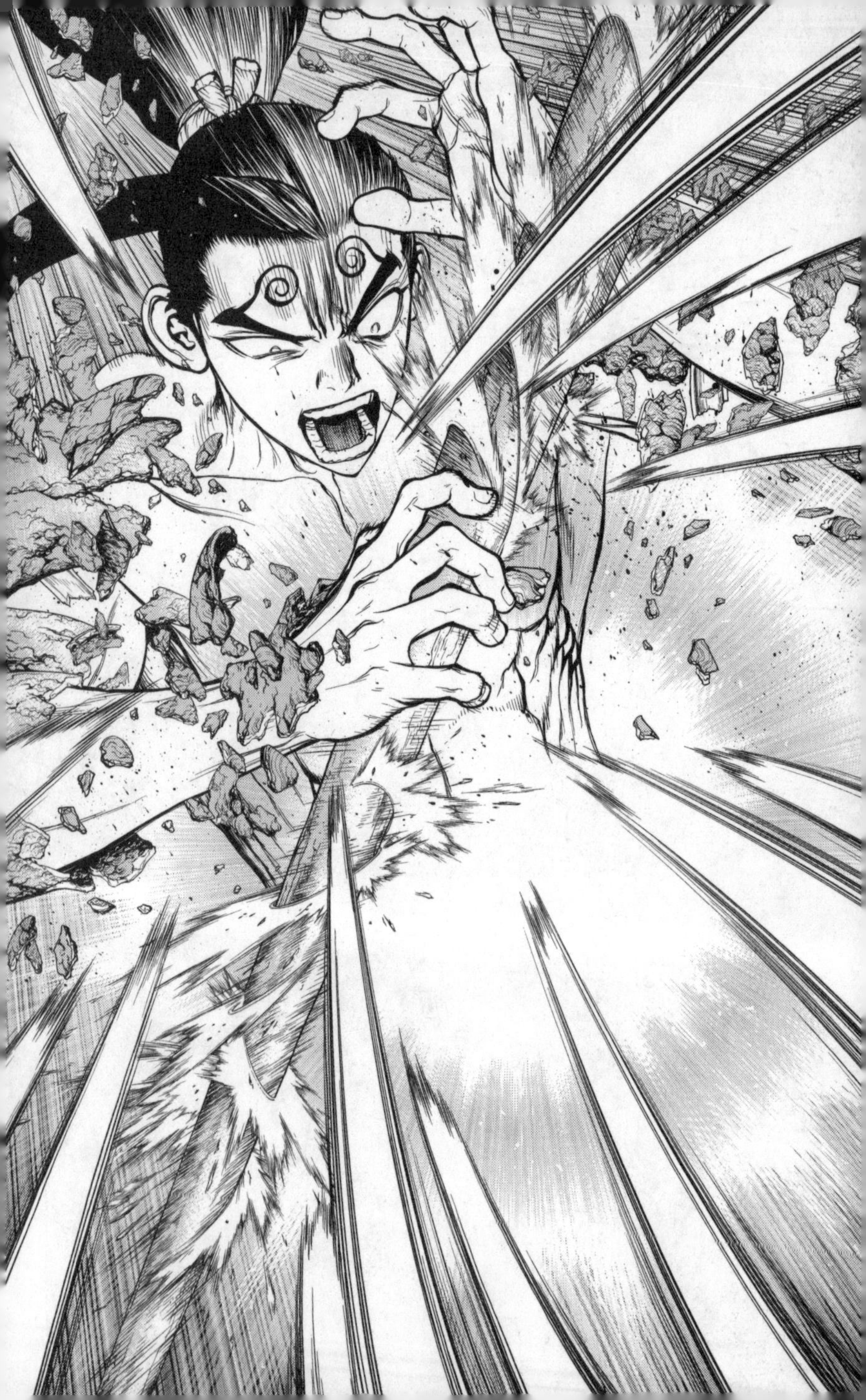

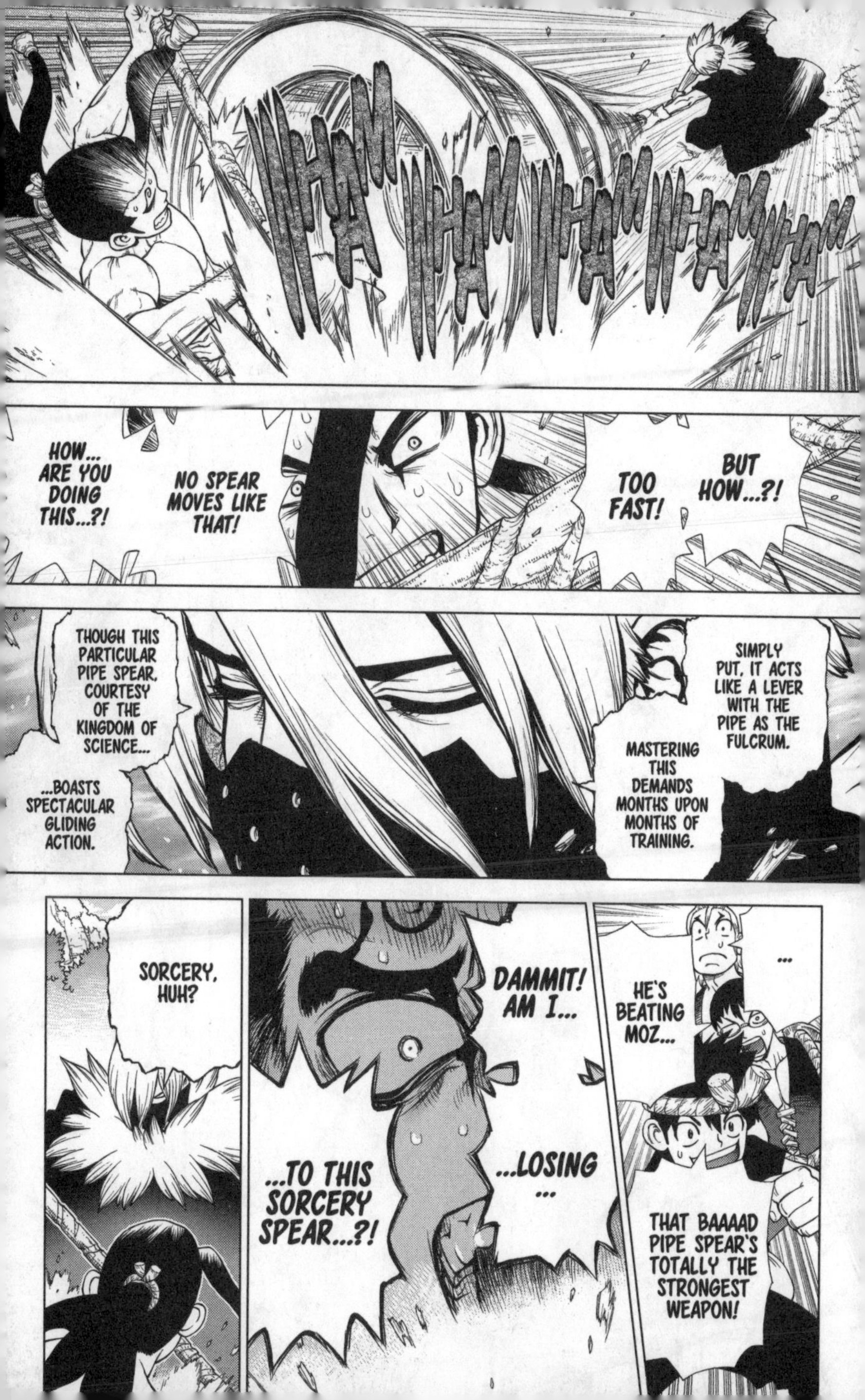
WHAM WHAM WHAM WHAM WHAM
BUT HOW...?!
TOO FAST!
NO SPEAR MOVES LIKE THAT!
HOW... ARE YOU DOING THIS...?!
SIMPLY PUT, IT ACTS LIKE A LEVER WITH THE PIPE AS THE FULCRUM.
MASTERING THIS DEMANDS MONTHS UPON MONTHS OF TRAINING.
THOUGH THIS PARTICULAR PIPE SPEAR, COURTESY OF THE KINGDOM OF SCIENCE...
...BOASTS SPECTACULAR GLIDING ACTION.
...
HE'S BEATING MOZ...
THAT BAAAAD PIPE SPEAR'S TOTALLY THE STRONGEST WEAPON!
DAMMIT! AM I...
...LOSING...
...TO THIS SORCERY SPEAR...?!
SORCERY, HUH?

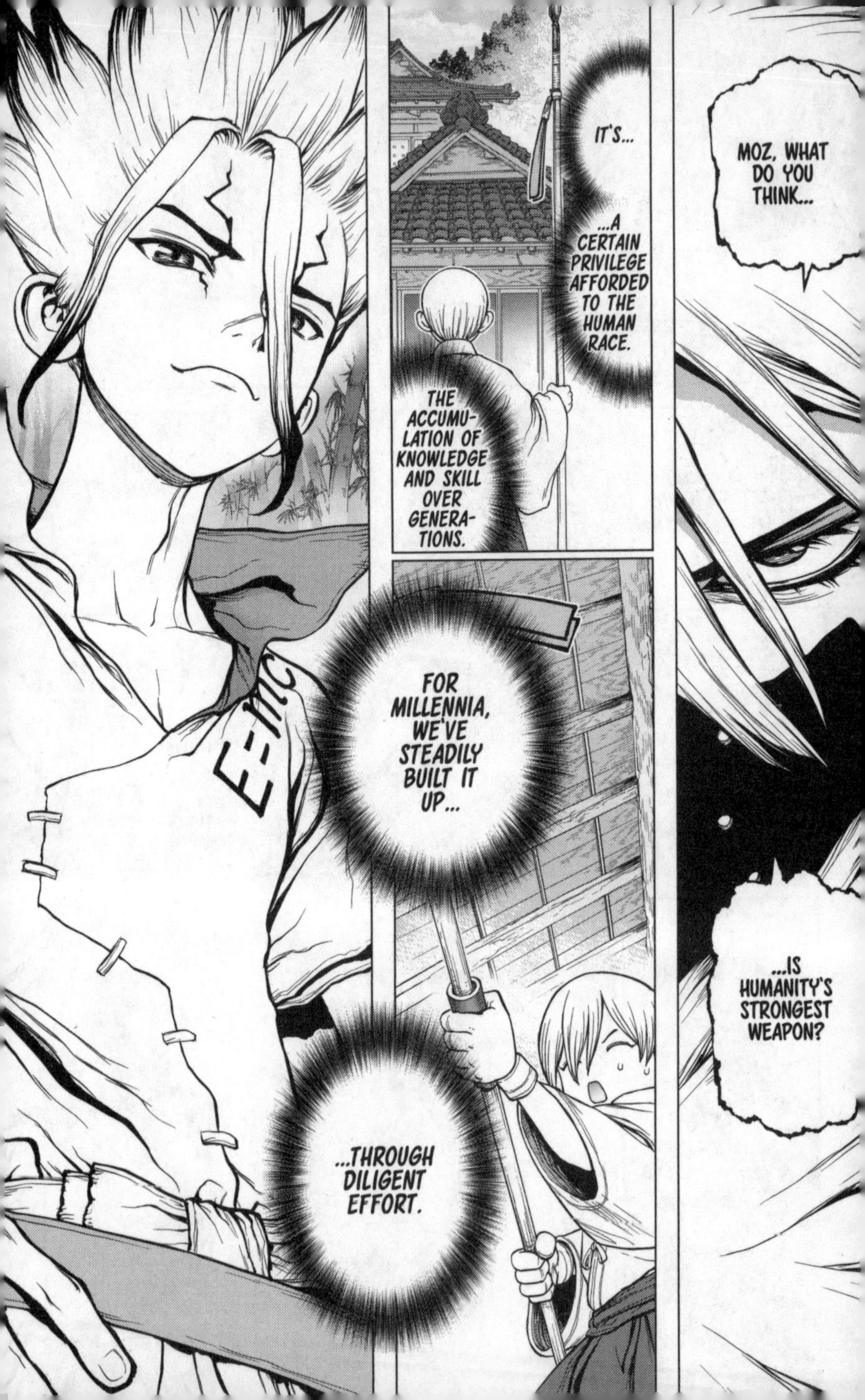
MOZ, WHAT DO YOU THINK...
...IS HUMANITY'S STRONGEST WEAPON?
IT'S...
...A CERTAIN PRIVILEGE AFFORDED TO THE HUMAN RACE.
THE ACCUMULATION OF KNOWLEDGE AND SKILL OVER GENERATIONS.
FOR MILLENNIA, WE'VE STEADILY BUILT IT UP...
...THROUGH DILIGENT EFFORT.

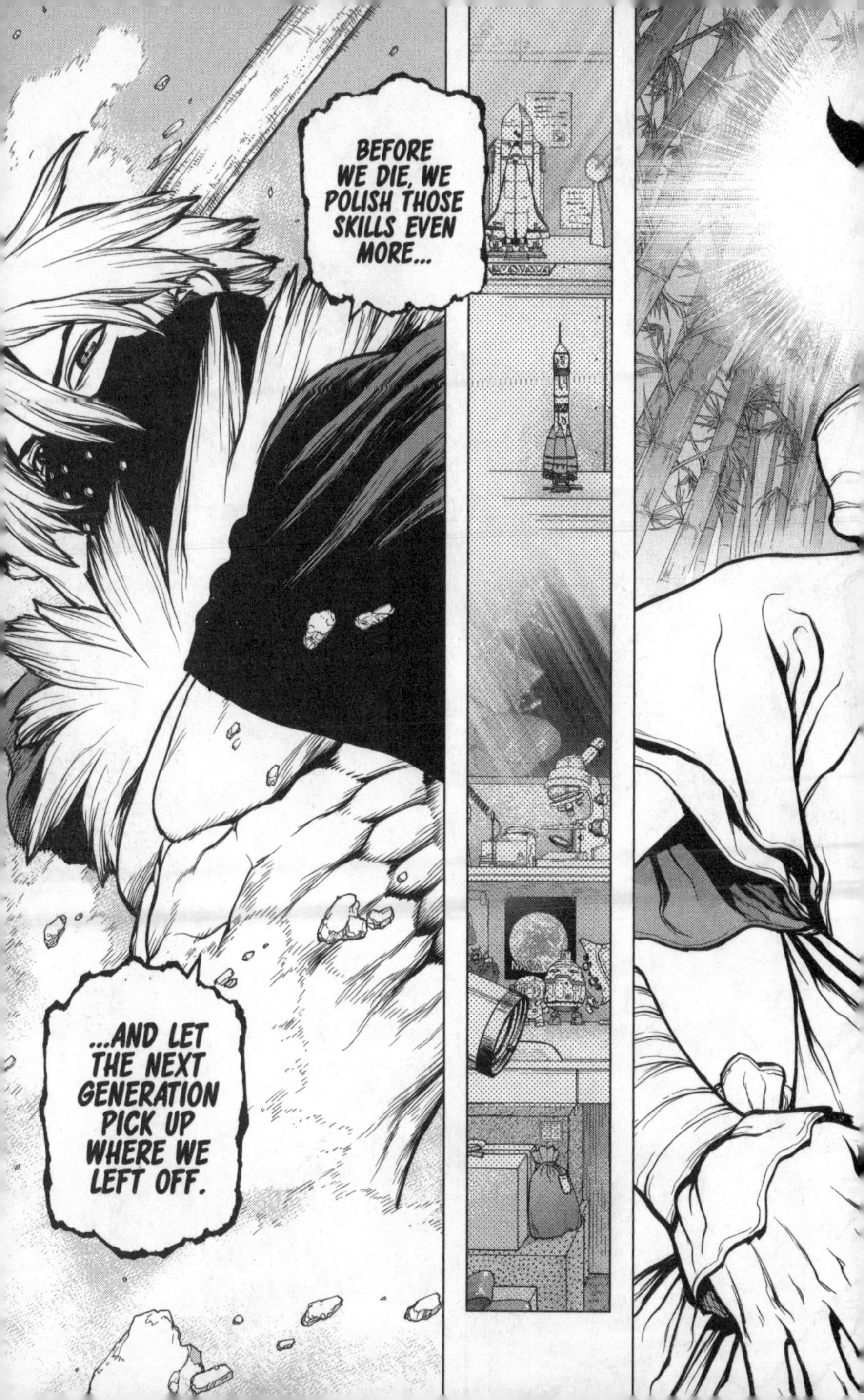
BEFORE WE DIE, WE POLISH THOSE SKILLS EVEN MORE...
...AND LET THE NEXT GENERATION PICK UP WHERE WE LEFT OFF.

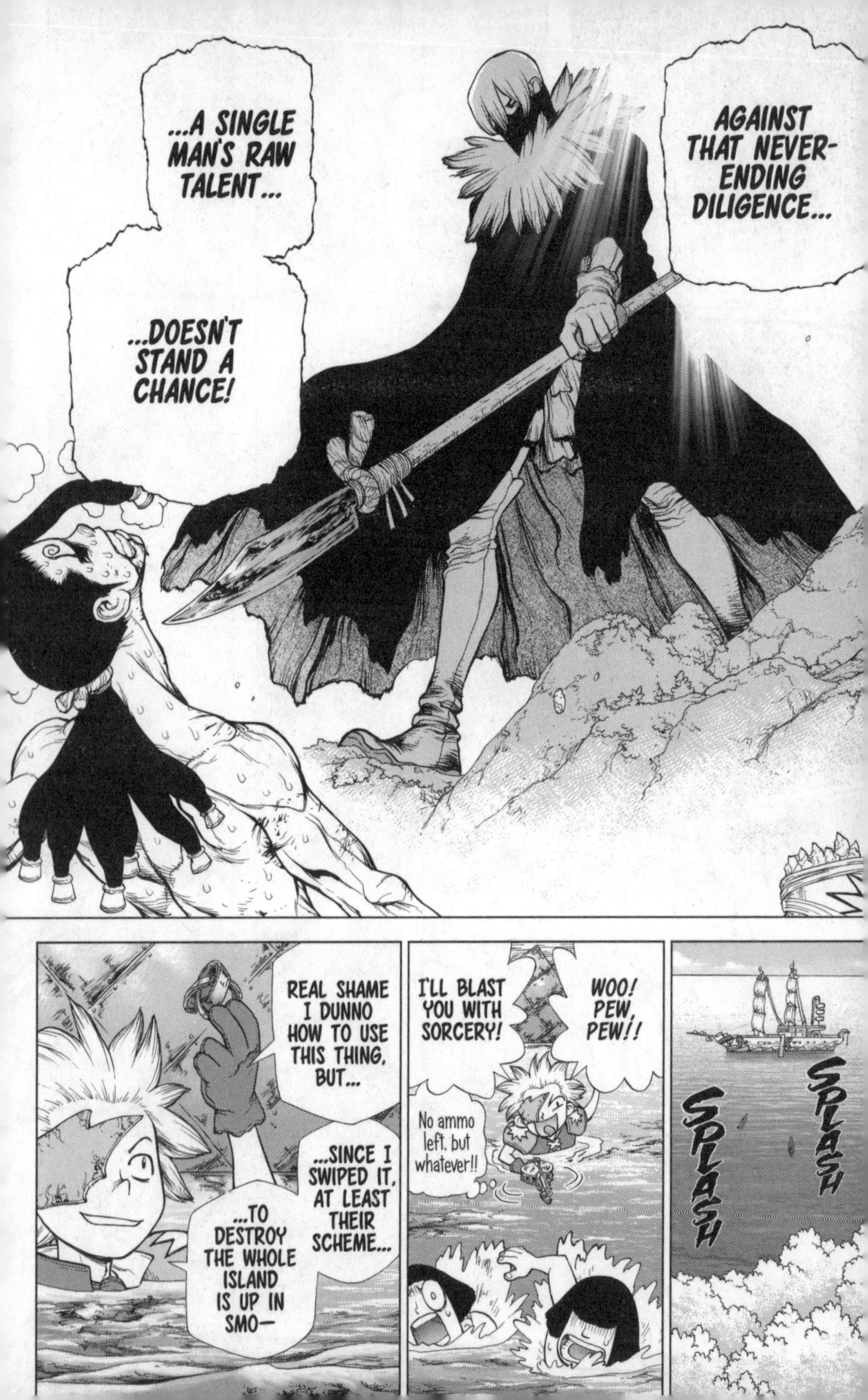
AGAINST THAT NEVER-ENDING DILIGENCE...
...A SINGLE MAN'S RAW TALENT...
...DOESN'T STAND A CHANCE!
SPLASH
SPLASH
WOO! PEW, PEW!!
I'LL BLAST YOU WITH SORCERY!
No ammo left, but whatever!!
REAL SHAME I DUNNO HOW TO USE THIS THING, BUT...
...SINCE I SWIPED IT, AT LEAST THEIR SCHEME...
...TO DESTROY THE WHOLE ISLAND IS UP IN SMO—

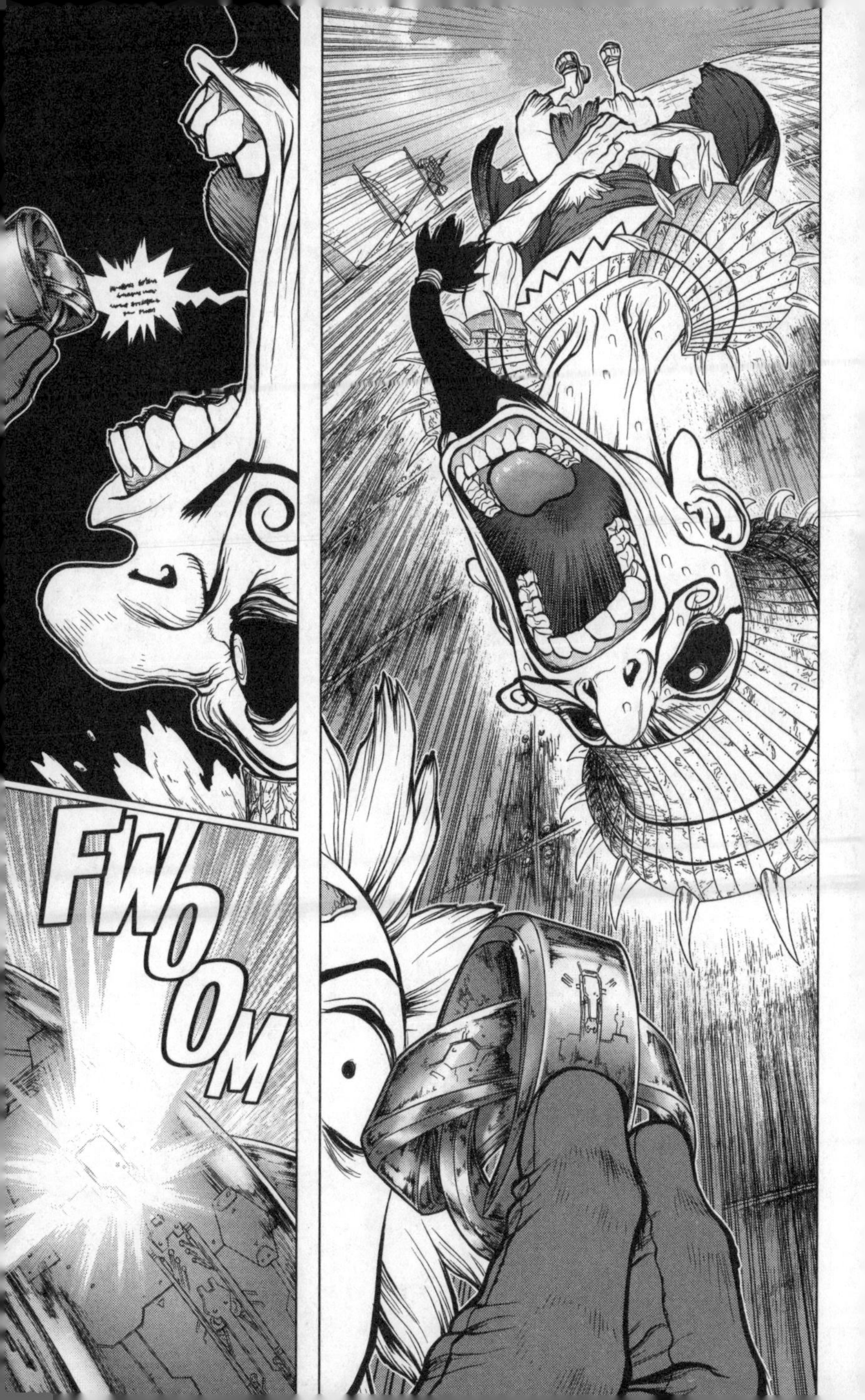
FWOOM

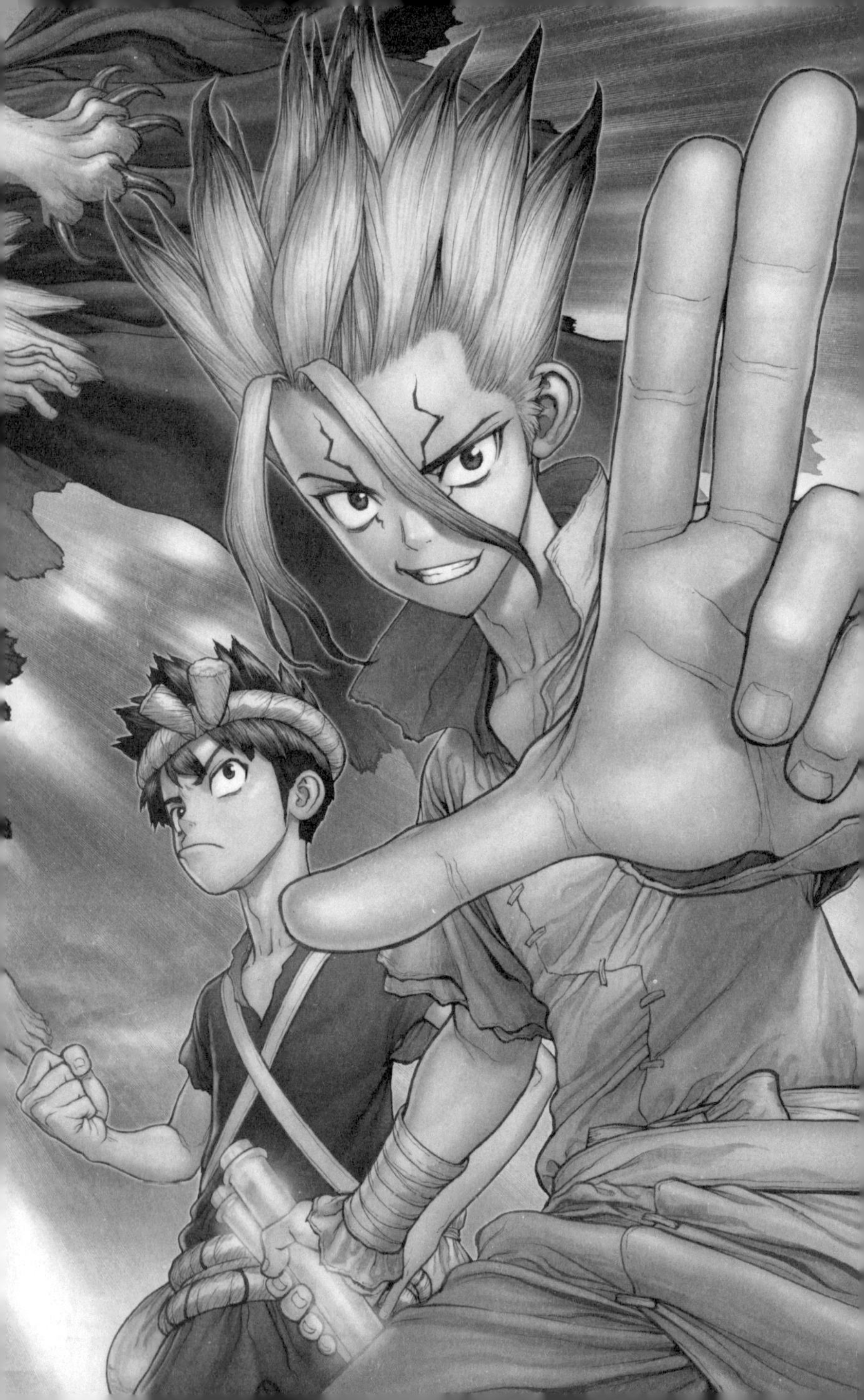

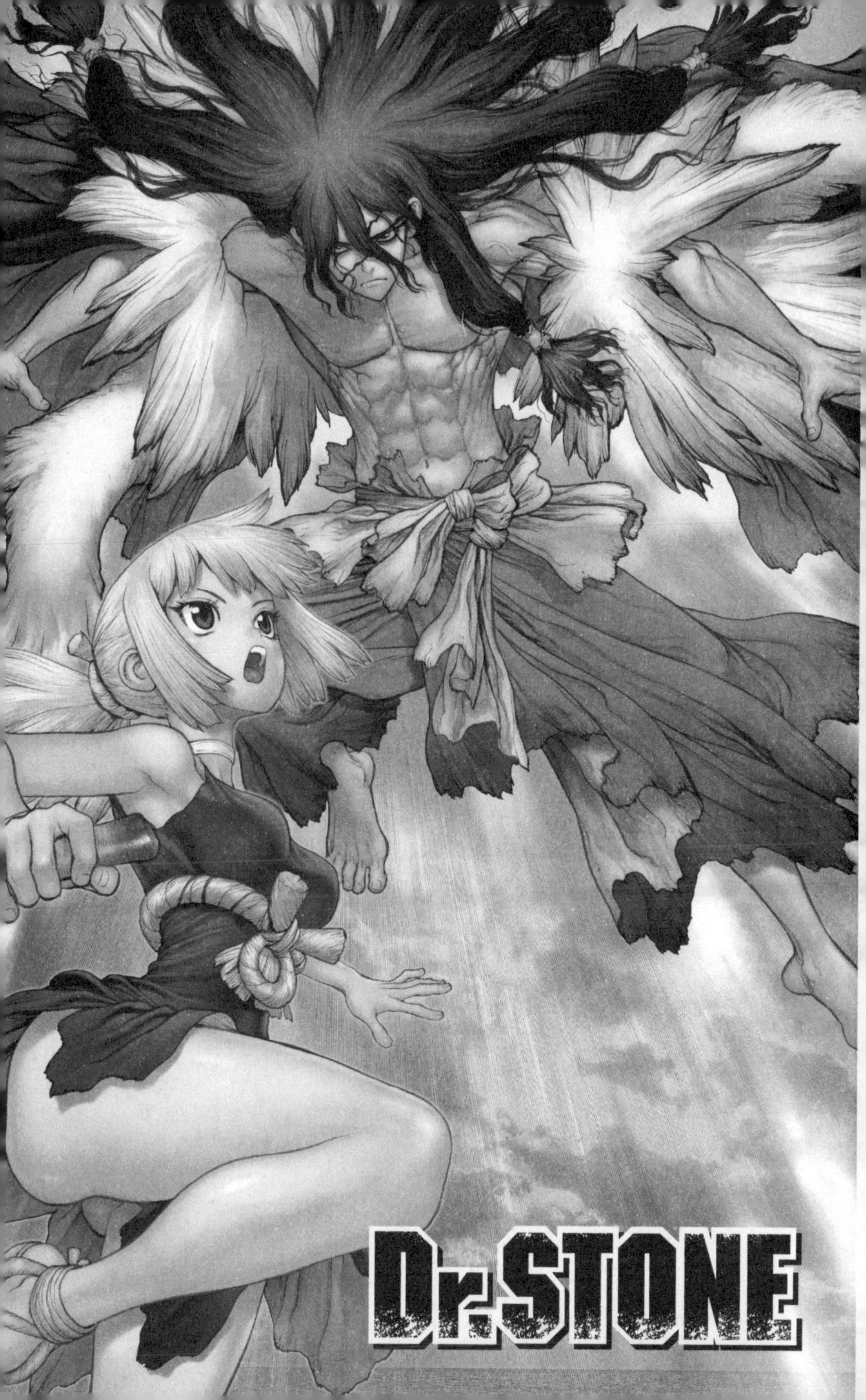
Dr.STONE

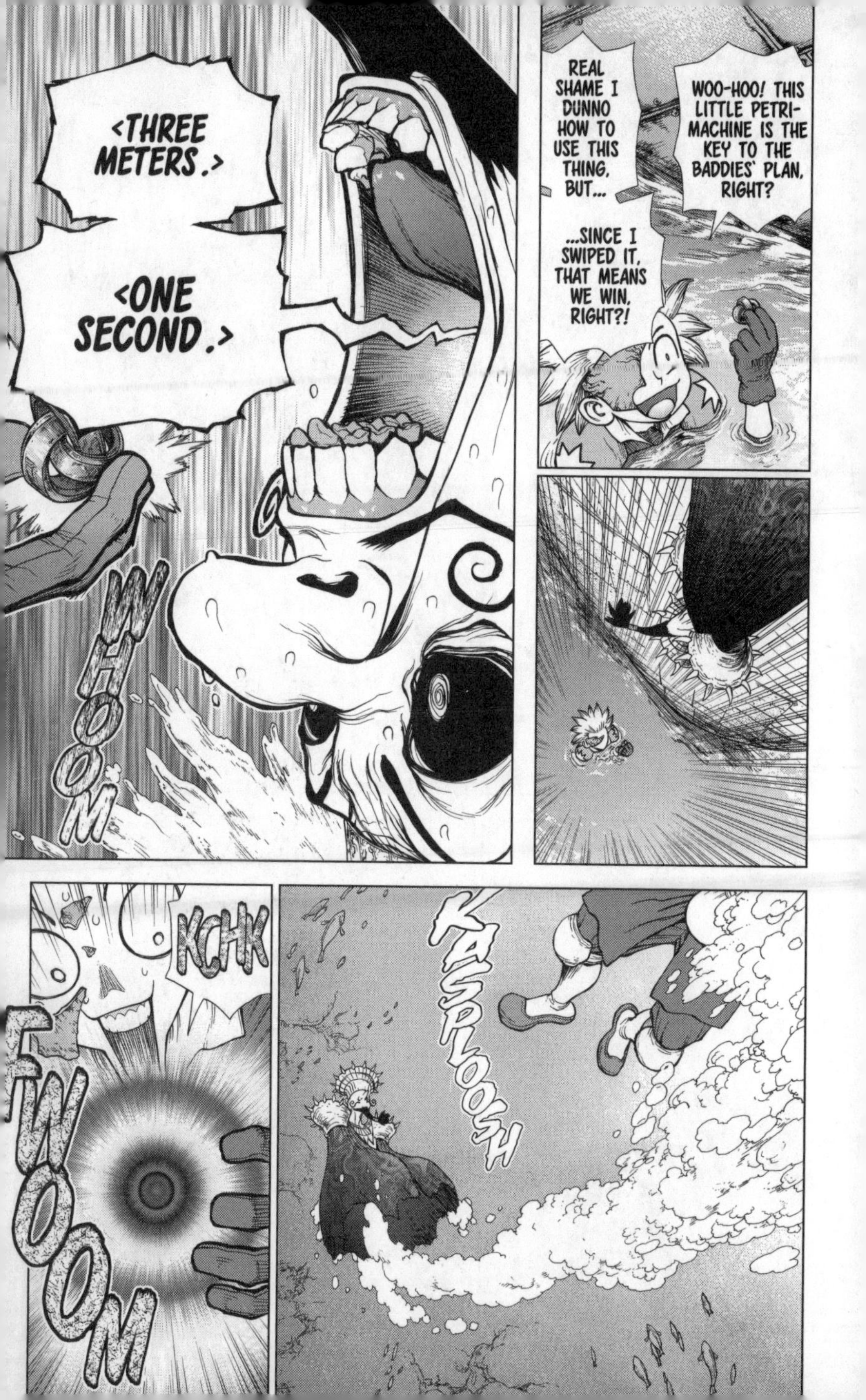
WOO-HOO! THIS LITTLE PETRI-MACHINE IS THE KEY TO THE BADDIES' PLAN, RIGHT?
REAL SHAME I DUNNO HOW TO USE THIS THING, BUT...
...SINCE I SWIPED IT, THAT MEANS WE WIN, RIGHT?!
<THREE METERS.>
<ONE SECOND.>
WHOOOM
KASPLOOSH
KCHK
FWOOOM

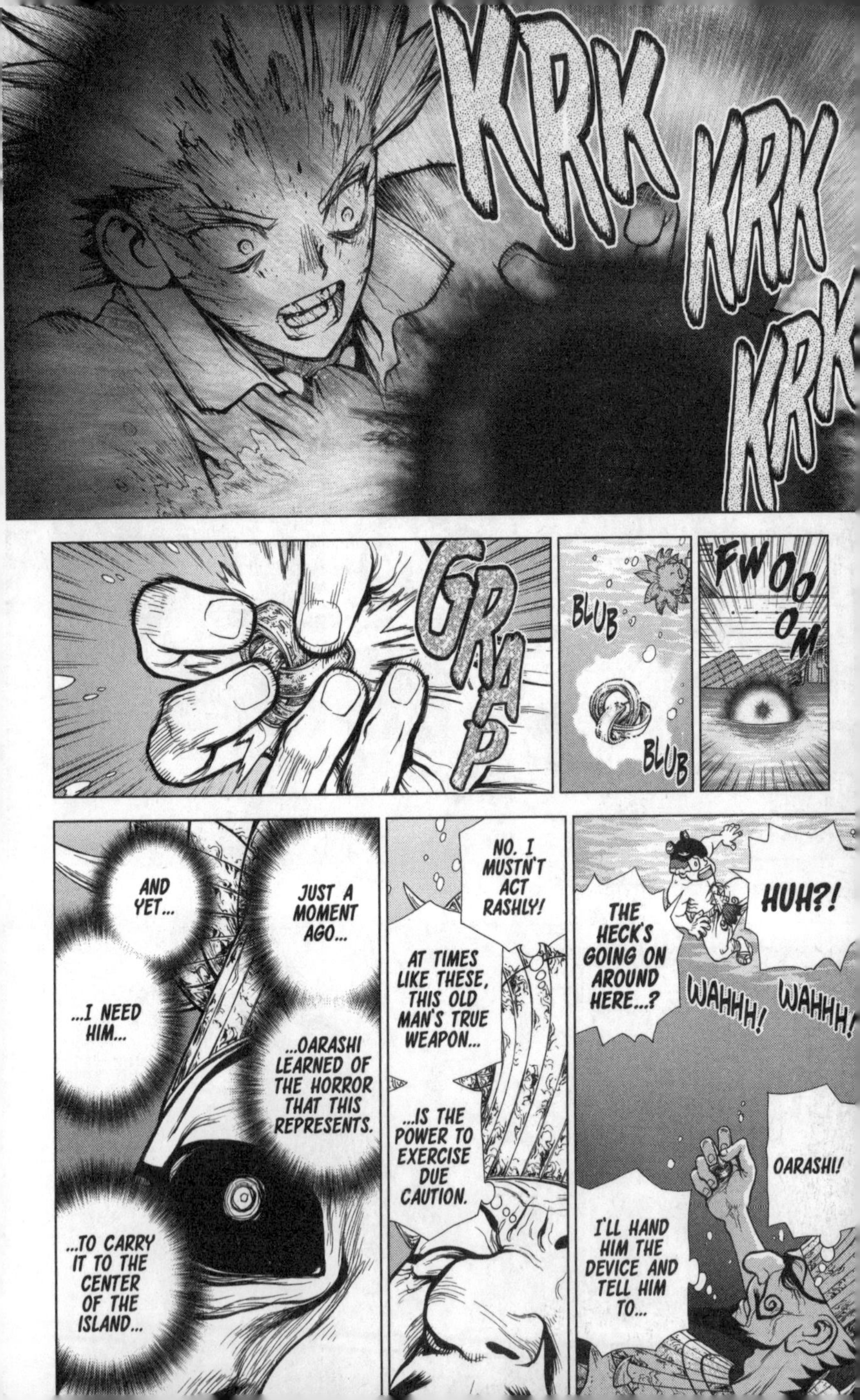
KRK
KRK
KRK
FWOOOOM
BLUB
BLUB
GRAP
HUH?!
THE HECK'S GOING ON AROUND HERE...?
WAHHH!
WAHHH!
OARASHI!
I'LL HAND HIM THE DEVICE AND TELL HIM TO...
NO. I MUSTN'T ACT RASHLY!
AT TIMES LIKE THESE, THIS OLD MAN'S TRUE WEAPON...
...IS THE POWER TO EXERCISE DUE CAUTION.
JUST A MOMENT AGO...
...OARASHI LEARNED OF THE HORROR THAT THIS REPRESENTS.
AND YET...
...I NEED HIM...
...TO CARRY IT TO THE CENTER OF THE ISLAND...

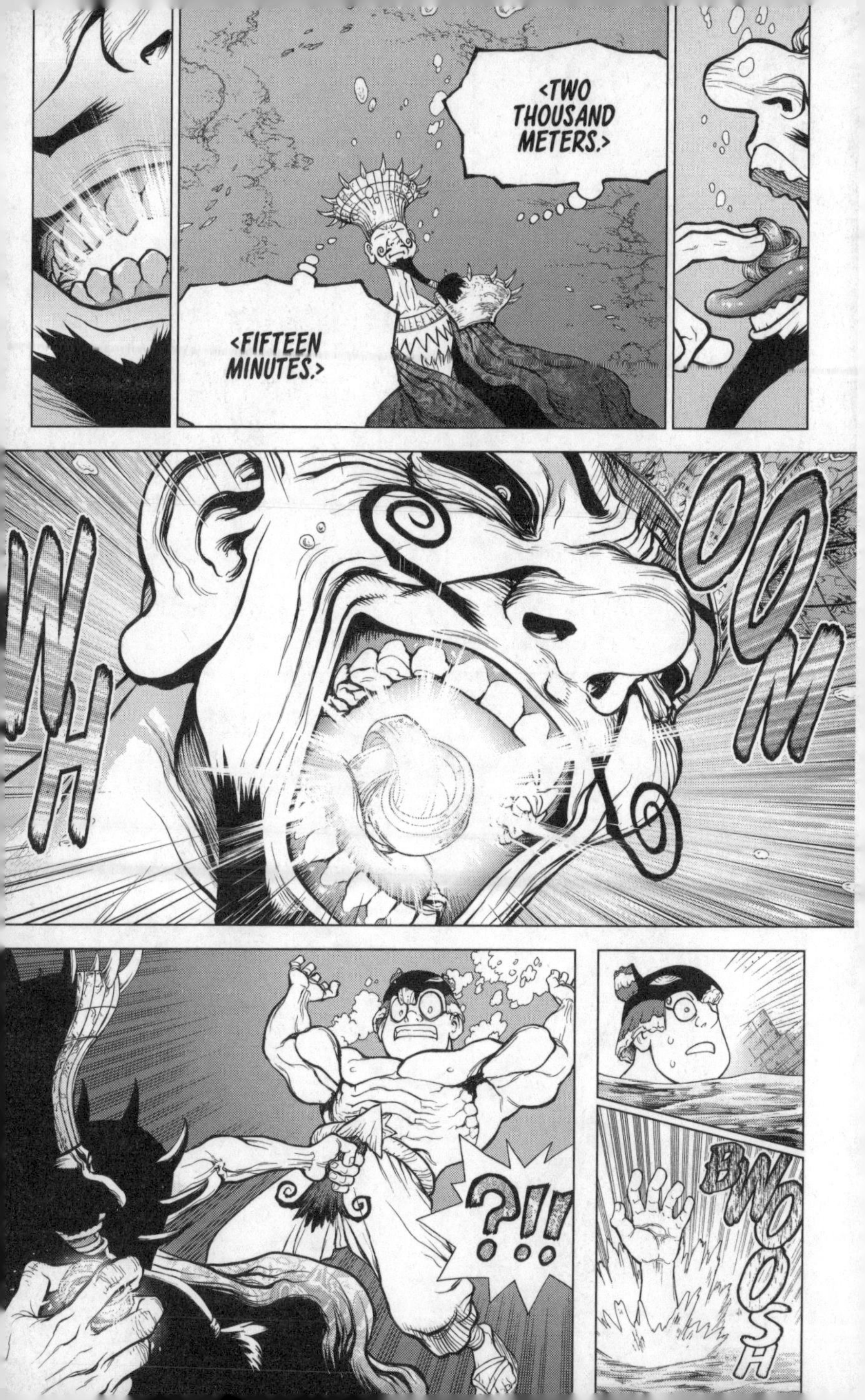
<TWO THOUSAND METERS.>
<FIFTEEN MINUTES.>
WHOOOM
BWOOSH
?!!

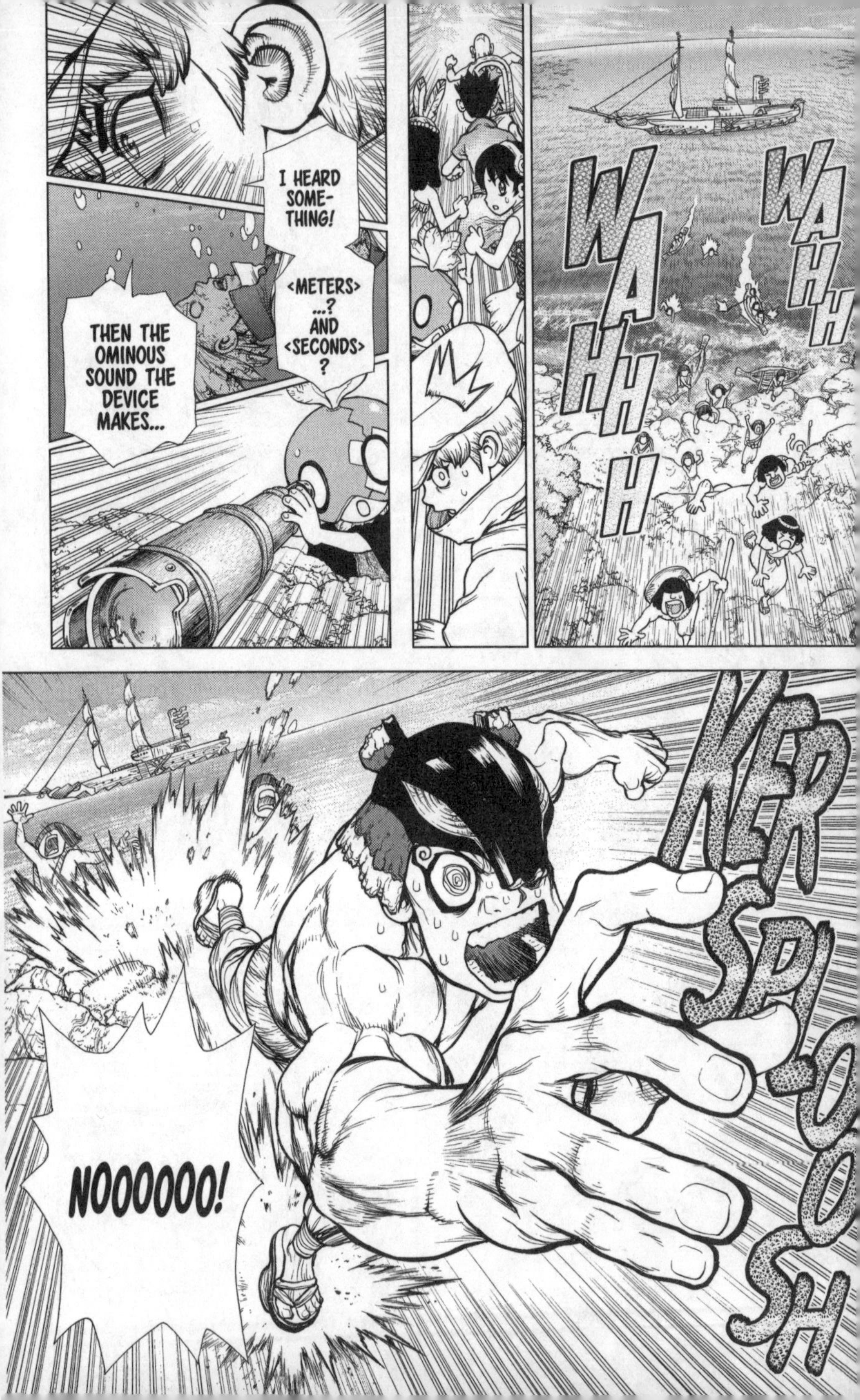
WAHHH
WAHHH
<METERS> ...? AND <SECONDS> ?
I HEARD SOME-THING!
THEN THE OMINOUS SOUND THE DEVICE MAKES...
KERSPLOOOSH
NOOOOOO!

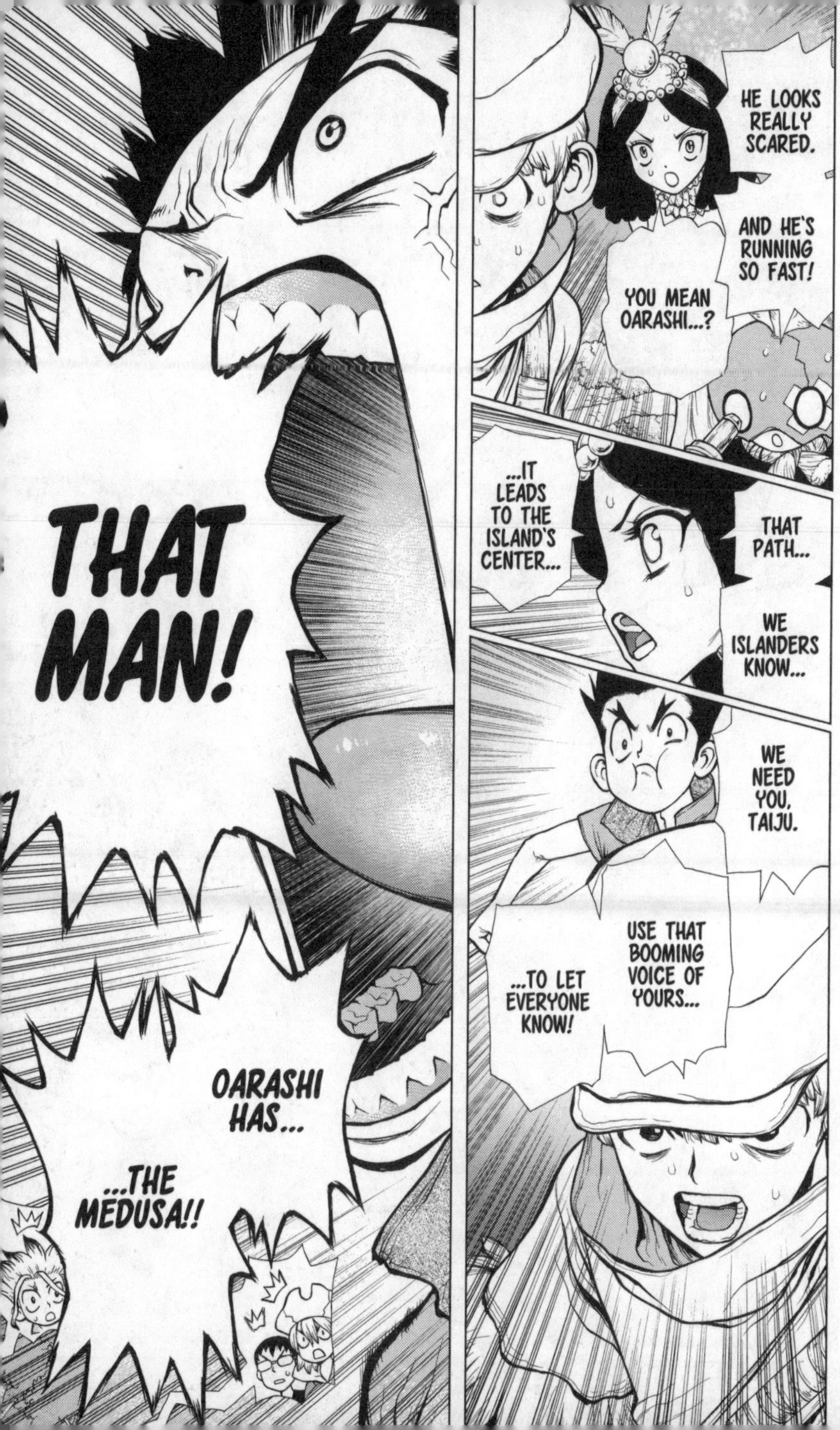
HE LOOKS REALLY SCARED.
AND HE'S RUNNING SO FAST!
YOU MEAN OARASHI...?
THAT PATH...
WE ISLANDERS KNOW...
...IT LEADS TO THE ISLAND'S CENTER...
WE NEED YOU, TAIJU.
USE THAT BOOMING VOICE OF YOURS...
...TO LET EVERYONE KNOW!
THAT MAN!
OARASHI HAS...
...THE MEDUSA!!

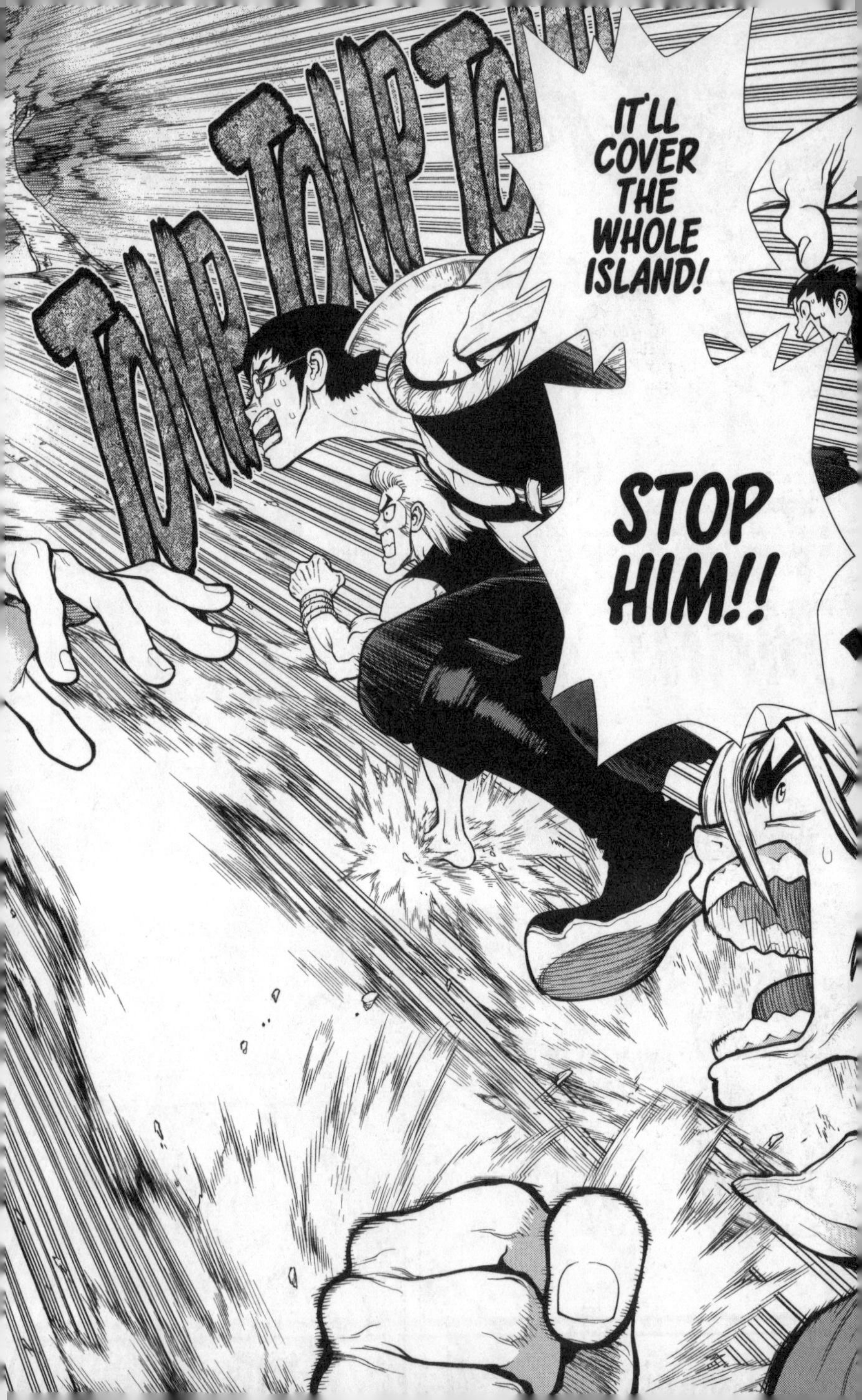
IT'LL COVER THE WHOLE ISLAND!
STOP HIM!!
TOMP TOMP TOMP

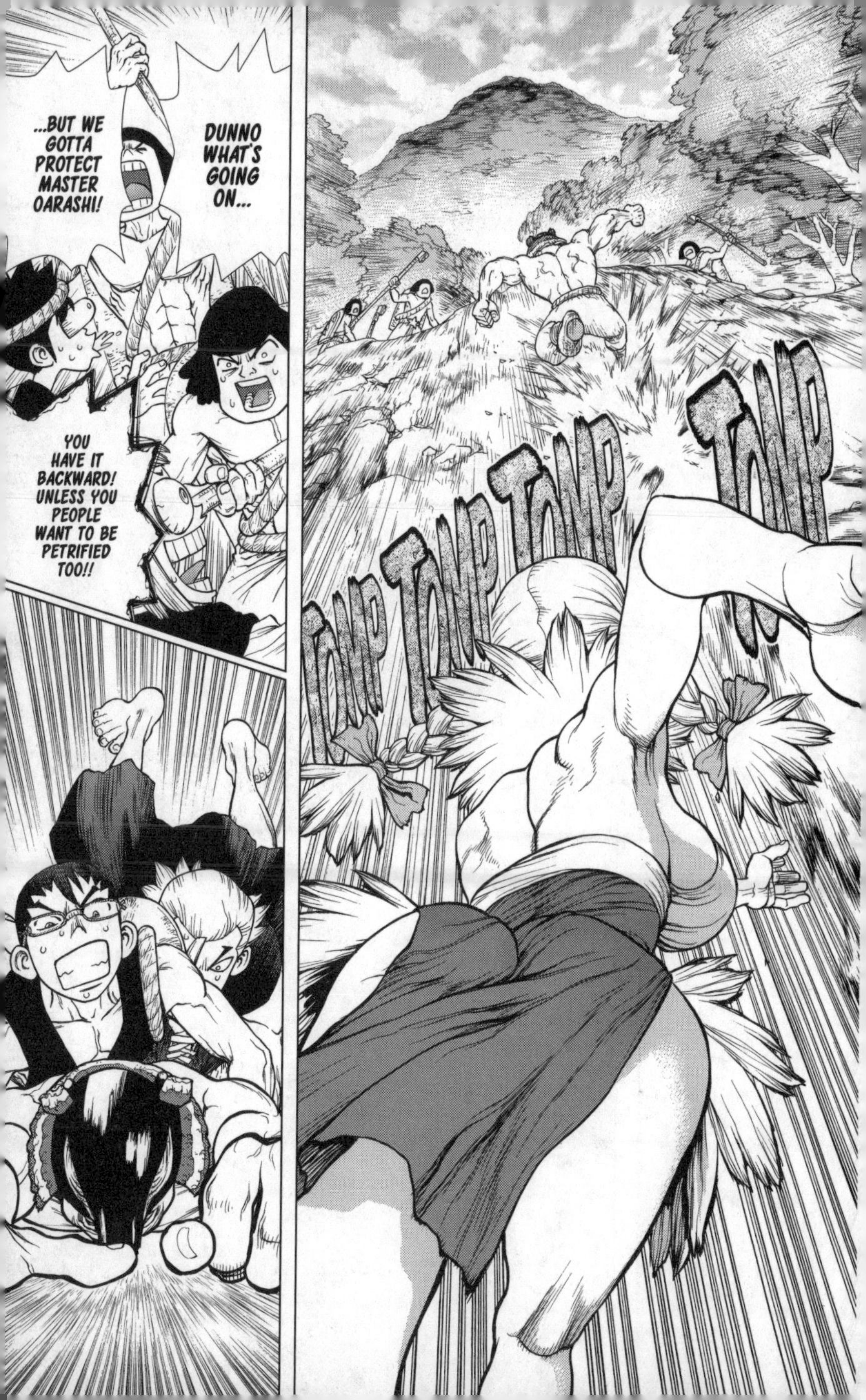
TOMP
TOMP TOMP TOMP TOMP
DUNNO WHAT'S GOING ON...
...BUT WE GOTTA PROTECT MASTER OARASHI!
YOU HAVE IT BACKWARD! UNLESS YOU PEOPLE WANT TO BE PETRIFIED TOO!!

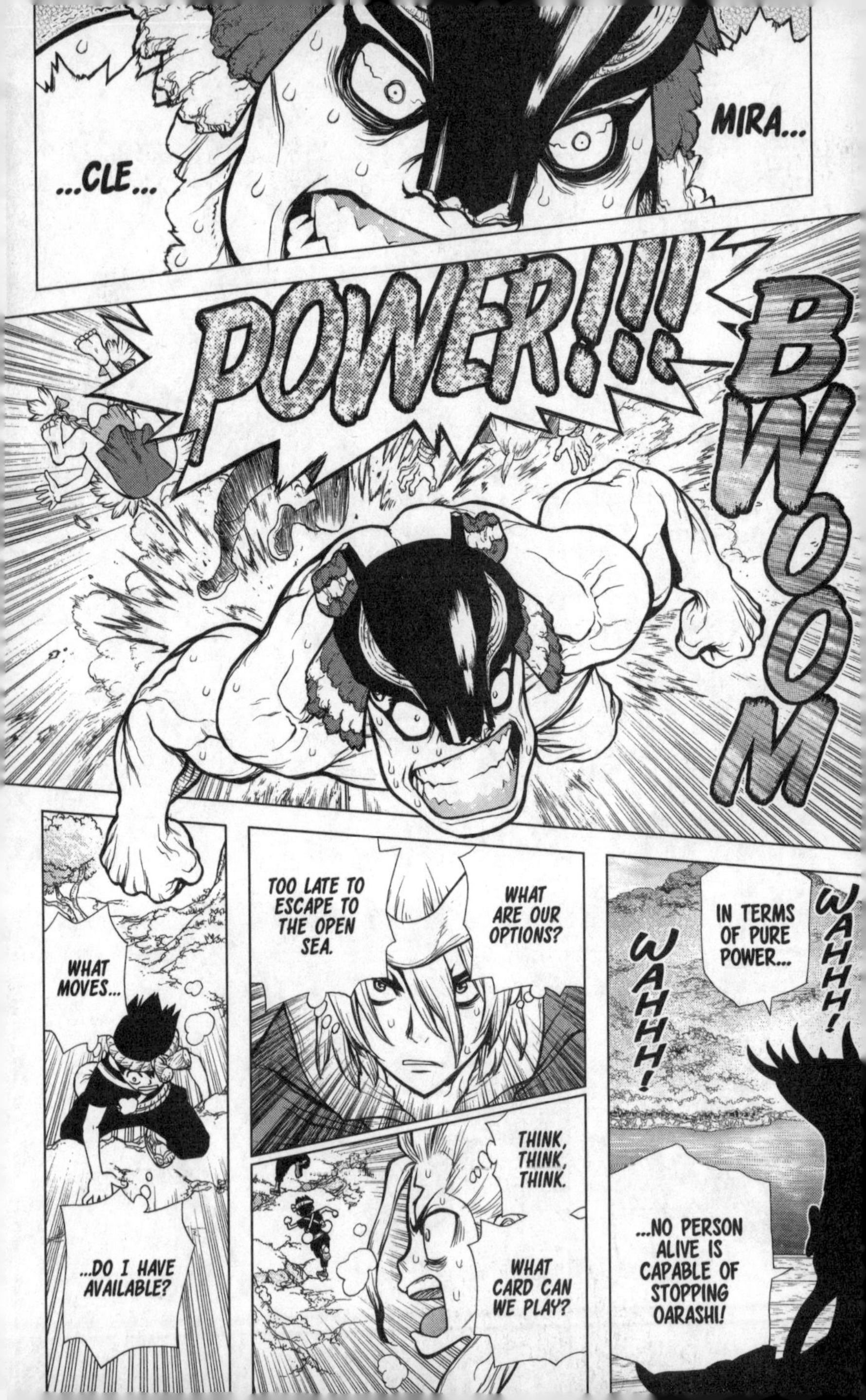
MIRA...
...CLE...
POWER!!!
BWOOOM
WAHHH!
IN TERMS OF PURE POWER...
WAHHH!
...NO PERSON ALIVE IS CAPABLE OF STOPPING OARASHI!
WHAT ARE OUR OPTIONS?
TOO LATE TO ESCAPE TO THE OPEN SEA.
THINK, THINK, THINK.
WHAT CARD CAN WE PLAY?
WHAT MOVES...
...DO I HAVE AVAILABLE?

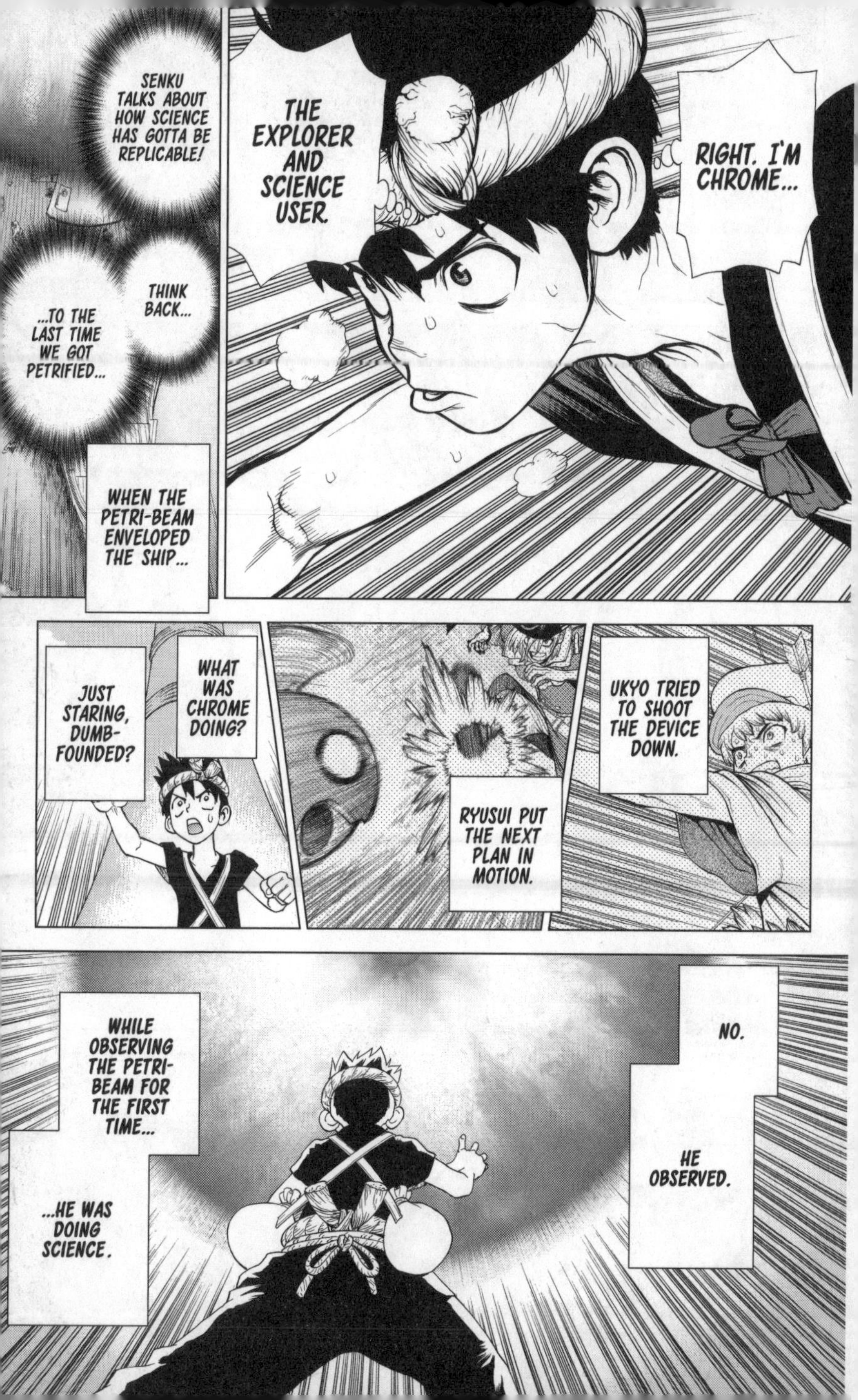

RIGHT. I'M CHROME...
THE EXPLORER AND SCIENCE USER.
SENKU TALKS ABOUT HOW SCIENCE HAS GOTTA BE REPLICABLE!
THINK BACK...
...TO THE LAST TIME WE GOT PETRIFIED...
WHEN THE PETRI-BEAM ENVELOPED THE SHIP...
UKYO TRIED TO SHOOT THE DEVICE DOWN.
RYUSUI PUT THE NEXT PLAN IN MOTION.
WHAT WAS CHROME DOING?
JUST STARING, DUMB-FOUNDED?
NO.
HE OBSERVED.
WHILE OBSERVING THE PETRI-BEAM FOR THE FIRST TIME...
...HE WAS DOING SCIENCE.

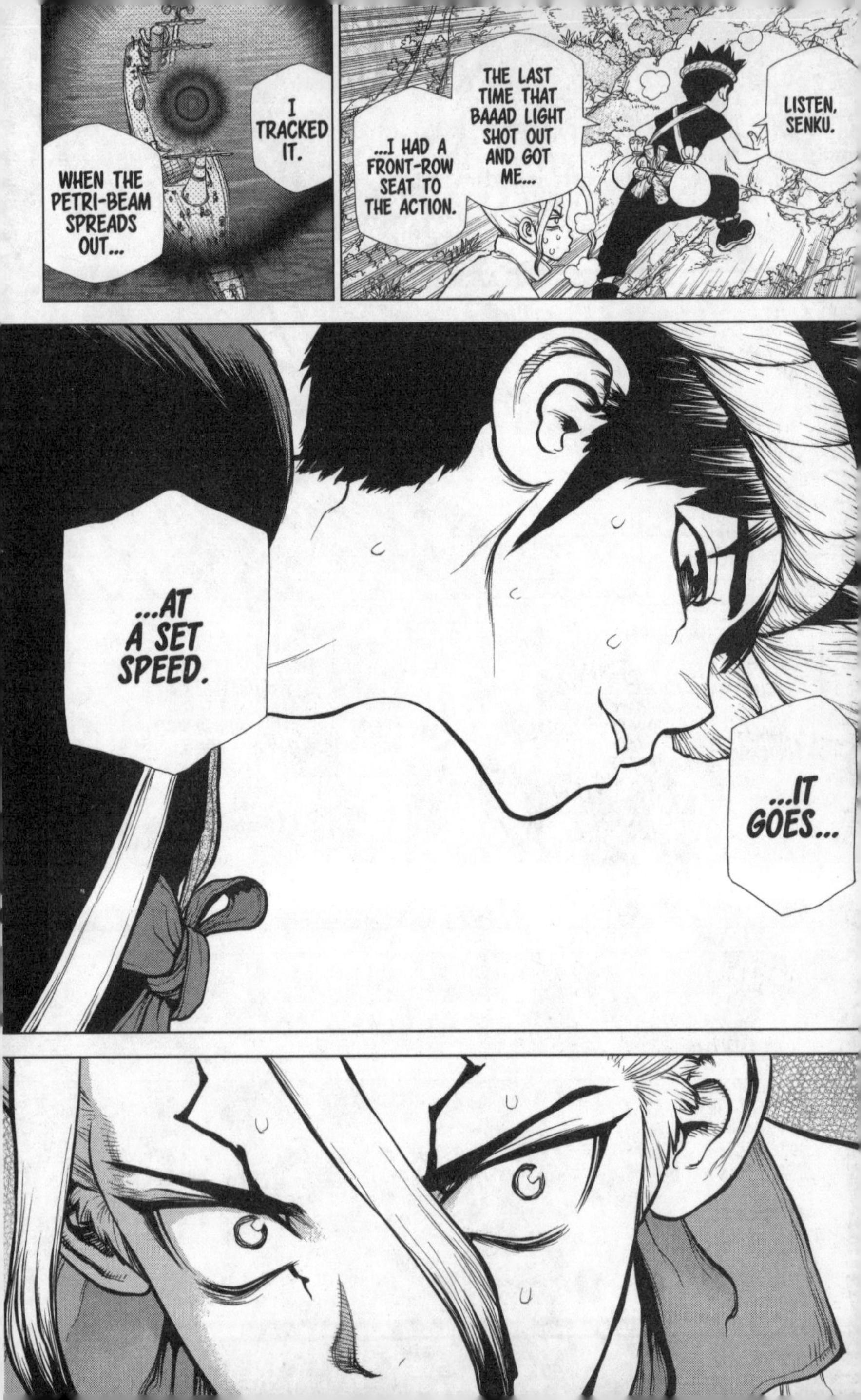
LISTEN, SENKU.
THE LAST TIME THAT BAAAD LIGHT SHOT OUT AND GOT ME...
...I HAD A FRONT-ROW SEAT TO THE ACTION.
I TRACKED IT.
WHEN THE PETRI-BEAM SPREADS OUT...
...IT GOES...
...AT A SET SPEED.

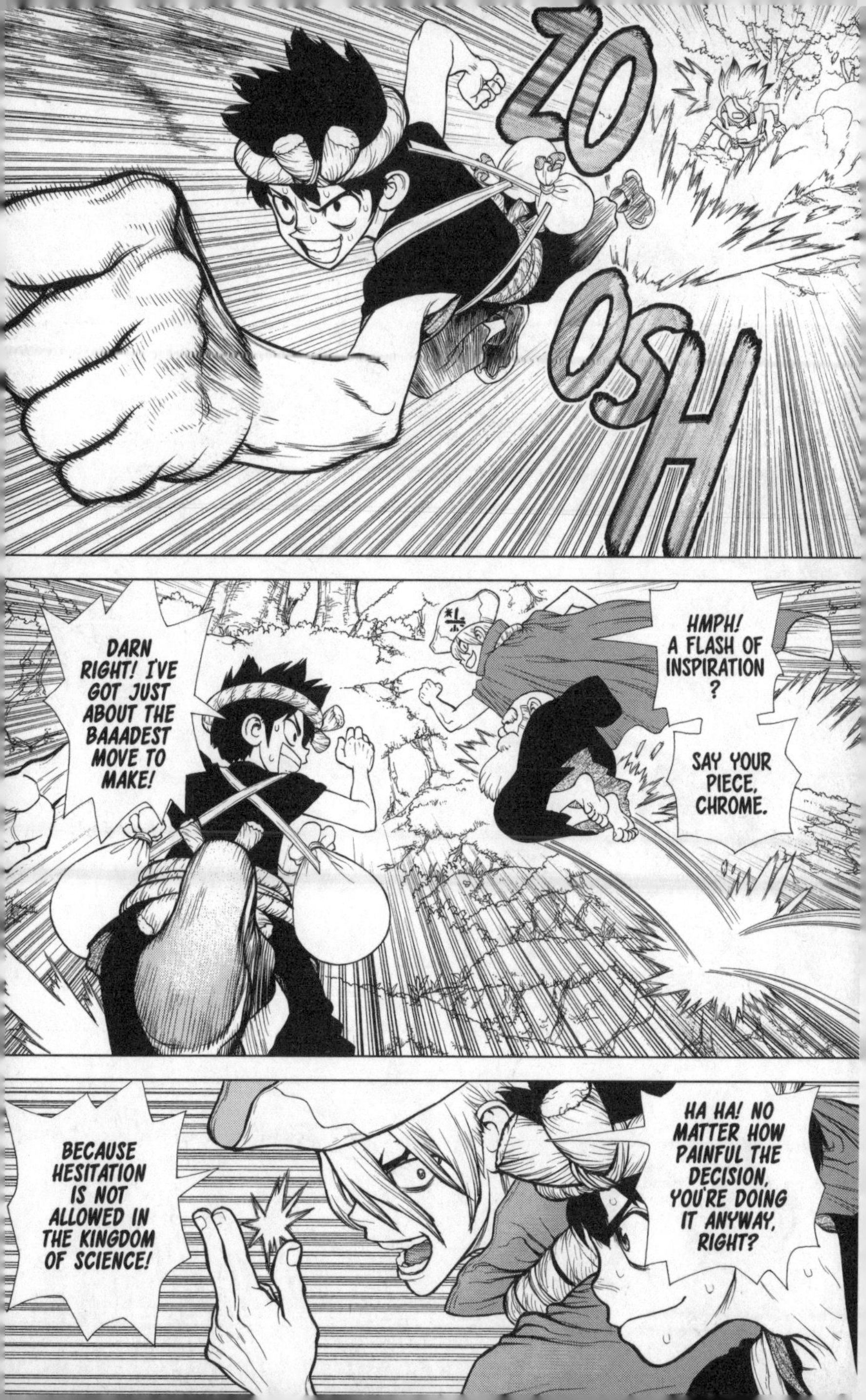
ZOOOSH
HMPH! A FLASH OF INSPIRATION?
SAY YOUR PIECE, CHROME.
DARN RIGHT! I'VE GOT JUST ABOUT THE BAAADEST MOVE TO MAKE!
HA HA! NO MATTER HOW PAINFUL THE DECISION, YOU'RE DOING IT ANYWAY, RIGHT?
BECAUSE HESITATION IS NOT ALLOWED IN THE KINGDOM OF SCIENCE!

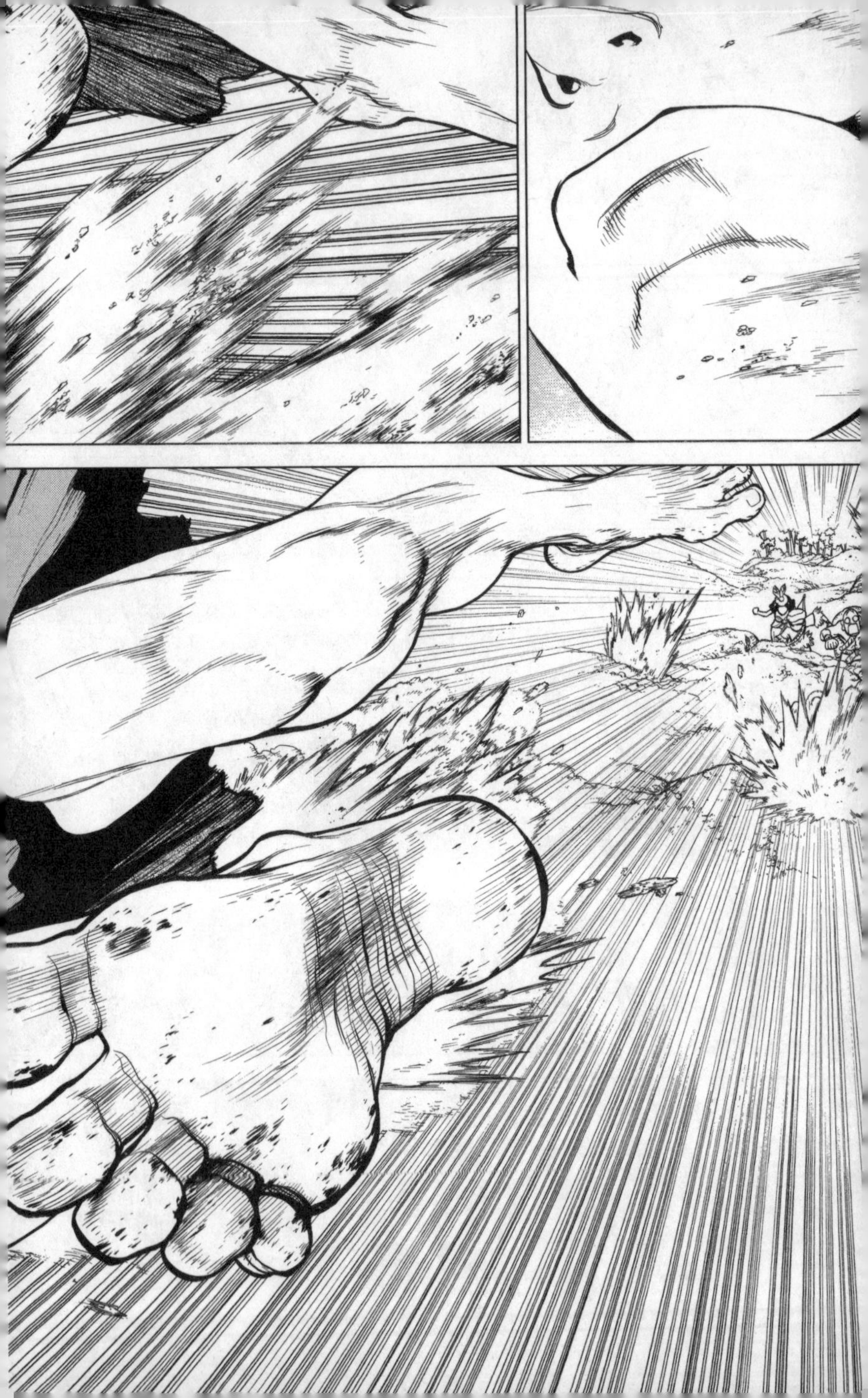

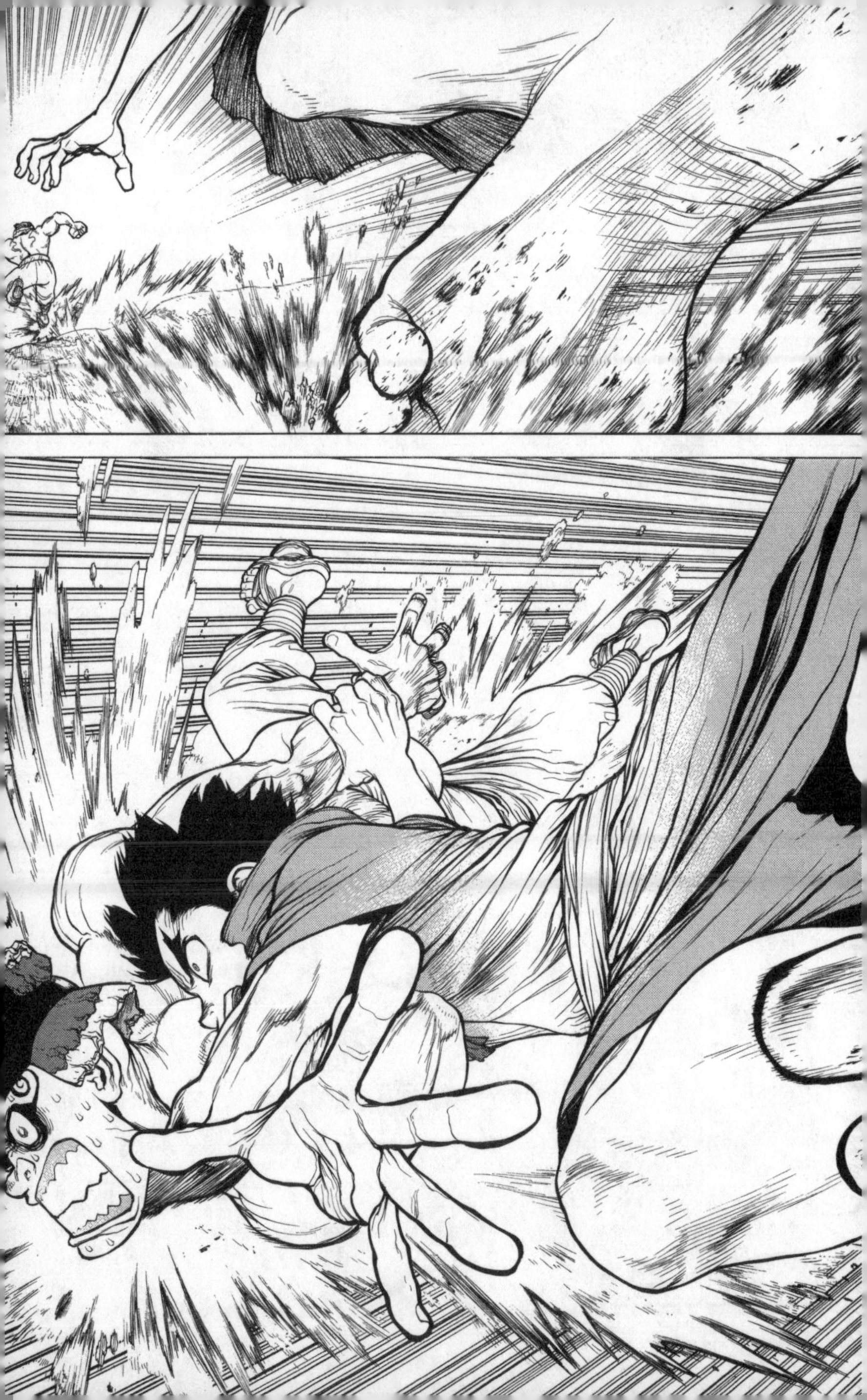

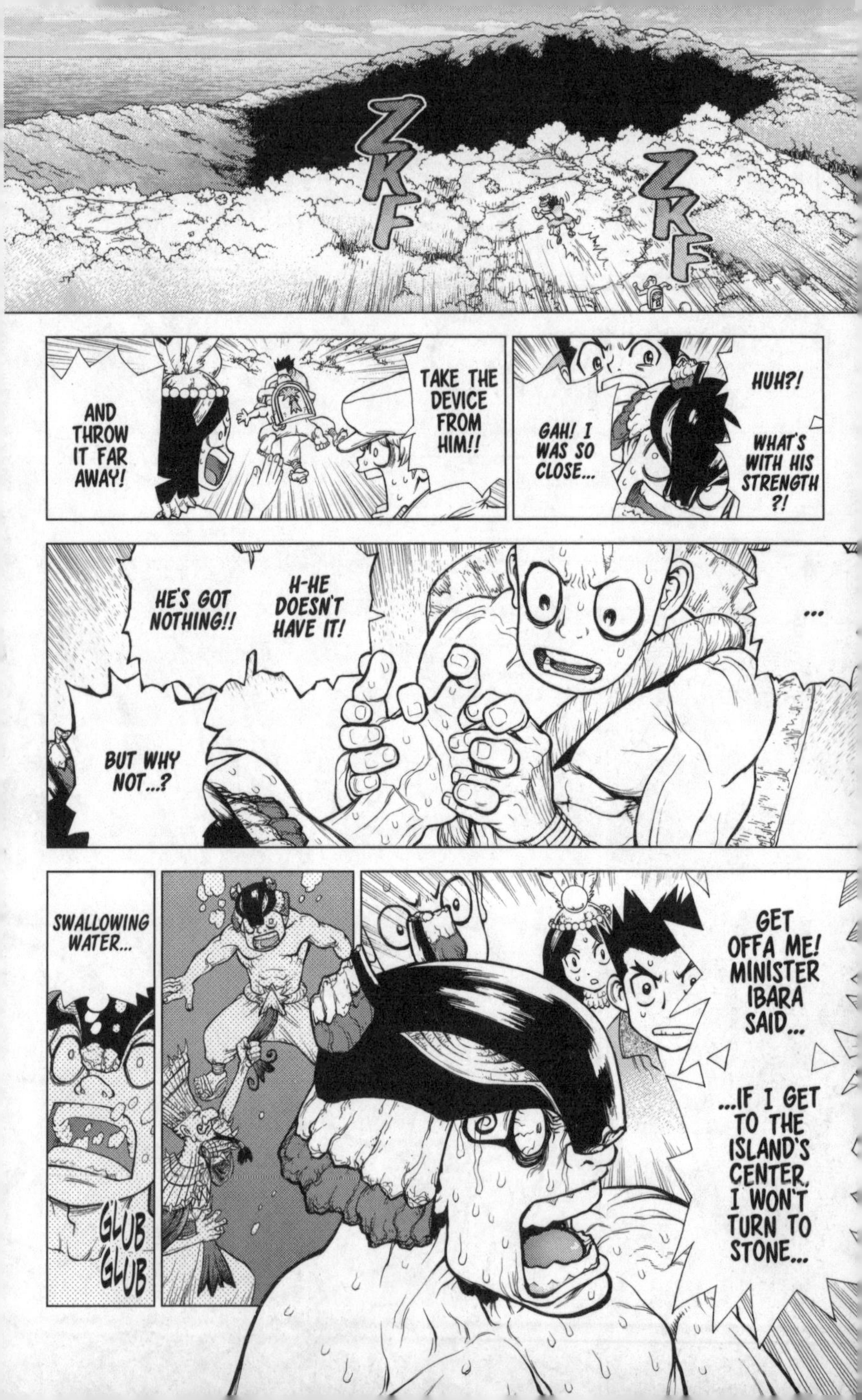
ZKF
ZKF
HUH?!
WHAT'S WITH HIS STRENGTH?!
GAH! I WAS SO CLOSE...
TAKE THE DEVICE FROM HIM!!
AND THROW IT FAR AWAY!
...
H-HE DOESN'T HAVE IT!
HE'S GOT NOTHING!!
BUT WHY NOT...?
GET OFFA ME! MINISTER IBARA SAID...
...IF I GET TO THE ISLAND'S CENTER, I WON'T TURN TO STONE...
SWALLOWING WATER...
GLUB GLUB

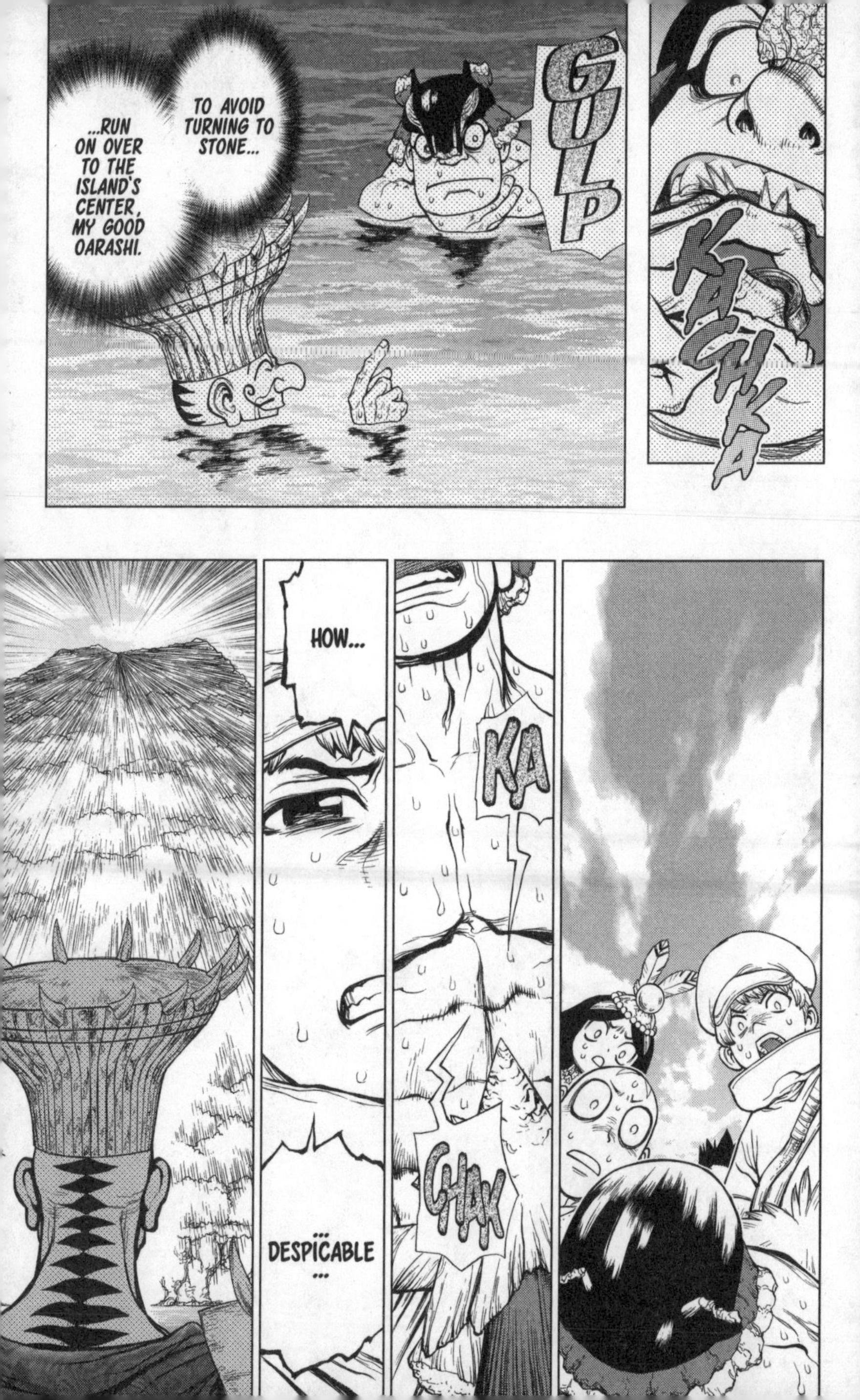
KACHAK
GULP
TO AVOID TURNING TO STONE...
...RUN ON OVER TO THE ISLAND'S CENTER, MY GOOD OARASHI.
KA
CHAK
HOW...
...DESPICABLE...

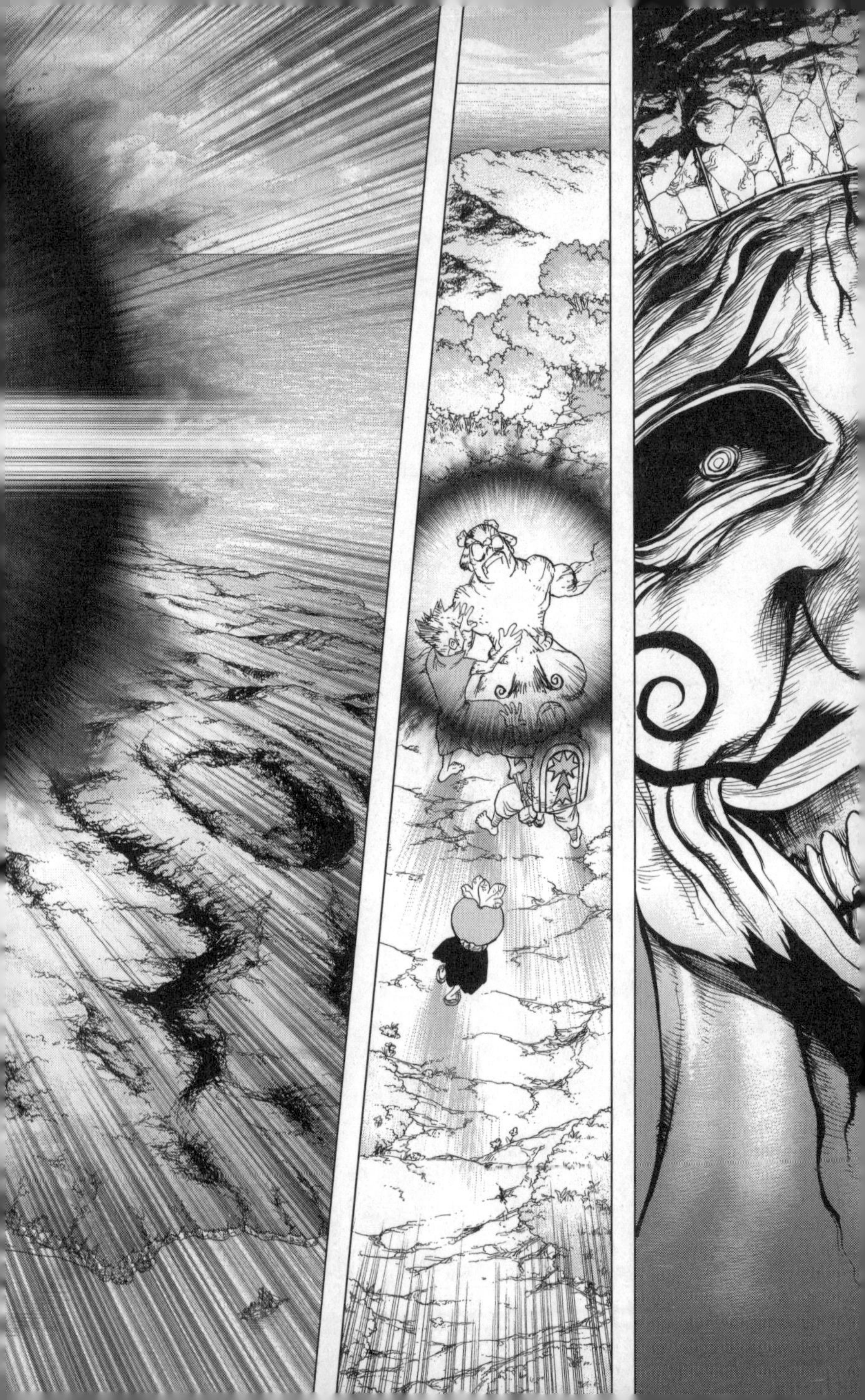

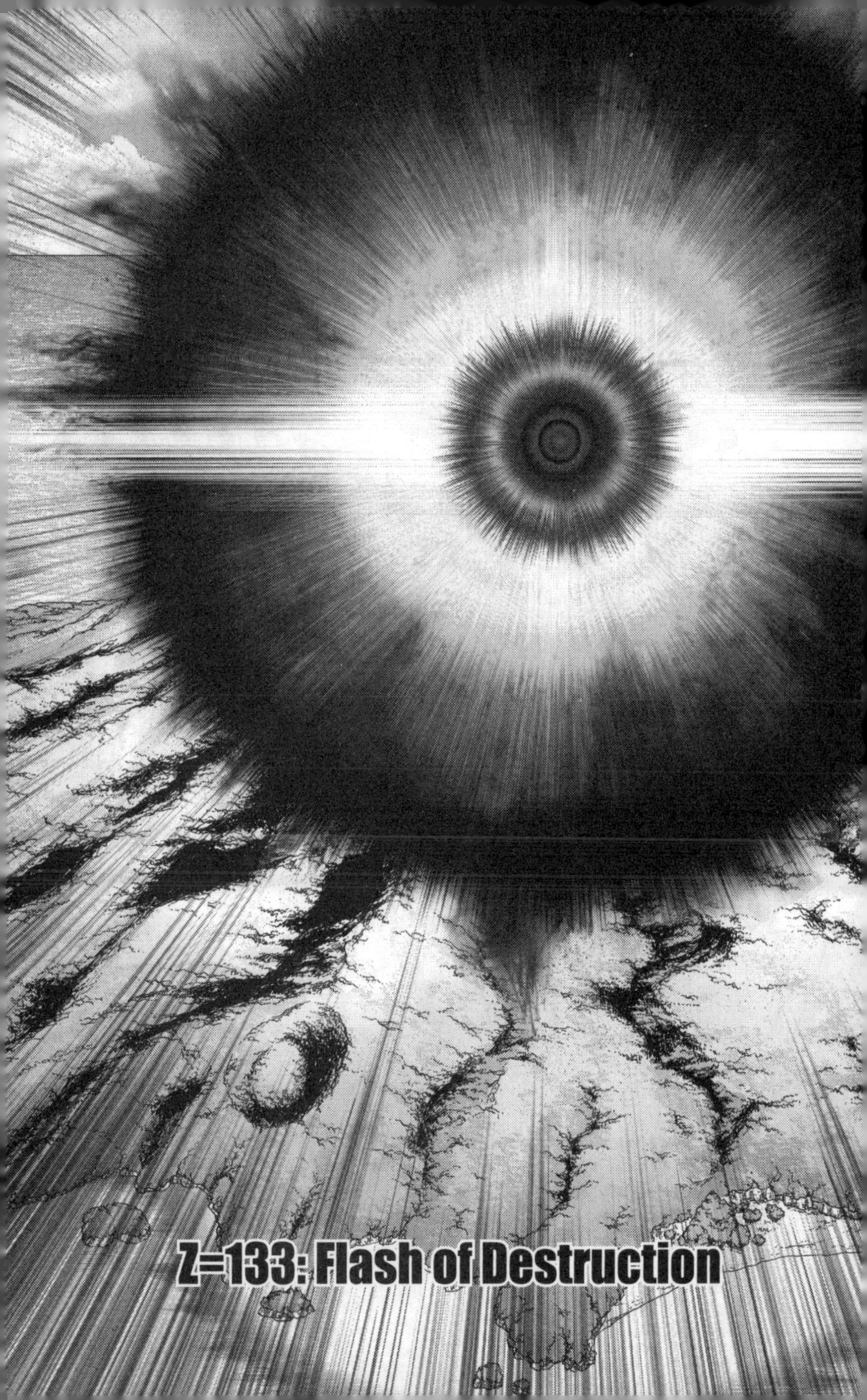

# Z=133: Flash of Destruction

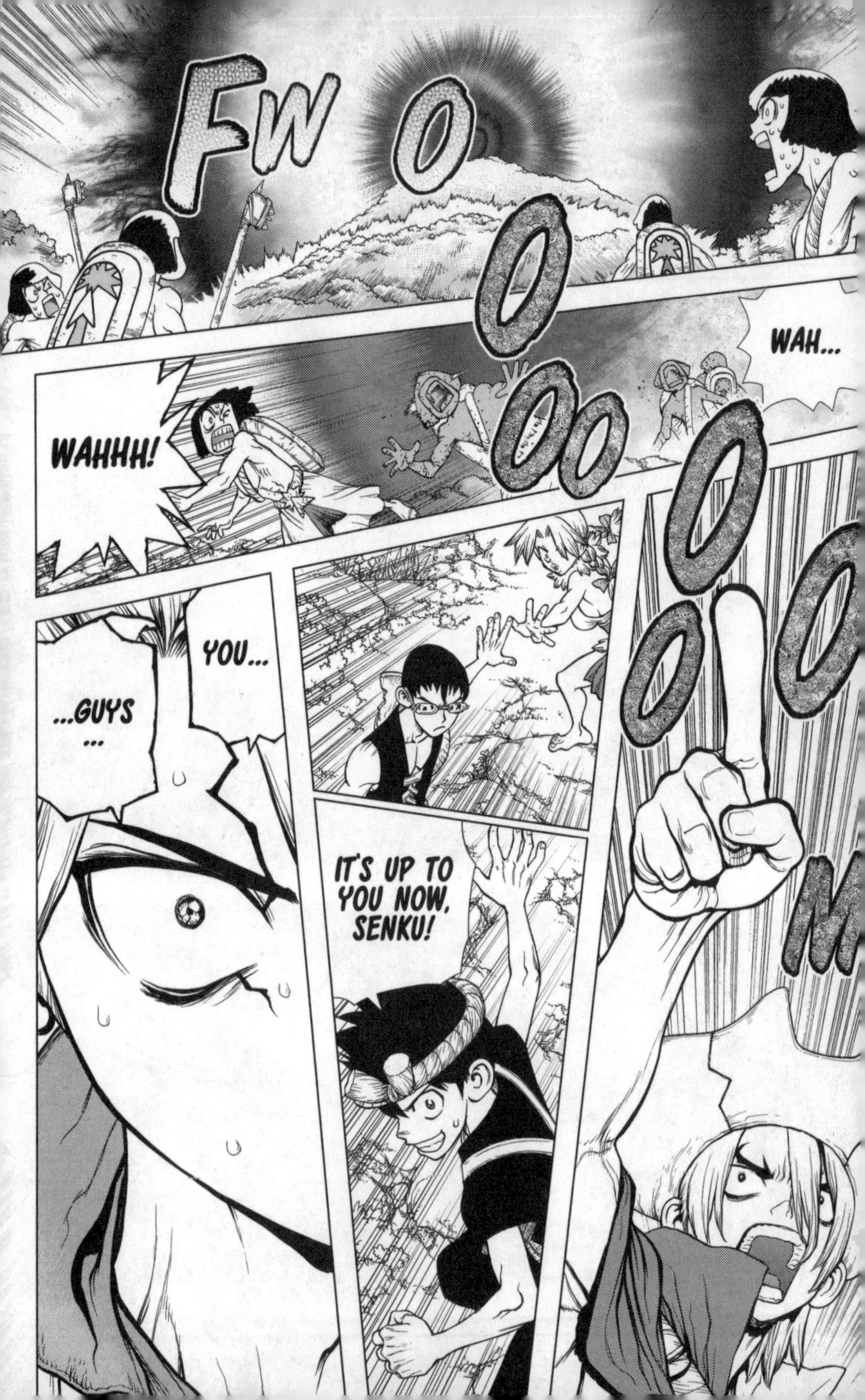

FWOOOOOOOOOM
WAH...
WAHHH!
IT'S UP TO YOU NOW, SENKU!
YOU...
...GUYS ...

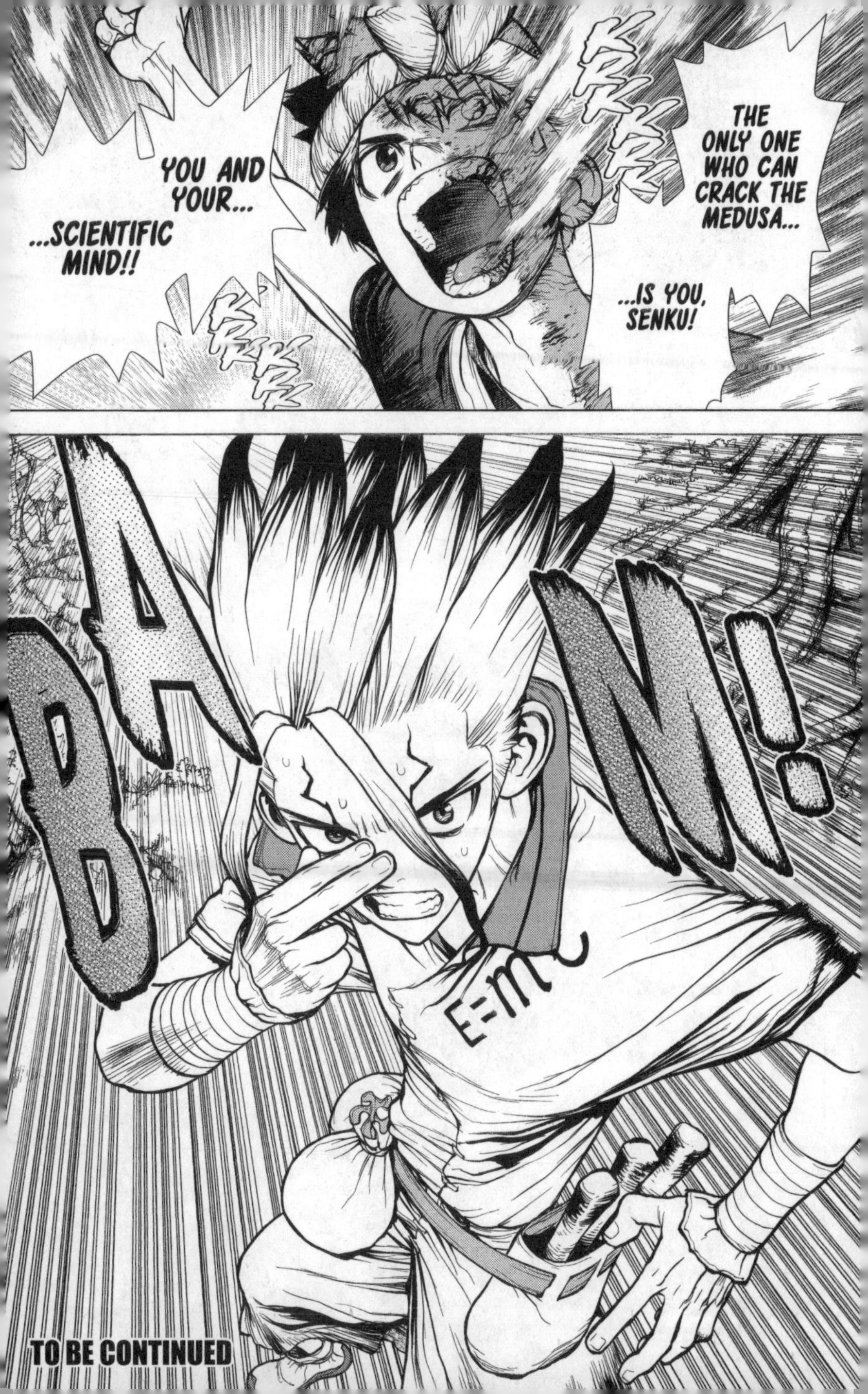
THE ONLY ONE WHO CAN CRACK THE MEDUSA...
...IS YOU, SENKU!
YOU AND YOUR...
...SCIENTIFIC MIND!!
BAM!
TO BE CONTINUED

# ASTRA
## LOST IN SPACE

**CAN EIGHT TEENAGERS FIND THEIR WAY HOME FROM 5,000 LIGHT-YEARS AWAY?**

It's the year 2063, and interstellar space travel has become the norm. Eight students from Caird High School and one child set out on a routine planet camp excursion. While there, the students are mysteriously transported 5,000 light-years away to the middle of nowhere! Will they ever make it back home?!

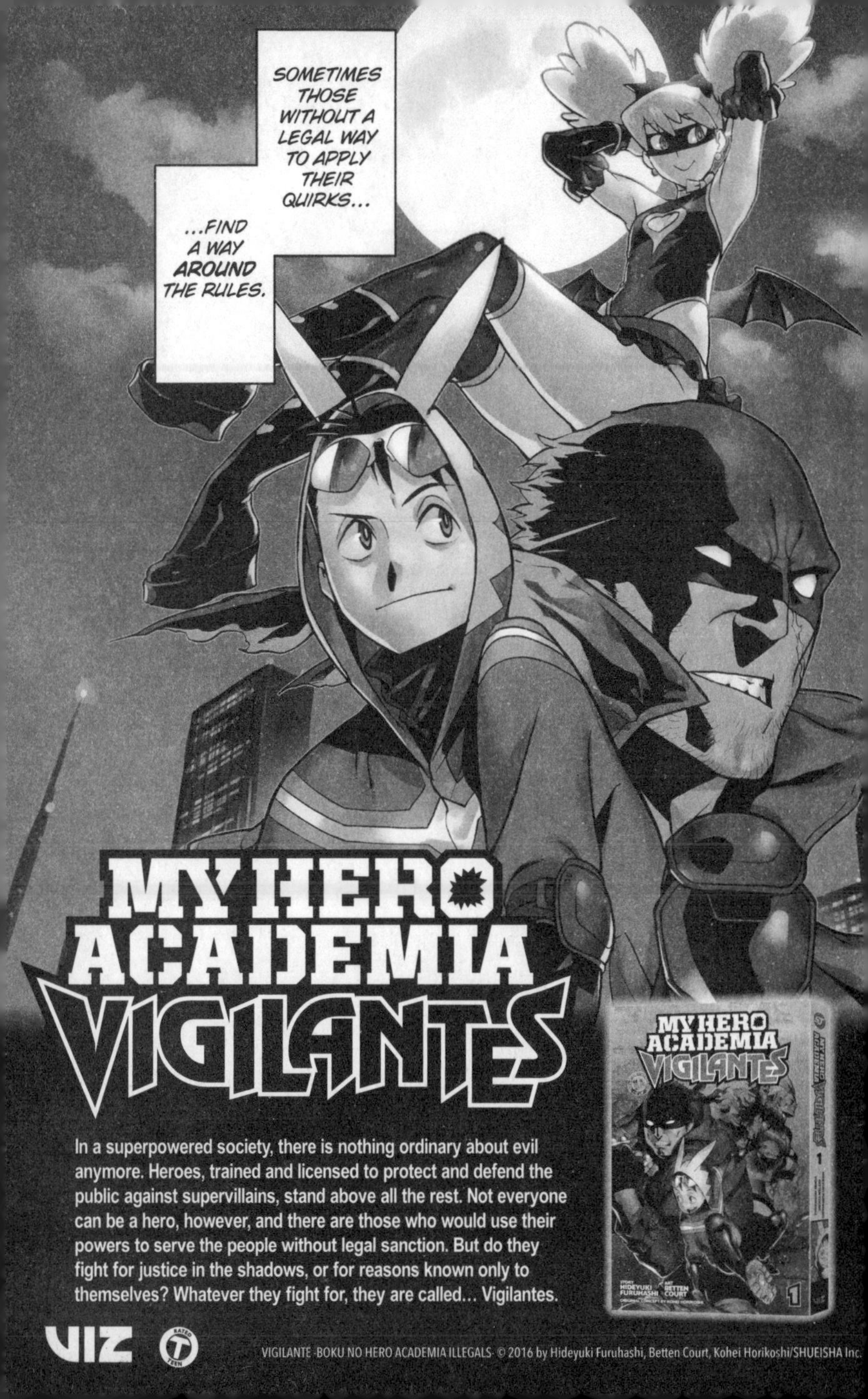

SOMETIMES THOSE WITHOUT A LEGAL WAY TO APPLY THEIR QUIRKS...
...FIND A WAY AROUND THE RULES.
MY HERO ACADEMIA VIGILANTES
In a superpowered society, there is nothing ordinary about evil anymore. Heroes, trained and licensed to protect and defend the public against supervillains, stand above all the rest. Not everyone can be a hero, however, and there are those who would use their powers to serve the people without legal sanction. But do they fight for justice in the shadows, or for reasons known only to themselves? Whatever they fight for, they are called... Vigilantes.
MY HERO ACADEMIA VIGILANTES
HIDEYUKI FURUHASHI
BETTEN COURT
1
VIZ
RATED T TEEN
VIGILANTE -BOKU NO HERO ACADEMIA ILLEGALS- © 2016 by Hideyuki Furuhashi, Betten Court, Kohei Horikoshi/SHUEISHA Inc.

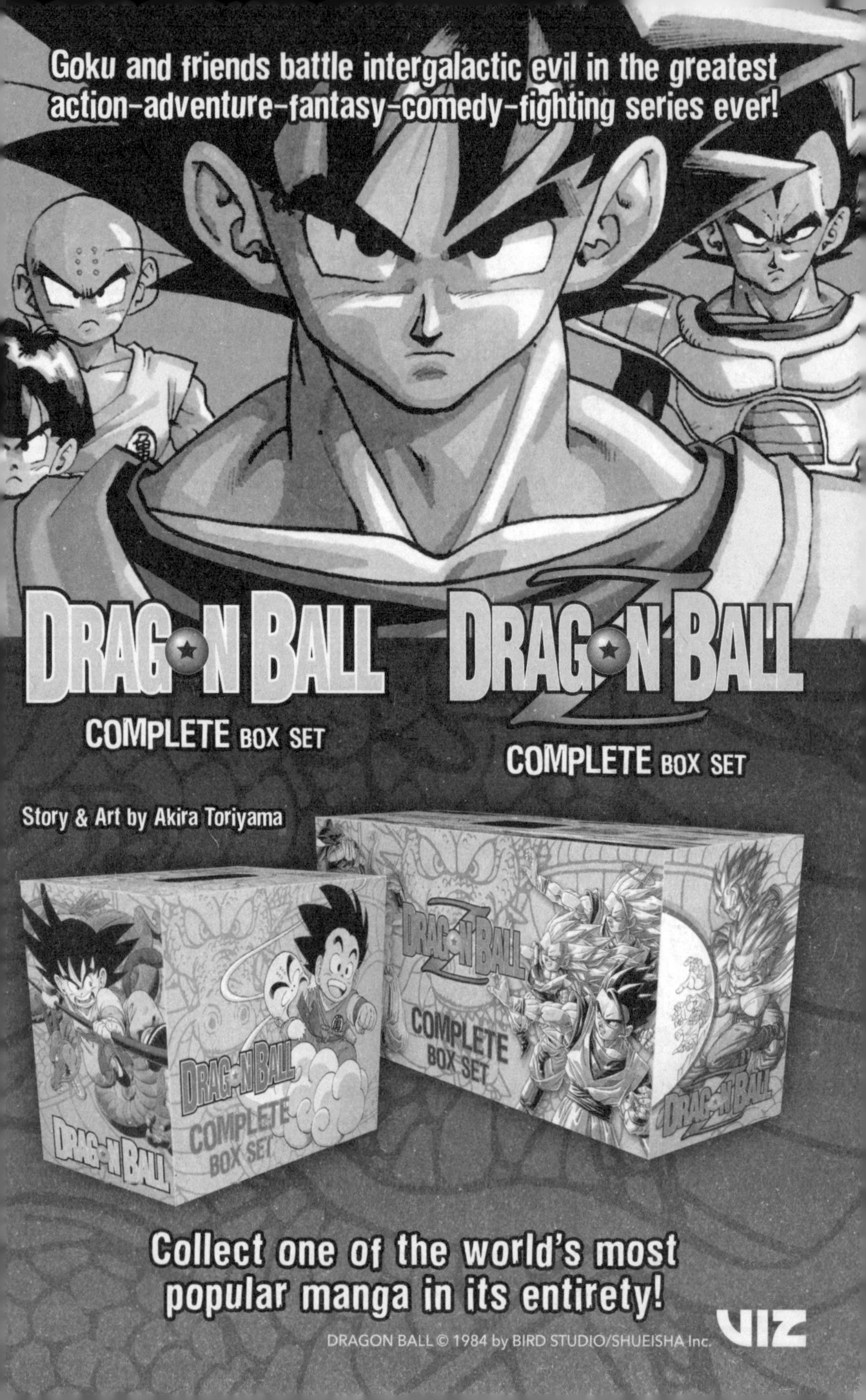

Goku and friends battle intergalactic evil in the greatest
action-adventure-fantasy-comedy-fighting series ever!

# DRAG☆N BALL
## COMPLETE BOX SET

# DRAG☆N BALL Z
## COMPLETE BOX SET

Story & Art by Akira Toriyama

# Collect one of the world's most popular manga in its entirety!

VIZ

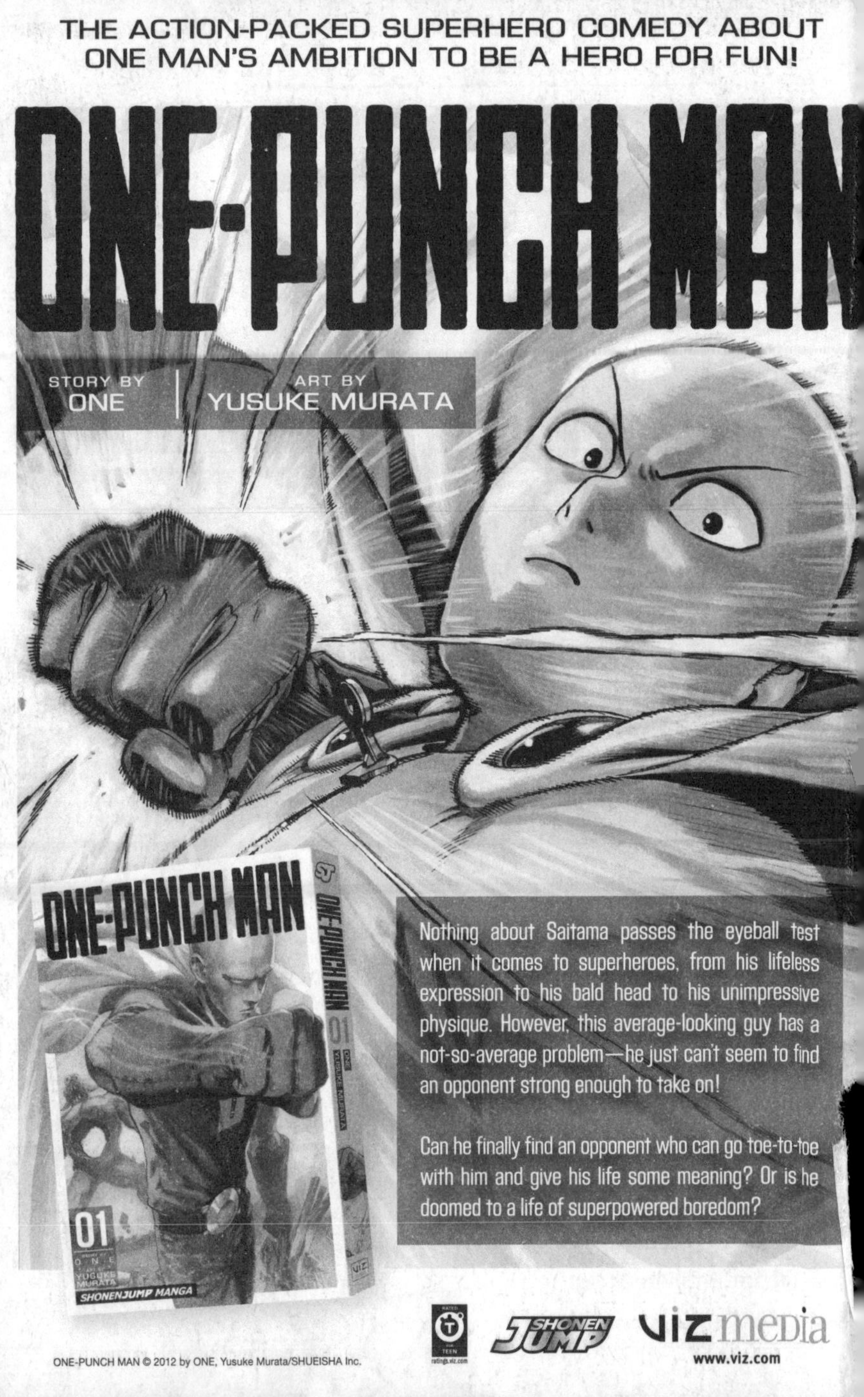
THE ACTION-PACKED SUPERHERO COMEDY ABOUT
ONE MAN'S AMBITION TO BE A HERO FOR FUN!
ONE-PUNCH MAN
STORY BY
ONE
ART BY
YUSUKE MURATA
ONE-PUNCH MAN
01
ONE
YUSUKE MURATA
SHONENJUMP MANGA
Nothing about Saitama passes the eyeball test when it comes to superheroes, from his lifeless expression to his bald head to his unimpressive physique. However, this average-looking guy has a not-so-average problem—he just can't seem to find an opponent strong enough to take on!
Can he finally find an opponent who can go toe-to-toe with him and give his life some meaning? Or is he doomed to a life of superpowered boredom?
SHONEN JUMP
VIZ media
www.viz.com
ONE-PUNCH MAN © 2012 by ONE, Yusuke Murata/SHUEISHA Inc.

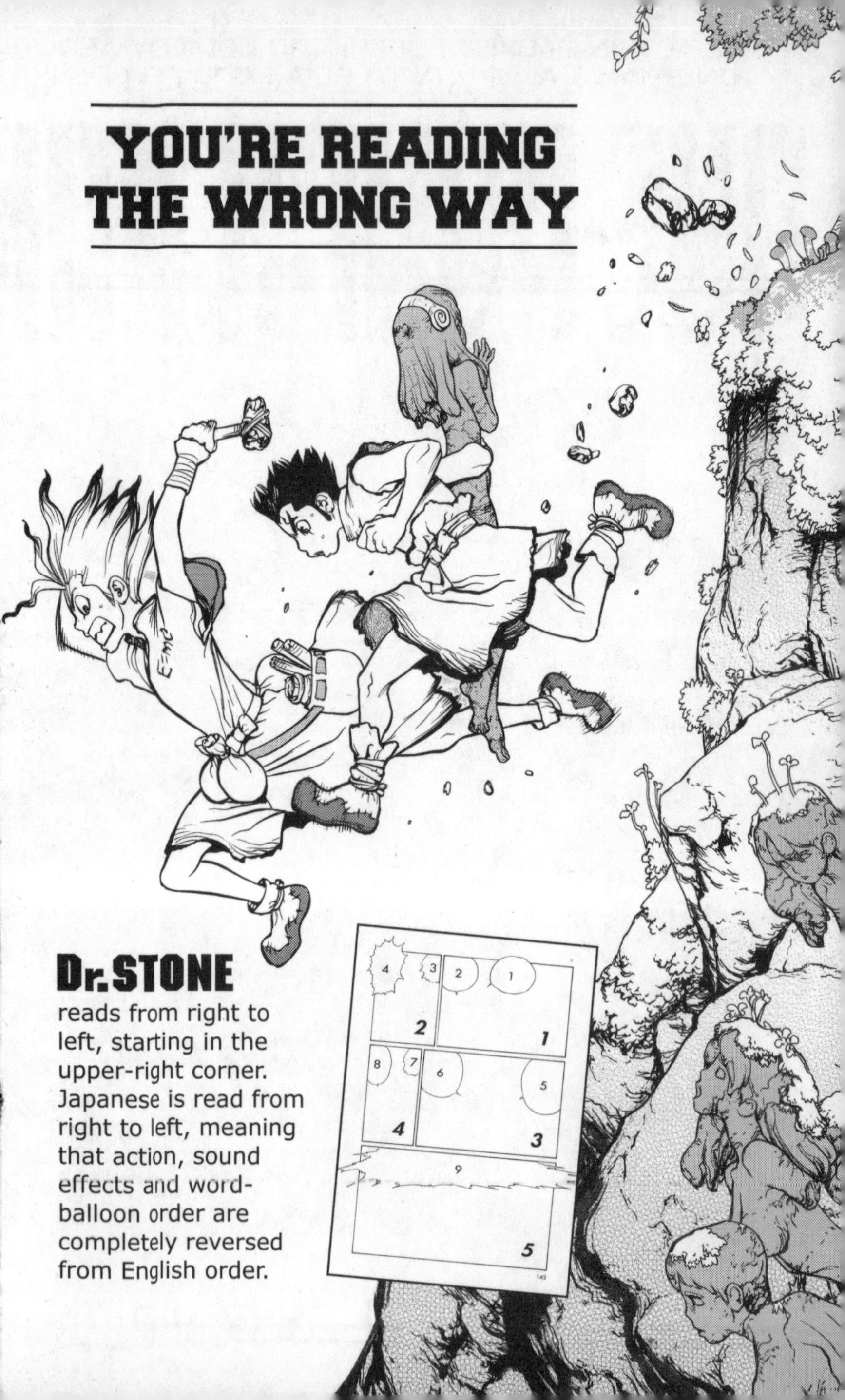

# YOU'RE READING THE WRONG WAY

**Dr.STONE**

reads from right to left, starting in the upper-right corner. Japanese is read from right to left, meaning that action, sound effects and word-balloon order are completely reversed from English order.